THE BOOK OF ALL SAINTS

Adrienne von Speyr

The Book of All Saints

Part One

Edited with an introduction by
HANS URS VON BALTHASAR

Translated by D. C. Schindler

IGNATIUS PRESS   SAN FRANCISCO

Original German edition:
Das Allerheiligenbuch: Erster Teil
© 1966 by Johannes Verlag, Einsiedeln

Cover art:
Dance of the Angels and the Just in Paradise (detail)
Fra Angelico (1837–1455)
Museo di S. Marco, Florence, Italy
© Erich Lessing / Art Resource, New York

Cover design by Roxanne Mei Lum

© 2008 by Ignatius Press, San Francisco
Softbound edition published in 2017
All rights reserved
ISBN 978-1-62164-212-1
Library of Congress Control Number 2006936320
Printed in the United States of America ∞

CONTENTS

FOREWORD

A convert from Protestantism, Adrienne von Speyr entered the Catholic Church on the Feast of All Saints, 1940. During the next twenty-seven years, Hans Urs von Balthasar, as Adrienne's confessor and spiritual director, carefully observed her interior life and was convinced that she was gifted with a special mission in the life of the Church—to revitalize personal, as well as communal, faith and prayer.

Working in close collaboration with von Balthasar, Adrienne received these intimate portraits of men and women, both inside and outside the Church, in conversation with God. Through a unique charism, she was able to put herself in the place of various individuals to see and describe their prayer, their whole attitude before God. Not all of her subjects are saints in the strict sense of the word, but all struggled, with varying degrees of success to place their lives at the disposal of their Creator.

"The *Book of All Saints* is a wonderful gift to the Church because it shows how the saints pray and because it invites us—by contagion, as it were—to pray ourselves."[1]

Vivian Dudro
January 4, 2008
Feast of St. Elizabeth Ann Seton

[1] Hans Urs von Balthasar, *A First Glance at Adrienne von Speyr* (San Francisco: Ignatius Press, 1981), 74.

I. GENERAL INTRODUCTION TO THE POSTHUMOUS WORKS

The vast number of Adrienne von Speyr's books that appeared during her lifetime frequently provoked astonishment because of the comprehensive breadth of her theological and spiritual horizon, the decisiveness and clarity of the positions she took, and the contemplative power with which she penetrated the most profound mysteries of the faith. They thus gave evidence of an extraordinary charism of prayer and life. At the same time, the reader felt as if he were gazing on a brightly illumined landscape without being able to look directly at the sun that was casting its rays. The publication now underway of what might be called her more properly mystical works (*Posthumous Works*: PW) will reveal the radiant center of this wholly unusual—perhaps even incomparable—mission. Though the themes presented in these volumes branch out in different directions and may therefore seem to lie at quite a distance from one another, they not only converge around a clearly defined personal task, but we can see that they are also objectively ordered into what is almost a geometrical figure, once we have caught sight of the mission's simple and fundamental themes and thus also the axes that join together the individual themes. As in the Church's great missions, the themes engaged are always guiding answers that heaven offers to the open questions of a particular age, answers that the age perhaps did not expect (or else the age could have come up with them itself) and perhaps was not very happy to hear, but which—if the age is ready for a *conversio*, which always implies a penitential effort—help in a much more fundamental way than the superficial advice it would have offered itself.

The purpose of this general introduction can thus be only to sketch out the basic arrangement, the knowledge of which is indispensable for appropriating the details, which can be disorienting in their abundance. The principle is simple, and everything else follows from it with strict logic. Once one has grasped this principle, and thereby acquired an overview of the "mystical" (that is, "esoteric") works, one will open up by the same stroke an understanding of the rest, all of the generally accessible (that is, "exoteric") works, which have already been published or will be published. In this way, it becomes clear how artificial it would be to draw a dividing line between the two groups of works, since, with the publication of the latter, only the result, the finished work, was offered, without indicating its provenance and the history of how it came to be. The very fact that it was possible to do so, that in other words the published works were able to speak for themselves without having to justify themselves by an appeal to their mystical quality, the fact that Adrienne von Speyr's works (and thus also her mysticism) possess this objective character, can and must qualify as the decisive criterion of their authenticity. One must constantly refer back to this objective character when the mystical graces give rise to misgivings on account of their singularity and thus their improbability (for the theological mind given to categorizing).

The commentaries on Scripture and the other books that have already appeared were dictated. Dictation would always come, without additional preparation, after general prayer; and yet if a person presented A. [Adrienne] with basically any texts from Scripture on which she had not been focused, she spoke just as peacefully and confidently about them (nearly ready for publication) as she would about a verse that was part of a commentary she was in the process of making on some book of the Bible. The fact that, as a medical doctor, she was not a reader of Scripture either in her youth or later will be seen in the two biographical volumes. She dictated quickly (so that it was not easy to follow her with shorthand, and I thus often had to ask her to wait a moment so I could finish a sentence), about twenty minutes a day. This peaceful work rhythm was interrupted at certain times by the sudden outbreak of events, "transpositions", ecstasies, experiences of the Passion, of "hells", of "pits", visions, aural experiences, and so forth, a report and account of which will be given in the present volumes.

If these volumes cast a direct light back onto the "exoteric" works, they also no doubt cast an intense, indirect light on their author's life, which however does not stand in the foreground in these published volumes, since what is at issue here is a hermeneutic of a literary corpus; testimonies concerning the life and radiance of her personality, which were often enough present, are not collected here.

It goes without saying that we also will not attempt to produce evidence that Adrienne von Speyr's mysticism is "genuine"; in the following, we will present only the documents that will have to be studied in order to illuminate the question of authenticity. The following texts will content themselves—by means of a sort of phenomenological *epochē* regarding everything that concerns the question of authenticity—solely with illuminating the essential contexts, among which also belongs the claim of the documents to reproduce, for example, the saints' voices and opinions as well as expressions of their will.

In Chaux-de-Fonds on Christmas day, the six-year-old Adrienne encounters on a steep city street a man who looks poor and has a slight limp. This man speaks to her and asks her whether she wants to come with him;[1] in later years, especially after her conversion, she sees him—Ignatius Loyola—on countless other occasions. Adrienne's entire path and her entire work is stamped by him, and for those who know him, the boldness of her project, the severity and intensity of its demands, the significance of what it makes known, bear his signature. Later, the young Protestant girl astonishes her classmates and teacher with the naïve and yet profound and luminous compositions and presentations on the Jesuits. After an endless waiting for the hour of conversion, it is finally a Jesuit who leads her into the Church in 1940. The extraordinary graces that she receives in the subsequent years initially and for the most part concern the Society of Jesus, and the new development of the Ignatian life was intended for the Society. It was only after my separation from the Society, which became necessary in 1950,[2] that these graces directly concern the new communities that were to be founded in the saint's spirit—and through them of course the entire Church, which receives from them a great theological and spiritual treasure. But already in kindergarten, "the man" shows the little girl how, with round, colored cards, she can form not only the letters "I" and "L", but also a "J": this is the man's friend, whose name is John. It is John, the final interpreter of the revelation of Jesus Christ, with whom Ignatius discovers a special relationship in heaven and in whose theology he broadens his own mission. John will be the first who one night will pick up the small New Testament from Adrienne's nightstand and open it to his prologue, so that over the course of many nights he can interpret his entire Gospel. He later does the same with the Book of Revelation and his letters. Ignatian obedience (which was always understood in the *Suscipe* as love) will now be interpreted in the context of Johannine love; this love gives its stamp not only to Christology, but (which is ultimately the same thing) also penetrates the very heart of the doctrine of the Trinity.

In comparison to this Johannine accent, the other New Testament and Old Testament accents are complementary accompaniments: Peter and James come forward with their particular spirit in the commentary on their letters. In relation to Paul, four of whose letters were

[1] PW 7.
[2] *Journal* 2.

3

commented on by A., there exists a slight but noticeable tension: his emphasis on personality ("Imitate me") constantly gets on the nerves of one schooled in the spirit of Ignatius and John and devoted to pure transparency and self-effacement; Paul also gives very little "dictation" and, instead, merely offers occasional "tips", leaving the work of interpretation to Adrienne.[3] As for the Old Testament, individual missions stand out;[4] A. interprets large sections of Isaiah, but above all she forms a lively relationship with Daniel, who appears in his essence and in his apocalyptic task as John's forerunner. Thus, the starting point and direction of Adrienne von Speyr's mission can be summarized succinctly in the following way: the Ignatian, in a new, bold, and powerful expression intended for our time, expanded in the medium of the Johannine as the concluding interpretation of biblical revelation.

In her mystical charism, Adrienne von Speyr will make clear what perfect obedience out of perfect love is capable of when God makes use of her surrender in order to fashion from it what he wills. What I had attempted years ago to verify theologically under the impression of what I was permitted to witness—the substantial inseparability of *charis* and *charisma*[5] (since all of the sanctifying graces entail a task and mission)—was confirmed in this great mission in a unique way: it is the unreserved readiness for anything (in Ignatian terms: indifference and obedience) that gives divine grace the possibility to begin and carry out with a person everything that lies in God's saving plan. In relation to the mystical, this results in an explicitly *objective* mysticism, because the transparency of the obedient person fundamentally excludes subjective aberrations and distortions, insofar as this transparency consists in nothing else but love, that is, in the most precious thing that a person in his subjectivity and in cooperation with grace can offer to God. It is not hard to guess that, if there were previously a certain tension with Paul, in the realm of the mystical one could expect an even starker tension with the explicitly subjective coloration of the mysticism of the great Teresa as well as with all forms of ecclesial mysticism in which subjectivity displays itself instead of being purely transparent to God's word.

What it was that God desired to play on this instrument, which offered itself to him in such a way, is impossible to anticipate or even

---

[3] See also "Paul's hell" in the hell of mission (PW 4) and many things in the journals as well as in PW 11.

[4] *The Mission of the Prophets*, trans. David Kipp (San Francisco: Ignatius Press, 1996).

[5] *Besondere Gnadengaben* (German ed. of Aquinas, vol. 23, 1954), and "Charis and Charisma", trans. Brian McNeil, C.R.V., in *Spouse of the Word*, Explorations in Theology 1 (San Francisco: Ignatius Press, 1991), 301–14.

imagine ahead of time. Nevertheless, very clearly defined and determined themes were played over the course of many years. As distinctive and unrepeatable as each may be, they are nevertheless bound together by invisible and unbreakable threads; indeed, considered more closely, they prove to be—often extremely bold and unexpected—variations on a single, basic theme. It would do no violence to Adrienne's work to lay out eleven of these basic themes; in what follows, each will be briefly characterized both in its particularity and in its connection with the other themes.

B. THE ELEVEN FUNDAMENTAL THEMES

1. Once again, *obedience* has to be mentioned first among the individual themes. It is the central notion, on the basis of which A. interprets the revelation of the Old and New Covenants: in Jesus Christ, the center of revelation, obedience appears as the way in which God the Father can and does appear to God the Son. This obedience is not only Christ's fundamental attitude (Phil 2:7f.) in the economic order (for the sake of the redemption of the world), but it is also trinitarian: it is the revelation of the Son's eternal love for the Father, and *in* this obedient love it is the revelation of the Father's love. Obedience is therefore *love*: the preference of the Thou over the I. And both obedience and love are therefore *faith* (understood in its rich biblical sense): the preference for the truth and insight of the Thou over my truth and insight. Obedience is the readiness of the entire I for every will and command and counsel and sign from the beloved God, and this readiness is not only expectant (as indifference), but it always already facilitates the beloved's demand as *surrender*. Obedience is the innermost characteristic of Christ in relation to the Father, but it is also the innermost characteristic of the feminine Church in relation to Christ. Here, Mariology takes a central place:[6] Mary is bride because she is handmaid, and she is mother because she is the ready virgin. Obedience in the Marian Church to the Lord and in the Lord to the Father in the Spirit: this therefore has to be the primary characteristic of Christian spirituality.

To obedience as *exclusivity* of readiness and of the surrender to God there corresponds in Adrienne von Speyr's work an interpretation of the *state of the counsels*, which she understands at every point as the

[6] See *Handmaid of the Lord*, trans. E. A. Nelson (San Francisco: Ignatius Press, 1985), the *World of Prayer*, trans. Graham Harrison (San Francisco: Ignatius Press, 1985), and many unpublished Marian texts.

primary and fundamental state of the Christian and the Church: theologically and existentially it is the believer's most immediate participation in the existence of Christ and the Church. For man, in the religion of the Bible, obedience (in faith) corresponds to what awe before the divine (*religio*) is in the extrabiblical religions more generally: what in the latter remains a modest reticence before the unfathomable abyss is inwardly transformed in the former into obedience, where this abyss reveals itself as the free God—and thus as the *Deus semper major*.

A.'s obedience is perfect and complete, which both natural and mystical trials proved over and over again. All of the ten subsequent themes were able to be elaborated only on the basis of this absolute obedience. Her soul was pliant clay out of which God could fashion whatever form he wished, without resistence. It was a thing so completely handed over that the Holy Spirit was able to risk imprinting upon it central aspects of biblical revelation and (cf. themes 6 and 10) to present them for the first time in this new elucidation of Christianity.

2. The second basic word is incarnation, *embodiment*. So begins the New Covenant in Christ and Mary. Like Hildegard of Bingen, Adrienne von Speyr is a doctor, entrusted with the entire realm of the body, from the physical, through the physiological, to the ethical dimension. While she was still Protestant, she was twice married, but her mystical autobiography (PW 7) shows that the marriage bond lay heavily upon her—not at all because of what it is in itself, but because she knew that a "bodily mystery" was intended for her, one that remained yet veiled but for which she knew herself to be reserved. In her Catholic period, it became immediately clear that God needed her body in every conceivable way for the embodiment and testing of her obedience, in particular for an experience, in every precise and candid detail, of Christ's Passion in her own flesh (PW 3: "The Passions"), but also for other mysteries (for example, Mary's state during the period of expectation, birth, and nursing of the child, and also the various states of purgatory, and so on). From this mystical use of her bodiliness as a touchstone for all of the Christian truths connected with the Incarnation, there arose a further, special task: to recognize and articulate the Christian theological significance of the entire sexual realm simultaneously from above (PW 12 on "Sexus and Agape"). Indeed, there has rarely been a human being—in contrast, for example, to Teresa of Avila and other women mystics—who was less "susceptible" to the erotic in a sort of turbid sense than Adrienne von Speyr. A combination of perfect childlikeness and the modest realism of a doctor characterized her during the many decades I knew her. She was created in order to

penetrate the sexual sphere from the heights of the gospel and the evangelical counsels and to carry into the deepest heart of this sphere the purifying fire of *agape*: "*in* this world, but not *of* this world". In a special mystical task, she worked out the general program of the *world communities* (secular institutes) (though of course not in this sphere), for which her work as a whole provides the decisive theological foundation: the penetration of the world without any succumbing to the world. She left the communities that she was instructed to found a bold and, for Christians, very demanding legacy. It is undeniable that the foundress, as a practicing doctor—a profession she practiced with passion and complete devotion—was providentially prepared, even from a worldly perspective, for this particular task.

3. A third basic word is *confession*. This sacrament, which according to Adrienne von Speyr has its due place next to the Eucharist, is praised and interpreted not only in the book devoted to the topic but throughout all of her commentaries and other writings: in the Eucharist we participate in the sacrificed flesh and outpoured blood; in confession we participate in the Cross as the event of redemption: the total confession of sins by the Crucified One, the Father's total absolution in the Resurrected One. This christological understanding of confession, however, takes on an additional Ignatian-Johannine coloring: confession is an act of obedience on the part of the sinner in relation to the Redeemer (and the Church), an act that demands perfect *transparency* to the core, an attempt at dis-closure (and thus truth) out of obedience, undertaken always and increasingly as constant readiness for showing forth (*Her-zeigen*), giving away (*Her-geben*); thus, the habitual "confessional attitude" converges once again with faith, love, and surrender. In several of her mystical works, she takes this confessional attitude as the touchstone for holiness: To what extent was this or that saint ready to keep nothing veiled, to keep nothing for himself, to be transparent to his very core? The Johannine face-to-face encounter between light (grace) and darkness (the sinner) is a theology of confession, in terms of which she interprets (PW 11) the Ignatian demand to drop all defenses (*Hüllenlosigkeit*) in the *Exercises* and in the Order. The sinless Handmaid of the Lord, who opens up everything before the Lord and puts it at his disposal, embodied of course the most perfect confessional attitude before God.

The properly mystical dimensions of this complete defenselessness lie in the aforementioned trials of her obedience, but also and above all in the *Book of All Saints* (PW 1), in which the attitude of prayer and life of the saints of all the periods in history are measured and judged in relation to the perfect confessional attitude. Adrienne von Speyr's mission of confession is important for the present age, insofar as the Eucharist has been placed so much in the foreground in the past decades that confession—which is the properly existential sacrament—has suffered. A. sets in clear relief the distinction between sacramental confession, the guidance of souls in faith, and, on the other hand, psychology and psychoanalysis.

4. A fourth theme is *childhood*, which is a fundamental concept in the New Testament kerygma and which has today been unduly exiled to the shadows because of the "coming of age" demanded of Christians. All her life long, and in spite of her almost manly decisiveness and resolve (she was similar to St. Teresa in this regard), Adrienne's relationship to her own childhood was always absolutely alive. An abundance of the tiniest experiences and episodes were constantly present to her and remained important to her, with all of the fragrance of what she felt at the time, whether joy or sadness. This is the natural[7] basis for a purely supernatural "experiment", which resulted from her obedient readiness for anything and which had to be carried out by me as her confessor and spiritual director over the course of many weeks (in every case for the space of time of her dictation) as a task enjoined on me by St. Ignatius. The task consisted in returning Adrienne "in holy obedience" to various years of her childhood, her youth, and so on, and to have her describe her life, her feelings, and in particular her relationship to God and her prayer. I myself came to Adrienne when she was a little girl and, later, a sick person in Leysin, a student, a married woman, and a doctor as if I were a friend to whom she was allowed to say everything and who became for her the embodiment of a moment that yet lay a distance away and was awaited with great longing: her conversion to the Catholic Church. The document of this experiment is presented in the *Mystery of Childhood* (PW 7). For the moment, it is crucial to see that the "childhood" theme arose as nothing more than a variation of the theme of obedience and confession and that it was pure obedience (and by no means a power of suggestion or parapsychology) that allowed both the "regression" and the wholly unselfconscious childlike candidness of what was said.

5. With this, we have already come to a fifth, difficult, and wide-ranging theme, that of the *theology of mysticism* in general. Adrienne

[7] One ought not to forget, however, that she had mystical experiences in her early youth and had a vision of the Mother of God when she was fifteen (PW 7).

von Speyr's lucid mind, together with the transparency of her obedient readiness, resulted in an optimal precondition for giving a theoretical account of what she herself had experienced in such a rich and multifaceted way. Her theory is distinguished in a negative sense from earlier theories first of all in the fact that she lays the accent, not primarily on the experiencing (*noesis*), but on the object of the experience (*noema*): the mystic is, like the prophet and the witness of the Bible's Revelation, before all else a "servant of Jesus", even when his name is John (Rev 1:1), commissioned to pass what he has received on to the Church. The point is the objective dimension alone, but the ability to pass it on in purity requires that the one who sees, hears, and experiences have as pure a heart as possible. For this reason what comes to the fore—again, putting it negatively—are not the subjective stages, but rather the unclassifiable abundance of the possibilities of the God who will not allow himself to be fixed in any system.

Such a theory of biblical mysticism can be developed in two different directions: on the one hand, from the side of the subject (PW 5), wherein the conditions of transmission and the various ways it occurs are treated in a critical way; and then, on the other hand, from the side of the object (PW 6), wherein a "dogmatic" theology needs to be developed, at least piece by piece, in relation to the experience of the various truths of faith. For if the Holy Spirit, according to Thomas Aquinas, conveys his charisms to all those who love with a living faith in such a way that they somehow receive an experiential knowledge of what they had previously "merely" believed—this general experiential knowledge would be a sort of pre-stage of what could properly be called a charismatic mysticism—then the object is not the "*Deus nudus*". Instead, it is the *Deus incarnatus* in the entire spectrum of the relationships described in revelation, wherein to be sure the accent has to be placed on *Deus* (the experience of God *as* God).

In relation to the tradition on this point, Adrienne von Speyr's theological (biblical) theory of mysticism will be something that speaks against the unbridgeable gap that is supposed to exist between word and mysticism, faith and mysticism, and thus will be able to revive the conversation with Protestantism on this theme. Moreover, it will overcome the long-standing Catholic discomfort regarding the relationship between dogmatics and mysticism.

6. As a surprising particular case of the aforementioned theme, there is the task of undergoing herself *John's visions of the apocalypse* as the visionary of Patmos underwent them and of interpreting them on the

basis of this direct experience. This unbelievable, but undeniable, experience, which began for A. during a retreat in Estavayer, will be described in detail in the three volumes of journals (PW 8–10). She was convinced that an enormous storm had irrupted (though the weather outside was beautiful) and described for me in great anxiety and excitement the vision of the woman and the dragon in Revelation 12, without the slightest clue what it was she saw. She then recited the text by heart (the stenograph of this dictation still exists), a text she had previously read only once in a casual way as a student, and could not believe it when I told her that the text was right from the Book of Revelation. In the period that followed, she dictated—with many interruptions, ecstasies, and "hells": it is the "most apocalyptic" manuscript that I received from her—from the twelfth chapter to the end of the book, then began in the other direction, with Ignatius interjecting many comments into the passage on the "seven seals", in order finally to examine the conclusion concerning the heavenly Jerusalem. After having reached the first verse, she worked out a complete theory of the apocalyptic visions, which is wholly based on the principle of pure disponibility and, thus, of obedience. In the vision, the seer, who is neither on earth nor in heaven, is fully objectified "in the spirit"; he becomes a pure "witness" of what occurs before his eyes between heaven and earth.

Branching off from the apocalyptic vision, there is the state, or rather the fluid chain of states, into which Adrienne was often "transposed", when she was supposed to turn off or "bracket out" her subjectivity, in order to turn it into a pure "voice", a pure "task". She named these states "hells", borrowing from her experiences of hell (PW 3); the accounts of these "hells" will fill an entire volume (PW 4). Adrienne also saw the great visions of the Book of Daniel in just the same way as she saw John's apocalypse, with no less immediate perception, and described them while she had them.[8]

In the power that was given to me as her confessor to "transpose" Adrienne in obedience ("ecstasies of obedience"), I was also able (this is an ability that cannot be explained by any general psychological categories but was an utterly unique gift) to make her a pure mediator in obedience (which is a particular form of ecstasy), in order to communicate to me the word of our Holy Father[9] and, indeed, to allow me to pose questions and receive his answers. This occurred in a completely

---

[8] Appendix to *Isaias* (1958), 251–84.

[9] [This was the name Adrienne von Speyr and Hans Urs von Balthasar used for St. Ignatius of Loyola, often writing it in Latin: *Sanctus Pater Noster* or abbreviating it as "SPN".—Trans.]

Christian sobriety and without the slightest hint of the turgid or magical element that tends to give "channeling" experiences a foul smell. A "discernment of spirits" will be necessary regarding the objective aspects (the noematic), regarding *that which* has here been conveyed as a whole—in other words, regarding its scope, importance, and fruitfulness for the Church. From this perspective, we may ask in anticipation: Judged according to this criterion, what "private revelations" in the course of the Church's history can be compared to this?

For the publication of Adrienne's commentary on the Book of Revelation, I gathered together from the manuscripts everything that was an objective interpretation; one can glean from the commentary the mystical experiences that lay behind it, but everything directly related to these experiences has been left out; it will be included partly in the "hells of mission" (PW 3) and partly in the "journals" (PW 8).

7. Adrienne was a woman of great prayer, indeed, she prayed without ceasing; one of her most fundamental concerns was to renew and revive the Church's prayer, especially her contemplative prayer (primarily in cloistered monasteries). All of Adrienne's works are pure fruits of prayer. Her teaching on prayer is scattered throughout her writings; it is collected in books such as *The World of Prayer* (1951; Eng. trans. 1985) and *Gebetserfahrung* (1965). But even in these, the properly mystical element is more inferred than directly seen. It is different in the *Book of All Saints* (PW 1), which is again based on an incomprehensible charism, one that has its foundation, once more, in the total transparency of obedience. As her confessor, I was given the instruction and thus the authority to "transpose" her into the spirit of many saints and other believers of the past, in order that she might understand from the inside how they prayed. In this, the object was in every case *only the saint's attitude of prayer* (and often the attitude of confession that was connected with it), which can be quite distinct from his or her intellectual achievement. The first thing that surprises a person in this book is the infinite variety of prayer styles, which change from personality to personality, the fullness of the dramatic life, the struggle, the failure, the success, and that strangely transcendent perspective of divine grace, by which the one who falls away is somehow snatched up and reconciled once again in the whole. It is perhaps in this work that we can most clearly see the Catholicity of Adrienne von Speyr's soul. She prays, not only *in* the Church, but in a mysterious way precisely *as* Church. The fact that the saints in heaven give their consent, in a sort of public confession before the entire Church, to lay bare even their deficiencies and failures is an ultimate confirmation of the

Ignatian-Johannine teaching about the attitude of confession and self-revealing obedience, which echoes, too, in the open letter of the Book of Revelation.

8. In connection with the Book of Revelation, and then later independently, Adrienne began to speak of certain numbers, especially in moments of rapture. These were *primary numbers*, at first specifically the first seven (after the numbers up to ten, which were reserved for God) from eleven to thirty-one. They were interpreted in terms of the foundational "orientations" that certain saints, the "pillars of the Church", represented. With these numbers began a peculiar mathematics. Soon the system of primary numbers extended to fifty-three, the number of the apostle John; then followed all the primary numbers occurring up to the number 153 (which represents the fullness of sanctity in the Church's net), and then everything once again in descending sequences. In this system, each number represented a particular saint with a unique mission, and in this way whole biographies of saints, whose names were at first unknown, could be sketched out in numbers (which Adrienne often received with extreme rapidity). Each number was at each step complemented by addition or multiplication with other numbers until it reached the total sum of sanctity, 153. Often it was left to me afterward to figure out who the intended saint was, and often my guess was confirmed or challenged, or much later a name would emerge, as if as an afterthought. The whole nexus was unveiled step by step or retrospectively, and at last a vertigo-inducing system emerged, likewise in extreme rapidity. Ignatius himself claimed to be the "inventor" of this highly provocative play of numbers; his purpose at the time was to encourage us in our mission by allowing us a glimpse into the heavenly interweaving of missions and, later, in order to give us a sense of the precision that was reflected in the things done on earth as they are in heaven, although he always emphasized that the earthly numbers were only an analogous reflection of the ordering of the heavenly Jerusalem; but finally it was to carry modern man's number-thinking home in the most unexpected way into the fabric of revelation. The primary numbers are the great missions, and the missions are created in heaven and conveyed to those who have been chosen and who present themselves as willing in obedience and readiness for the reception of such missions, for the identification of their existence with such missions. The numbers' precision, which expresses the precision of the missions, thus shows that the obedience to mission, indeed, all faithful Christian obedience in general, cannot be approximate but must correspond to the exactness of God's demanding word. It was

not for nothing that, quite often, the shocking penances laid upon Adrienne herself (not the ones she chose!) were governed by the numbers of the missions. Anyone who is familiar with her thought and contemplation, however, will have to admit that the superabundant fullness of her theology of love is not in any way narrowed or formalized by this aspect of precision. On the other hand, the notion of mission, which one finds everywhere in Adrienne von Speyr (as an expression of the objective quality of her obedience), here celebrates a victory that can hardly be surpassed. What the *Book of All Saints* displays from the subjectivity of so many praying individuals—the communion of saints as an inconceivable wealth of love and grace—is revealed in the *Fischernetz* (Fishers' Net, which will be the name of the book on numbers, PW 2) according to the aspect of a divine, lucid order, as mysterious as the view of the starry heavens in their cosmic, mathematical array.

9. The last three themes are stronger than the previous ones, which up to this point have concerned dogmatics; they form the heart of this mission. First, the *passions*: participations, especially during Lent and Holy Week, in the Lord's suffering. The beginnings, which were accompanied by visible stigmata, will be reported in the journal (PW 8). Adrienne's mission, however, included not only the subjective suffering of bodily pains along with Christ and the soul's undergoing of the abyss of suffering, but also their precise theological articulation. She has thus penetrated more deeply into this mystery than any other mystic in the Church to date. On the one hand, what is at issue is the presentation of the mystery, how it is that obedience enabled the Son of God to bear the whole of the world's sin, what this bearing of sin meant for him experientially, what inconceivable landscapes of suffering emerged here—constantly new views, perspectives, unexpected changes, in which the suffering is deepened and intensified—how the experience of time is thus eliminated, what the anxiety, the abandonment by God, the separation from men and from the Mother mean for the Son, and so forth. This presentation constantly takes place in the dialectic between distance and proximity, the complete separation and then once again the reconciliation of the suffering sinner, as something Adrienne feels with the suffering Lord: though experiential, her participation is indirect; to describe this in a proper way belongs to the most difficult and important aspects of her mission to undergo the passion.

10. At the first genuine passion, I expected that the suffering would have essentially come to an end with Jesus' death, at three o'clock on

Good Friday. As it turned out, the part of the task of suffering that would prove in the following years to be the most decisive and consequential had only just begun. Indeed, this part must be seen in general as the most surprising of Adrienne's entire mission: the inner participation in *Christ's descent into hell* (from Friday afternoon until early Easter Sunday morning), the articulation of which outlines for the first time in the Church's history a proper *theology of hell*. This theologumenon, to which the poets of our age have laid claim but which has been almost completely neglected by theologians because it cannot be transmitted further within the old form, will be retrieved both with the *Zeitgeist* and against it, in a manner that cannot have been anticipated.

Christ visits the kingdom of the damned, which is a mystery that belongs to the Father (as the Creator of human freedom and the world's judge), as one who is himself dead; he can be led into this kingdom only as one who has died, who in obedience to the Father has entered into the furthest extremity of Godforsakenness. But hell is the world's "second chaos" (the Creator brought order to the first), which arose through sin and henceforth can be separated from sinners through the Cross of Christ. In this respect, Christ contemplates his own work of redemption in the darkness of hell: depersonalizing sin dissolves into the chaos. This is an understanding of hell from the perspective of salvation history, as taken up into the process of redemption, an understanding that is, indeed, trinitarian in its depths: It is the encounter between the Father and Son, but in the mode of turning away, of abandonment (since the Son seeks the Father precisely in that place in which he *cannot* be found), and all of this no longer in the sense of the subjective pain of one who suffers, but in a totally objectified "suffering", immediately from the side of the Cross that faces eternity.

These few remarks cannot convey anything of the richness of Adrienne von Speyr's theology of Holy Saturday. Every year during Holy Week, this same fundamental experience repeated itself, but always from a different perspective, as if one were slowly turning round a sculptured image; the fullness of aspects is so rich it overflows any systematization. It points to the fact that what we are dealing with here is an unfathomable mystery that pervades every area of theology: the doctrine of the Trinity, Christology, soteriology, the doctrine concerning man as redeemed, concerning the theological virtues, the Church, the sacraments, and eschatology. Holy Saturday is the center that binds together Good Friday and Easter, and it is only from the perspective of this center that we can receive some sense of the act of redemption in its ultimate depths and universality. In this theology, apparently opposed partial aspects of the tradition finally reveal themselves to be reconcilable: Origen, for example, receives his due place next to Augustine, but only insofar as both are subsumed into a higher point of reference. One could say that hell is definitively "demythologized" here, in order finally to be theologized in truth: the mystery will only become illuminated in its dark depths once it is understood, no longer anthropologically, but only christologically and, in fact, univocally as a function of the Son's *obedience*.

11. As the final, all-pervasive theme, we have to mention the *doctrine of the Trinity*, which must constantly and consciously be borne in mind, not of course as an abstract idea, but as the supporting foundation that illuminates every aspect of every event of salvation. The Christ event is the "opening up of the Trinity"; it has its movement within the eternal movement of the Son, who proceeds from the Father and returns to him, and the understanding of this movement is mediated by the Holy Spirit. This is of course in a central way Johannine thinking, into which the Ignatian opens up: obedience, readiness, and self-gift have their place in the Son's movement and, through grace, are identical to it. In this, even the Ignatian notion of the ever-greater God (*Deus semper major*) is completely removed from the merely formal God-relationship that one finds, for example, in Plato's and Plotinus' philosophy (in which the essence of God always remains more unknown than known) in order to be transformed into the God of the ever-greater and therefore ever more inconceivable love, just as the Son experiences the Father and just as the Father reveals himself to the Son in the Holy Spirit. Our age—which is deeply distrustful of the subjective relationship with God, of prayer, and of the childlike love for the absolute—needs such an understanding of God more than it needs bread.

These eleven points do not provide an exhaustive description of Adrienne von Speyr's ecclesial mission; they merely set into relief the aspects of her mission that are especially characteristic and especially remarkable. It will be evident that these points are primarily related to the parts of the properly mystical works introduced here and thus do not characterize her work as a whole. This work goes beyond the sketch laid out above in many places, insofar as the whole doctrine of revelation and the entire Christian life pervades it in ways that never cease being new. Thus, many essential things have gone unmentioned here, for example, the theme Adrienne often treated of the relationship between heaven and earth, between the God who reveals and offers himself in creation and redemption and the human being who constantly lives within what God offers[10] (an understanding basically opposed to the ideologies of man's distancing himself from God in a "worldly world"), the complex differentiations of her teaching on prayer, the teaching on the states of life in the Church that she developed in both a theoretical and practical sense,[11] and so forth, which is connected with the founding of new communities in the evangelical counsels.

C. THE TWELVE VOLUMES OF THE POSTHUMOUS WORKS

Included under the title "Posthumous Works" are the properly mystical works of Adrienne von Speyr, which have been described above. In addition to these posthumous writings, there are other works that have not yet been published [as of 1966]; these will be published in the same form as the books by A. that have already appeared. These include several writings on the Old Testament, a few shorter texts, an autobiography, which Adrienne wrote by hand at my request (the first part in French, the second part in German), a large number of meditation points (on the Gospels of Mark and Luke, the Acts of the Apostles, as well as those written for individual feast days or other occasions), aphorisms, prayers, remarks on the Rules of the communities, and many letters. Moreover, there are sketches for a book on medical ethics, shorter literary essays, and so forth. These will not be discussed in the present context.

The twelve volumes of the Posthumous Works are divided as follows:

Volume 1: *The Book of All Saints*. This book has two parts; the introduction will follow below, pp. 20–24.

Volume 2: *Das Fischernetz* (The Fishers' Net), or the book on the primary numbers of the saints, which are contained in the number of perfection of the Church's holiness, 153. The dictations that occurred intermittently over the course of many months are reproduced here without any alteration in detail, though they have been arranged in an objective order. In an appendix, there appear several "mission-hells" that bear some relation to the numbers (cf. vol. 4).

[10] For example, in *The Gates of Eternal Life*, trans. Corona Sharp (San Francisco: Ignatius Press, 1983), *The Boundless God*, trans. Helena M. Tomko (San Francisco: Ignatius Press, 2004), and *The Countenance of the Father*, trans. David Kipp (San Francisco: Ignatius Press, 1997).

[11] *The Christian State of Life*, trans. Mary Frances McCarthy (San Francisco: Ignatius Press, 1986); *They Followed His Call*, trans. Erasmo Leiva-Merikakis (San Francisco: Ignatius Press, 1986).

Volumes 3 and 4, grouped under the title *Kreuz und Hölle* (Cross and hell), contain the theology of Good Friday and Holy Saturday. Volume 3, *Die Passionen* (The passions), sets into relief in each case the particular periods of suffering from the context of the mystical experiences that Adrienne had over the course of the Church year: above all, the days of the sacred Triduum must occasionally be referred back to Lent or Holy Week. Because the experience of Good Friday always passes over into the experience of Holy Saturday, the theology of the Cross and the theology of hell are joined together in this volume.

Volume 4 contains a large number of *mission-hells*, that is, objective ecstasies that occur for the most part in hell-states or states very similar to these, and simply serve to communicate insights or tasks. Some are more directly related to the theology of hell; others are more distant; there are also questions of obedience, of dogma, of mysticism, or of the states of life, treated in ways that are for Adrienne characteristically relentless and often humiliating; moreover, various typical heretical figures are shown, in order negatively to accentuate what is true. A mission-ecstasy (at the end of the dictation on the Book of Revelation) in the heavenly Jerusalem forms the conclusion. This volume can be seen as a supplement to the *Passionen* and to a number of other treatises.

Volumes 5 and 6, grouped together under the title *Wort und Mystik* (Word and mysticism), treat the theology of mysticism mentioned above in point 5, and they do so in a way that corresponds to the two perspectives outlined there. Volume 5 contains the *Theologie der subjectiven Mystik* (Theology of subjective mysticism) from the point of view of the experiential act (*noesis*): the presuppositions, elements, and modes of mystical experience measured against the criterion of biblical theology and ordered to the service of the Church.

Volume 6 treats the same theology from the point of view of the object of experience (*noema*); it shows, through examples, how the objects of faith are incarnated in such experience and are undergone in a fully human way. Christology, pneumatology, and the doctrine of inspiration are also not neglected here. A particularly noteworthy treatise is the discussion of purgatory, the experience of which (contrary to what Origen thought) is altogether different from the experience of hell.

Volume 7: *Das Geheimnis der Kindheit* (The mystery of childhood), which was mentioned above in point 4, is an autobiography that I recorded on the basis of a regression into the level of consciousness she had in the years of her youth and adolescence, a regression carried out in obedience to my request. This mystical work is not to be confused with the aforementioned autobiography that A. wrote by hand from the present perspective of the consciousness of a mature woman, by means of her normal memories of the past. The first covers in a summary fashion the time leading to her conversion (1940), while the second breaks off at the year 1928.

Volumes 8–9: *Tagebücher* (Journals). These began immediately after her conversion, since it was just at this time that the first mystical phenomena occurred. Initially, I took notes without Adrienne's knowledge; I would copy down at home what she recounted to me in the house on the Münsterplatz. Shortly afterward, once the dictations on *John* began, I henceforth recorded it and other things in her presence. The first volume treats the turbulent first years of her conversion, as visions and experiences, external and internal sufferings, befell her, stigmata suddenly overtook her (once out of the blue during my meeting with her), soon after she was overwhelmed by the storms of the Apocalypse, and so forth. The more the dictations and, with them, the "objective" mysticism took center place, the less I followed along taking notes; the journal breaks off in the middle of her fiftieth year. The last years were filled with countless individual experiences, which Adrienne dictated (especially in regard to the experiences of prayer in the midst of the Night), and which on account of their more personal or occasional character were not recorded in the volumes on *Wort und Mystik*. Volume 8 is directly connected with 7: the great longing, the thirty-eight-year wait, that the former describes leads to the superabundant fullness recounted in the latter.

Volume 11: *Ignatius Loyola*. This volume remains unsatisfying to the extent that, ultimately, the spirit of our "Holy Father" permeates all of the posthumous works and, in fact, Adrienne's entire corpus, which, as he himself emphasizes, is due to his initiative. Thus, for example, the selection of the "holy numbers" in volume 2 has a distinctly Ignatian coloring, and even the theology of the sexes (volume 12) bears his seal, not to mention the entire theology of obedience, of election, and of the states of life, which pervades even the Bible commentaries. Nevertheless, there were many things pertaining to his special significance that had to be collected into a single volume. Included in this volume is the following: (1) a commentary that he himself gave on his own autobiography (*The Pilgrim's Report*), in which he shows in a straightforward way ("no sensationalism!" he says at the outset) the particular life circumstances, the inner coherence, and the motivations of his actions.

The purpose of this commentary was primarily to bring life back to the image we have of him, though something new in his spirit also ought to become apparent. As I surreptitiously began to bring forward other sources for his life that were not included in the *Pilgrim's Report* and to ask corresponding questions, I was told quite strictly—just as P. Gonçalves was (cf. the introduction to the *Pilgrim's Report*)—that I had, in obedience, to adhere to what he had arranged. (2) Countless things that he said about himself, his first companions, about the *Exercises*, at both a practical and a theoretical level, about spiritual direction, treatments of mystics, and many other subjects. (3) Things he said about obedience (which stemmed in part from the dictation on Revelation 2–3, in which Ignatius always juxtaposed his own view to John's; his thinking is for the most part included in a brief, condensed form in the printed commentary, and it will be published here in a more extensive form). This volume, moreover, also contains the countless "tests of obedience and readiness" that he arranged in great detail in the form of strict penances for Adrienne to perform. These tests too were often "objective mysticism" to the extent that (in a manner analogous to volume 1) the degree of readiness of other saints or mystics were to be "measured" by them.

Volume 12: *Sexus und Agape*,[12] which was described above in point 2. This is the biblical theology of the Christ-Church relationship (which is itself rooted in the Father-Son relationship), which extends into the life of Christian virginity and finally is reflected in the relationship between Adam and Eve, man and woman (Adrienne also did a brief commentary on the *Song of Songs*), in which the difficult problem of the original, paradisiacal meaning of sex is constantly addressed.

This overview of the posthumous works ought to be taken as an anticipatory account, which intends to divide up the material in very general ways. As the books begin to be published, certain details may be changed.

---

[12] [The name given to this volume upon publication was *Theologie der Geschlechter* (Theology of the sexes).—TRANS.]

2. THE PARTICULAR INTRODUCTION TO THE PRESENT VOLUME

This work came into being over the course of several years, as new portraits were constantly added on occasion or at my own request. In the beginning, Adrienne was shown individual saints during times when she was not at all thinking of these particular people. For the most part, they were shown in their general disposition and, then, often in prayer that was particularly characteristic of them. Adrienne was each time able to reproduce their disposition when we recorded the dictation, and the words they spoke in prayer were given to her again during the dictation. Once the dictation was over, she would most often completely forget what she had seen and heard, as always was the case when Adrienne had "settled" something in obedience and put herself at the disposal of a new task. In the first period, she was also often given the vision of a saint during the night while she was at prayer, and she would report to me the next day that she had seen this or that saint, asking whether she could tell me about him or her. Frequently, she would be shown the essence of the person she saw without knowing exactly what the person's name was. Once she said, "Today I have seen Gregory." "Which one?" I asked. She confessed that she did not know there was more than one; she had no idea which person it was with whom she had interacted. I asked her then to begin, and after just a few sentences it became clear to me that it could have been none other than Gregory Nazianzen, as the section in this book will confirm. Later came Gregory the Great and Gregory of Nyssa to join him. Another time she said to me, "Today I received Catherine", and to my question, "Which Catherine?" she could only say, "Not the one from Siena; I know her." With the description, I guessed that it must have been Catherine of Genoa, whose life I myself had never read; a subsequent comparison with her biography and especially a comparison of the prayer with the account of the visions Adrienne had received gave me the certainty that it could have been no one else.

Later, the choice of the saints that were to be described was increasingly left to me. At first, I would jot down names for myself on a scrap of paper, and it might happen that, when I placed the paper before Adrienne, she would immediately say, "I can do this one." Another name she might take with her into her nightly prayer and then describe him to me on the following day. Later, I was able to request from her whatever saint or special personality I wished: a brief prayer would transpose her to the "place" of vision, she would close her eyes, look for a moment in the Spirit on what was shown her with intensity and inner excitement, and then the description would begin, slowly at first, in very clearly stamped words, and then more quickly, without the slightest hesitation, making new judgments with every sentence. Those who were still alive, and whose fate still lay in their free decision, were not shown, or (as, for example, with Therese Neumann) only in very brief glimpses. The definitive text on the little "Resl",[13] as well as on John XXIII, were written only after their deaths.

Adrienne had either no knowledge or just a glimmer of an idea about the majority of the personalities whose names I presented to her. Quite often the outcome of her description took me completely by surprise; I had expected something altogether different. I also presented her with names that were for me nothing more than names; I got some of them from a list of people who had received the stigmata,[14] above all, in order to see what sort of piety or attitude in each case lay behind the phenomenon; a few names were taken from the book by P. Herbert Thurston,[15] behind whose purely psychological and physiological descriptions the properly religious and Christian destinies and decisions remained hopelessly hidden and unrecognizable. What might the truth be, one wants to ask, about a Maria Castreca or the enigmatic Maria de la Visitación? In most cases, I did not verify the answers with documents that may finally have come to my attention; but the things that were shown, which were always extremely precise and bore a unique personal quality, already arranged the individual and disconnected traits into an internally plausible portrait.

It is important for the reader to bear in mind that the only thing intended to be shown here is the particular person's prayer and attitude toward prayer in relation to God. This attitude can in some cases be considerably different from the person's other achievements in the world and also for the Church (as, for example, the surprising and indeed shocking portrait drawn of Thomas Aquinas shows). The degree of integration between inner life and external work can vary quite significantly in the different saints, as we see, for example, in the description of Gregory of Nyssa.

---

[13] ["Resl" is a diminutive for "Theresa".—TRANS.]

[14] Franz L. Schleyer, *Die Stigmatisation mit den Blutmalen* (Hannover, 1948). Almost nothing about the interior life of those discussed comes to light in this doctor's descriptions.

[15] *Die körperlichen Begleiterscheinungen der Mystik* (Lucerne, 1956).

Particularly in the earlier periods of this work, Adrienne possessed an altogether extraordinary need for purity and transparency. Each time, she would ask, almost with anxiety, whether she was in fact "clean enough", whether I was able to see perfectly through her soul. She preferred to go to confession every time before she undertook this work, desirous as she was to be in every case in a perfect state of confession. In this regard, she dictated to me the following sentences:

> As long as a person lives in this world, he always clings in some sense to the things that belong to him. In confession, by contrast, a person must set the things that belong to him free; he must let the world go; he must bring forth everything and hand it over to the Church. He must become like a child. Then a person can allow everything God wishes to pass through him. Everything the Spirit says. But in confession a person gathers together all his sins, 'as God sees them'. He becomes dispossessed of his own judgment over himself in order to leave judgment to God alone. Only when a person leaves judgment to God alone can he, when he is shown a saint, say how it is that the Holy Spirit sees him. The Holy Spirit's judgment often turns out to be different from what the saint himself expects. For this reason, it can happen that something is shown of which the saint and those around him were scarcely aware; the Spirit underscores certain things that *he* takes to be important in the saint's soul, whether they be positive or negative.

The state of confession, in which Adrienne sought to remain, means: pure openness and readiness, the whole of the soul being nothing more than a photographic plate, able to take up and reproduce anything that is given to it, just as it is given. If this purity were not there, according to Adrienne, it would not be possible to see "how much of what was given belonged to the saint himself and how much belonged to me. In fact, it would disproportionately increase precisely what I had kept of my own, hidden in myself, in the transmission of what came from the other, and would thus make the objectivity of the portrait impossible." The more absolute the obedience demanded was (and here it was truly demanded in an absolute sense), the greater would be the guilt if someone wanted to keep something hidden. It is clear, however, that such an "experiment" could be performed only with a soul that had been completely purified. The complete self-effacement that was demanded has of course nothing in common with Buddhism and Zen; it is a pure work of Christian love; it is the highest possible approximation to the Church's attitude as the Bride of Christ, in whose bosom and spirit all the saints and those who pray find their shelter. It is the attitude of the soul that has been known, since Origen's time, as the *anima eccle-*

siastica, the ecclesial soul,[16] it is the perfection of the Ignatian *sentire cum Ecclesia*.

Adrienne takes the prayers of the saints and other believers into her soul through a perfect reenactment of them. That is why she occasionally shows some awkwardness when she has to reproduce an imperfect prayer: she herself would have preferred to pray a different way. Or, if the prayer contains traces of vanity (as, for example, in Gregory Nazianzen), she feels afterward somewhat stained. On the other hand, she feels personally enriched by all the things in the prayers that are good. She receives all of this with her own "organ of prayer". If she herself had not prayed so much, she would not have been able to transmit any prayers, and if she did not herself have some experience of everything that appears in all these prayers, she would also not have been able to reproduce them. Nevertheless, she was not permitted to be anything but an instrument in the moment of transmission. Moreover, she was not able to carry through these transmissions in the presence of anyone but her confessor, because the whole was a work of obedience.[17]

If, on Adrienne's part, it is a work of obedience, then on the side of the saints it was a work of humility. Of a heavenly humility that does not shy from displaying itself before the earthly Church in an unshielded attitude of confession. If Péguy considers public confession to be an indispensable principle of the earthly Church,[18] how much more validity it holds for the heavenly Church, where nothing private exists anymore! The examples will show that nothing happens outside of love and discretion, for the sake of mere curiosity, and that everything that is shown is an aid in some sense to Christianity on earth.

---

[16] [Balthasar's translation of the Latin as *verkirchlichte Seele* would be literally rendered into English as "ecclesialized soul".—TRANS.]

[17] The one attempt I made to request something of this sort in the presence of a third person (a young Jesuit priest, who was a friend of ours, was present) was such a torture to Adrienne that I immediately perceived the falseness of the endeavor and never repeated it.

[18] "Publier le privé, c'est le principe même, c'est la méthode ecclésiastique même. Le vieux principe de la confession publique court sous toute la chrétienté. Le chrétien dans la paroisse, dans la chrétienté, est toujours le premier chrétien, le fidèle antique toujours prêt, toujours soumis à la confession publique, à la commune et comme mutuelle confession" (*Un Nouveau Théologien, Oeuvres en prose*, vol. 2 [Pléiade], 875). [To make public what is private is the very principle, the very method of the Church. The old principle of public confession flows under the whole of Christianity. The Christian in the parish, in Christianity, is always the first Christian, always the ancient believer, who is always ready, always subject to public confession, to a common and, as it were, mutual confession.]

The various series came to be at different times. In the first series, one finds sections included that occurred at a later date. The series dealing with the threefold attitude and the series with the recited prayers came into existence within the space of a relatively brief period of time. When Adrienne had finished her description, I was given the freedom to ask questions in order to fill in some blanks. These questions, or the answers to them, can be recognized in the text because they are preceded by a line space. It is significant that Adrienne, who was doubtless in a form of ecstasy, nevertheless heard the voice of her confessor by virtue of her obedience, understood his questions, and was able to answer them in view of what she saw.

The choice of the saints' portraits remains of course arbitrary; there could have been many more such portraits to be had. Regarding the wording of the dictation, very little has been changed; nothing at all has been changed in terms of the meaning, though the sentence structure was here and there tightened; French words (Adrienne's native language was French, and she was not always able to find immediately the fitting word in German) were often left untranslated. A bit more variety was brought to her somewhat poor vocabulary through the occasional use of synonyms.

In judging these portraits, the reader ought to focus his attention on the center of the things said rather than getting caught up in the margins or in trivial matters. Certain details might be expressed in a one-sided manner, perhaps even badly characterized. But no one is going to deny that Michelangelo is able to draw well just because in one of his drawings there happens to be a "stray" line. In reading, one reads the Spirit in the illuminated background, not in the letter. No one who reads the following pages can fail to see the power of the things said, whose intellectual differentiation and characterization presuppose a wholly uncommon natural intelligence and a just as uncommon supernatural discernment of spirits. It should be clear, however, that this work is given to the modern, prayer-weary Church in order to awaken in her an astonishment over the riches of the "world of prayer" and a new joy in praying.

The second part of the *Book of All Saints* will fill out things in this first volume in a variety of ways.

Hans Urs von Balthasar

FIRST SERIES

Briefer descriptions, occasionally with responses to questions

I see his pious prayer. He is of simple heart and perseveres in the openness of a surrender that he will never fully grasp. But he does not need to grasp it, because God did not fashion his mission as one part of a dual mission. His relationship to the Mother of Jesus cannot be compared, for example, to that between Benedict and Scholastica or between Francis de Sales and Jane de Chantal; here, by contrast, one mission stands adjacent to the other, and it is Joseph's task to give support to Mary's mission in a very modest way. Just as you could not call them a couple, a married couple, so too you could not call theirs a dual mission. Joseph, the righteous man, is involved in something that at first frightens him; he does not understand it. But then grace brings him a certain understanding, even if it remains incomplete. Through the angel, he receives a confirmation of the correctness of what happened, and from that point on he knows: This is my path, and my path has God as its source. But he will never fully comprehend what happened with Mary the Virgin. And if he endeavors to stand by her and to be a father to her Child, he nevertheless is always aware that he is only a foster father. This is as far as his understanding goes. And he prays more and more that God will show him the paths he will have to prepare; not that God will give him a definitive understanding. When he looks upon the Mother with her Child, he understands that it is an inconceivable grace to be present here and to be able to watch and to contribute his help, and he grows in faith and he grows in joy, without having to follow the difficult path the Mother has to take. If he, too, experiences difficult moments out of concern for the Child, he also has a taste above all of the joy of surrender, the joy of participation, and his prayer is one of gratitude—not very comprehensive, but still faithful and pious and kind. Whenever some aspect of the Son, some aspect of his growing up and his mission, opens up to Joseph, he takes it immediately into prayer, because it belongs together so intimately with his own path that he must keep watch over it, too, in prayer. He loves, and he works, and his help is the sort that never counts the cost. Once the angel spoke to him, he was set at rest once and for all, and this calm radiates over everything he does. He knows none of the disquiet that comes with reckoning. He knows that he has a share in many mysteries, even if it is not his responsibility to explore them. He is without curiosity, a simple and pious man.

He has had some experience of contemplation. The very fact that he sees the Mother and the Child and sees what unifies them is already contemplation; for he sees it in a spirit of prayer; and he carries it into his prayer as another mystery that has been given to him, which he must in some sense meditate on in the hours of his own prayer. To meditate on and not to explore, but rather to allow it to permeate his prayer in a fruitful manner. And his prayer develops, but from first to last in the Son. It grows, even if it does not grow in insight.

BARNABAS

I see his prayer, which is at once deliberate [*überlegt*] and reflective [*überlegend*]. He wants to be a good representative of the things concerning the Lord, but he feels distanced from him and asks the Lord to initiate him better and to give him the grace of perfect imitation. He also prays a good deal to God the Father and wants to receive many graces from the Holy Spirit, in order to be able to distribute them further. He is not as gifted as St. Paul, but he is very aware of his mission. And he makes an effort to live in poverty in the midst of his mission and not to receive anything without passing it on to others. He follows his path step by step, not so much in a blind trust, but rather as part of a deliberate reflection. He is perfectly aware that the first disciples after the Lord's departure from the earth have to travel down paths that remain paths that can be imitated. Thus he wants to remain wholly within what is real and not allow himself—either by faith or by the other apostles—to be carried away into things that would lie beyond his oversight. This is due, however, not at all to a need to be constantly assured he is right, but rather to the awareness of having been called by God to a mission of overseeing things, a mission that it is his responsibility to manage in such a way that it becomes clear. He prays a lot, primarily for the others. He does not have St. Paul's need to have others pray for him; rather, he has the need to watch his prayer *disappear* into God. He also has contemplative prayer, in which he holds firmly to what he knows about Christ and his life on earth, in order to arrange these things as part of new scenes played out in heaven and to be able to contemplate them thus. Also, the Our Father, which the Son gave to the world, is a prayer dear to his heart: to be able to pray it as the Son himself prayed it and so that the Father's will may be done on earth.

His relationship to St. Paul is a hard relationship: he has accepted this relationship in obedience to God; afterward, the roles were in a certain sense reversed, and the one below became the superior. However, there was no personal resentment in this, but rather a responsibility that he carries before God and that he cannot allow Paul to take from him. He is convinced that they have many things to give one another, indeed, that this exchange is indispensable, even though their missions cannot be substituted for one another.

I see his prayer, which Paul transforms into a priestly prayer. For him, Paul embodies the Church; he is the vessel of obedience perhaps even more than the nascent Church. Indeed, Paul is obedient, and Titus is meant to live in obedience. He thus lives on what Paul gives to him; not in a distance from the Lord, but all the same in a renewal of what Paul has to be; by accepting what Paul is and reproducing what Paul mirrors in him.

He prays; the prayer that he himself fashions is not particularly important; more important is the prayer in him that awaits, which corresponds in a certain way to contemplation. It is an emptiness, which he creates in himself in order to make room for the message. This message primarily means the words of St. Paul. It is practice in obedience, preferably in that form of obedience known as indifference. Paul has disposal over him as he would over a thing, and Titus allows himself to be thus directed. But he must learn to be thus directed in the name of the Church, which is also in the process of learning, in the name of the answer that all of those responsible to St. Paul have to give. To create an emptiness in himself means to look away from himself, his plans, his talents, and their effects, in order always and at every moment to do whatever it is that is given to him to do, and to do it in such a way that he carries his obedience even farther than the superior's words dictate. This means: to make the superior's words so much the rule of one's life that, where the words cease to reach one, one nevertheless continues to obey their meaning and thus carries out the superior's primary intention. In this way, it is practice in contemplation, in becoming empty, and practice in indifference, which occasionally appear as separate from one another. And then Titus sees in Paul a direct translation of the Lord's qualities and thus comprehends what constitutes the essence of sanctity. And he remains respectful of Paul and respectful of the Lord, as he walks down the path God has laid out for him. His prayer is humble, but deeply stamped by the accents of waiting, of a refusal to anticipate. He is more an imitator than a creator; but wherever imitation ceases for want of an image to follow and demands the task of creativity, he becomes a creator out of obedience.

TIMOTHY

I see him at prayer. He does not pray a lot, just as the first Christians do not pray a lot, because everything is so new to them. They nevertheless make an effort to enter into a unity with doctrine, which produces an atmosphere of prayer in every conversation. He is thus minded to act as apostolically as possible, to free himself from his faults, but he does so more as action, making use of all his capacities; the attitude of allowing things to happen and the attitude of indifference are not at all as clearly defined in him as they are in Titus. He sees Paul before him, the one who works and acts, and sees himself as one who acts with Paul. And everything in himself that he sees change and improve he believes to be due directly to Paul's influence. He thus prays for the Church, for himself, and for St. Paul, but in an extremely active form: he wants to see the fruits. He asks for the visibility of whatever he undertakes; he counts.

But he is zealous and untiring and is in fact almost more devoted to St. Paul than he is to God; he cannot imagine what would have become of him if Paul had not imposed upon him that form of life which lay on Paul, a form of life that Timothy feels is suited to him. He also has opinions concerning his life and the Church and the world that bring what was mentioned above very clearly to expression; he believes that people must hurry because the last days are imminent, and he sees— even if the concepts of action and contemplation have not yet been defined—that, in everything that happens, his particular function and role lie in action. *Et sa prière s'en ressent* [and it can be felt in his prayer]. He remains active even later, as a bishop, but is altogether magnanimous. He does not measure things out in terms of his own capacities, even when he is tallying results.

APOLLOS

I see his prayer, which is perhaps not very warm, but nevertheless very zealous. He tries to grow in Christian understanding by means of his prayer. He would like, with the whole of his being, to help give Christianity and his faith a broader basis, to translate it into the various levels of the spirit, to multiply possibilities in everything that occupies the human spirit, to safeguard the participation of the Holy Spirit, in order from the beginning to give every art, every science, and every realm of the heart a Christian coloring. And whenever he is unable to do this by himself and not yet able to recognize it in others, he nevertheless attempts absolutely to present this task as something that is both possible and necessary. His activity is a preparation for what is to come; he sees chests of drawers that as yet still remain empty, things for which there does not yet exist any use but which will belong tomorrow or the day after to the common good and which must be kept in mind already in advance so that, when their time comes, the Christian element will not have hardened into a rigid skeleton in the meantime.

He is humble in prayer, earnestly attempts to learn from God what he ought to do, and he does not allow himself to be confused by the things he sees with his human eyes.

He is still a great way from understanding what it means to pray without ceasing; he has a strong sense of the value of action and foresight. But he also understands quite well the significance of petitionary prayer and is perhaps the one who is least aware of himself in prayer, because he is quite occupied with the matter at hand: to give a good, viable form to his apostolic task, to the Church and her doctrine. He sees his own task in a certain sense in detachment from himself; what he undertakes he looks upon, not as his own work, but rather as a response to God's word. And then he is at every turn shocked at how little zeal he sees in people and how the Lord himself did not find anyone to take his place on earth. The first apostles seem to him—and this is perhaps also true of St. Paul—to be wholly filled with striving, to be immediately inspired by the Lord, but to lack the capacity to awaken the same intensity of enthusiasm in others. And he is anxious, with a real tradesman's anxiety, that Christianity could begin to lose its validity, because those who represent and cherish the faith could lose their strength, because, even though the number of believers is increasing, a superficiality has entered in at the same time. He thus tries to hammer and impress, in a busy zeal that perhaps here and there ought to make room for a deeper inwardness of prayer, a greater simplicity. He ought to return his attention to the value of individual souls more than to the standards that have been reached or to reassuring ideas. And then he sees that even he has disciples, just like the Baptist did, that he acquires a circle of followers, which terrifies and delights him at the same time; it delights him because he recognizes the necessity of keeping the Church alive; but it terrifies him because he fears creating divisions. He would not by any means want to play a role that was not accorded to him or that he himself did not seek. Precisely in the thought of division, an image of the later Church appears before his mind, an image that ought to be avoided at all costs and at the same time a sign of the sin that *also* exists in the Church, a sign of the proximity of sin *also* in one's faith.

THE SHEPHERD OF HERMAS (ca. 150)

I see him, before he begins to have his visions. He believes and he prays. When the visions start, his faith and his visions have no connection with one another. He receives faith as a grace; he attempts to live in its grace and makes an effort to gain a better understanding of it. Next to this are the visions, which arise from grace but which he looks upon for the moment as foreign images, without being able to see the point of access, without understanding how these images belong to his faith. He makes efforts to integrate himself ever more deeply into his faith, to allow himself to be determined by and taken up by his faith, indeed, to receive from his faith a way of life that has value also for others, that bears apostolic fruits, that could help bring others to faith or to a strengthening of their faith. In prayer, he begins to contemplate the events that he encounters in a natural way, the things that cross his path in his everyday life, and he wonders how these things look in faith, in the life of the Lord and in the life of heaven. He reflects; he begs for clarity; he accepts whatever stimulation comes to him from the outside or whatever is given to him from the inside in faith as an enrichment of his faith, and he tries to live in the unity between faith and what he has experienced.

And now the connection between the visions and his faith opens up to him. And once this insight enables him to acquire a certain training in seeing, he begins to see things in a different way. At first he had immediately seen only with the eyes, even though he was aware that these were not his own eyes that saw, not his own ears that heard, and that his perceptions were not tied to his senses in the usual manner. Now he suddenly understands that these senses have received a new intensity through faith and that his visions therefore belong to his faith. He must accept them as a gift of grace, though he is obliged not only to look on what is shown to him, but also constantly to grasp it in such a way that the meaning of the vision is incorporated into the meaning of faith and that he must never grow tired of asking questions until he has understood. What occurred up to this point on the periphery must now become the center of his mission; the contribution he must make is not directly concerned with God's word as other people are able to perceive it, but he is meant to enrich God's word by his experiences, by approaching it, so to speak, in a roundabout way. He is meant to make known a kind of addition to the gospel (the word is a little too strong), to speak through a symbolic language, which employs images, colors, and similes that are different from the ones used by the Lord and yet contain one and the same truth. This new language ought not to set only him on fire as a Christian but ought to help overcome the difficulties that beset his fellow Christians, to clarify their thinking, and to facilitate the living out of their faith.

He is not allowed to leave off questioning until he grasps the unity of meaning. And since the essence of the Church and the essence of penance and confession are granted to him as his particular task, he must present the Church in herself, which he does by confessing and by doing penance, and he constantly becomes more and more intimately a son of the Church. But, using his visions, he must truly illuminate in a new way what is essential about the Church, what is indispensable in penance and the hope for confession; he must describe the loftiest mysteries of a wise Church with the means of a simple man. All of his visions have as much an immediate practical meaning as they do a supernatural meaning, even if the supernatural meaning is not as completely transparent. The practical meaning can and must be immediately translated into life; behind this, there remains something mysterious, something that points more or less clearly to the mysteries between the bride and bridegroom, and draws its life essentially from these mysteries. Most of the visions are those of a shepherd, containing images he recognizes, or perhaps occasionally also images he does not recognize, things that, on the natural level, at best could have inspired his startled imagination or his colorful hope. These images are foreign to him. He knows them—and yet he does not know them; he knows them by virtue of the natural gift of his senses, but he is not permitted to recognize them again within his vision, because here they become for him bearers of perfect, yet unseen mysteries.

In this familiar and yet foreign effect of the matter of vision lies one of the most beautiful possibilities of surprise that is caused by the reciprocal illumination occurring between what is natural and what is visionary: when God takes what is natural and perceivable by natural means and raises it up for vision into his supernatural world, it has an effect that is simultaneously familiar and foreign. It has to be so filled and recast by God's presence that everything about the faith, unto its innermost corners, is reevaluated; what was up to this point sketched out merely in a rough, provisional sense is now adorned with everything that God the Father, the Son, and the Spirit desire to give the Church both as ornamentation and also as an enrichment of doctrine.

"Hermas" sees in a wholly objective manner; in such a way that he lives solely from the perspective of his mission. To live from the perspective of mission is the most objective thing a believer can do.

GREGORY THE WONDERWORKER (d. ca. 270)

For him, prayer was the final place of refuge. Not only a place of safety in the spiritual sense; when he is in prayer, he feels himself surrounded by a wall that protects him and the things he cares about. He is completely whisked away to solitude. He forgets the world and speaks with God; but nevertheless, when he is addressed from outside, he is immediately able to respond and deal with the pressing questions. It is not the case that he strives after a permanently abiding disposition of prayer; rather, he swings back and forth between the world of others and the world of God and prayer. He always tries to carry the one over into the other as much as possible, in a manner similar to one who would gather provisions and clothing from a house for those who are poor and who suffer from the cold. He must always traverse a particular path. Thus, he knows nothing about any permanently fixed disposition of prayer (though one could say that this shifting itself permanently characterizes it), and he also has no experience of it. If he has to spend time with the people around him, it can become burdensome, and if he is required to give advice, he draws what he will say from prayer. There is, as it were, a pause between these two things: he does not feel himself to be so carried away that he immediately has a ready answer; he has to go speak with God; he must ask God's opinion; he must interact with the saints and find out their view. And he must feel that he has perfect solitude in order to be able to achieve this prayer.

Visions are not very common but are given in such a way that they provide powerful nourishment to his prayer, and he has to pray over what he sees and hears for a long time. In a vision, he discovers ever new material for countless prayers, for countless parables and explanations. If he performs miracles, it occurs, not through his prayer, but when he is surrounded by other people. The miracles therefore appear to him like lightning straight from heaven. If he were to recognize them completely as his own, he would be fully convinced that, in performing them, he is God's instrument. He would also have to confess that he does not understand why they are not in unity with the answers he receives in prayer; in other words, why the miracles do not occur in solitude, but only in the "other" time, and also why the miracles are not things that are useful for him or that he himself asked for. When a person asks him for advice, then he retires into prayer and returns with an answer. But when God performs a miracle, then God does not give him this moment of time; instead, God surprises him along with those around him with the miracle. God perhaps thus answers the person who requested the miracle, but not Gregory. And thus he has to allow the confusion that the miracle causes in him to be tempered once again in prayer. But he is himself perfectly unimportant; and he is ashamed that the miracles that occur through him cause him confusion. He thus attempts to pray even more zealously, in order to forget himself more and more, so that he will not lose the thread that God placed in his hands and will at least be faithful in prayer, because whatever comes to pass outside of prayer always affects him in an odd way. If he could do what he wanted, he would never come out of the solitude of prayer, and his longing for silence grows with the years, his longing for the silence of God's voice, so that it becomes a torture for him—and this torture is a part of his cross—to endure the human circus and its demands. He also has the gift of being able to see through people, to see how pure their intentions are and how necessary their requests. If their hearts are not pure, then he sees them as if covered by an opaque veil, and this shows him that he can gain no access. He is not the great purifier, but the great discerner. This discernment of spirits, which is given to him as God's gift, never leaves him and makes him constantly more sensitive to those things that concern him. What does not concern him remains opaque to him. Occasionally he can give sharp admonishment, but his realm is more the strengthening of the good that is there, encouragement, help, and illumination. And the world of his visions and his prayer is for him the real world; the world of heaven. The other world is the world to be ransomed.

He also sees the Lord's Mother and John; not only once, but several times. John, in part together with Mary, explains Scripture to him, so that he may get a better understanding of it and can use what he understands primarily as the foundation for his prayer; he learns from the visions how to pray into the visions. It is not a verse-by-verse commentary. Occasionally, even pericopes are interpreted for him, or even the spirit of the Scriptures as a whole is shown to him; the heavenly world is explained to him. If Gregory ever needs an answer for some request, it can happen that the question gets completely objectified, as if it henceforth had little or nothing to do with the person asking it, and then John shows what Scripture has to say to this question and perhaps what result it had with him or with the Lord's Mother. And then it becomes possible to draw a response from this to the person who made the request.

CONSTANTINE, EMPEROR (288–337)

There is more to report about his disposition than about his prayer. The fact that he converted to Christianity means, for him, that he strives to have a Christian disposition; he acknowledges the greatness of the Lord, and he accepts the faith, which becomes eminently important to him. But he has difficulties behaving like a Christian, because he is, so to speak, blinded by the greatness of Christianity. He tries to find his way in it; he converts a lot of people—though in fact more by force than by the power of persuasion—but he is so preoccupied with the idea of what it means to be Christian that very little time is left over for himself and for his taking up of prayer. He does pray a little, to be sure, but this little looks sort of like compulsory prayer; as an army general quickly commends himself to God before the battle, so he commends himself often to the Lord before he undertakes something, without ever passing over into a longer prayer, without above all making any real attempt at contemplation. It would be unjust to say that his prayer has too little weight. But it has a different weight; it bears more on his determination and disposition. For he genuinely *wants* to be Christian, just as a man wants to be a soldier. And the fact that, as a Christian, he is also the emperor imposes on him an immense responsibility, which he is perfectly willing to bear. In this, he knows that there are many things that he strives for that he is personally unable to accomplish. He is, however, convinced that he has received from God the mission to be a Christian emperor, while the monastic life, the life of withdrawal and contemplation, are things that do not concern him personally. He will in any event attempt to encourage others in these things; he will listen with goodwill whenever such things are spoken about. Nevertheless, his task is above all one of Christian politics. The Church remains for him in a certain sense a burden; there are many things he wishes were different, and the question is alive for him how many of these things he ought to take upon himself. For he also recognizes that this is not right; he sees other tasks to which he turns his attention. Nevertheless, in all that he undertakes, he is a man of great honesty. Even in those cases where he gives too much weight to diplomatic paths, he tries, at least in God's eyes, to be clear and honest, to serve God in the nobility of his position as emperor, in the obligation he possesses before his Lord. He has a very comprehensive notion of what it means to realize Christianity in the world: he wants to bring about a Christian world, to be able to establish an Order that is capable of enduring through the ages. But he pursues this goal more with the strength of his understanding than with that of his piety.

(PSEUDO-) MACARIUS (ca. 300–390)[1]

I see him at prayer. And prayer is indeed a need for him, but especially ascetic prayer. He needs discipline in order to pray. Then he takes joy in it, when he is inside it, a joy similar to that which he experiences in doing penance: the joy of giving, the joy of knowing about the one thing necessary. He has a peculiar way of making contact with God,

[1]The author of the so-called homilies of Macarius, PG 34:449–821.

insofar as he seeks and finds him in every word, and at the same time he remains quite aware of his own unworthiness. He is also in part sad that he cannot pray in a more spontaneous way, that, though his soul has a constant thirst for God, he experiences it almost as a penance to pray. Every time, or almost every time, he has to overcome himself. Once he has done this, then he prays willingly. It is sort of like someone who does physical exercise and is happy that he no longer needs fifty minutes anymore but only forty minutes. It moves along. It is not the feeling of being finished more quickly that makes him happy, but the feeling of order.

He prays for the world, and he also prays a little for himself. He is happy once he has prayed. He is also happy that he has been able to persevere before God in the attitude of prayer. Often it seems to him that this attitude slips away from him, as if he were too great a sinner to be able to attempt to persevere in it. Nevertheless he does make the attempt. He prays the prayers of the Church, but he also prays freely; his contemplations are more conversations with God. Christ is for him in the first place a man who went about on earth among other men; he unfolds his concerns before Christ and then has the feeling that he has been helped: Christ the man understands him, his fellowman, and God in Christ can help him.

(*The devil?*) He experiences him in a powerful way as the "power of evil". He also sees the effects of this power in the fact that prayer seems to him to be an ascetic practice. But he sees evil above all in himself and in his fellowmen. It is this that he struggles against. In his thoughts, his prayers, in his entire disposition. But he sees the devil's tricks.

(*Visions?*) I do not see it so much as a vision. Rather ... as a powerful experience. As something supernatural, which he is able to appreciate as such.

(*The Church?*) Nothing extraordinary. He has the nature of a fighter, which means he tries to divide. He wants absolutely to be orthodox. He harbors an anger against anything that is not orthodox. Perhaps he has a powerful view of heresies as coming from the devil.

GREGORY OF NYSSA (d. ca. 394)

He was educated with great care and in his later years is a great reader. From his reading springs the powerful need to cooperate in the building of theology, to cooperate in fashioning doctrine. He reads philosophers and many of those who already wrote about Christian doctrine before him. He maintains an active correspondence with many people who had significance in the Church at that time. He sees the earlier writers' level and also that of his contemporaries, and he would like the contemporary one to be as high as the earlier one. He suffers a lot on account of the fact that people are simplifying Christian teaching; according to him the exposition of Christian doctrine ought by no means to rank below that of the pagans. Christianity is superior and also ought to find a superior expression in the intellectual realm. It would not be fair to call him an aesthete; but he finds nothing less bearable than the vulgarization of theology. If even the old pagans made such an effort to express philosophical things about God with care, how much more ought we to do so! He participates in all the intellectual currents. He is subtle in differentiating his opinions. He does not content himself with an abstract construction of doctrine, but he makes connections with everything around him. He writes above all for cultivated people; or at least that is his intention. On the one hand, he dealt with the basic questions of dogma, on the other hand, he raised several side questions. His belief in Christian doctrine is faithful, but he also grows in a sense with his results. Here and there he succeeds in a great project; if, in this particular area, he thus no longer sees any contradiction, if everything seems to him to have been proven, then his faith is thereby strengthened and encouraged. But he distinguishes well between what is part of the canon of the Church's faith and what is mere speculation; in this, he is faithful to the Church.

He does not pray an enormous amount and makes a strong distinction between prayer and work. This is why his faith is strong. He tests his work carefully against Scripture and tradition, but he does so more in faith than in prayer. There, he receives illumination, more in philosophical and theological thinking than in his immediate relation with God. It is as though simple prayer, the straightforward falling on one's knees, seems too simple to him. He is not a mystic; if he is at all, it is at most on the intellectual level. He is the opposite of a John of the Cross, who always molds things on the basis of his experience in prayer, while Gregory proceeds entirely from the tradition of "great thinkers". In particular, in the ancient Greek thinkers he sees the *beauty* of thought, and he is attracted by a certain rhythm. He thinks: This beauty is something we ought not to lose; it should come alive again for us, in the dancing and rhythm of the soul. In his reading, the musicality of his soul is awakened in him, and he gets carried away. He then projects this experience into the Christian sphere and attempts to capture this value and to translate it in a genuine way (and not just externally). He does it ultimately, not for his own sake, but for the glory of

God. He enriches the Church by the foreign treasures he brings to her. He is like a lover who learns new customs of love from foreign peoples in his travels and then describes them to his bride upon his return and introduces them to her, for example, by giving her jewelry of a new sort or new clothes to dress in, and so forth.

His work and his increasing knowledge have little effect on his prayer. It is as though he is unable to take up into his prayer the worship to which his work lends powerful expression. He is a little like a dressmaker who makes the most extraordinary gowns for her clients but who uses the simplest of clothes for herself. On the other hand, he has a whole circle of people around him who take an interest in his work and to whom he is able to pass on many things.

EPHRAEM (306?–373)

From the beginning, he knows about the reality of faith. This faith is initially for him something completely bound up with people. He sees himself as someone who believes, and he wonders what is supposed to come of it. He understands that he has to pass it on. And he reflects: Should I perhaps do something extremely simple, go around a bit through the country and preach, go to assemblies and talk with people, open up a school for children? ... He envisions the life he would lead if he were to pass on his faith in this way. He sees the external work, but then the image of the internal work also appears to him: how much it would cost him to live in such a way that his life would truly be an expression of the faith he professes. How would it be if he could focus his faith in such a way that it would comprehend his entire existence? At the same time, a life of study rises before his eyes as an ideal: what it would mean to understand the living faith, which has been personally appropriated, also now in an internal way. For he is intelligent; he has a clear grasp of what consequences the ideal he sees would entail for him. Up to this point, the faith and its demand stood, so to speak, next to one another; the demand was restricted immediately to the sphere of "moral life". Now he recognizes that, in order to create unity, he would have to refashion his life from the ground up on the basis of his faith. And while he reflects on this, the demand appears to him as *God's* demand. Once again, the two things at first stand apart from one another: here there is the faith with its laws and demands, and there, as if at a remove, is God with his wholly immediate personal desires. He accepts the first in a very naïve way, almost more with his heart than with his understanding and will, as something restful, something calming, traditional. The second at first remains for him, as it were, abstract and intellectual. Almost pretentious, even. He sees that God can personally call a person in rare individual cases, and indeed even to an intellectual mission, precipitously upward and into that "faith" that he thought he already possessed.

He thus stands in a new place. It is no longer an either-or between religion and study, a personal choice of what one likes more. He has now seen the possibility of a personal vocation to theological study. There is such a thing. God does such things. But he is still at a distance from imagining that he himself could be meant.

At this point the first and the second converge: How would it be if one were called to study *in* faith, and not next to the faith? He begins to understand the concept of vocation: a vocation either to a simple practical apostolate or to study in the faith. Both would be a service to the faith. Thus, the question becomes very concrete for him.

He is talented, and he knows he is. But he is humble. And he does not trust himself to ask God questions. He also does not have the prayer life that would be necessary in order to receive an answer to this questioning. He will not throw himself at God's feet and offer everything to him and assail him until he answers. Instead, from his capabilities, from his position and his talent, he derives a sort of obligation to put his abilities at God's service, to test his possibilities and thus to come to a choice. He says to himself: I am not less talented than others; I can take the responsibility of placing the gifts God gave me at his service.

He thus begins to work, to write, and his work acquires satiety and strength. Alongside his work, his prayer and his inner life likewise develop. He takes up individual themes and proceeds from the concepts that are given and are at hand and advances by relating them to one another, by weaving them into one another.

There are people around him with whom he has active exchanges; he is successful. He sees that what he achieves is good, and he continues with it. He infers from his growth and progress that he is on the right path, that this is truly what God wanted from him. He would never say, from his own perspective: God called me to do this . . . , but: I humbly hope that this is the path that God intended for me.

He discovers Mary in a way that is similar to the way he discovered his vocation; initially, he takes an intellectual interest in her, as it were, and then becomes involved in an increasingly central way. His prayer to Mary awakens through his work, since the fullness of contemplation and prayer always flows from his work; he sings the praises of his object, and this is what gives him an entry into prayer. But he is more a scholar than a poet; the poetry is an expression of his scholarly work. His humility remains naïve in him.

DIDYMUS THE BLIND (ca. 313–398)

He is childlike. The fact that he is so certainly has something to do with his blindness, and perhaps it is even more because, aware of his blindness, he possesses an infinite trust in God's light. His darkness seems to him to stand in an absolute contradiction to God's light, but this opposition is overcome by the light-knowledge [*Licht-erkenntnis*] of God in God's grace. It is almost as if, by taking away the light of his eyes, God gave him the grace-filled capacity to live in the light of his knowledge. He does not thereby think that God has favored him over others, but he knows explicitly that he has received a gift from God that sets him apart. Through God, his lack of light has become for him a way to God. It is for him a sort of symbol for the fact that a person has to sell everything in order to follow the Son and that God can foster this selling of everything by appropriating for himself even what a person is unable to give but which is nevertheless a possession. But God took away the light of his vision only in order to strengthen his inner vision and to give him a certitude concerning the things hidden in God. This is something fundamental in his work, although he otherwise refers very little to himself. He tries to accomplish in his person as a whole in relation to God what God has shown to his eyesight and never more to look upon himself. It is his desire to be robbed by God of his external light, not in order that he might illuminate more profoundly his own interior being through the light of grace, but only in order to be able to pass on the light of God that he has received. God cleared away his obstacles so that, for the benefit of others, fewer obstacles would be felt in his theology. He is joyful and objective in his work. What he loves most in God is his light in its communicability, in the triune life, and he also loves very much God's relations to human beings, all the eucharistic mysteries, grasped in the broadest possible sense and always leading to the commandment of love.

EPIPHANIUS OF SALAMIS (ca. 315–403)

I see his pious prayer, which does not vary much. With prescribed prayers, especially when he adheres to a text, he has all sorts of difficulty grasping the meaning in such a way that each word takes on a meaning. But when he is able to pray in a way that suits him, his prayer is simple and devout. It is at the same time the stammering of a creature who feels his distance from God and knows that he cannot find or form the right words and a simple gesturing, a simple expression of what he has to say to God. The content is his own life, the life of those entrusted to him, and otherwise a few ideas. He is of a simple intellectual disposition, but extraordinarily faithful and good-natured. Once he understands something, he has truly understood it, that is, he understands it in the context of his surrender, his mission, the will of God. Everything that strikes him as incompatible with God's will is not only foreign to him but hateful. It thus happens that he develops his understanding through battle. When he does not understand something, but only after he receives a confirmation from outside that it is not intelligible, then he blindly launches an attack against it, with great zeal, with the same zeal that characterizes his whole life. When he remains among familiar things and sees the goal of his task, and also recognizes the goal of those who are entrusted to him, then his prayer is somewhat richer, because it is full of trust and surrender. But when he is entrusted with tasks that surpass his capacities, then he becomes unhappy, and his prayer in fact loses almost all of its consistency, because he cannot recover the inner peace he needs in order to pray.

He lacks the flexibility of mind necessary to undertake very differentiated tasks. But he achieves something extraordinary when he is truly at home in his material, when the arguments are within his range, when he has become familiar with the things by carrying them from his prayer and bringing them into prayer. He is very honest, but somewhat simple; he is zealous, and, when he has recognized something as his path, he is perfectly at peace. He only becomes restless when he is affected by things from outside that are beyond him. And he loves God, he loves Christ with his whole heart. His path is characterized at its core by love. Monasticism is for him the unconditional form of obedience to God; it is love's answer to love. His views on this are simple and straightforward and very beautiful.

BASIL (ca. 330–379)

He is at once intelligent and humble. His humility constantly causes him to raise questions about the things he has discovered in his personal work. By contrast, his intelligence causes him to hold fast to something once he has truly come to know it. He reflects and formulates until he reaches a point when new insights arise that are false or skewed. He has to come to terms with these things. His humility inclines him to accept others' insights and formulations a priori as correct, while his intelligence compels him to keep a distance, to criticize, and to point out mistakes with precision.

His prayer also stands in a way within this same dilemma. It is a very zealous, humble, and above all extremely scrupulous prayer. Scrupulous in preparation, in all the attendant circumstances. But also scrupulous in its tenderness. For a man, he has a very tender disposition. He knows the sort of prayer that is neither dry nor particularly filled with consolation, a prayer that remains altogether constant. He experiences it as such a grace, just to be allowed to pray, that he always tries to keep his prayer at the same level, in a way that is slightly pedantic. He is completely overwhelmed by a feeling of awe, as much in relation to himself as in relation to the God who reveals himself in such a way. The constancy he desires and strives after allows him access to God. God lets him lead his life of prayer freely and, doing so, keeps him within certain limits, because he observes the tenderness of his prayer and because he does not need anything particular from him in this area, but rather above all in the area of the development of doctrine. The subdued grace that God bestows on him in prayer grants him the feeling of peace in prayer. He would be suspicious if he possessed this peace by virtue of his own resources. But he knows that he receives it as a gift that God gives him again and again in prayer. And he would not be equal to the agitations his work causes the soul if God tossed him back and forth too strongly in prayer between dryness and tangible presence, and so on.

Prayer then allows him to find the correct balance between knowledge and humility. It is prayer that always provides the way out of the dilemma, the guarantee for what is correct and what is false. It gives him the strength to defend his own good insights and to take up battle against false new ideas. Prayer becomes the regulator of his existence and his reactions. God gives him knowledge in prayer—because it is humble—and then allows him in humility to carry the certainty of correct insight into his work. If he were not such a man of prayer, he would be a man of the most extreme uncertainty. His humility would quickly degenerate into despondency and sickliness; his cleverness would easily turn into an all-too-great self-assurance. Prayer is, for him, the means that clinches everything. Because he knows the instability of his talent, he also comes to know daily that he can place no trust in himself, that he must seek all reliability in God. Thus, despite the pendulum swing between hesitation and certainty, he can carry out his task in a completely systematic way.

In his work, he always comes to a proposition in which he, so to speak, embraces the conclusion as an acquisition. But this conclusion must always be brought in prayer over and over again into the field of certainty and peace before he is able to incorporate it into his work.

He is very good-hearted with people; but because he is called to be a theologian, he must be steadfast in his ideas. This cuts him off from some people. In important ecclesial questions, he knows no compromise; he knows that everything he establishes must be unshakeable for the long term. It is his prayer that teaches him this. He has no right to form a private friendship on personal grounds unless a consent to the Church's doctrine has already been tested and confirmed. Otherwise, he would feel that he had betrayed his mission. He takes this mission very seriously, almost solemnly. In defending it, he is harsh. No one ought to suggest that he did not know the truth. He feels himself to be a Church Father.

His Rules have the same balance as his other study. But he formulates them to a large extent by his own lights. He measures them against himself in order to see what is good. In this respect, he is completely different from Ignatius, who advises what seems to be good for each person in particular. What connects him to Ignatius is the primacy of reverence, a certain rationality, the possibility of perseverance, and the humility of prayer.

JEROME (342–420)

I see his prayer, which is very much alive. He prays the way a person wages battle and brings everything he knows into his prayer. He fights, in fact, with God—over things. Over things that concern him personally, over virtue and purity and zeal and love and surrender, but he also fights with God over the concepts he uses. He prays in a way that always retains the character of a fight, even where he would like to hand himself perfectly over to God, inasmuch as he cannot calmly wait in God's presence to find out whether God has something to share with him and what it is. He is full of enthusiasm but also full of the will to fight, and, when he grows tired, he is not without bitterness. This means he would like to count his fruits as a child would; he would like to see what it all comes to. Perhaps less concerning him personally than concerning his fight with God. This is not a preoccupation with calculation; rather, it belongs to his fighting nature to want to conquer and make full use of things. From the outside, he often displays great humility and simplicity and love, but he blames himself when he sees himself become too gentle and soft; he attributes it to his fatigue or his mood and asks for more strength to fight. His main fight is a fight with God. And if he also has to fight through many things in the world, if he does not evade arguments and seeks sharp ways of putting things, he is nevertheless in general very lenient with other people because he has gathered experiences from the bitterness of his inner struggle that incline him to be gentler with other people. He possesses a form of mercy of which he actually becomes ashamed once he is alone again, because, in accordance with his nature, he has the feeling that a person ought to stand before God as a knight and forge others into knights. Character-wise, he is quite intense; his first reaction is generally that of intensity. But the second is always once again humble and gentle. He knows he is superior to his opponent in intelligence and dexterity, but he does not think of these things as virtues. Instead, he believes they simply show that God has given him weapons that he must use.

In terms of time, he is much acquainted with contemplation; he also considers contemplation the highest form of prayer. But he perhaps does not possess enough peace and quiet to be able to carry out contemplation in a daily manner; this does not correspond to his ideal of a fight. And when he has experienced passive prayer, which always returns and is always very well carried out, then he believes he has received sufficient strength from it, so that he must absolutely return to the battle prayer.

He erects no borders between his own agility of mind and the intensity of his heart; the latter therefore does not appear to him to be a fault. And he does not fight in order to be better than others.

DIADOCHUS OF PHOTICE (fifth century)

He prays, strangely, in batches. At one time with a great flood of words; then once again there are only individual words, upon which he dwells for a long time, surprised, overcome by their power, by the goodness in them. He did not realize that a single word could say so much; it overwhelms him anew each time that the word "Father", or some other word, could be so filled with truth, with gifts, with aspects, colors, entire landscapes, and with so much obligation, ascesis, restraint, and mystery. One can scarcely give voice to such a word, it is so heavily freighted. Then, once again come effusions, many sentences uttered immediately one after the other, which press upon one another back and forth, because the words also form sentences, and the sentences can say so much.

Another time, he feels he is no longer worthy of praying because prayer consumes too much of his Christian substance, it claims too much of his will to give himself, because in fact all he wants to do anymore is pray. He deals forcefully with himself, demands much from himself, but he knows that God the Father demanded much from the Son, and God the Spirit constantly places demands. He also tries to pray without words, simply through his attitude alone, and thus to remain before God in prayer. Often he would like to transform the whole of theology into a prayer; theology seems to him too stiff, too dead; everything, even knowledge, and even every conversation, ought to become prayer: that would be his goal.

(*Consolation and desolation?*) Perhaps in a way that parallels his words and wordlessness: everything is only a single word, which contains everything. Desolation, in this case, would result from the inability to integrate everything into the unity of prayer. But in this he also receives a lot of consolation, because if he had been in deeper desolation he would perhaps not have had the strength to pray so much and to seek so much.

(*Visions?*) Hard to say. Is it really a vision when prayer dominates so much that a person thinks he is having visions? When the word acquires such a fullness that it always already contains the image and reveals itself thus as an image of eternity? He is a little like a small child to whom one tells stories and who from the start experiences and "sees" everything you tell him because it becomes so vivid for his imagination.

PSEUDO–DIONYSIUS THE AREOPAGITE (I) (ca. 500)

I see him. He is a humble and learned man, who does everything to glorify God and forgets himself more and more. He is caught in a fierce struggle with himself, with his nature, with his longing in the broadest sense, which also includes his aesthetic needs, his desire for knowledge, his desire for recognition, for fame, for visible achievement—so that he will do nothing in the end but what God asks of him. The struggle would be destructive, if it were not the case that his humility before God is at the deepest level untouched by his desire for fame. He has a genuine humility before God and lives an inner life of penance. And he prays long enough for God to root out whatever obstacle there may be keeping him from God. If after a couple hours of prayer—there is also a lot of prayer at night and much fasting—he has not reached anything, but instead sees that he is the same as he was before, then he perseveres longer and does not stop. And the achievement is never such that he ascribes a part of it to himself. It is always God's victory over him, indeed, against him. This struggle with himself would, in his judgment, be enough to fill his entire life

46

if he had not understood already at the very beginning of his struggle that he has a mission and task, that God has chosen him for something else in spite of his unworthiness, that the struggle against himself ought to unfold within a fight for God's glory, that he is allowed in a certain sense only to use the time left over for the struggle with himself. He belongs to God, and so does his time and his particular task. Thus, in his renunciation of the struggle, of the rigorous struggle conducted in a way that admits description, there lies a second struggle, which is simply the struggle of his mission: a struggle into his task, and only secondarily, out of this struggle, a struggle with himself. He possesses such power for the vision of God—in the context of the problems he has been given—that he sometimes finds himself afterward in the greatest astonishment on the other side with the pen in his hand. He is carried away by what God has shared with him and given to him to work out.

The fact that he claims to have known the holy people at the Lord's time is a very remarkable story. It is the consequence of his visions and to a certain extent the consequence of his childlike faith. Viewed externally, it looks like he misrepresents himself, historically speaking; but something more real corresponds to it. At bottom, he is so completely who he is that he is at the same time who he is not. The Lord's words also do not lose their power with the passing centuries; the words of the Gospel have today the same vitality as the words that Christ once spoke on earth. Thus, with his mission, he can stand right next to Dionysius. His mission points from the words of Scripture to him. Even if there is no historical continuity, nevertheless, there are no ruptures, similar to the way in which Christ is the fulfillment of a particular event or a proverb from the Old Testament, which has to be grasped simultaneously as being and as becoming. Or a seed that happened to be left over from the historical time of Christ; it fell upon fruitful soil, but it is only the rain that brings it to sprout.

PSEUDO-DIONYSIUS THE AREOPAGITE (II) (ca. 500)[1]

I see him in prayer. This prayer often seems like a step that has to be leapt over. Perhaps one could say it has a twofold character. There is the prayer that affects him personally and embraces his work as a whole. And then there is the guiding prayer, which belongs to the work itself and out of which the work is formed. This second prayer is separate from the sphere of his person. One cannot call it a prayer of

[1] Dictated several months after the preceding sketch.

the understanding; it is a prayer of work. It is prayer that flows directly into his work, and, because his work is suprapersonal and, through mission, is submitted to his supraintelligence, it remains suprapersonal. To be sure, he asks for clarity of expression, for the gift of form, for the correctness of understanding, and his prayer is born from this; but, in a certain respect, it is more like the whole Church's prayer for a particular grace that she needs. In this moment, he always embodies the whole Church, anonymously—for only a few hand themselves over with their work—and there is a purity that pervades his work, a fullness, a grace, which in a certain way do not even touch him but, rather, pass through him and flow into his work, so that he becomes an instrument in this respect that stems from God and is used by God.

Precisely because he is not without vanity, he needs this possibility of prayer; it assures the purity of his work and lends to it the greatness intended for it. The act of adoration lies almost more in his work than in his personal prayer. It is not as if he had no desire to worship; but when he worships, he disappears into his work. The work is in fact more divine word than personal prayer; it is the condensation of the Most High, what God wishes to communicate to him through grace. Of course, there is for him nothing higher, more sublime, more worthy of adoration than God. He would do anything in order to please God. But because he has his faults and his struggle with himself and his renunciations, one cannot call this preparation for the act pure prayer. Of course, in everything he manages to grasp of God's greatness he feels overwhelmed, and he is not only astonished but shaken by what God allows him to say about God. But, in this, not only does the fruit of prayer become visible to him, but also something of prayer itself, and he has an intimation of how much it surpasses him.

He is like an artist who invents strict ascetic practices that allow him to bring into being the most beautiful work of art. For Dionysius, the artwork is the presentation of the divine; thus, his ascesis is perfectly Christian. But it is as though he did not have the time to finish with himself completely, to finish with all the things that, in himself, obstruct his way to God. And thus he begins adoration "beyond himself". He begins at a point at which he is no longer to be encountered as a man with his good and bad. He prays in the absence of his person. That is the leaping over of the step.

BEDE (672/673–735)

He prays well, in an abundance of words and thoughts, which he immediately carries with him as already formed but which he then submits to God as if for his assessment. He is full of love, and it is love that drives him to prayer; he abides in love while in prayer, and, returning from prayer, he radiates love. This love is noble and gracious, considerate and humble. When something keeps him from praying, he becomes unhappy. He has greater ease living with God than with people; his interaction with people is always a bit of a penance, but one that he offers to God as a sacrifice. Often he longs to be able to do nothing but pray. Often, too, especially as he gets older, it will appear to him that a life spent in contemplation alone would have been too easy for him.

His trials consist especially in the fact that he is tempted to fall out of love. There are moments when he in fact recognizes the devil's hand in this. In relation to other things, he becomes uncertain; but when he devotes himself to prayer, he once again acquires certainty.

He is, on the one hand, attacked by the people in the cloister, and, on the other hand, he is deeply loved. He is surrounded by both groups for the entire duration of his life. One sees how radiant he is when he returns from prayer; one feels what it is that radiates from him. Many people do not want to acknowledge this radiance, while others, by contrast, live from it and learn from it their own humility and love.

(*Ecstasies, visions?*) Both in a natural sense, so to speak; it is probably better to say: visions as ecstasies, because he passes over to the other side with great self-understanding. This is for him a sort of constitutive element of his prayer: heaven is included in this.

(*His relationship to the Church Fathers and theologians?*) I do not have a clear perception of this. I can tell that he knows them well, knows many things about them, and looks for things in them. But I cannot tell how much he takes from them. Actually, he is himself a Church Father in his own way, insofar as he spontaneously learns very much from the same things the Fathers experienced.

CHARLEMAGNE, EMPEROR (ca. 742–814)

I see his prayer and his anxiousness. His attitude is a mixture of trust and anxiety: trust concerning the ultimate future of the world and his own eternal life, but always anxiety about the present moment. He is aware of having a mission, and his awareness grows with time; but there are moments when this awareness completely leaves him, when he wanders like a child lost in the woods and the propositions of faith, propositions that he himself formulated, Scripture, and tradition seem completely foreign and confusing to him, when he no longer recognizes the truth that had otherwise inspired him. He can pray like a child, in the joy of a praying child who suddenly receives a share in a foreign, beautiful, vast, and mysterious world; in relation to God, he is like a child in his father's arms; he receives everything from his hand, takes delight in it, and wants to honor the things he has received. He is just like a child who receives an object from his father's hand, an object that is meaningful only to the father, but the child is proud that the father entrusts him with something that comes from his own belongings.

From this prayer of trust, he tries to form an abiding attitude of Christian trust, which ought to belong not only to himself, but to all those who are entrusted to him, as much those immediately around him as entire peoples. He would like to bring about the Father's world on earth. His thoughts are ultimately very simple; they almost breathe the air of the Lord's parables; they are meant to be clothed in words that are easy to grasp, but they always mean for him something ultimate, insofar as he means everything he says in an absolute sense and knows that he himself is duty-bound to the Absolute. And if he suddenly prays once again in a certain weariness or downtroddenness, which follows his many deeds, it can happen that he fails to understand what he prays; he no longer feels the Father's presence; he believes himself to be unworthy, indeed, even ridiculous in relation to the saints; he no longer understands the path he has followed with consistency; what a little while before still seemed to him important, clear, and straightforward, he now finds confused and inextricably entangled. Then he is assailed by the anxiety that, in order to please God, he forgot to do whatever it was the world needed from him; he mixed up his role; he imagined it as too great; he took the Father's world so seriously that the world of man that was entrusted to his care suffered as a result.

But then he turns back, walks once again step by step in the certainty of faith, in the confidence of action, and if his personal power grows, then this becomes for him a proof that he is walking confidently in the ways of God. He only has a little experience of indifference, since he engages himself with his entire temperament on behalf of God's concerns, and he already takes this engagement as a proof for the correctness of what he is striving after. Defeats depress him; they drive him to anxiety. But it is not really the anxiety of the Cross; it is more the anxiety of one who is all too certain. He has built a little too firmly on his own foundation, has occasionally confused "Thy will be done" with "my will be done", not out of a bad intention, but rather out of a conviction about the validity of his task and of its correct execution. In spite of this, he is humble before God, and also often before his neighbor, and his prayer is quite substantial, because he takes pains to contemplate the things of this world in such a way that it almost always leads into prayer, indeed, it almost always becomes a Christian contemplation. He is also completely uncompromising in relation to his own faults and weaknesses: like the converted sinner in relation to the sublimity of confession, he thus has a clear awareness of his unworthiness in relation to his mission. If he can confuse every once in a while what is God's and what is his, nevertheless periods of genuine humility and clarity always follow, in which he accuses himself of arrogance and pride. Moreover, it is not easy for him, because he possesses so much earthly power, which has to be placed in the service of manifesting the power of God's glory. It is difficult for a person to see the borders of his self stretch out so far without taking notice of his service and his effectiveness.

HENRY II, EMPEROR (973–1024)

I see him at first occupied with his destiny, which he regards as a vast cloth out of which many things can be made. He sees all the things he is able to accomplish. Progressing from detail to detail, he sees how the most variegated possibilities could be produced from this cloth. And he reflects and prays. In prayer, he suddenly recognizes: So much power and ability is not given to everyone; therefore, he ought to abide by what is great. His destiny is laid upon him so that he might accomplish great things. Now he asks God what these great things might consist in, for he himself, because of his piety, would be more inclined to stay with what is small. He would be inclined to say small prayers, to do small penances, to avoid small sins, to devote small moments of time to the Lord. But he sees that this would be inappropriate in his position, that he must entrust himself to the Lord in the *one* discipleship that God expects from him. His daily work before God, his prayer life, his contemplation, and his practice of penance are not permitted to fracture into countless fragments; they ought to reflect *one* love, *one* attitude. And now it becomes clear to him: the very same thing that holds for him personally in his private responsibility before God also holds for his responsibility before God for his entire work and his worldly position as ruler. He thus endeavors to be a Christian ruler; his ultimate intentions ought to be Christian; he aims to make all the people in his realm, all his friends, each person he happens to meet, attentive to God, to their responsibility, and to their task.

Here and there he is able to found something. But all of the individual things are always and every time summed up in the one thing: the greater glory of God. Whatever he builds, founds, esteems, commands, and begins is in fact always an image of the *one* Church, the *Catholica*, which he is meant to establish and fortify. When he founds monasteries or advises friends to enter a religious Order or to form groups, he always has his eyes on the idea of perfect unity, never in order to produce a special form of religiosity or adoration or responsibility before God. And he seeks to achieve such unification also in the realm of his prayer, of his interior life before God. He sees the measure of his mission and understands that he must stamp this measure on those who fall within the sphere of his responsibility during his time. He does not want to urge upon them the particular prayers and forms of contemplation that he personally follows, but he stands before God and asks him to determine these forms himself. He is the sower, who entrusts his harvest to God and who accepts all the seeds that God entrusts to him to sow. He does not abuse his power, because he remains completely humble. If there is a concern that lies particularly close to his heart, it is this: that his people be humble. For him, the greatest faults are arrogance and presumption. Whoever is of humble heart will more quickly attain to perfect purity. And if he has to continue to struggle with himself, he nevertheless knows with great certainty that victory lies with God, and he need only hand himself over to God, he need only pray to him and implore him, and God will use him personally as a ferment in order to bring about what is impersonal, what is suprapersonal, in the whole kingdom.

CUNEGUND (d. 1033)

I see her prayer, and I see her Night. It is something she knows well. When she prays for a long time, there are periods in which she ends up in the Night again and again, precisely through prayer. But she does not do anything to avoid it, because she recognizes that the Night is God's will. Her day-to-day prayer is idiosyncratic and personal. Idiosyncratic because she converses with the Lord without asking advice just as she thinks she is bidden to do, and in doing so she constantly offers herself in order to receive certain *burdens*. When she then receives these burdens as the Night, as desolation, as spiritual torment, she abides in them until the Night yields of its own accord. She has no one who can really advise her. Thus, in spite of her inner certainty that she is on the right path, she has to labor in order to persevere on her path. If she had a proper advisor, the Night, to be sure, would not lessen in darkness, but nonetheless it could be fashioned in a more fruitful way for those around her. She could grant more good things to others out of her desolation.

In between these periods, she is consoled, but she is so in a certain noble reserve that she lays upon herself. She does not allow herself ever perfectly to relax and recover; there, where God would have lightened her burdens and been prepared to show her images that would have brightened her mood, she turns away out of fear that she would thus become unfaithful to her duties in prayer. She does not understand that precisely the relaxation that God could give to her, indeed, wants to give to her would be beneficial for these interim periods, because then her Night could be even deeper. She tries to give form to her everyday life on the basis of her prayer, to be fully surrendered to God and to love him completely. But her love for her fellowmen is made difficult for her, because she has a lot of difficulty making connections with them. She lacks a certain external equanimity, which would make her conversation and exchange more intimate in a human sense. Nevertheless, when she suffers from this, then she does so in a Christian way and inside of prayer; insofar as she thinks that this form of stiffness was laid upon her in connection with her inner Night, she thinks that all consolation has to be saved for heaven and ought not to be enjoyed already now in unnecessary interaction with human beings.

Her prayer styles are not simple; many of them she arranged for herself, which she repeats as her daily task and in which she never forgets to ask for desolation, suffering, and torment. Her spiritual gifts, which are not few, moderate her, insofar as she seeks to gather all of her interest and direct it to God alone. Whatever leads to God in indirect ways, whatever could be interpreted as distraction, she avoids in order not to lose anything of what she feels belongs to prayer. It is not easy for her to discover the right relationship to her Lord on account of her stiffness and her whole conception of life. She becomes anxious if she does not understand him perfectly, but she loves him with a love that is ready for any sacrifice, even if an ultimate self-Evidence is lacking.

PETER DAMIAN (1007–1072)

I see him at prayer. His prayer is simultaneously childlike and hard. Hard, because he cannot separate himself from thoughts of his responsibility; he has to come before the Lord as a disciple who is giving an account of his work, not merely concerning the state of the Church in general, but very particularly also concerning the thriving, the growing, the *emergence of love* in her. And because he does not perceive the signs of this growth, but on the contrary sees the hierarchy endangered by the lack of love and observes so much in his surroundings that seems to stand in stark contradiction to what God demands of those in office, indeed, of everyone, he thus stands before God as a person who has to give an account in the name of all people, because he has to bear responsibility for everyone. He bears it, not as an office that has just recently been placed on his shoulders, but rather as something that involves the whole of his existence: he feels guilty not only for the things he could perhaps truly have changed, but just as much for the situations that were already in place beforehand and that he could not influence. His prayer is burdened by all this, and this gives his prayer a certain hardness. It is also as if God had to reveal to him, point by point, what is now part of his office, what is part of his personal task, where he now has to begin, what he could take up and attempt.

But at the same time it is the prayer of a child. He stands before his Father; he knows that he is his child, who does not have to show anything but his belief in God's fatherly will, anything but his obedience, his surrender, his desire to hear what God has to say to him in order to arrange himself accordingly. And once again his prayer is a struggle, because he knows that every single prayer will carry consequences for him, the tiniest no less than the longest contemplation. Every time, he will receive a new call; every time he will have to learn to bear things anew.

GREGORY VII (1020/1025–1085)

I see his prayer, which is very simple and childlike and constant. In fact, he prays as much as he can. But it is not prayer filled with grand words or ecstasies or powerful feelings; it could not be farther from mystical. It is a prayer of tranquility. He has always arrived when he prays; it is perfectly clear to him that he has to give thanks, that he is permitted to raise petitions, that he can lay things out before God. And the things are for him tasks belonging to God himself; they possess a greatness that seeks out their equal. And if he sees a task in front of him that lies outside of prayer, if someone says something important to him, then it is his first concern to achieve certainty about it, to check whether it is thus willed by God and is included as one of his tasks. He shows the matter to God, in simplicity, from every angle, as if he had to present the pros and cons in terms of how it looks from a human perspective, so that God would have the possibility to weigh it from his position, that is, the position of a human being. And God chooses. Either this or that. And he disapproves. It is never the case that Gregory could say that he himself would have been of the same opinion. He feels that his opinion is not in the least requested; no one could say, though, that he is not involved, for he was the one who had to present the matter. But he lays it out the same way a salesman would show a customer a sample that he received from some neutral factory.

These samples are for Gregory what belongs to him and also what comes to him from the outside and acts on him. The customer would be God, who is left with perfect freedom to make his own choice. The salesman does not put any pressure at all on him to buy it or not to buy it, to choose it or to choose something else. If God disapproves, then not a single word more will be wasted on the subject; if he chooses it, then there will also be in general very little said about it unless Gregory does not see how to carry it out. But already when he possesses only a few details, he goes to work with them, and God gives him power, strength, guidance, and the Holy Spirit for this work. And he acts inside of the supernatural power that has been given to him by God, which always surpasses every human dimension. When he has presented something to God, something that seemed simple to him and that God chose, and afterward developments, obstacles, and objections arise that seem insurmountable, or Gregory seems to stand before an opponent who is vastly superior to him, then his mind receives such an acuity and power to reply as God would that it reveals its divine origin on its own. If he settles some affair, then he gives thanks as though it concerned himself, for he is so deeply unified with his mission that he takes every task as his own concern, because he was chosen by God together with the matter.

OTTO OF BAMBERG (1060/1062–1139)

I see his prayer, which is very pure and good. Not only vocal prayer or contemplation or spiritual reading, but his whole attitude gives his prayer this purity. In a way, he never stops praying, because he never wants to separate himself from the task God has given him, which he feels very much alive within him. His great desire is to remain faithful. But he does not pray in a trivial way for this fidelity; he does not worry anxiously about grabbing as much blessing as possible for himself through prayer, but he prays out of the necessity of love. This necessity is for him closely bound up with the office he holds. He is convinced that when a person fills an office in the Church, God lends him the grace not only to manage it properly, but to acquire greater insight into love and the need for it. But this insight cannot come from anywhere else than from God himself and, thus, from prayer. And if he receives a task from his prince or if he sees the need for battle and engagement, his first task nevertheless comes from the Lord: it is the same task that Christ gave to the disciples as he sent them out to teach the people. Otto feels himself to be an apostle. Not in the sense that would give him a value that sets him apart from other people, but in a wholly primitive and original sense, with respect to which he is convinced that it applies to everyone who wants to belong to God, especially to all priests. And if he attempts to pray without ceasing, he does not try to turn it into a theory; he does not have the feeling that this prayer is a cure-all, which he absolutely has to recommend to others. He also does not worry anxiously about gathering up the fruits of his prayer. He is almost more inclined to see the great amount that he prays as a sign of his weakness. To be sure, he knows that God needs a lot of prayer, but he is nevertheless convinced that he, Otto, needs a lot of prayer in order to be able to hear and follow God's voice and direction. He has great respect for the saints and is always mindful of imploring their help, in a certain sense in order to "relieve" God. The thought is very much alive in him that the saints have a genuine task and that he cannot master his own tasks without their help. The saints were sent down paths similar to his own; they have received the same task as he has; they simply carried it out better. It would never occur to him to consider himself a saint.

RUPERT OF DEUTZ (1075/1080–1129/1130)

I see his piety and his perseverance, the large amount of praying that he does, and the growing will to set in order his following of Christ. He sees that the world can be saved only through Christ, and he would like to place the reality of this salvation in a living way before people's eyes. He sees only one way to do so: to live out the following of Christ, but also to give order to it. That means: to point out the ways people can share tasks and to force every individual who wants to participate into perfect discipleship. He takes pains to write about the trinitarian God, about Christ and the Church, in such a way that the hearts of those who encounter these writings will be set aflame in the love of Christ and no longer be able to do anything but lay down their arms. Not in a passive resignation, but actively—as much in the sense of contemplation as in that of external activity.

He wants to have true followers, who first renounce themselves and then everything that belongs to them, in order to follow the Lord as closely as possible in a readiness that serves to provide the Lord with a practical disposal over people on whom he can count. And all of this in a very simple manner, without any eccentricity; obedience, love, and seeking God's will are for him the simplest of things. It is enough to have a childlike insight into the necessity of this service; then everything else will just follow. This is the same way he himself tries to serve; but he sees a part of his service to lie in inspiring others to the same service. God is everything to him; and in order to be able to abide in this "everything", he prays. He follows his path without straying, for he experiences the presence of God in a way that forbids him every halfheartedness or hesitation.

(*What significance does religious life have for him?*) Religious life is the only state of life in which the Lord placed his disciples. This is how he looks at it. And the individual religious Orders somehow embody the spirit of the individual apostles; the variety ought to be collected into a particular number, so that the thing does not fragment. He looks on the whole always from the Lord's perspective. Next to this, practical reflections on obedience, chastity, and keeping the Rule play a role; they likewise serve to simplify the whole, in a fruitful sense. He sees the Orders as something like work groups.

WILLIAM OF SAINT-THIERRY (d. ca. 1150)

I see him praying, and for him deed and prayer are essentially the same. Even his most contemplative prayer is pervaded by the impulse to act, is a deed of prayer, just as his deeds are prayers in turn. He exerts himself to find the perfect unity between the general disposition of his life and prayer. He sees this unity above all in the fact that he stands before God, never distances himself from him, and strives to recognize God's will in all things.

He goes to contemplate some word or sign from Scripture. And as he begins to contemplate, he becomes filled with something that he has to decide about, something that has to be done. For him it goes without saying that he ought to bring the things that are preoccupying him into prayer with him. When the time for prayer has passed, he usually knows exactly what now has to be done and no longer lets himself be distracted from it.

In spite off his masculine hardness, he lives, as it were, in a constant elevation, a state of enthusiasm or an active readiness for this enthusiasm, even in circumstances that would present an obstacle. In prayer, he is ready for the utmost and completely hands himself over to it. He prays a lot. But the energy he devotes to prayer does not prevent him from being open and present to his fellowmen. Indeed, they are a part of his prayer, of his decisions. And prayer does not form for him any sort of wall; rather, it presents an entryway that gives him access to his neighbor.

He loves the Son's readiness before the Father; in fact, he loves the Lord's humanness before the Father. The Son is for him a model for his own attitude, insofar as it is determined by the unity of deed and prayer. He sees this unity embodied in the Son. Just as he himself tries to be the same when he prays before the Father and the Son as when he is a fellow human being among others, so he sees in the Son the perfect openness to God and to men; he sees a perfect channel. The Son is for him one who fights for the Father among men. To be sure, he sees the greatness of God's merciful love; but his inner image of the Son is extraordinarily sober and masculine, in spite of all the enthusiasm of his love.

NORBERT (ca. 1082–1134)

His prayer has a hard quality. It is a prayer that is fundamentally unfamiliar with God's "letting be". It is a parade prayer, not in the sense that he would parade himself before God, but he presents himself to God in a sort of concern for objectivity; he lays out before him what he possesses and does so in a particular order. He is so actively preoccupied with displaying things, exhibiting them, recommending them to God's appraisal that he does not empty himself before God; he is unable to give God the entire place within him. Therefore, his prayer remains hard and rough. With people, he is friendly and makes an effort to understand them, but he does so in a sense by classifying them, which is felt by people less than by himself: he experiences it as a kind of limitation and must always get a running start in order to leap over the hurdle.

His unconditional will to serve is what is best in him. He is prudent and has a lot of common sense. He is extremely magnanimous; he wants nothing for himself. It is just that he does not notice that if he were to empty himself and stand naked before God, God would certainly give him some additional gifts and that even if he received nothing else, he would nevertheless be more humble, because he would then accept what God wills to give him. Everything would be more fundamentally removed from his discretion. He is good, but stern. And this attitude has more to do with God than with other people.

Occasionally, he has visions, which have to do especially with his Order. But every time he receives something to see, he immediately has to evaluate what he sees. To a certain extent, he breaks off his vision the moment he sees the possibility of bringing it about in reality. That he does so is only partially correct. In his whole disposition before God lies a certain activism. Externally, he has no doubt carried through his plans in the way God willed; but he has not established human relationships completely in the way God wants; the way of life, the Rule, everything that leads his fellowmen to God and binds them to God, is in order, it is only he himself as the mediator who has remained too hard; he has not become sufficiently transparent. The tiny fissure in his being is best seen from the perspective of prayer. In his work it is not very visible. For the ones who follow him it is a *good* work. But if he had given himself in a different way, then the first generation would have been more richly provided for; they would have experienced a more scintillating life at the source.

HILDEGARD (1098–1179)

In her professional activities, she proceeds in a very systematic way: she heals, and in doing so she uses the knowledge of her time; she does what is customary, making use of all of her cleverness, circumspection, clarity, and calculation. She has a particular approach to therapy, a scale of chances for success that she consults. But from the very beginning, there is a lot in her activity that is intuitive. She herself remarks on this: if she has a case that is perhaps more complicated than the remedy with which she is familiar, she adds something of her own to it, as if she were following an inner voice that went beyond her methods. She understands that the peculiarity of her way of working lies in intuition, which she brings into her knowledge when she puts that knowledge to use. She is not far from thinking that some sort of "power" must be coming from her, that in any event her intuition always offers the correct answer in a particular case.

Next to this there is the pious, faith-filled, and humble Hildegard, who prays for her sick people and for those around her, who leads a genuine life of prayer. And she does so in a way that is not obvious and easy but involves a struggle. Even in her faith she must constantly struggle anew for faith. It is not easy for her to accomplish; and thus her faith takes on an altogether personal dimension.

There is yet another dimension, namely, her mystical life, which represents, as it were, a third area of her existence, something altogether different from the other two. And it often seems to her that she is living several lives at the same time, each of which has its own unique quality. And then there is yet another sector: she herself in her difficulties. As a doctor, she has almost too great a knowledge of the bodily realm. And she has to struggle for her purity. But not at all like the great Teresa; there is nothing here that is sublimated and drawn up into prayer and into mystical experience. Hildegard's knowledge is nourished, on the one hand, by her own drive and, on the other hand, by her medical experiences. Beyond this, she is clairvoyant: she knows how she appears in the minds of others. She knows that she is attracting attention, that she has a vocation to be a doctor, but she also runs into strong forces of resistance. This bothers her a lot. She swings back and forth between an anger that sweeps through her whenever she runs into resistance and a feeling of joy whenever she achieves something beneficial; there is also an expectation that she will become better known. In between, however, a knowledge suddenly arrives that is not given to her in a vision, but occurs as if by accident: she comes to see that every professional intuition was no natural gift; rather it was a *grace*. That her activity as a doctor therefore does not stand outside of her prayer life, but both are and ought to be a single unity. From this moment on, her entire prayer life is transformed. She lets the grace flow into her prayer life that she had previously allowed to flow into her professional life. It is as if she allowed herself to be conquered in prayer, because she came to understand that she was already conquered by God in her professional life; where she believed herself to be the master of her art, she was already a handmaid of the Lord. And what she considered to be the work of her intelligence and a device of her skill was already God's work. God entered in through a door that she had not opened. In this lay for her a pronounced humbling. She understands the unity of profession and belief, and indeed not in an abstract sphere, but in her very own life. That is why she must now integrate the whole of her person together with her instinctiveness into a synthesis; everything she has must become serviceable to her profession and her prayer life. And it is only now that her visions become God's answer to her consent to this unity: her consent to the surrendering of her profession to God. Thus, the visions take on a completely new place in her life; they are from now on increasingly incorporated into this unity. Insofar as she has now given everything over to God, she can become the great and famous woman who is able to advise all the people, and so on. This no longer costs her very much because now all the glory belongs to God alone.

(In the contemplation of Hildegard's visions, A. feels as though she has been completely transported back into Hildegard's time, in the same way as when she herself commented on the visions in Revelation.)

Hildegard's visions are deeply influenced by her knowledge and her profession in the way she reproduces the visions, indeed already in the way she understands them. The more the whole of her existence is unified in God, the more the visions become for her a heavy burden. For she must adapt herself more and more perfectly, and everything is shown to her with increasing persistence. It is as if God wanted to show her how much *his* system surpassed hers. And at the same time, she is required to understand what is shown to her. But the visions that are shown to her are complicated, in fact they are often infinitely complicated and detailed. She sees thousands of details, which all have a meaning and always say even more than what she has already grasped and articulated. Thus, there is much that remains unresolved in her vision and in her descriptions. God wants to show her through images that he is "always greater": not only because she has a good eye to see what can be seen, but because she has a still better eye to see the aspect of the image that transcends the vision itself. The fact that she cannot interpret everything is therefore not a shortcoming; it is a particular way of communicating the "ever-greater". She must remain constantly aware that in spite of the complicatedness of her visions and her own lack of simplicity—which is a necessary and expected consequence of her scholarliness—she will never succeed in finding a formula that would be comprehensive and scientific enough and that would express the whole of what she sees. In this, what ought to make an impression on her is not only God's "ever-greater" character, but also the constant concreteness of what she sees, the concreteness that completely overwhelms her scientific soul. In her interpretation, she cannot even describe all the concrete things that God shows to her, much less convey their spiritual meaning.

In addition to this, she lacks a spiritual director who would take his share of the task. (A. says that she herself would become "crazy" if she had to try to interpret her visions as a practicing doctor; she leaves this to her spiritual director. He saves her from the torment of self-diagnosis: "Where do I belong?") Hildegard does not have this second person in her mission; she therefore sometimes does not know where she belongs. This has particular consequences: namely, that she constantly becomes an obstacle to herself in the interpretation of her visions. In obedience, a person is always freed from all self-reflection, even the reflection the interpretation demands. Hildegard does not have this guiding obedience; thus, she must include herself in her reflections; she is forced to pay attention to how she herself fits in. She herself must forge the synthesis between the natural and the visionary state; she cannot let both of them simply stand next to each other in a naïve way.

With her previous knowledge and her subsequent intuition, she stands, as it were, at the transition point between the Old and the New Covenant. In the first stage, she was, as it were, "Jewish"; intuition lends the Christian breath of the New Covenant without her being aware of it. Afterward, she recognizes the unity of the Covenants, which the Lord creates and which she must also establish in herself. But she does not have a precise knowledge of the transition, since there is a whole experiential gap or even tension between science and intuition that can never be precisely measured.

RICHARD OF SAINT VICTOR (d. 1173)

I see his prayer. He prays a lot. His prayer has three parts. He prays in the liturgy, and does so in fact with his whole soul, just as he is called to do. Then, he prays in a personal way. And finally, he prays for his work, as the Holy Spirit has commissioned him to do. This last prayer has a particular form. With someone else, one would probably have to call this a preparation for his work, a time of study. But it is his task to study himself in prayer, to unfold the state of his soul in the presence of God in contemplation, to clothe what he has received, even the most subjective aspects, in a form that is worth sharing and thus is able to find an entry into his writings. He then prays in the way a field hand waters the field in which the seed has been planted, in order that the seed may sprout and produce a harvest. Inside this third manner of prayer, he has a lot of guidance. Occasionally, he enters into prayer with the intention of arranging a particular problem in prayer, to lay it before the triune God, so that he might receive some inspiration from the Spirit, that is, to find out in obedience from the Spirit what aspect of things is pleasing to God, what could correspond with his mission. Then, what results is something altogether different; and he at first has the feeling that this may have been an intrusion or disobedience, because he ought to have adhered to what he had made up his mind about before prayer. With time, he notices that it is precisely obedience when a person remains docile also in those places where one already believes one is being led, and he allows himself to be carried wherever the Spirit wills. He has an infinite reverence for the afterworld; he is so convinced that God speaks from the beyond that a true believer, who has been liberated from sin, can and must live already here below in such a way that God is perfectly able to address him. Writing is not always easy for him; indeed, he writes in all different ways: sometimes things that he has completely mastered and is able to confirm (even after a considerable time has passed, he is able to say in a very precise way what his state of mind was in prayer, what he had in mind, what he was supposed to express); other things, which preserve for him a character of unfathomability, he writes immediately after emerging from prayer. Someone else (he thinks) will perhaps understand better than he does what is meant. For him it remains a bit hard to read, and he does not recognize it as coming exactly from him. When he reads such a text over outside of the context of prayer, he cannot reproduce the state of mind and is not certain whether what is described corresponds exactly to what God wanted from him or whether that which is opaque to him is somehow mistaken. Thus, with respect to his work, he is often overcome by doubts and uncertainties; at these times, the prayer of the liturgy becomes a consolation and also the very fact that he is able to pray without a particular thing in mind and is allowed to breathe the air of his spiritual home without some achievement being demanded from him. But the apostolic aspect is nevertheless something of great importance to him, which possesses for him in a powerful way the character of Christian witness. He thus turns his attention above all to those who in his opinion are very advanced in prayer.

His presentation of the stages leading to the highest contemplation is genuine and not merely literary. He believes one has to construct the transitional stages. He cannot imagine that the highest contemplation is something God would give for nothing; instead, he thinks that it requires preparation both on God's part and on the part of the person praying. He confuses a little bit his preparation for work with the contemplative ascent. God lays a foundation, and the person with whom God has begun something has the obligation to make further progress toward set goals.

JOACHIM DI FIORE (ca. 1130–1202)

I see his prayer, which is both very pious and very *touffu* [compressed]. He prays a lot and almost manages to get to the point of never praying in an empty way. His liturgical as well as his private prayer and his contemplation always have their meaning and their fruit. In fact he has a great capacity to gather up this fruit after every prayer and write it down, for he really receives something tangible; he is also very diligent and constantly attempts to carry out a twofold operation: to incorporate the fruit of his prayer into his study and to incorporate the fruit of his study into his prayer, in order to bring both of them to a unity, though it be a unity that he sees perhaps in too personal a manner. He is erudite; but in this erudition, which is tied to much prayer—prayer that is totally sincere, prayer that he does not want to mix up with his erudite knowledge—he nevertheless thinks that the moment will come when he will bring the two together, when he will be able to produce a system out of what he knows and out of what God gives to him in prayer. This leads him to let certain details go, to simplify things too much, and to identify, without really realizing it, what he has acquired through study with what God gives to him in prayer, what he learns in his vision.

But a lot of what he says is completely true, and everything ought somehow to be looked at in a way that brings out what is true and valid. Too often, people have measured him against a time-bound standard and contemplated his truth too much in terms of the fruits it produced. But he loves God, the triune God, with his whole strength; he loves the world and the people in it; he loves everything that God does in history as a sign of his omnipotence, of his presence and merciful help and concern for mankind and the Church. He is very selfless and trains himself always to love. It is not his nature to feel very close to people, but through his love for God, especially for the Son and the Spirit—as for the Father's loving gesture toward the world—he also tries to find the Son and the Spirit in man and his activity. His love for man arises from his love for God.

(*Are his visions genuine?*) Yes, surely. It may be that he lacks the talent for expressing what he in truth sees and means, and, on the other hand, he oversimplifies. But the people who deal with him for the most part insist on a standpoint that is also not correct, and thus both sides are unable to come together in what is important and fruitful in his mission.

What he says about the Holy Spirit is thus not altogether tenable, though there is still something to be said for it. But in relation to his mission, it was more the Unspirit than the Spirit that was revealed. Everything would receive its proper meaning if one constantly kept in mind that it is the Son who sends the Spirit and that in general the absolute relations between the three Persons pervade the whole history of the world.

INNOCENT III (1160/1161–1216)

I see his prayer. He prays with a kind of formality, since he sees himself as the administrator of the Church's property, who has to give an account to God of the state of things. His prayer is above all an accounting prayer and takes everything that constitutes the Church's life into the account. Not only in the stricter sense of inner concerns, but also external ones, which are also included in this sphere. He aims at the whole; as if he were the tenant or the manager of an estate, and the lord of the manor had commissioned him to take care of everything together: the seed, the harvest, the mowing, the fruits, the cattle, the small livestock, the state of the houses, and so forth, and as if he at the same time had to be an expert regarding any question that could arise. Up to a certain point, he is in fact right in this, since there is only *one* pope, to whom everything is subject; on the other hand, he chose his station in a much too personal way. To be sure, he was chosen to be pope by other people; but thereafter it was *he* who made the choice, without ever asking God his view of the matter; he himself in a certain sense has chosen *everything*, out of a conviction that God needs *everything*. His prayer was in this respect not sufficiently contemplative; in other words, he himself was not empty and peaceful enough to perceive God's voice in prayer, and he always already prayed from the same starting point: from the necessity of having to give an account of everything. He was always already resolved in the sense of this totality of the Church.

This one-sided manner of praying does not exclude the fact that he is humble before God, that he sees himself as the Church's lowliest servant, and that the burden of office often lies very heavily upon him. In the midst of this humility, however, there regularly arises a somewhat false conviction: I am dealing with everything now. This formality, which never lets him become a child before God, will always allow the harshness in his management and in his being to stand out ever more clearly. To be sure, he occasionally feels that something is not exactly right, but he is unable to retrace his steps; he thinks he has to push on through in any event. In one respect, he has a good grasp of the excessive demands that the Father placed on the Son; but the fact that these excessive demands are not an external imposition is something he does not see. If he had looked at these demands as something expected of himself, if he had, on the other hand, seen his partner or opponent each time more as a Christian and not assumed that this other person possessed the same gifts of the Spirit that he himself possessed, then he would have often made more progress. If he had treated other people with more goodness, accepted them in a fatherly way, he might have more easily persuaded them—at least if they were open. To be sure, he did not lack goodness. But he forced his personal qualities to bear the yoke of duty.

In later years, he prayed in a more childlike way and came to see certain faults. But everything was already so set in his prayer, in his basic disposition, in his conduct, that he could no longer adapt himself to the time; even in God's presence he was not sufficiently yielding—although some things improved. However that may be, he never attempted to distance himself from God; he was a man of a peculiar piety, though a genuine one, and he retained this piety to the very end.

FRANCIS OF ASSISI (1181/1182–1226)

I saw St. Francis at first in his old age, at prayer and sickly, of an indescribable cheerfulness and purity and humility. Everything in him, everything that constituted his life, all his difficulties, are now trans-figured and have become translucent. And this happened through prayer. The things that occupy him no longer contain anything at all that is purely personal, not a trace of annoyance or injury or resentment for the unjust things inflicted on him. God alone is left, as well as perfect service in the indescribable happiness of one who serves and in uninter-rupted contemplation.

His contemplation is of a particular sort. It knows moments of gran-deur that fall suddenly, over and over again, because a superabundance of visions has been given him, and in the periods between these visions his spirit occupies itself with great ideas and inspirations. He evaluates them, but he does so while remaining at a certain continuous height. It is as if a person were to offer him food from time to time and leave it up to him to get by at other times. He receives what is presented to him, with a spirit that corresponds to what is shown, and he is always particularly *grateful* to receive it. This is what his contemplation is like in his final years.

But such an impulse was always there with him. And his first reac-tion was always gratitude. He accustomed himself, in everything that happened in his life, always first and foremost to praise and to give thanks, even before he knows what it is, in fact, that he has received, even before he accepts what he receives, looks at it, and gives it shape.

(As A. saw his stigmata, she was deeply horrified. And she thought that everyone would have been horrified as she was.) Francis, who does not know what it is, but only that it is something that has to do in a profound way with the Lord, starts by giving thanks. He had previously thought a lot about the Cross; always with the feeling of gratitude. He had also reflected, without understanding, on the Lord's wounds. And now he sees the stigmata on his hands. They strike him as something foreign, as something that simply does not belong to him. As if the Lord's wounds were like two rose petals that accidentally fell into his hands as he gazed at the rose bush. And as if the petals served simply to allow him to contemplate the roses better. He does not think of himself as a "stigmatic". His wounds are simply there in order that he might see the Lord's wounds better, to understand them in a more intimate way. His peace is undisturbed. He has the certainty that everything that happens has a single object, namely, to praise God better. Only once he observes that the wounds stay with him does he recognize that they are a particular gift that the Lord has given him. But in his eyes they are nothing that sets him apart. Instead, they are an aid to teach him to pray in a new way, a better way to praise the Father through a more vivid memory of the Son.

He always offers his hands and feet to God. He would never allow them to do something that was not of the Lord. He has, as it were, loaned his hands and feet to the Lord and entrusted them to him. They no longer belong to him. The Lord has taken his limbs from Francis for his own use. Francis has a certain respect for these limbs, as parents would have for a son of theirs who became a priest. It does not occur to him to compare himself on some point or another with the Lord. To the contrary. He has become lost to himself.

When he was young, when he founded his Order in the bloom of his youth, everything was already service and gratitude and humility. But he was burdened with a lot of work. The poverty that was so dear to him was something he first had to learn for himself. He had to work out a unity between his life and his song of praise. His prayer outruns him; it is faster than he. It moves at a height that he himself has to expend great effort to reach. He is of such a humility that he learns something from each of his brothers, from every person that comes to him. In all the difficulties he encounters, he first gives praise; and once he has given praise, he is certain that the difficulties must have their meaning. And now he begins to reflect seriously on how he is going to deal with them.

His chastity and his obedience are from first to last the fruit of his poverty. Ever since the time he began to believe in a way that was completely alive, it was poverty that conveyed everything to him. It is as if Christ's poverty was the first thing he saw; this is what taught him how to give praise, to pray, to contemplate, and to live. Even his humility appears as a consequence of his poverty: when a person is so poor, then he has nothing but to be humble.

His fellow human beings present a lot of difficulties to him, because he loves them so much that they have a hard time living up to his love. He manages to love everyone just as if each individual were Christ himself. He comes with such a claim on them—to be allowed to love them—that they cannot begin to understand it. He is unable to adapt; he cannot soften his demand. This causes a lot of people to become alienated, and he suffers from this. But he has a very winning personality, and the good people begin gradually to understand. Until they have understood, he suffers, because in his simplicity, he does not comprehend how a person can think of the commandment to love one's neighbor as anything but the most urgent thing there is.

His own poverty teaches him to see a form of poverty in everyone, and this attracts him. Starting from external, corporal poverty, his eyes open up to every other form of poverty, even poverty of faith, love, and hope. And if he offers his personal love to a poor person, then he also offers Christ's love with it in spirit. But he does not confuse his love with the Lord's love, any more than he confuses his hands with the Lord's hands. He sees himself so much as a person who has been sent on a mission that he knows: the love he has to give is not his own but is the Lord's love. This does not cause him to live in an impersonal way—to the contrary. And his love, moreover, does not become general and average. It is similar to John's love for the Lord. The ones who hurt him the most are those who do not want to have anything to do with poverty.

He acknowledges the Church's hierarchy, but he does so under the pressure of external and increasing difficulties. The difficulties within his Order also increase and are brought to Rome. And Rome is not very willing to do what he desires. There are obstacles, delays ... He would have been happiest if he could have transplanted his ideal there as well, and he feels in fact a certain contradiction between his ideal and the official, hierarchical Church. He would also like to achieve a certain form of equal standing for all the brothers in his Order. In this respect, he is quite clearly different from Ignatius. At bottom, he would like to have everyone obedient to everyone else. Obedience in relation to an elected superior lifts him out of the ranks and makes him either richer or poorer. Francis is so pure in his simplicity that he trusts people all too much.

CLARE (1194–1253)

Compared to Francis, she is the smart, clear, and practically inclined woman who does honor to her name. Francis' entry into her life means something completely new for her. Thanks to him, she does not remain merely a woman of reason, but through her love for him—a love requited by him—she becomes his student. She believes and is willing, but she at first sees her service mainly to lie in the practical realm. In herself, she is a born Martha. The fact that she also receives a share in Mary is something she owes to Francis. But in obedience she must continue to be Martha: as the superior, who understands and deliberates and arranges. She has henceforward come to see that contemplation is the mother of action. Through Francis, she has learned what personally given love is; her love becomes a *response* to what she has encountered in Francis. Only because she has learned to understand prayer through him does her love for the Lord become a truly personal love. Everything in her relationship to the Lord now becomes concrete and an end in itself, while previously it was more like a means to an end. She was at first like a person who wants to improve bad habits and then discovers that Christ offers a good way to order one's habits properly and who for this reason gets involved in Christianity. But Clare truly found the Lord on this path, and found him for his own sake.

Her prayers are full of excitement, but they are also of a perfect virginity. Because she discovers proper love relatively late, she becomes in prayer a young lover. Her prayer has almost the same naïveté as a young girl's expressions of love, a girl who has just learned what love is. Her mind is filled with ideas. Moreover, she has work enough in her cloister. But this does not prevent her from always being able to find the time for new discoveries in prayer. She also introduces her sisters to this form of prayer. She describes the Lord to them in such a real way, with such a tangible love, that the others learn to see and love the Lord through this love. When a person hears them pray, love, and speak, one gets a sense of how much spontaneity has been lost in the life of the cloister nowadays. She loves in a completely pure, but extremely expressive, way.

While, for example, the little Thérèse develops her piety in a completely normal manner—when she is twelve, she prays like a twelve-year-old; when she is twenty, she prays like a twenty-year-old—Clare has a sudden blooming. But there is also a man who is part of her love, which was never the case with the little Thérèse. For Clare, love takes on a concrete reality in Francis. Because Francis is a whole man, and perfectly pure, Clare is able to see the Lord through him. Francis and Clare possess a common task of making love for the Lord concrete. The wounds that Francis receives are a form of this concretization. Clare does not need to have them because Francis already possesses them. And their missions are connected.

She has much less trouble with fellow human beings than Francis does. Perhaps the reason is that she sees the difficulties that Francis has and, also, that she is a woman and is not as demonstrative as he is in the way she offers love.

Learning to pray in a Franciscan way required of her a great renunciation: it cost her a lot to distance herself from her drive to activity and success in action and to become a contemplative. Work for its own sake was much more demanded of her than of Francis, because she had to renounce what was the primary feature of her character: her reasonableness, which she possessed and rightly possessed, and the facility for helping and serving. It is more difficult to renounce something that is good and beneficial than something problematic. At the beginning of her contemplative life, she would have often preferred to leave contemplation to others; not simply because of her disposition, but on rational grounds. However, she allows herself to be fashioned into what God wants to make of her.

ELIZABETH OF HUNGARY (1207–1231)

In the beginning, she is very cautious, careful, a little scrupulous. First, there is prayer. She prays a lot and quite willingly, she is very pure. Her prayer, in the beginning, is very much that of a young girl, the "prayer of a little blossom". In her spoken prayers, she loves the decorations, the pretty images, the little baby Jesus with his smile, his tiny hands, and so on.

And already as a child she loves to bring joy to people. Even in this she is a bit cautious: Is she doing the right thing? Is this really the right way to make this person happy? She at first directs her alms to the servants around her. She cares for them, bestows her help, such as she understands it. Everything she undertakes has this "little flower" style. Perhaps she dwells a bit longer on the secondary matters than on the main issue. Indeed, she has not yet developed the habit of looking at the main issue. For example, she might bring a poor person flowers instead of a hearty soup. The way she practices her love is completely in harmony with her prayer.

Then she begins to discover the world of contemplation, half by herself and half through the suggestions of a priest. In the beginning, she contemplates in a way that fits in with her spirit up to this point, in an altogether external manner. Perhaps she makes up her mind to contemplate the Child Jesus; but she almost never attains to her object because she gets caught up for such a long time with the flowers in her hand. Nevertheless, because she is pure and light, this does not cause her any concern. It is as if the main thing were kept in reserve for the time being, and she does not want to anticipate anything. She thinks: It will come soon enough.

Up until now she has prayed the Our Father as something that has been handed down and that goes without saying. She has prayed it with seriousness, but not really with as much fervor as her other "decorated" prayers. It is too masculine for her. But she does not notice this. One day, however, while she is praying, she discovers that the petitions it contains are in fact huge demands. That nothing greater can be conceived than what the Our Father contains. She sees this suddenly. In the same moment, it becomes clear to her that when the Lord gave us this prayer and commanded us: "This is how you are to pray!" he had always already recognized the Father's demands in it and took them so seriously that he became a man in order to carry them out. And that the Cross is nothing other than the Son's answer to the Father's question: How ought my will to be done on earth? How ought my world to be redeemed? Perhaps the Son could have made this a secondary question; he could have allowed himself a little relief here and there in the redemption, or he could have remained in heaven with the Father and saved the world in an easier way. But he wanted to do the utmost, only the most difficult was good enough for him, in order to fulfill the Father's will. Elizabeth sees this, and although she has been pure and good up to this point, it is for her like Saul's being knocked from the horse. And now she sets things in motion. Her anxiousness is blown away, so to speak; in God there is only one answer possible: the whole! From this day forward, she gives herself away. And that means: she now gives what is asked of her and no longer what she herself chooses to give. Her works take on a new spirit. No job or offering of help is too coarse, too demanding. Her prayer, too, is completely transformed. Everything has been brought to a simple and stark line.

She loved her husband very much. But she had difficulties with him. These external difficulties are what brought about her last great purification, liberation, simplification. She sees the Cross directly and immediately through these difficulties. Ever since the decisive turn in her life, nothing is trivial to her anymore, even in relation to her own internal life. Everything in her now is at full strength.

CELESTINE V (1215–1296)

His prayer is childlike, pure, and good, and God regularly takes him up into heaven and shows him the mysteries of his saints, the hosts of angels. God also shows him the Mother and her relationship to the saints and shows him in various ways the little Child Jesus. And he feels at home in heaven and is happy in heaven. He also sees the Church, how the good Lord introduces her into the mysteries of heaven, hands over to her the keys of heaven, makes her his bride in heaven, and bestows every authority upon her.

When an official duty calls him and he has to interrupt prayer, when he has discussions, he is always shocked to see how different earth is from heaven. And since he stands at the peak of the earthly Church, he feels that he is responsible for the way she is on earth. And he *cannot bear* this responsibility because he sees all too clearly how everything ought to be, how things are with God, how things look in heaven. Moreover, he believes he is unworthy. But this feeling of unworthiness is something altogether simple and childlike. It is not a complicated problem that weighs down on him, but something completely straight-forward. And of course he is right: no human being, if he were pope, would be able to turn the earthly Church into the heavenly one. But if he sees other good human beings, he always thinks to himself: perhaps this one or that one would be able to do it. And finally, he has such a respect for his office that he believes: Whoever has this office is required to be able to do it—if not perfectly, nevertheless better than I can. And so he thinks that the best he can do, the way he can most correspond to God's will, would be to pray without ceasing, to pray as much as possible, to do nothing but pray. This is the way the Church would be helped the best, for this is the way to work toward the realization of the heavenly Church. And thus he simply resigns. He does not at all have the feeling that this is an escape, although it is easier for him to go than to stay. And it is no great tragedy for him to think that he was once pope. Nothing from this previous life sticks with him. He is afterward just as much a child as he was before and during his time as pope.

LOUIS IX OF FRANCE (1219–1270)

I see his prayer, which rests on two main ideas: he desires to practice the love of neighbor in the realm of his people, to be one of them in order to love them. The other is a desire to practice love as king, as one who has received the ruling office from God. Everything else stems from these two notions, which have the greatest importance for him. Thus, his prayer, his pronouncements, his plans, and his thoughts can always be understood as descending from above. He does not strive upward from below to God; rather, he establishes the highest and God-given thing as a golden rule and makes sure that it is kept. And he prays a lot, with the aim of bringing about a general recognition that each of his people ought to love the others, not out of self-serving love, but out of Christian love. He is wholly convinced that Christ himself placed him in office, and he earnestly prays that Christ's expectations might be fulfilled. He prays more strongly for the result than for the path and the progress and the goals to be reached along the way. When he has internal difficulties, temptations, or fits of doubt, then he prays much less for the personal strength needed to fulfill his task than simply that it be fulfilled. It would not matter to him if someone else were to do it, if this was how God would have it.

But he knows that he has to remain in office. He knows that God wills him to be there. And thus he accepts this office daily in a spirit of great indifference. This can once again be explained by the "from above" character that ought to be aspired to. He sees each word of God as something that can be carried out, as a task that is given to him. This is how his deeds can be explained and also the peculiar manner of his contemplation, which he makes at intervals for the affairs of state and which is for him half prayer and half rational weighing of circumstances: the affairs are integrated into prayer, and they are so not so much because Louis himself invented this kind of prayer as because it is given to him in this way. Other monarchs will distinguish their prayer very clearly from their affairs of state, even those who are saints. Louis is not able to; he needs the air of prayer, the atmosphere of God's presence, in order to have a clear vision of the goals that must be met.

There is nothing he would rather achieve than to form France into a perfectly Christian, peaceful, and loving country. Everything he undertakes bears the seal of the greater glory of God. He wants to bring back to God more people who love him and believe in him, in the spirit of the command to "Go forth and teach all nations." And because he receives the capacity in the power of prayer to see things from a different standpoint, nothing seems impossible to him: he *presupposes* the intervention of grace in everything, whatever it might be, assuming that he has properly understood God's intentions and that God desires to accomplish a thing through him. This "through him" once again belongs to his indifference. Because he brings the affairs of state into his prayer, he thus also brings his prayer into all the affairs of state; he thus detaches himself from his private life in order to allow his life to become public; he detaches himself from his personal encounters with God in order to make them into God's encounters with his people.

MARGARET COLONNA (d. 1284)[1]

I see her love for the Lord, her ecstasy. And the *regularity* of her prayer. There is a rich variety in her prayer. All the forms and possibilities of prayer are given to her as a gift. She does not believe she has a preference for any particular form of prayer, and yet at the same time she is greatly affected when the Lord imposes periods of dryness on her. She then feels that she has been abandoned and is useless, when she would want to be a spring of love. And she has no one who really guides her and shows her how to bear the vacillations of experience with equanimity. And so she grows sad, reproaches herself, tortures

[1] A Poor Clare, the sister of Cardinal Colonna. She was a stigmatic who was beatified by Pius IX.

herself, when the signs of her being Christ's bride are not sufficiently evident to her. She has a great inner impatience, which she must constantly curb. She manages to do so in her interactions with other people and in her earthly trials but is unable to do so when she stands alone before God. Then she expects particular forms of fulfillment.

When miracles and signs happen to her, she is then in her element and is happy and at peace. She is even happy when they are sufferings, persecutions, and misunderstandings, for she recognizes God's hand in these and sees the signs of his providence. The mysteries of the Lord's life, his Incarnation, and his words are for her a constant occasion for wonder and gratitude. She does not grow tired contemplating the same mysteries over and over again; so much life springs forth from them for her that she feels refreshed and can squander herself further; she is amazed that not everyone shares in the Lord's being, in his miracles and words, to the same extent. Occasionally, she worries that perhaps she is guilty, because of her lack of virtue, her impatience, her hesitation to describe her own experiences, if others do not also discover the great joy and nourishment that she has found in the Lord.

LUKARDIS OF OBERWEIMAR (1276–1309)[1]

She has to place herself in a very strict obedience, which in fact runs counter to her spirit's inclination. She is far from being scrupulous or narrowminded or a person who pays more attention to the letter than to the word and spirit. But God leads her down paths that run against her grain. So much so that she at first always thinks that it will not work. And that it is not possible that she would have to be educated and led to God through this form of obedience. As if everything were a mistake and meant for someone else. When she would like to stretch out over a wide arch, she is led very narrowly, so that there is no more room left for her. She must take the tiniest of steps, one after the other, and each of these tiny steps is meant to appear to her as seven miles. For her it is like walking or stomping in place; she does not feel she is making any progress at all.

And once her eyes open up, and she comes to see that God truly does want this of her, that he wanted her to be bound in such a tight way, she actively submits. And tries to give even more, to walk at an even slower pace, to cease to long for any more flight for the soul. To desire nothing other than what God meted out to her in such an apparently meager portion.

[1] A Cistercian nun who received the stigmata.

She desires the stigmata for herself. But her desire arises from an obedience. From a spirit of mysteries, which desires even deeper mysteries. The spirit of obedience is her distinguishing characteristic; it constitutes her sanctity. Whether a person understands her or not, she remains open and naked before God and stripped of any self-will. What God wants and demands and carries out she deems right. She wants only one thing: to persist in obedience. With time it is almost as if she is stripped of her own mind, her own soul; alienated from everything that does not have a place inside obedience.

HADEWYCH (1300, Holland)

I see her prayer, which is pious and humble, and her visions, which actually are not visions at all. It is very difficult to describe these visions, because they are not something she invents and yet they are not really something she sees either. They are prayed; both thought up and experienced. She cannot find the right words to characterize her situation. It is, to be sure, always similar to the state of rapture from which she returns, and yet it is not a vision. It is an outflow from her prayer, which is bound up with a lot of imagination, something like a falsely understood *applicatio sensuum* in the Ignatian Exercises—as it can happen to disciples of St. Ignatius when they do the Exercises without enough guidance and thus give their power of imagination so much room that they can no longer distinguish reality from what they are imagining. Hadewych employs a symbolic language that she carries too far. One cannot blame her for it; one cannot say it is a sin; for it in fact is not one. She should have said the same thing with different words, in which case it would have been true, but she does not know these words. She does not know that there are levels that are neither visions nor realities, levels at which, however, the words of prayer, the forms of prayer, and figures of the imagination receive *contours* that correspond to the ideas. And thus she is like a poet who substitutes different words for those that are perfectly fitting in order to preserve the meter or rhythm. She knows that the Lord had this or that to say to her and that the notion she has of the Lord could be broadened and deepened. And insofar as she goes into prayer with this knowledge, she is humble and pious. But then she transgresses the limits of knowledge insofar as she characterizes what she has thought up as something she has seen. Nevertheless, she has a mission: it is right for her to give an account of these things, even though they are not entirely true in the way she says them. Hadewych should have formulated them as theoretical truths, which were learned in prayer and contemplation and reflection—this last plays a great role! She paints for herself what she pretends to see; she claims to hear things that she herself ultimately shapes. And yet everything is so close to genuine that one can hardly raise any objections against her. If she had had real guidance, then both ways would in fact have been open: that she would not have expected for herself anything other than what was given to her; or that through the elimination of obstacles, she would have been led to genuine visions. It is the extremely rare case that the offer of visions in some way was there and yet could not be grasped. Concerning her attitude, one could say that she never deviates but is constantly occupied with the Lord and the things that concern him.

CHRISTINA OF STOMMELN (d. 1312)

I see her very peculiar prayer, which displays a mixture of great piety and her own extreme fragility. She promised herself to God in a great burst that was perfectly free from self-seeking. But then she became deeply terrified once she saw what she had done, because she knew herself and was afraid of herself. She was afraid of the days of luke-warmness and stubbornness. She was also afraid that she had promised herself in a demanding way, in an attitude of pride and self-superiority, in a certain "à nous deux!" [just the two of us!]. And if God accepted this promise, then that means that he had to take upon himself all the consequences, also the consequences of his conquering her. In her defiant mood, which at the same time is a kind of lukewarmness, she always thinks she knows better; in this, she is in a sense honest and is afraid of the consequences of her dishonesty. And thus God uses this odd self-gift full of hesitations; he takes her seriously; he overcomes her and conquers her. He takes her so seriously that the temptations do not disappear but become increasingly intense, so that she is torn between God and the devil, between what she wants and what she does not want. And in what she wants there lies what she does not recognize. And in what she does not want lies what she does recognize. So that she has to promise to God a Christina that she *is not*, and she almost is obliged to give to the devil the Christina that she is. This pendulum swing within her struggle is extraordinary. One would almost have to say that the more she belongs to God, the more she is assailed by the devil, that is, the more she is tossed back and forth, and she is spared no struggle. And God increases even her vehemence, so that she falls dumb before the enormity of his power. Then everything becomes simpler and more surrendered, and her prayer becomes pious. When the strongest temptations are over and overcome by a sort of weakness, then she again receives an abundance of strength, in which she can pray and adore. Her stigmata are the sign that she is supposed to possess in the devil's hour in order to know that this is right; but at the same time they are the sign that she is supposed to show to the Tempter so that he knows that he does not possess ultimate power over her. And yet he is left enough room to drive her almost to insanity, although to be sure to an insanity that always ends in God's arms.

TAULER (after 1300–1361)

His prayer is like a little stream that almost threatens to dry up; then, it is suddenly nourished from above and swells to a tremendous river. With him, it is almost as if the visions conveyed his prayer, rather than his prayer leading to visions. When his stream merely trickles, he has an active quality: he is then slow, reflective, even diligent about praying properly, anxious, not setting sail and apparently not risking anything. Suddenly, he sees something, or something is given to him, something that would fulfill his prayer, an unhoped-for fulfillment, even though his previous prayer was moving in that direction but was only a tiny, weak piece of wood, unable to furnish a whole frame. And yet the whole picture of this vision lies upon this piece of wood, which in the same moment becomes a robust tree, and the stream becomes a massive river that carries everything away. When his prayer thus achieves such dimensions, he almost ceases to recognize himself; everything in him gets washed away; he is no longer able to swim and only barely manages somehow to keep his head above water. His prayer threatens at the same time to swallow him up. It is no longer he who prays; rather, prayer happens in him. And in the midst of the river flow images, parts of visions, that were carried away by the current: there a movement, here an intuition, something of heaven, there once again the answer to a question that arose in prayer. And then it can happen that the images find one another and come together, in order to produce a whole vision, and when such a thing happens, when the river acquires an order that brings things together through a vision, then it is as if the river once again had to dry up so that the images could once more come to rest on dry land. And now one sees them like memories; they no longer have any life in them because they are no longer being carried by the stream, and they are unable to bear such an existence; they fade away, and the prayer once again reverts to the strength of a trickle. And the little man that up to this point had to fight so much with the river and against the current limps behind, as if this dry, impoverished, and unimaginative prayer were what he was still able to manage and as if he had no desire for anything else. And things go on like this for a while, until the whole process starts all over again.

God plays him a little like one would a harmonica. God seems to want to show him these higher and lower possibilities [*Übermöglich-keiten und Untermöglichkeiten*], and, although he possesses a genuine awareness of sin, he is meant to understand that none of this depends on him in any way. As if everything were sent to the wrong address.

What God gives to him he accepts in a proper manner, although certain personal things, a certain vanity (in spite of his modesty and humility), constantly get in the way. This relationship between vanity and humility is particularly unusual in him. He has a certain vanity regarding his Order, a feeling that more fundamentally lies in his appreciation of his Order than of himself and, then, nevertheless affects him somewhat retroactively, precisely because he belongs to this Order. As a priest, he can be inspiring, but then once again completely mediocre. This mediocrity most comes to the fore when the river carries him, because he no longer has any idea how to behave; during the periods of dryness, his mission becomes evident in a more pronounced way, and he also throws himself more powerfully into his preaching.

BRIDGET (1302/1303–1373)

She hands herself over completely in prayer; she is as pure and transparent as a child. Her prayer is so warm that she constantly listens in it; this means that she feels she is being responded to. She has no experience of dryness in her spontaneous prayer; it is nothing but warmth, fullness, and goodness. And, from her prayer, she draws the strength to go on praying. Her prayer generates prayer. She has a poignant way of allowing herself to be borne in prayer, hauled along to wherever God wills: there are whole periods of time in which she forgets that she is present, in which she serves God alone in prayer, in perfect selflessness. Her external deeds and decisions flow with complete naturalness from this prayer.

None of this has yet anything to do with her visions. It instead forms their indispensable basis. Her first visions are not particularly "appealing". They arise in the middle of her prayer, almost as illustrations: she sees what she is praying; it is like an accentuation of her prayer, from one content to the next. And yet they are in fact genuine visions, though they seem to have no other goal than to be the sight of the things prayed about. But then the visions begin to develop on their own, as it were, and they become more difficult for her to understand. In this way, a certain activism arises in her attitude toward the visions, in which she does not simply allow herself to be led by God. She constantly has the feeling that she could and ought to "make something" out of these visions; they are, so to speak, an invocation to something or other. And because she is not able to interpret this call, she seeks too much within herself. What she is lacking is a person to remove the burden of her vision and to tell her: "Leave me to deal with, interpret, and answer for the visions; let it all be. What they mean will become evident in good time." But she is therefore compelled to figure out an interpretation on her own, and this costs her in a sense her naïveté. Since she has to find solutions, she brings the visions into a connection with her immediate surroundings; she now comes to see in her visions a host of details that concern her surroundings and often hold little interest in themselves. This arises from a failure in interpretation, which is itself due to a lack of guidance. It is this reflection that she assumes she must carry out that causes certain things in her vision to become somewhat trivial. If she had some place to deposit their meaning, without grasping it, then, although she would have had less knowledge, everything would have become bigger and would have had, moreover, a share in the fruitfulness of obedience. The person with the visions is never an adequate agent of interpretation. If he wants to be, then he takes his own format, that is, the format of his own knowledge and world view, into his interpretation and unwittingly limits the meaning of what is shown to what he himself is. The meaning is thus lopped off and fixed, precisely where it ought to remain open. Bridget is obedient, and she interprets things in the context of her obedience, as she understands it. She wants to share what she ought to share, to give the advice that she ought to give, but the others are not sufficiently obedient. Perhaps because of respect. Certain confessors see only the sanctity of the recipients of grace they encounter and are so impressed by it that they forget their own task. They prefer simply to gather when they ought to lead. This is how aspects of the fruitfulness of the visions get lost.

Because Bridget is truly obedient, the aforementioned lack does not cause any breach in her holiness, but it does damage her mission. If she had been able to hand everything over to her confessor, her mission could have been more relaxed, more effective. The confessor's exaggerated respect for Bridget's holiness contains within it a disrespect for God and even for Bridget's own person, because her mission thus becomes darkened. Often she receives only impressions, and she lacks any of her own means of connecting them. But she felt herself obliged even to tighten the threads that bind the various elements together among themselves, to weave together the whole into a "story", while in fact everything should have been handed over—both what she saw as well as what she handed over to her guide—to the ever-greater mysteries of the Lord.

The fact that Bridget, the saint, does not understand her own visions also causes no breach in her visions themselves. To be sure, these were meant to have been greater and would in fact have remained greater if she had not interpreted them. One sees in Bridget that one has to raise saints as one does children: as much the visionaries as the martyrs and everyone else. Saints must preserve a perfect childlikeness with respect to their mission; they must not be permitted to entrust their own tasks to themselves out of an unenlightened zeal, tasks that have a necessary connection with their mission only in their own eyes. Thus, Bridget's mind is overworked, and even her body has to adapt itself to these tasks. She is assailed by a spirit of external restlessness, which does some damage to her mission. It was no doubt fitting that she involved herself with the founding of monasteries. But she adds to this a host of unnecessary trips, visits, and so forth. Where there should have been contemplation, one finds action. Her confessor mistakenly placed the measure of obedience in her rather than kept it himself: and thus she herself became the measure of what "was supposed to happen", that is, her own ideas and what she understood to be her tasks. She seeks to "draw in" as many people and events as possible, and since her confessor looks on all these ideas as stemming from her holiness, he supports her. And because she is supported, she believes she has to do even more things along the same lines. Ultimately, she would much rather have been freed from all of this and to have been permitted to be a simple child before God. For God laid a great desire for childlikeness in her soul.

Because she has genuine holiness, she shows her fellow human beings a poignant love. She is attracted very much by other people. She wants to be meaningful to all of them, and she is in fact very meaningful to them. But here, just as in her prayer, she is more hindered than helped by her busyness. Those whom she accompanies she is never able to lead completely to the destination; because no one in fact ever entirely presented to her the importance of what she does and what her age required. And the interpretation of her visions occupies her a great deal: her visions are so multifaceted and rich, so many things impose themselves therein, it is almost like a kaleidoscope. And since there are in the Church many people who take an interest in her and have a great respect for her, she feels herself obliged to keep the affected people in mind when she interprets and also to project them into her interpretations.

At precisely the time when her visions attain this fullness, she becomes acquainted with dryness in prayer. It is like a warning from God: she ought to notice that something is no longer altogether right, that she explores too much. The dryness is like a deprivation that God lays on her because she has given up something of her childlikeness. It is as if she were punished instead of her confessor. For ultimately her mission is not a mission of suffering, but she is nevertheless granted suffering in the experience of dryness in a secondary way.

MARGARETHA EBNER (d. 1351)

I see her very stormy but pious prayer. It contains an infinity of love, a love that is at once the love of a child and of an adult, the love of someone who is without a clue and of someone with a lot of experience. In more than one point she can be considered a forerunner of the little Thérèse. She sees the concreteness of natural love, even in the life of the cloister, and she has a sense for this life and also a sense of humor. In the prayer she has before the time of her visions, she attempts to bring the things of everyday life into the things of heaven and to give the things of heaven a meaning that could be captured concretely in words here below. And with each word she catches, whether it be in a conversation or a homily or wherever, her intuitive basis becomes richer but, at the same time, always a little more disorderly. There is so much unkempt stuff that she piles up there. Now, she attempts to do this with the childlikeness that represents a basic trait of her being; and God gives her a flood of images as if he took a certain pleasure in this disorder in her. Her visions enrich her knowledge; now she swings back and forth between a prayer without vision and a prayer that is so determined by visions that she is pushed up against it as though she were up against a wall and does nothing more than gaze anymore and no longer realizes she is praying. She is like a collection of many missions, which lie in the confusion of her many notions. She desires the good, she is very spontaneous and full of love; but she sees that the good constantly overflows her and, indeed, not in the serious excessive demands made on the Christian who accepts it precisely along with the Lord's ever-greater character, but rather in a sort of disordered flood, as if even the vision itself were making fun of her and took pleasure in causing confusion. And not in order to bring her to confusion, but because God destined her to be a point of convergence, where many things ought to discover something for their further path.

Things are mixed up with one another and juxtaposed to one another: there are Christian notions that have existed from the beginning and others that are meant to be embodied by Christianity in a new way and still others that must first be reflected upon and translated in order that their essence may be added to the Church's store. And she receives all of them and writes down some of them; she prays and feels herself drawn by them. She is like a young pupil who receives a lesson in a classroom in which many grades listen to their lessons in proximity to one another: she herself sits in the first grade, but she tries to catch many of the things meant for the third or the seventh grade, and she takes it in in a very childlike manner, without properly distinguishing the ideas. Or as if she were reading dry reports of information in difficult books whose texts were not meant for her and noticed that here and there was something that fits with the title of the book, without really grasping the content. But God is not concerned with the confusion; he simply lets her be the way she is; and even when she expresses several things one after the other and seems not to recognize things properly, she nevertheless lives in faith and in trust and remains childlike, because she is a genuine child of God. Like the little Thérèse, she ventures unabashedly into the most difficult things; she feels that she is not excluded from anything in heaven, is welcome everywhere, and all of this occurs in a completely natural manner.

Her relationship to Nördlingen is completely in order, even if it is affected a bit by her enthusiasm and the storms of her personality. There is essentially nothing that would need to be changed in it. For him it is important that she exists, and for her it is essential that she is able to be "combed" by him from time to time. In the broadest sense one could speak of a dual mission here.

HENRY OF NÖRDLINGEN (d. after 1379)

I see him praying for absolute love, in the clear awareness that Christ loved the world with an inexhaustible love, which is therefore able to enkindle a boundless love in man's heart. He desires love in order to carry out his mission, love in order to produce more surrender in himself, love in order to show others the way to love. By "showing", he does not mean an individual and personally colored deed. Showing and being shown ought to be one and the same, just as the Son sees as he prays, loves as he is loved, and the Father reveals as he is revealed. It is thus his concern, and also his office, to take care of all of those who want to love. And he knows that the highest love reaches its condensation point in prayer; it finds its form in religious life, and so he is grateful that his task has brought him here. Insofar as he gives spiritual direction, he allows himself at the same time to be led, because he sees in each guided soul a soul that is turned toward God, one that quietly whispers mysteries that have been entrusted to it by God and passes them on to the director so that what is entrusted may be handed over into the Church's safekeeping and the bud may be brought to full bloom. And what he shows to the souls he directs, so that they may give shape to it, ought again to serve to form others so that once again they may be fashioned even as they fashion others. Such a guiding in being guided is for him a mystery that corresponds to loving in being loved. And he has a great respect for the souls he loves and in which he sees God's garden, which he must water to a certain extent in order to be able to pick the individual flowers and bring them to others. He prays a great deal, also for other people, and includes many people in his prayer so that in this giving and receiving of prayer the Church might be strengthened. For wherever God is loved, he sees the Church and desires her unfolding, development, and complete fulfillment. For this reason, he worries anxiously about never falling out of prayer. And when he has the feeling that he has been without prayer for a moment, or has made decisions without having been sufficiently guided, then he tests himself anew in prayer and does not shy away from confessing possible errors, not only before God, but also before other people. For, to him, the highest truth lies in love, and the highest love lies in conversation with God.

CATHERINE OF SIENA (1347–1380)

She does not have a great facility in contemplation. She cannot just slide right into it; she must first prepare herself, especially by means of penances. She also has to have a solid footing, in two respects: on the one hand, her contemplation must have an object; on the other hand, it must have a goal. She has to know what it is she will beg or request from God and, then, fashion her contemplation accordingly. Thus, the whole preparation for contemplation contains something painful. For example, she might have at heart the conversion of a particular hardened sinner. She formulates this into a petition. Then she places herself inside the person, who may be someone she has never seen. She knows why she prays for him; this becomes the thing that moves her to understand him in an interior way. Then she chooses a theme for contemplation, which corresponds in some way to the person's need. For example, if this sinner loved his mother, if this seems to offer a way into his soul, then she might choose one of the mysteries of Mary's motherhood in order to meditate on it. At the same time she builds a bridge. Once she finds the theme, then comes her turn. She finds that the primary obstacle for the person's conversion lies in her, a sinner, and she begins to do penance for him, indeed, a horrifying and completely extraordinary penance. Exhausted by this penance, she then moves finally to contemplation. And if she comes up against a wall in contemplation, if it is not working anymore (perhaps simply because, humanly speaking, she has run out of matter for contemplation), then she feels once again that she is at fault and starts over with her penances. Though her prayer is very pure, all of this makes it something hard; she does violence to herself in almost measureless ways, but not in the least for her own sake, as though she wanted to achieve some graces of prayer *for herself*. Indeed, she wants nothing for herself; everything she wants is for her task, for others. She is so merciless with herself that it calls for compassion. She lacks an ultimate restraint; although she is not at all indiscreet like the great Teresa, one wonders whether watching all of this self-torture does not begin to make the Lord a little sorry. Her whole being is somehow obdurate, inflexible.

A. adds: It seems that she herself [Adrienne] has also gone too far in doing penance. Afterward she has a "bad conscience" and says so to me ... most of the time. (That is correct; but I also see that, when she really has gone too far, she nonetheless has not violated her obedience, because the task of doing penance stood so vividly and exclusively before her eyes that she forgot everything else.) Catherine also knows that she goes too far, but she believes that she has to and that she is allowed to. She takes nothing back afterward. She does not have a clear idea how far obedience extends in this area.

There is a moment in contemplation when a person is passively drawn into it. There is also a moment like this in penance: when a person no longer determines for himself how far he will go but simply carries on. It is not seldom that Catherine *substitutes* the passivity of contemplation with the passive being carried away in penance, by means of a certain ecstasy of penance. When ecstasy in prayer comes to an end, then she places herself in the ecstasy of penance; she transports herself willfully beyond the limits, where she knows she will no longer have control over the penance. She knows from experience that this will help her be able to go farther once again in contemplation. This trait is admittedly only one detail of her prayer. But it is characteristic of the stubbornness of her existence.

Nevertheless, her prayer has nothing to do with arrogance or pushiness. She is utterly and completely humble in relation to other people. But the moment her task or her relationship with God is at issue, this hard feature emerges. This is also connected with the fact that she lives in the *world* and has to do things from this position. She thus lacks the slow guidance, the leading, that happens in the cloister. And because her mystical development already begins in her youth, her natural development follows, so to speak, in tandem with it and thereby acquires a slightly inhuman character. In the world she plans and acts in an independent manner, even if she does so in complete humility, and thus she also not infrequently takes matters into her own hands in prayer. Things ought to go according to her wishes. Her development makes her very deliberate. (A. suddenly sees the advantage of a late conversion for her own part: she has not been fixed a certain way through any personal development.)[1]

VINCENT FERRER (ca. 1350–1419)

I see his task and his misfortune. Vincent is gifted with words and determined to give his talent entirely to God. But this occurs in a choice that is not fully carried out. He gives his talent rather than giving himself; he gives words rather than giving himself. He takes joy in his talent and in his words, in formulating them, in their having a good resonance, in their success. He possesses this joy even before he enters the Order and begins his missionary work, even before he has in fact made his choice. And then he has a desire to give himself, to follow God's path, and he is inspired to do so by various lectures and conversations. But he knows his worth. This does not mean that he is vain. He is not. It is just that he has in a sense an all-too-precise awareness of his capacities. It is these particular capacities that he wants to offer to God, without offering himself, indeed, without it ever having occurred to him to offer his talent to God in such a way that God himself could decide whether he wanted to be served by this talent or not or whether he did not have a better use for this man somewhere else, perhaps in the silence of contemplation. This is Ferrer's misfortune, which accompanies him the whole of his life. He always has the sense that he has only partially handed himself over. From the people he converts, from those he leads to the religious life or to priesthood, he requires for the most part the sacrifice he himself made, in the same reduced form, which he himself however does not perceive as such and which no one ever pointed out to him. He is incredibly zealous, tireless, and when he really does become tired and can do no

[1] Essential things are added to Catherine's portrait in the second volume of the *Book of All Saints*.

more, he nevertheless shows no consideration for himself; he forges on, believing that *he* has to manage to bring *his* talent to bear even there. And he is no doubt right from a human perspective: another person would not have achieved his success. But he thus fails to understand the value of prayer, of obedience, and of renunciation.

At a certain point, he realizes that he has not handed everything over; but it is somehow too late for him then. He is unable to go back easily. But something nevertheless changes, and in fact does so in a serious way: namely, his prayer, which now becomes very humble and indifferent, into which he completely throws himself in order that it may be blessed by God, in order that it truly become able to bear fruit. And now he feels that the effectiveness of prayer finds expression in his words, and in this he recognizes a new danger for himself. He is never able completely to resolve this problem, that is, the problem of measurement, of evaluating himself according to a value of which he himself is aware. Still, he grows in good will, and he also grows in his trust in God. But a division remains in him until the end, even where he seems to be perfectly at peace, because he never manages to drive away every evaluation, to let go of what he has withdrawn or held back, even in a form of anonymity, so that God may have complete disposal over him according to his own will. But he loves his fellowmen and delights in their conversion, in a joy meant to be God's own.

GERSON (1363–1429)

He lives in a tension between the activity of the ordinary world and the activity of God's truth. He experiences God's truth, not primarily as a truth to be grasped, which has an impact as such in this world, but rather as a mystery that remains impenetrable and nevertheless is reflected in the world without the believer being able to say exactly how.

He stands between his office and his prayer, between his worldly obligations and the inner impulse to occupy himself with things that refuse to yield to him the ultimate mystery of their being. In the everyday world he knows precisely what he has to do; he learns what he needs to; he is smart; he can be prudent and discreet, but he can also act impulsively if necessary, and he looks with a realistic eye on whatever happens. Thus, he can fulfill his tasks in an extraordinary measure. And he sees this, too, very clearly. But he separates this insight from his life in prayer, to which he wants to ascribe an ever-greater reality. A reality that is not contained in the realistic words that he speaks, a reality that is not of this world but is completely supernatural, so much so that even the character of the supernatural escapes him. It is like a deer that more shyly takes flight the closer one tries to get to it. But he knows this too. He thinks of mystics as people who were permitted really to possess the transcendent even in this world; they were able to see God's mysteries open up even in the ordinary light of day; they were able to possess a true being in their visions and intimations, something of the boundless essence of God was made accessible to them outside of God in faith; as God's creatures, they were able to be taken up into the truth of their Creator. And he wonders: Is it possible to be like them?

He prays a lot, and he prays with precision, insofar as he is careful to stand before God unimpeded, truly to perceive God's voice and not to confuse his own desires with God's plans. In this precise prayer, however, the prayer of those whom he attempts to imitate takes up a large place. He begs God for the humility and the obedience of his mystics, for their simplicity and their clarity, fully aware that there is no such thing as an immediate imitation because mystical graces are personal. Nevertheless, it is his opinion that there must be a lot of things that one can take from the Christian mystics of the past that have value for today. And when he prays in imitation of what others before him have prayed, whether it be in the rapture of vision or in the simplicity of an ordinary evening prayer in a cell or in church, with this prayer he thus desires to penetrate more deeply into the truth of these praying people, in order to help, to serve, to complete their task, to respond to God.

This therefore means that he perfectly recognizes, as much in life and in his attitude as in the silence of prayer, the *singularity* [*Einssein*] of God's will, in the mystics' prayer as well as in the action needed today; and since he does not want to fail in the political sphere, but also does not want to give up his worldly position, he thus seeks shelter with the mystics, in order to satisfy the obligations of his profession from this place. Life and prayer both show an expansive faith and service; we can see this also in the fact that he refers back to what has already existed in a Christian sense in order to crown what is to come, and in order to be the person God desires, hidden in his hand.

FRA ANGELICO (d. 1455)

I see him (*A. smiles*). He loves the path that leads to God and is caught up in a constant contemplation of this path. His entire prayer is nourished by this path, and when he became a religious and chose God above all things, it was in order to remain on this path. And when he paints, he always paints this path. The saints he paints, the angels he portrays, everything is for him an expression of this path. And in everything he experiences—even theologically or philosophically, even when it is something extreme, something that remains inconceivable to him—he apparently can figure it out only when it can be brought into harmony with this path. The moment he enters on this path, everything becomes clear to him, and he even becomes capable of drawing extremely subtle distinctions. It is as if God had selected him specifically in order that he might depict the path to God. Thus, all the things that are given to him in contemplation, all the things he experiences in prayer and in his daily life, are always related to this path, which leads to God.

It is the path of childlikeness and of God's childhood. It is the path of holiness, the path of renunciation in love, in love of neighbor, which unfolds to such an extent that one always sees the Lord and his holiness in one's neighbor.

His art is given to him. He did not choose it himself. It is so completely his gift and corresponds to him so much that *it* chose him more than he chose it. But for him art is one with religion, with love for God. He is in fact Franciscan all the way to the core of his being, in the same way that one imagines Francis himself in his youth. He is one of the smiling saints.

JÜTZI SCHULTHASIN (author of the *Schwesternbuch* from Töß, fourteenth century)

I see her prayer, which is for her an absolute necessity. She has to pray just to stay alive. And when she prays she comes to knowledge, and this knowledge embraces her entire life and reshapes it. She lets grace happen. And the *good* confessor helps her to bear everything and to receive everything just as God wants her to bear and receive it. These two things are not entirely coextensive: what she has to bear is completely clear to her in terms of importance and duration and heaviness; but the suffering is so passive that in the suffering itself lies very little knowledge. The reception, by contrast, consists in infinitely many insights, great and small, which, lined up next to one another, offer a reflection of Christian doctrine, but *lived* doctrine. She responds to it with her life and with her resolve to sacrifice precisely as God would have it, so that her life acquires an aspect that bears God's stamp.

In fact, it is confession and the confessor's advice that keep the devil and every form of temptation at bay. She is too childlike to be prepared with insight and a perfect defense when evil wants to slip in, but she takes refuge in obedience, and the obedience and the explanation from her confessor take effect just where they are needed, so that she may remain pure and childlike. She is a paradigm of the expansion of the effectiveness of obedience in the religious life and of obedience in confession. Absolute obedience begins at the point at which she in fact has confessed and has been perfectly absolved. And thus it is the obedience that is achieved in relation to her confessor and his word that is borne by the Spirit that forms her contrition.

The times of vision and the times of non-vision flow perfectly into one another, just as the time of Christ's earthly existence passes perfectly into eternal time. She sees love more clearly than obedience, but practically speaking obedience prevails in her.

In vision, it is her task to take in; reproduction is less necessary. Her sisters ought to catch her whole, contagious grace; to report in detail what she sees and hears is not part of her mission, which above all lies in the realm of obedience. The key for her is an absorption of the subjective element into objective obedience: her personal perception and listening, that which the ego ought to answer to God's deed, falls somehow into the background, insofar as it is absorbed into the Son's greater obedience to the Father. The humanly subjective obedience is brought to fulfillment in the objective divine obedience.

THOMAS À KEMPIS (1379/1380–1471)

I see his prayer, which is carried by and filled with the word—with the word of Holy Scripture, that is, which continuously moves him and leads him farther. In prayer, he learns more and more profoundly not only that God needs more love, but he also learns the pathways that God uses for the cultivation of prayer. And these pathways are closely connected with the pathways of the first apostles, who were nourished day by day by the Lord's words and after the Ascension were constantly led by the word they heard and experienced. Thus, he wants to lead men to God more and more by the word, to bring them to prayer by the word. The *Imitation of Christ* is meant to be a way of doing this; it is meant to open the human mind for what is essential in the following of Christ, to fill prayer with it, and to introduce people into God's presence. It is therefore much less the sacraments than the word that moves him. He himself has an incredible endurance in prayer; it does not tire him but rather refreshes him. This quickening also constantly gives him new insight into what God needs. And when he guides men to deeper prayer, then he knows that he always conveys to them *the* great gift that God has to give, and he is astonished when people do not immediately realize how important and multifaceted it is. To him, prayer is more important than eating or sleeping. It is not only the content of his life, but it is also what leads him consciously to new life. He wants to renew the world, not through a popular movement, but always through *individuals*; even when he forms communities, he has in mind the individual, which is what matters to him. Communities are meant to exist in order to promote the strength of the individual, in order to facilitate his path to prayer and his own experience. His prayer does not cease to grow deeper and deeper; everything he sees and hears and experiences, wherever it may be and whatever the circumstances, is transformed in his prayer, is tested and purified there, and it enriches his discipleship. It enriches it not only in what he records in writing, but also in the sense of an increase in his apostolic power, of an increased personal gift of self, which as such becomes immediately a fruitful gift to others. He now guides them better and can help in a more effective way. He is very humble and struggles against his faults in the unconditional understanding that God needs saints and that it is the Christian's first duty to become a saint. For him, the concept of sainthood is merely the presupposition that forms the sole basis upon which everything else that is so urgently needed for the apostolate can rest, everything that leaps over the boundaries of one's own sanctity, which proceeds—and *must* proceed—through the I into the Thou, by means of the activity of an I that belongs to God.

NICHOLAS OF CUSA (1401–1464)

His prayer takes many different forms. The variety is not due to him and his attitude, because he is always ready for prayer; he enters willingly into it and takes joy in it. Then he becomes entirely transparent in prayer. He needs only to say a few words in order to stand before God completely pure, bright, translucent, and radiant. Even when he fears God, because he has a powerful image of God's justice, even when he experiences God's grace as overflowing everything, he beams because he reflects God's light back to God. The variety of his prayer arises from the fact that God constantly transposes him to another place. There are extremely simple and childlike prayers; the child stands before the Father in order to receive things from him, in an absolutely clear relationship, which perhaps represents God's primal relationship to his creation. Then God brings him again into the suffering of his Son, and his prayer can become a pure prayer of suffering, a prayer of uncertainty, of impotence, of questioning, even of doubt. But all of that remains embedded in God's love, and he himself remains transparent and ready to achieve what God entrusts to him and demands from him. Then there is the prayer that lies within unfathomable mysteries, in the light of God himself, in his triune light, or in some other tiny mystery, a mystery that has not yet up to this point been explored, tiny, not because any of God's mysteries can be tiny, but because it allows itself to be presented by just a few words. Then he listens; he feels his way through; he questions, receives, attempts to understand; but in this attempt, he remains so submissive, so surrendered, that he is never indiscreet. Everything he begs for or questions remains within a *fiat*, within the Father's will.

The Church is an extraordinary concern for him. But he suffers on her account, chiefly in prayer and especially when he brings the Church before the Son in prayer, as one commissioned by the Church to request something or disclose something: then he suffers greatly because of her deficiencies; he would like to straighten her out, to bring her as a radiant bride to the bridegroom; he suffers because of her stains all the more because he knows precisely how she could have looked if she were wholly pure.

JOAN OF ARC (ca. 1412–1431)

A. sees her first as a child: she is completely naïve, childlike, and at the same time clever and crafty, a true peasant girl. There are tons of things she knows because she grew up in the country, and people know these things there. But she has this knowledge in complete innocence. She is totally natural, without being prim or prudish. Her virginity is the last thing she is worried about. Her prayer remains even in the later years of her youth the prayer of a little child. She especially likes to pray the prescribed prayers, in the morning and at night. And also in the times between. It makes her happy. She is a little like children who tell stories, who have the need to recount things to their parents or siblings. She recounts her stories to the Mother of God and to the saints. And because the stories in the prayers seem to her more beautiful than the ones she makes up herself, she recounts these stories from prayer. At this point she is about ten years old.

A little while later something changes in her. As if there were something in her that she did not want to admit. At certain times she still prays as she did when she was younger; at other times—in the evening, for example—she does not. Perhaps she prays during the day a little more in order to have permission in the evening to pray less. That sounds a bit too harsh; she herself is not able to express what is happening. Something has awakened, something that is related to her future. And she is not able to look this Something in the face; she steers clear of it. It fills her with desire and at the same time with anxiety. When she thinks about the Mother of God and about the Child Jesus, this anxiety becomes present. With others, she is happy to pray together to the Mother of God, but the moment she is alone, the inhibition is there. A dark foreboding. Before, she was happy to be alone. Now she much prefers to be with other children. For when she is alone, peculiar moods come over her. She never talks to anyone about these. Everything remains set aside; it is not meant to be touched. The suffering on account of the mission has the external effect of an evasion of suffering.

Just before she hears the call, it is as if the anxiety came to an end, as if she managed to preserve herself through this evasion so well that peace was restored. For this reason, what now lies in her soul is concern for the country, anxiety regarding the war. This brings about a new and peculiar tension in her. She is a peasant girl who hears the stories that people are telling in her presence. But there is a second person hidden inside this young girl: a little peasant boy who wants to fight. She stamps her feet, finds it unbearable, is no longer able to take it, having to listen to these stories. She is robust like a boy. And completely separate from this, there lives in her soul another feeling, which is like a relative of her earlier anxiety: an inner feeling of defeat, a sense for suffering, a feeling for the defeat and the downtroddenness of her fatherland. Here she is affected in the core of her being. Here she is no longer the naïve little girl who lives in the country. This new sensibility is something she has developed entirely out of her prayer, and it continues to undergo new developments. She reacts to the external reports as the boy, but in prayer she allows God to impart to her inmost being a feeling for the humiliation of defeat. And it seems to her as if God himself were no longer able to hear her prayer, because he himself was suffering too much. Now she can once again think about Mary and her Child: almost as if *she* now had to console the Mother and Child and as if it were a consolation for them to look on what she is undergoing. (Herein lies something extremely tender, which can scarcely be expressed.) As if the Mother at least were waiting on her prayer and as if the Child took joy in this. As if the Child loved it, like other children do when someone sings sad songs for them. And then she becomes again so proud that the boy in her does not like to think about the person at prayer. How can someone be so weak, so unforgivably weak, internally to go along with this in such a way! And thus she has the feeling that she has to hide the mystery of her inner suffering way down deep in order to be strong.

Then the call, the breakthrough. Before her call came through, the boy was by far the dominant presence in her. The whole interior world of prayer and suffering was as if swallowed up by the tumult of the war. It goes without saying that, in all circumstances, she preserved the tact and the delicacy of a little girl, and of course she continues to pray. But the only thing she has on her mind is her task, and she measures everything else against this. At this point, she does not have the slightest understanding of the fact that the two things are united: her interior suffering and the external battle. The fact that the voice she heard was an effect of her prayer, which the voice had itself prepared. She thinks that the voice related only to the fighter in her. The fighter in her is naturally a believer, one who is pious (although not exaggeratedly so) and completely pure. But he received the task only because the little praying girl stood behind him; the savage action arose entirely from praying and suffering contemplation.

Once she achieves her first victory, her contemplation begins gradually to grow stronger. But it is only when everything has gone awry and she is caught that she begins to understand that everything was one. She separates herself from the peasant boy that she was, and she now becomes simply a woman, a virginal woman, a woman who prays. She retains from the boy only as much as she needs to defend herself; in God's presence, she is already completely handed over. She is soft and gentle and bears what is given to her to bear: before, she had borne things for the Christian king; now she understands that her mission is expanding and that she has to bear things for all believers. The end is not "heroic", but completely pure, without blemish, as simple as only a childlike faith can be, and perfectly trusting. She does not think for a moment about what effect she might produce or about a show of bravery she would have to perform. She must simply remain true to the Christ Child, who has in the meantime grown into the Lord. Before the jury she gives completely unequivocal, clear, and true answers. But she is already so completely detached from herself that she scarcely has any human conception of the significance of her situation; she is merely convinced that the whole stands within her mission and cannot proceed in any way other than the way her mission requires. She has placed everything in God's hands; he should be the one to decide what to do with it. At first she did not think she would have to die. But deep inside she is ready even for this and knows that she is.

Her visions: Initially, it is mostly voices that she hears. Voices that are scarcely accompanied by visions, but extremely imperative and directed specifically at her. She never hears: "*One* ought to ...", but always "*You* ought to!" And she hears it as something that is impossible, but she nevertheless adapts herself to it: she will achieve the impossible without knowing how. The voices break in on her at first in a completely brutal way, like the penetration of a surgeon's knife. They are tuned to the young boy in her. It is only later that she begins to live in the vision, when the sufferer and contemplative enter into the masculine aspect. Her dual existence extends even into her mystical life: It is as if God could reach the boy in her only by going through the suffering girl, who however once again through the boy knew a kind of defiance. For the many visions do not correspond to the boy, since they strengthen the girl in her surrender, and again the rough command form of the voices corresponds, not to the girl, but to the boy.

The visions have a certain setting, a particular splendor, which is in fact "ecclesial pomp". Bernadette sees only the pure figure of the Mother; Joan sees the figures in a whole surrounding scene and atmosphere, which is as essential to her as the figures themselves. Then particular places also play a role in her visions and what is played out in these places. She sees, for example, the place where the king has to be anointed. In her visions, it is not geographical contexts that unfold, as a sort of supernatural battle plan. But certain strategical points, goals, are laid out for her. She can then immediately look on the map and see where it is and order her plan accordingly. These are aids for a particular stage of her mission's path; if something has been carried out, then for her it is completely over with; she does not retain anything about it, or if she does, then only in a very vague way. It no longer concerns her. That is why she has so much difficulty afterward reconstructing how it was.

The first voice she perceived remains present to her in total clarity. At that time, she spoke her assent from the core of her being and wanted to obey the voice entirely. Later, in the attendant revelations, she is always grateful when it is confirmed, when the goal is reached. Especially, too, because people begin to disconcert her. She was least able to hesitate at the beginning of her mission. But when she then has to say a lot of things before the jury about which she is no longer completely sure, even things she does not understand and never knew, it becomes more difficult. She tries to rescue herself from this confusion by always bringing everything back to the simple truths of the catechism. As if she had to cling to what is unshakeable in the catechism in order to be sure to speak the truth even in a personal sense. Her recantation arises out of this confusion, since she simply no longer knows where genuine obedience lies. The first voice had demanded the most complete obedience in the most complete certainty. Now she recants out of a presumably new obedience, which they called forth in her artificially through confusion. One sees here that God often leaves his saints with nothing but their human capacities. That it is truly possible to bring even saints to confusion, that her mission becomes obscured and lost—at least for moments at a time. Joan now does, "to the best of her knowledge and ability", what a human being can do, while at the beginning of her mission she did only what God wanted, without the slightest concern for human measures. But in death, she wins back complete simplicity. And, with it, the return to the first obedience, which is perfectly fulfilled in her death. Insofar as she is wholly and completely obedient, she turns God's eye away from the disobedience of the others. She redeems the guilt of those who burn her.

At bottom, she has no strong personal interest in her fellowmen. As a child, she plays with the other children, in a cheerfulness that is not very obliging. Later, she sees other people in the light of her mission and appreciates those who are able to help her. She retains a certain difficulty in making the leap to the Thou. She stands at the disposal of other people, when they are in need or in straits. But she carries out such service in a peculiar objectivity. She bears a tender love for the king, but it stems entirely from the love of her mission.

CATHERINE OF BOLOGNA (1413–1463)[1]

I see her prayer, which consists above all in praise and thanksgiving. Something odd emerges with her: she did not grow slowly into prayer, by striving to pray more and better; instead, prayer lays hold of her; it overwhelms her, and she now, after the fact, has to take stock of how to deal with this overpowering force. She *hears* prayer; she *sees* prayer; she feels prayer. And everything that she would be able to do—even willing to pray, even having to pray, even forming a prayer, even bringing herself into a prayerful mood and getting rid of obstacles— everything is already taken care of in her. She has to see from the perspective of prayer how to deal with reality. She has in fact to rescue herself from prayer in order just to be. God's atmosphere, the air of prayer, indeed, all of the prevailing aspects of prayer are primarily at her disposal, but because she is a human being among other human beings and has to live with them according to a given manner, the struggle does not consist in moving from life to times of contemplation

---

[1] A Poor Clare sister; author of the *Liber de septem armis spiritualibus*.

or prayer, but, on the contrary, in finding time for everything else in the face of prayer, which she is able to carry out in a perfect way, in order just to be a human being and not a person who prays and does nothing else. But she receives from prayer a clarity about how to lead her life. It is immediately marked out in her, and her obedience is so closely circumscribed that she always sets out with the certainty that this is the time for her to go. Prayer—God's world—is her home, and whatever she does is dictated to her from this house of God, from prayer. When she speaks, she does so with the certainty that she is saying what she must, even inconsequential or fleeting things, but also good things, things that endure and that belong to her apostolate. That is what is most peculiar in her: that she does not grow into but has to grow out of prayer in order to be what God wills. That he binds her so strongly to himself that everything seems pure and completely self-evident in relation him and that she has to take a step that is not self-evident from there into the world of sinners. The normal relationship is reversed. She perdures in the beyond in order to come from there to this world and to cut the figure in this world of a person whose home is elsewhere. She herself experiences this in a fundamental way and nevertheless has to live as one human being among others.

Her prayer is praise, thanksgiving, and joy. She possesses the deep joy of those who know. Quite often it happens that prayer gives her energy, cheerfulness, and alacrity in her conversations and social interactions, which help make the service of God look to others like something that brings joy.

Her visions, in a sense, have the breadth of Christ's life; she sees the saints, the angels, the Mother of God, and Christ; she also sees his suffering and is invited to share it, but only within prayer. If she steps outside of prayer, she must once again become the person she normally is; she must be able to lay aside her share in Christ's suffering, for it is her mission to be joyful among other people. No one would guess that she suffers so much in prayer; her suffering is enclosed within prayer and is thus of the deepest mystery. When she speaks with others about the Cross, then it is above all about its fruit, about the redemption of the world. In prayer, her suffering can be a dark Night.

AUTHOR OF *THE CLOUD OF UNKNOWING*
(fourteenth century)

Yes, I see him. I see him praying quietly. As if he had laid aside the burden of everyday life, the burden of his own self, the burden of the sins of the world, and whatever else that is causing him to suffer. He lays these burdens aside as if they no longer concerned him. As if the moment had come to speak to God and to participate in a form of the Church's eternal adoration, to drink up all that the Church and God offer without any regard for anything else, to pray for the sake of prayer and for it alone. To rejoice, to understand, to love, to marvel. And everything in complete peace and as a matter of course. It is not possible to say that one is consoled by prayer, because one has not brought any suffering to prayer. It is also not possible to say that one is strengthened by prayer, because there is not any weakness one has brought to prayer. Everything rests in itself and is just as it is.

Then his memory slowly catches up with him. He recalls all his burdens. He brings them before God. Then his prayer turns perhaps into a wordless groaning. Or it may also sometimes become something that resembles a discussion: Why? Why? Why? As if he were complaining, in a very precise way, and as if he had taken the opposing argument—for a moment—into consideration: There is so much pain and suffering in the world; but we live for you, we love for you: Can you not do something for us? It is almost an accusation. And at the same time it is a little like a fixed program, something he has set his mind on.

After this he is able to return peacefully to his prayer. Every prayer in fact ends with an act of thanksgiving. Gratitude for being able to pray, gratitude that God does not drive us away from him but rather takes us into battle with him and that God enables us to love him and to sing his praises.

(*What is the cloud?*) It is always that which renders invisible, that which separates, that which leaves one to intuit more than one is able to understand. It can be something to take very literally: a casting over of heaven, not as an eclipse of the relationship to God, even if the objection mentioned above could be characterized in such a way, but something that casts a pall, that poses an obstacle between God and humanity on account of sin. Also a non-appearing, a closing of understanding, a greater non-grasp that enters into every further grasp along the way. So that everything we see at the same time serves to make the unseen even more greatly manifest. That is for him extremely important at certain moments. He is in fact a very simple soul, but at the same time very refined and intelligent. He feels entranced by the cloud.

(*His surroundings?*) He is a monk. With a great matter-of-factness. But I do not see any Rule, or any indication of a Rule. The Rule is in him. But he is definitely a monk.

I see his prayer, which always proceeds from the same point, namely, from the Lord's question on the Cross: "My God, why have you forsaken me?" This question is for him proof that the most extreme severity is necessary in Christianity, because God the Father treated the Son in such a severe way that he permitted this abandonment. An abandonment in the objective sense, even though the Father remains present. What is white one says is—*must be*—black. And with this ultimate gift of the Father to the Son on earth, the Father gives completion to the Son's mission. Francis, as a saint, stands on the opposite side of extreme severity, because in spite of all his love—and he is able to love like a child—he sees the Son's experience of the Cross as the most essential element of faith as a whole, as man's preparation for the encounter with the Father as well as a preparation for the Son. In his prayer, this is always his point of departure. But his prayer is a prayer of fullness, in which everything that befalls him is alive, in which he lays everything before the Father, out of a need to contribute something to the vision that the Son constantly has of the Father. Not as if what he contributed carried any importance, but he believes that the Father wills it so. If the Father accompanies the Son into every little event, if the Son sees the Father in every miracle, but also in the most ordinary everyday thing, then—in Francis' eyes—man must substitute this vision with the analysis of what he experiences. And thus his prayer is filled with all the people who are entrusted to him, with religious life, with the questions that occupy him, with all the minor details as well as with the great things and with the constant petition to God that he might bless it all. But he always sees this blessing in the form of the Father's presence on the Cross. For this reason, it would be impossible to achieve half or to demand half. And if he himself has to perform miracles, then this always happens in a totality of intention, insofar as he stands humbly before the Father and the Son and the Spirit and leaves them the choice and the measure and all the circumstances of the miracle and is present, as it were, only to confer his blessing in the final moment. Thus, it is as if he were never anything other than a presence embraced by the encompassing presence of God. Miracles, for him, are always followed by a dark Night, which accompanies and veils them, and he himself moves through this Night with the greatest difficulty, but he is aware of it, in fact, he understands it and allows himself to make no judgment about it; he would never ask that this Night be changed or shortened. He sees in it the Father's severity, which is for him the most important thing, and, when he finds himself in the Night, he needs a lot of strength and prayer in order to take hold of the stillness of letting be and to persevere in it.

BOTTICELLI (1444/1445–1510)

I see his prayer and also his thoughts. His thinking is often directed to what he wants to do or what he has done, because he is not without ambition, and he feels that he is surrounded by his talent, as if this talent were a person who laid demands on him, pointed out things to him that he had to portray and, once he brought them into being, showed him how far he was from accomplishing what was demanded. This is one side of his being. On the other side, he is pious and he prays. His prayer is full of humility; he begs for more humility, more love, more faith. He strives to acquire a deeper understanding of the things of faith, to comply with these things in his personal life. And suddenly, one day, he realizes that a Christian life ought to have a unity: not talent here and piety there, for God is in fact the giver of both and both ought to be brought to perfection in God. A discrepancy between the two is sin, because it is necessary for the two to form a single service. And now he becomes afraid of having alienated himself in his mission as an artist and its demands from what God requires from him as a pious man. And now he makes moving attempts to see God as the one and only, to serve him as such, to place his talent in the service of his piety and no longer to place his piety in the service of his talent.

He prays a lot; it is a slow, evenly flowing prayer, from which forms emerge and colors come forth; prayer itself gives him insights into things and relationships; he has a sort of painter's view of what ought to be realized. If he feels uncertain in achieving these things, he begins to pray again and begs God to perfect what he himself cannot bring to completion. Thus, there is in his work a sort of interplay of question and answer with God, an anxiousness about creating a distance, a will to do God's will.

He experiences in his work an asceticism that forms a part of his personal ascesis, since he introduces penances on occasion, and days or hours of silence, and sets aside times to listen in solitude to God's voice. He tries to let humility get the upper hand on his personal intensity, not in the sense that it would be he himself who planned and carried out the victory, but always in the sense of letting God become the victor over him. And if he manages to produce a genuinely pious work, he is able to pray to God as he stands before it, and the more modest and transparent the prayer becomes, the happier he is with the work. He believes he has achieved the highest of his abilities when he has created genuine images of prayer, when he has expressed something that gives rise to prayer through his art.

The Lord's Mother is very important to him. He loves her; he has a strong sense of her being the second Eve: all of the beauty he is able to see in a woman is, in his view, perfectly fitting for her; she is for him the most beautiful creature on earth, and he is never embarrassed to lend her the features of beauty.

If a painting has turned out to be something that inspires prayer, he is happy: but as it is coming into being, he tortures himself, because it never seems to correspond. And yet, when it is finished, he allows himself to take delight in it, at least for the most part. It remains a suffering on account of human impotence, but even this is transformed in relation to what is achieved in prayer.

STEPHANA QUINZANI (1457–1530)[1]

I see her pray and pray and pray, in obedience, in faith, and in humility. It is very strange how little concern she has for herself; how everything she perceives in relation to herself she immediately lays aside, without reflecting, without looking at it as a possession, without wanting to be remembered for it, in a certain sense like works that have been finished and now lie behind her. Like a woman who knits clothes for the poor, and once she finishes a piece, she sets it in the basket and no longer concerns herself with it. It is also true that her mission does not include the task of contemplating the various things that happen to her and registering them and attending to them in a way that makes them useful. She is therefore a "plaything of the Child Jesus": every time something new happens, the game is already over, the Lord already turns again to something else, even if this other thing also involves her; but she has no other way of playing along than by allowing things to happen in this way.

The most remarkable thing is that she does not strike one in conversation as displaying a special objectivity, a self-withdrawal, or self-effacement. In fact, the opposite might be truer. But the moment a matter affects her, this is no longer an issue for her. She remains faithful to the matter. She prays a lot; she contemplates in an intense and loving way. She only takes care in this not to get in her own way; she has a sort of anxiety, every time she thinks of herself, about feeling rejected and becoming aware of her inadequacy and unworthiness. The

---

[1] A third order Dominican and stigmatic. She was beatified by Benedict XIV.

Lord, who gives her suffering, wants her to persist at the same time in a sort of cheerfulness, and this would include the times when she thinks about herself, when she raises questions about how and why God acts the way he does. Not only is she not curious; she knows not to be curious in this regard on account of her mission.

JOHN FISHER (ca. 1459–1535)

I see his prayer, which has something very harsh about it. He is not acquainted with properly contemplative prayer, because he distrusts himself, and vocal or liturgical prayer seems to him to offer more security; it seems right to him. He prays a lot, and in the periods between prayer he does not distance himself from the strict Christian attitude that characterizes him. His faith governs his life in a definitive form with an enduring validity. He has never desired to test this validity, because he considers himself unworthy to allow or desire any sort of change. His credo is somehow complete. Insofar as he affirms one of the propositions from this credo, he at the same time affirms all the others, even those to come. And thus he has no experience of the inner struggles that befall talented theologians, who recognize what is inadequate, what is not permitted, what has not yet been formulated, and devote their entire talent to shedding new light on whatever it is that strikes them as necessary. For him it is settled.

On the other hand, he also has no experience of struggles concerning his person; he is so conscious of lying in God's hands that he sees everything he encounters as something God has permitted. He is not one of those people who can shed tears over their own fate, but he is also not one of those who regard the actions taken against them with a certain humor. He possesses a certain stubbornness and cultivates it. But this stubbornness cannot be described in any way other than as a child's trust in his father, a trust that is so unconditional that everything the father desires is good. Any speculation or conjecture about the consequences of his behavior, any weighing of how much a person can handle, simply has no bearing. He is ready. And his readiness never flags. To be sure, he is a man, and, as man, he can easily allow himself to get caught up in a certain sentimentality. He is aware of this and avoids it all the more meticulously. He wants to fall back with his whole being into God's bosom. And because weakness and failure are things he hates, he lets God arm him against them and makes use of his strength in order to fight against other faults. It is as if he did not want to be attacked on all sides at once; he knows where the trials lie for him, and thus he remains unaffected by challenges wherever it concerns judgment against him and the adherence to dogma. And he prays to the end with the clarity and severity that is his wont in prayer.

OSUNA (d. ca. 1540)

He prays with passion, always with passion, but very irregularly. He brings his entire passion with him into prayer, and when he does he is totally present to God, truly only to God; he lets God speak, act, and purify him. At other times, however, he is, so to speak, possessed by his worries, his joys, his bad moods, his subjectedness to God. He takes it all, in its wild disorder, into prayer and thus obstructs contemplation; he interrupts God's speech, and afterward he is surprised when he is not able to move on to the next thing purified and strengthened. It takes a long time for him to realize where the cause lies; because his temperament in a certain sense pervades him, discernment is difficult for him or seems unimportant, because he might forget to examine his conscience, to prepare himself for prayer, or to open and empty himself completely for God. He comes to prayer too burdened. He prays for this or for that and brings along too much of his own judgment about individual things and the impressions they make on him. Nevertheless, he likes to pray, and his prayer is often accompanied by great supernatural insights; it can also be the case that God deals with his overly burdened prayer in such a way that it becomes effective and brings him closer to God. But as long as he dwells on earth, he remains somewhat deficient in discernment regarding himself. He prays the Church's prayers, those that are prescribed and those that have become familiar to him from other places, but he also prays his *own* prayer, and that remains for him the most vivid, the most ardent, for he not infrequently has trouble adapting himself entirely to what lies before him. He is convinced about the necessity of an order, an *effacement*; but carrying this through is extraordinarily difficult for him, and he always forgets his insight. Then he goes in a false direction with great presumption, although much more often he enters into good, proper, and open prayer.

LAS CASAS (1474–1566)

I see him, with the commandment to love one's neighbor that compels him to enter the Order. He is, as it were, possessed by this commandment, which at first is somewhat formless for him, insofar as he has a precise sense of neither who his neighbor is nor in what love ought to consist. In love he sees something like the crown of glory the knight receives for performing heroic deeds to please his lady and who joyfully *allows* them to be reported to her. The reports the others give of these heroic deeds and the honors they earn for the knight gradually became for him a likeness for the Church's prayer, for the devotion to the Lord, for the nameless things that were nevertheless done by individual believers. It is an *apport* [contribution]. But he knows in the meantime not to start anything with this love, which is demanded of each person and has to be extended to each person, until he has come to see that it has its foundation in love for the Lord; that the Lord loves each person through each person, that he acts through each person in whom he dwells, that he is no respecter of persons insofar as he makes everyone who loves him his servant and takes them all into his service, as it were, in an anonymous way, which is what constitutes the Church.

Thus, the Order of Preachers becomes the refuge where he seeks it. His prayer during his first period is a prayer schooled according to the Order, which remains foreign to him. He has trouble doing what his brothers in the Order do; he has trouble being one among many, until the moment in which he has a new experience, through the Order, of the vitality of the commandment to love one's neighbor. And he experiences it this time with a violence that henceforward never leaves him in peace; he learns second what he wanted first; retrospectively he experiences what his entrance to the Order actually meant, indeed, what his being a Christian means, and, ultimately, what his life from the first prayer on, from the first encounter with the Lord on, ought to have meant. And the reflection he enters into when he weighs this meaning for himself translates immediately into a fulfillment of love of neighbor, into the anonymity of service, into the knowledge that every person is his neighbor. And from now on he wants to elevate every person to the status of neighbor. Thus, not only does the difference between persons, races, and peoples fade away for him, but the difference between individual things in general; they all appear to his eyes from the perspective of love. That means: he loves a priori. This acquaintance, that person whom he has not met, this person about whom he knows nothing at all, that person about whom he has heard something: he loves them all in a comprehensive sort of way, but in this love he knows that he has to represent the Lord, who loves each human being personally. And thus he risks everything in order to be allowed to love. He makes himself a bearer of the word, and this word is love of neighbor; he knows no diplomacy, no compromise. He has no desire to know anything at all; he wants only to love. His entire temperament, all his gifts, everything he is and at the same time everything he is not, everything he neither knows nor expects from himself, it all makes use of his voice to defend the rights of the oppressed. Even when it goes unspoken, he acts in the name of the Lord and his commandment to love. And in the midst of his battle, of his darkness, his Night of prayer, which often descends upon him, he knows no uncertainty regarding anything that has to do with the commandment to love. He is indifferent to every obstacle: his mission and his awareness of not being able to do otherwise are so great that they carry him over everything. And for him this being carried over means something that corresponds to ecstasy, rapture, transference, the transcending of space and the sensible world.

His holiness consists in simple obedience to the commandment. On the basis of this commandment, everything he has to do in obedience appears to him as an unconditional obligation. He follows his path in faith without straying.

MICHELANGELO (1475–1564)

He has, so to speak, a double piety. The one is inherited; one could also say it is tied to the Church; he says the Church's prayers, receives the sacraments, carries out the practices of worship, just as the Church stipulates them for good, average Christians. And while he carries out these prayers and practices, his mind remains narrow in a sense; that is, he does not reflect on them. He prays in a straightforward way; he is pious; he gives alms whenever he has something to give; he attempts to do what other Christians do, without questioning it, without a need to enter deeply into the Church's problems or into the words of her prayers himself. He is in this respect like a Christian with a relatively small soul. And this piety is meant to be the resource that makes his work a Christian achievement.

But the moment he begins to enter into this work and to be an artist, the moment he catches sight of a task, the moment it becomes clear to him what he intends, what he wants, what he plans, he then prays around his work, the work that is meant to be a pious work: he prays that God would give him support, that his angel would help him, that the saints might not forget him, that the Lord's Mother might grant him her particular protection. And this is where the second prayer appears: for the work, into the work, and—even before the work has begun to take shape—*out of* the work. And then he is carried away: by his talent, by his vision of things, his desire to be pleasing to God, indeed, by the certainty that he is in fact pleasing to him. And now his prayer no longer knows any boundaries, and his ascetic practices and

his devotions take on an unsuspected breadth; as if they were nourished by his work, as if they were produced and borne by his work,
they take shape, they overflow every fixed boundary and time, they
become supremely personal. Now he has difficulty accepting the earlier, meager prayer again and yet endeavors not to be unfaithful to it,
because it belongs to his essence, because it belongs to the tradition
that is for him and around him, because he has an intimation of times
to come when his spirit and his talent could fail, grow mute, and, with
them, his inspired and living prayer. And he does not want to find
himself suddenly without prayer.

In everything he does, and in his human life, the artist in him always
does battle with the very pious man, but he attempts to transpose the
norm of the pious man into the world of the artist, to be what God
expects of him, to offer to God that for which God made him. Here
and there he worries that the world might see him as too pious or
even that those who are pious might see him too much as nothing
more than an artist. And for his own inner equilibrium, he needs to
show Christians that an artist can be a Christian and to show artists
that a Christian can be an artist. In this, he recognizes something of
his apostolate, which is bound neither to the limitations of his creativity nor to the demand to produce devotion through his work.

LUCY OF NARNI (1476–1544)[1]

I see her pray twice. Once in ecstasy, in a state of inspiration, in the
joy of an encounter with the Lord, his Mother, and the saints. She is
transportée, not only because she truly does have an encounter, but also
because the encounter takes place in this supreme joy, in a state in
which she completely loses sight of herself, a heavenly state. She raises
no questions concerning the scope of this state, which transports her
completely out of the world; in this state she is no longer aware either
of her earthly joy or of her suffering, because heavenly joy fills her to
the full.

And almost in the same moment she is brought back to earth, in the
desolate dryness of a non-encounter, in doubt. It is above all a doubt
about her own path, a doubt also in the very moment it seems to be
going well, a doubt about whether she is doing God's will. She feels
far from God, from his intention and his will. She strives with all her

---

[1] A third order Dominican. After thirty years of a virginal marriage, she founded the
cloister of St. Catherine of Siena in Ferrara. She was a stigmatic and was canonized by
Benedict XIII.

might toward the Lord, but she does not reach him, and this inability, which contradicts her will, stands out with particular clarity to her. She would like to annihilate herself in prayer, to turn into dust and nothingness, if only this nothingness lay in God's will and he to a certain extent had cleared her herself away like an obstacle, in order to do what he wishes.

Her love swings back and forth between these two poles: between the totally inspired love and the anxiety of despair, because it does not seem possible to give any more of herself. She attempts to transform everything that constitutes her life into prayer, and yet it is precisely when *she* wants to pray that she falls most into doubt. In ecstasy, she is simply carried away, so much so that she is not even permitted to desire it; if she has desires, then the other, difficult thing comes; and if she is in the more difficult time, then moments of such doubt arise that she condemns herself for having expressed the desire for prayer, because she knew how it would turn out. But every time there is a lot of genuineness in her anxiety and despair. It is as if God wanted constantly to confront her with herself so that she would become merciless and inexorable with herself and would no longer be able to bring to light anything good in herself.

(*And the contempt of her final period?*) She looks on it just as little as she had taken heed of the honor paid to her earlier. Concerning everything that comes from the world, she sees herself simply "put there". Her vision and her love apply so much only to God and lie so completely in him alone that everything that comes from outside this means almost nothing to her.

LUTHER, THE MONK (1483–1546)

I see his prayer, which is quite pious in the beginning; indeed, it is good prayer. He himself is inspired by a great need to dwell in God's presence, and his suffering on account of the Church is a genuine suffering. He sees all the imperfections and faults that have crept in, and it would be his cross to bear these faults in the simplicity of a man who knows that God has stewardship over every cross. But he cannot liken his cross to the Lord's Cross. This suddenly strikes him as a sort of confusion; it seems to him that there is a temptation in this thought and in everything that would have helped give his cross an ultimate authenticity: the persecutions, the empty discussions, the insight into more and more abuses, the apprehension of their provenance, at this point get transformed, since he no longer wants to take up the Lord's

Cross himself, into moments of alienation, insofar as he sees the Church now as standing in opposition to the Lord. And thus he becomes disobedient in relation to the Church, in order ultimately to become disobedient to God, in two stages:

At first he thinks he is able to be disobedient to the Church without losing a nearness to God, and as he is driven out he tries to cling to God with all his might. But when he then observes that this does not work, he invents a new theology, which allows man's clinging to God to appear useless—because it turned out to be useless for him—in order to lay everything on God and his grace. In spite of this, his prayer becomes a coercive prayer; it is like an insisting within a conversation that has long since broken off, a coming back to things about which one's partner no longer has any interest. In the recollection of his former prayer, there are still times when he believes he is being carried, and yet it remains the case that, in between these moments, he has a precise experience of alienation and estrangement.

EMPEROR CHARLES V (1500–1558)

I see in him the notion that *Unum necesse est*, "There is one thing necessary", which takes hold of his entire personality. And he desires to pray; he desires to be what God wants him to be, in order to be able to serve God's designs. He lays out every intention, every plan, indeed, every constructive thought, in his prayer, so that it can be tested and weighed by God: in terms of its provenance, its acceptability, its possible usefulness. If a thought is handed over to God's designs and stands firm, then Charles has the certainty that this thought comes from God: if God accepts it, he is also the one who gave it. And thus he prays in the certainty that he does not have to rule alone but that God has employed him to rule in the world. That God wants to rule through him and together with him. That in his governing of things in relation to God's sovereignty, he therefore has to submit himself to God in everything. He sees himself established, incorporated into the hierarchy that God sanctioned so that he might be king, but in order that, as a king, he might serve. He works zealously on himself insofar as he keeps a check on his passions, his ambition, and his impulses, in order to serve God alone. He would like to be a good instrument in God's hands and knows that he can be that only by God's grace. He often feels very lonely; he suffers a lot of betrayal, but he does not take it personally, so to speak. Instead, he understands that a Christian, who has a mission, is brought closer to the Lord's Cross with every betrayal. The fact that he has to fight against the treachery is clear to him, but also that he may not suffer more profoundly from it than is allowed, that there is always a limit, which the Lord establishes so that man does not carry his own cross but helps the Lord carry his. And if after he has wrestled with his own ambition he still always displays a sort of zeal, then it is a zeal for God in view of the task that has been given him, in order that he may order himself in the proper way. He knows that he is able to achieve something only through prayer; his need for prayer grows stronger day by day until his life consists almost solely of prayer and meditation. This meditation makes use of the images of his time, which he incorporates into the images of the Lord's time and which are also given back to him by the Lord with a certain fruitfulness, so that his spirit becomes constantly richer and more apt. He can begin his prayer with perfectly worldly images, but these images are brought before God so that God can make a divine story out of the worldly story and can initiate him, the man at prayer, always more profoundly into his mysteries and grant him an abundance of sanctity, which stands not only his own prayer in good stead, but also the Church's treasury of prayer and the whole turn of things.

PIUS V (1504–1572)

I see his prayer, which at times displays a great intensity and a thoroughly sacramental character. Prayer, for him, is not only conversation with God, a sinner's personal conversation with his God, but also a sort of confession before the judge. Confession plays a great role for him. Not that he goes to confession with particular frequency, but he knows a lot about it, and his knowledge primarily concerns *clarification*. For him personally, confession means setting into relief his unworthiness in the face of God's majesty and, then, extinguishing this unworthiness through both confession and office. For the holding of office is for him like a higher level of confession. The sinful man who accepts an office is required to be naked in relation to the office, to be dispossessed of his imperfections, his little habits, his evasions, in order to grow into the office and to be taken up by the office. The office is for him once and for all, while confession is something that is repeated; nevertheless, there is a precise correspondence between them. Confession, too, is for him the sinner's being taken up by God's grace into the form of absolution and at the same time the necessity, not only of seeing his guilt and confessing it, but also of carrying out an authentic contrition. The genuine appreciation of one's unworthiness in office in fact corresponds precisely to this authentic contrition. Thus, he prays in a certain sense the way a person confesses; not in the sense that he dwells at length on the confession of sins, but in the sense that he brings to mind the things he has done but ought not to have done, the ways in which he has been halfhearted and imperfect; he thereby places himself, as it were, in a state of contrition. In this state, just as in confession, he becomes able to request absolution, which in prayer means drawing sustenance from God's grace. Then he translates all of this into the terms of office, which is for him often completely violated. Although he lives with the mind of the Church in the most extreme sense, he always thinks his election was a mistake. They ought to have chosen someone else. He sees men around him whom he would not begrudge the papacy, because he is convinced that they have achieved more than he has. But his confessional disposition does not impede him; rather, it provokes him to increased activity. Even when he has the feeling, before God and man, that he stands in the wrong place, he nevertheless desires to do as well as he can with it in order to balance out the mistake they made in electing him. As for him, he does not think this is possible—he does not believe he is qualified—but perhaps his deeds can make up for what he as a man cannot do.

When he has prayed for an extended period of time, he can sometimes lose interest in a certain respect; he feels as if he were under pressure. The thought that his election was a mistake then seems consoling to him. Afterward, he recovers; he increases his penance; he increases his prayer; he is ashamed of his halfheartedness; and he tries to make everything better again. But there is always this shifting, which never becomes evident externally, because he is very regular in his work and because the well-being of the Church is something he takes with profound seriousness. But, oddly, his prayer turns more around himself and his office than around the Church, while the Church is emphasized much more in his deeds and what he says and his entire activity. He also has the feeling that many things in his prayer have to remain private in order that he may better ripen in his task.

JEROME NADAL (1507–1580)

I see him at prayer, which exhibits a bit of a manic-depressive character. Manic when he sees before him a work or a task. This is when he has his strongest need for prayer, and he attempts to derive as much as he can from it. He prays obediently; he listens in prayer and is receptive; he consents to everything God wants; he feels God's presence, on a level that is difficult to describe but that he accepts as something given, something he has received. And as long as this presence is effective in him and he feels it, he acts in a way that corresponds to its laws. He feels alive and confident. Like someone who, having a certain color of paint on his paint-brush, is happy as long as the paint is flowing smoothly without changing. Once the task comes to an end, then a certain depression shows up in his prayer. Then it is for him as if he had to give up a certain level or color of being-in-God, because it was intended for him *ad opus*. With the completed work, the source of this paint has also dried up. In a sense, he finds himself unable to pray, which is however not the same thing as suffering. It is perhaps his human weakness that is expressed therein. He needs the stimulation of a task in order to carry out his prayer, and in the interim periods it is absent.

He understands Ignatius well, even when he often personally finds him relentless. At certain times, he has difficulty following him, difficulty seeing the tasks that Ignatius gives to him as so important, like a child who loves his mother but who at the moment does not see exactly why he has to interrupt his game at precisely this moment in order to do some little service for her. It is his personal difficulty with Ignatius, which is always repeatedly overcome. It is as if a slight alienation from Ignatius emerged because of the sterility of prayer in the times of depression, an alienation that always disappears again with each new task. But the instability in his relationship to Ignatius is much less important than that in his prayer.

In carrying out his tasks he can be very dry and pedantic; this fault comes from the fact that God withholds from him a certain communicativeness, because he does not want to pray into his emptiness in a spontaneous way. His good moments in prayer lie completely in the line of Ignatius; they would correspond in a sense to his "tears". These "tears" are in fact not easy to understand. But this is precisely where Nadal stands. When one otherwise looks at the Society, even from its best angles, one does not in fact exactly have the impression that everything is built upon "tears". Instead, one sees the founder more as a "dry-eyed" man. What was said at the outset about the "manic" aspect of Nadal would translate, with Ignatius, into the state of "tears".

Inside of his tasks, he is always correct as a leader and organizer. The correctness stems perhaps more from the task and from his obedience in relation to the task than from his personal character.

TERESA OF JESUS (1515–1582)

I saw her praying. Often, she completely lets herself be led; other times she keeps prayer in her own hands. She knows exactly what she wants to request from the Father, what she wants to request from the Son, and what she wants to request from the Holy Spirit. There are times that she quite clearly sets aside, this time for God, the other time for a particular saint, and so forth, according to her daily needs or further plans, for a house, a person, a foundation. She is then so resolved that one has the impression God cannot change a single iota of what happens to her desire. One is a bit shocked in seeing this, but then one sees that her will is given to her by God himself, that her organizing corresponds to previous experiences in prayer, that being led is something lying well in her past, and that the sentences she speaks, just as the intentions she harbors, are the fruits of this being led. The whole can sometimes take on a military sort of character. One is shocked: that is not how a person should pray! But if one keeps watching, one smiles and thinks: perhaps one has sometimes prayed in this way oneself earlier. Nevertheless, it strikes a person as not being altogether sufficiently humble. It is as if in her writing and instructions, often also in her conversations with priests, she used more humble words than are actually fitting for her. On the other hand, these words of humility are perhaps like warnings that she is giving to herself. What she says in this way she would also like to experience in the same way, but she never quite manages to achieve it on this score. Then she undergoes a sort of crisis of humility and sees where she is lacking. And then she makes bitter accusations against herself before God and sometimes also before other people. She knows very well how things ought to be, what the proper thing would be, the ideal.[1]

PHILIP NERI (1515–1595)

I see his prayer, which is cheerful, cheerful because he loves God so much that it is a need and a joy to converse with him and cheerful because he has a secure grasp of his service as a cheerful service of love. This does not prevent him from seeing difficulties in love, especially in others. He therefore wants to experience so great a love that it could bridge everything that causes them difficulties and thus keeps them from God. He gives God in prayer as much love as it is possible to give. And after every time he adores the Child Jesus or the adult Lord or Christ on the Cross or God the Creator or the Holy Spirit, he tries in prayer, but also in the periods of time that lie between serious prayer, to prepare surprises for them, to give them

[1] More is written on Teresa below and in vols. 2, 5, 8, and 9.

some gift, to prepare for them a little joy. This is not an excessive anthropomorphizing of God, but rather the need to be so demonstrative of his love and to be able to reveal it so much that he would never come up short when he has to love other people. He prays a lot, and in his contemplation he sees the Lord and his concerns from the perspective of doctrine; he sees the Church and her need, men and their lack, and he constantly has love alone as the means to see, to experience, and to help. The love of God, which man receives and is permitted to give in return. He is an apostle of love. His love bears a very human quality, but one that pleases God greatly: namely, the desire to cultivate variety. In a sense he has to watch out so that he does not adore God every day in the same way. He does not want to bore God. And the fact that he himself never gets bored by God allows him to see that the paths of God's love have an infinite variety.

What he most desires is to carry love to those who have never experienced it, in order to bring them the great surprise of love in his joy. Thus to make them marvel, because they are receiving something they did not expect, something that was unknown to them. And sometimes, when he adores God, it seems to him that God has at bottom still never experienced love from human beings, except for the love that the incarnate Son showed to God the Father. And he would like himself to give God the joy of love, but he would also like to encourage others to do the same: he would like to found a covenant of love.

To be sure, he can look foolish from time to time, in the manner of a person who is not particularly well educated, a person, too, who is so possessed by love that he is not able to control himself completely anymore and who has a passion for generating new love through surprises. But there is nothing awry in all of this; they are just simple pleasantries.

TINTORETTO (1518–1594)

His piety is pugnacious. He fights with himself in order to come to know God. He has constant temptations, and he initially does not run away from them, because he believes that being tempted belongs absolutely to his calling. He possesses a gushingly enthusiastic love for nature; he loves women, loves beauty, and gives himself over to it, in order later to tear himself away from it in new fits of piety, contrition, and surrender. Indeed, he is decidedly not one of those who get out of temptation's way ahead of time and consider temptations to be harm-ful. Instead, he has once and for all come to terms with his sinful nature and reconciled himself to it in order then nevertheless to raise himself up against it and, as it were, to seek new paths to God in a sort of constant revolt.

And the path to God is not a simple one, because God, for him, is not a simple God; and all his paintings ought to be witnesses to his seeking, but also to his finding. And if the material he chooses is infinite, which, on the one hand, never ceases to be a provocation and a voice, nevertheless, on the other hand, it bears the same traits he does, for it lends the various stories of the Old and New Testa-ments the face of divine might, which penetrates all things; every-thing has at once the same content, even when this content points to the Cross. In every event of the Old and New Testament, he comes into contact with God's perfect power; to lend this power tangible expression, which would be worthy of it and allow the mysterious background to be intuited: this is what he sees as his mission. The easily and unproblematically sketched image means nothing to him; there has to be character and particularity in it; it must show that questions are raised here, and it must always make God's presence visible in a radiant center, in a particular light. In fact, all his works ought to be an image of himself, who in the midst of all his world-liness has never failed to feel something of God's presence. He gives himself over to this presence; he would like to radiate it; his moments of excess and his confusions grow briefer with time, because he is filled ever more unconditionally with God's power. (By "moments of excess" is meant also purely spiritual excesses; many of his tempta-tions have their entire significance at the level of spirit, even when they have consequences for the flesh.) The way back to God, which he follows a countless number of times, is for him of such fullness and beauty that he does not want to miss it even in his ascetical times. He enjoys being in the state of a converted sinner. But he prays, and he prays a lot; he prays as he paints, and his painting gives him material for prayer. There is, with him, a sort of contemplation that has hardly any interruptions, for even when he gives himself over to sins, he arranges their features; he looks upon them almost like a mask, in order then to be able to reproduce them in his paint-ings in a way that gets rid of them. His stupendous knowledge of Holy Scripture and the events recounted therein could have made him an exegete, who could have used words as well instead of merely painted images. But he knows that he was called to make paintings, and with painting he stays.

I see her humble prayer, which always begins with her presenting herself to God, similar to the way in which a maid offers herself for the service of her lord. She then has no possibility of overseeing the further course of prayer or even to guess or anticipate what its form or content might be. For as soon as she stands there ready for God, the Holy Spirit takes her perfectly into his possession and makes out of her what he wishes, which is something she cannot imagine. He accompanies her through every possible vision, allows her to hear many things, things that shock or delight or cheer her, in a motley variety in which it is impossible for her to find her place. She is left incapable of doing anything other than placing herself at the outset of prayer perfectly at God's disposal. What happens afterward is a pure *having* to let be. She suffers, she rejoices; she sees suffering more profoundly than she ever had before; she receives a joy that surpasses all measure, but all of this never with an introduction, a prologue, an opportunity to prepare her mind for what is to come. Everything is abrupt, unanticipated, but it all comes as a whole and in a binding way.

When she is given the task of suffering, then for those who observe it from outside, it follows a very determinate path. For her, this path is completely new every time. She has some sense, because of her knowledge of Holy Scripture, of what course the Lord's suffering followed. From her own experience, however, she does not know it, because each time it will be the way it has to be, in a manner that cannot at all be anticipated beforehand. And when she rejoices, then it is like a child rejoicing over a new toy; joy, too, arises in her each time in a completely fresh way, and the events that she activates, as new joys in God, are formed in such a way that she experiences them as brand new, with immediacy and perfect naïveté.

Later, there are the relationships with those outside, in which she has to be something for the people of the world. But she is unable to grasp this part of her mission—the enlivening of God's being, especially the communication of his active intervention in the laws of nature. She sees with clarity that she stands before God and has to present herself to him, that her *fiat* is one of her obligations; and she also knows that life in the cloister is the life she is meant to live, that she ought to lead her community in this and no other way and ought to

---

[1] A Dominican nun and admirer of Savonarola. She was a stigmatic and corresponded with St. Philip Neri and with St. Mary Magdalen dei Pazzi. She was canonized by Benedict XIV.

present to her sisters precisely what she presents to them. But this communication beyond the walls is something she does not understand; and this lack of understanding is a part of her cross; it sets into relief the distance that lies between God and man. And when people come to her with questions, she thus finds that her fellow sisters would be more suited to speak with them about these things; she would be happy to pray constantly for the people, but the immediacy of contact wounds her in a way she does not understand, so that she does everything she can to avoid this contact. Her nearness to God or God's nearness to her never acquires a certain constancy but is always shifting and taking new forms, so that the unanticipated character of both the shocking and the joyful things never dulls, and she is never trained to impose regularity on the unanticipated events, for that would drain the significance from God's plan.

CAMÕES (1524/1525–1580)

I see this sort of steadfast prayer, which endures in him and yet cannot be compared to the strained efforts others have to exert in order not to fall away from prayer. It is sort of like being possessed by prayer, a being taken into possession by prayer. On the other hand, a gentleness, like a perpetual prayer, attains it, without asking for possession or striving after it. It is just that he cannot do anything else than look toward God with all his passions, insights, inner struggles, in all the things that happen to him or stand in his way, less in order to offer everything he encounters to God than to preserve a vision, an audacious vision, as it were, beyond human vision, a spiritual vision. As if he had not only to know about the Spirit's loftiness but also had to climb constantly toward it and take hold of it, in order to contemplate from these heights not only what happens to himself, but also what the things and events of the world mean. Thus, his prayer is a sort of battle with the elements, in fact, with the Spirit and his gifts, in order to be allowed into them, to reach the place where the Lord offers himself to the one who sees. And this truly as prayer, not only as spiritual exercise. It is prayer, because at the same time he asks for the proper comprehension, because he knows that God alone can measure, weigh, and anticipate things in truth; but he lays claim to this measuring providence as a possession that falls to him, because he in fact must be a poet, and his mission is to present things, a mission he carries out as a Christian who has to show how things truly are. Everything ends, even before it has begun, in a victory of Christianity; nothing else at all is possible. Perhaps there are moments when he has the desire to contribute to this victory by increasing his piety and surrender. But this is not very essential. What is decisive lies in the vision and in the struggle for it; often it is almost like a duel with God, who for him is always the fighter, in order then out of the peace he achieves in God—for God will always be the victor, but he is also magnanimous—to contemplate what happens.

He is not only bold; he also never grows tired. And he has a profound inner need to produce his work. But if one were to ask him about its foundations, he would always point to heaven. For he also depicts things that he does not absolutely believe in himself but is convinced that they belong to God's truth and that he himself is simply too weak to be able to affirm them as well in his innermost heart.

LUIS DE LEÓN (1527–1591)

I hear his prayer, which at first is very much spoken from a book; it is a liturgical form of prayer that, in spite of all his piety, he *speaks* without putting anything else into the words other than a general expression of *other* people's surrender and perhaps also his own. He prays often without an immediate internal desire, more in accordance with the intellect, almost with the attitude that when he does this he at least does not do anything that could offend God. But then he experiences something that is not altogether different from a conversion, though it is not limited to the space of a particular period of time but lays claim to the duration of his life. Suddenly, with the flash of an inspiration, it occurs to him: the words are full of meaning, there is an abundance, in fact, that they already possessed in Scripture and that transcended the understanding of those who wrote them down, an abundance of meaning in the Church that was established by the Holy Spirit himself and that is not of human origin. The words always say more than a person intends; indeed, they say so much that each word contains the whole of faith: the faith of the Church, which is distributed among one's fellow Christians but yet remains the *one* faith. This insight allows him to grow into each individual word, and the word allows him to find faith: he is taken up into its fullness, in order to experience it, in order to receive his life from it, in order to be capable now, by virtue of the attitude of a person borne by the word's fullness, of strengthening others in their faith. He acts by means of his admonishments, his conversations, but most of all by means of his prayer, insofar as God makes use of this prayer in order to give more support to the saints of his time. Thus, on the one hand, he has a personal effectiveness, which can be verified, but, on the other hand, he has at the same time a supernatural effectiveness, which belongs to the essence of his mission: namely, to increase the Church's treasury of prayer and to give of the fullness of the word to those who are unfilled—the beginners, the seekers, the dissatisfied, the believers who want more, the lovers who have not yet understood the meaning of love. He is squandered on a level he does not see; his fruitfulness is great, but the fruits fall to others. Those around him can see the fruit of his prayer in his change of character: he, who had a tendency to fly off the handle, becomes gentle; he reprimands with temperate words, and yet this temperance is not indifference but the transfigured expression of an endured inner storm. He prays in a gesture of great surrender, but in this surrender, he must experience the mysteries of the Lord, his night, his suffering, all of which has for him a double face: the face of sharing Christ's suffering and the face of having to suffer from adverse conditions, from unruly people, from ambition and the quarrels people carry out in his presence. These fights tire him out and wear him down to the utmost degree, but he does not leave off praying—this is part of his mission—until he follows it through to the end, until he has achieved peace and gentleness and is capable of acting with tenderness even when he has to reprove. He is perhaps not always conscious of all the fullness contained in the word in a theological sense, although he does know many things. But his knowledge remains closely connected with the battles he wages, and he uses the inner struggle he has to carry out in himself to fight out the battles in the realm of the Church. God uses him, the individual person at prayer, and allows his activity to benefit a multiplicity of people, primarily members of the religious orders. And if he preaches and gives an account of the heights of mystical struggles, he always does so at a distance from his own experience that keeps him from making public what happens to him. For him the experience has already grown old, though it still belongs to his present task: he has to bring precisely this experience to others, in order that, in a sense related to his own personal struggle, they may be stirred up and continue to grow.

PHILIP II OF SPAIN (1527–1598)

I see his mission, I hear his prayer. For his part, he considers himself perfectly inessential. His prayer has a life-forming significance for him; it permeates everything. Everything that is mediocre or halfhearted strikes him as cowardice; he speaks what he prays as a man's word. He is king and thinks of himself as the lowest servant, but one who possesses a mission that is completely visible to him, one who administrates it and who calls it his own only because it has been lent to him by God. By God in his prayer, but also by God in the prayer of his ancestors. He was ordained to be king. But he is also a Christian; and he knows himself to be both king and Christian in the unity of mission. And no word of Scripture, no sign of his faith, no content of his prayer remains unintelligible for him, because, in order to understand it, he stands above himself, in a place where he certainly does not look at himself, but where he lives in prayer. There are no visions or raptures, but it is the state of prayer, of which ultimately every Christian has some inkling, and which is perfect reality for Philip. From here he arranges and accepts things just as they are given. He does not concern himself either with propositions of faith or with personal weaknesses and failures, with his inadequacy, with the distance that separates him from God, for he stands at the proper point, at the place that is willed by God, that was chosen by God, a place that he, Philip, fulfills insofar as he is precisely the king, sovereignly Catholic, who serves in a universal way, the slave of all, but a servant of the most high Lord, and he stands so much in his mission that he fights to the end for what he recognizes as proper, without worrying about the consequences.

He does what is right in two respects: insofar as he desires what he has to desire and insofar as he accepts what he is given in response. He is one who has *been forever favored by God*. For everything comes to him from God, but everything has to return back to God. His love for God is made visible through his life; not only through his life as king—which can constantly be grasped, without fluctuations, in a totality—but also though his prayer life, through his constant standing before God as a servant. He experiences weariness and exhaustion; at times he experiences resignation and the feeling that he is at the end of his strength; but this occurs without anxiety, for ultimately it is God who has given him this body and this soul; it is God who has entrusted him with this task and laid this mission on him. He is the knight; he is the most obedient vassal, who lays all his capacities at the service, not of his people, but of his God and thus serves his people through God; through God he is the knight of his faith; through God he chooses the harshest order of life. All his decisions, whether to rest or to move ahead, stem from this higher level of prayer. And it is due to his humility that he accepts the order from this standpoint, even when it appears to him impenetrable and unclear. His obedience is not entirely the Ignatian black-white obedience, and yet it is quite similar to it, because he allows what comes from God to be precisely what it is and because he attaches no significance to the way he himself sees things or the way he reacts to their particular shading. And when he engages himself on behalf of the Catholic faith and against heresy, he does so on the basis of his mission. The highest good of truth has been entrusted to him; he must defend it. This mission is entrusted to him not only in the Church, but explicitly as king: he must protect the ecclesial hierarchy; he must protect the hierarchy of the kingdom; he must protect the life of believers; he must protect the death of believers. He must bring everything to a unity. He embodies this unity in his castle, which remains a cloister, in an austerity that does not refuse itself any splendor, because he does not need to swing from one standpoint to another but is permitted to accumulate, because he has to represent in his life, in what he builds and brings to completion, the unity of the triune God, the unity of life and death, the unity of faith and office, the unity of world and Church. And it is not the case that he stands above these things as a man, but God stands over all things. And he knows that God makes out of his prayer whatever God needs, moment by moment, and that therefore God's answer to him at every moment contains what is necessary to him as a Christian king. There are neither scruples nor worries nor asking around for advice, but only the infinite certainty of one who believes in truth, of one who has received grace, of the saint, to whom it is granted that his holiness possess before men no other face than the certainty of faith, the fidelity to mission, obedience, and never seeking one's own, never wanting to allow his personal existence to become hardened, but the face of one who understands everything and does, receives, and prays through everything as a servant of the Lord.

BALTASAR ALVAREZ (1534–1580)

I see the "letting be" in his prayer, which is at first without equilibrium, because he wants to "let be" even there where there is in fact nothing that is supposed to happen. When Mary speaks her consent and carries the Son inside her, she is indeed able to persist in the attitude of one who has let it be, but she does not need to let be again what has already happened. Fr. Alvarez had also given a consent at the beginning of his contemplation that fructified his contemplation; he allows the contemplated word to guide him in prayer and bear fruit in him. But at other times, when he is torn away from contemplation by worldly tasks, concerns, and distractions, which he did not bring meticulously enough into his prayer, he tries nevertheless to "let be" now within a void (which corresponds to a certain alienation) and remains open to a nothingness (which is comparable to a *grossesse nerveuse* [false pregnancy]).

With time, these states disappear; on the basis of his prayerful "letting be", he acquires a genuine life in prayer, a certainty for the things of God, an attitude that is similar to the attitude of unceasing prayer, so that the contemplations he carries out in peace are perfectly fruitful. The imbalances of the beginning were due to his character, perhaps also to a lack of reflection. At that time he did not have a proper perspective on the point of departure, the moment at which he started out. Looking to Alvarez, a person can construct a thoroughly valid theory of the life of prayer—his theory—but it would be valid only for the one who prays in a true way, who does not allow himself to be forced away from total prayer, to whom even pastoral or scholarly work means prayer, a growing into God's demands, a better adaptation of the self to them.

To him, however, it never becomes entirely clear that there were fundamental uncertainties and instabilities at the beginning of his prayer. He learned so much from the times that he was successful, from the edifying experiences, that he later forgot the slight improprieties of the beginning. He had discovered a grace-filled way of praying, perhaps even committed the mistake of clinging somewhat one-sidedly to this, proclaiming it a bit too rashly to be the right way. The rejections that he experienced were from those who saw these mistakes as greater than they were but were right insofar as they recognized the dangers that lay in these deviations better than he himself, on account of their greater distance. Nevertheless, they were very much inspired by a spirit of bias against him and the desire to teach him something. It would have been better not to persecute but to explain; that would have given him the opportunity to fix things and come to see his one-sidedness, and the spirit of envy that prompts such persecutions would not have needed to be so widespread and to bear such bad fruit. At the times when Fr. Alvarez lacked a bit of understanding, the superior's understanding could have intervened in order to bring everything into the proper track.

MARIA DE LA VISITACIÓN (Lisbon, b. 1541)[1]

(*A. gives a long sigh.*) I see her humility. And above all I see her in front of the angel, to whom she looks in order to find out what God wants from her. An angel accompanies her, and, for her, it is as if he were always so present that she could speak with him at any moment, look to him, and receive immediate instructions from him. She is so used to him that she never prays, contemplates, or makes an inference without

---

[1] A Dominican nun. She was condemned by the Inquisition as a fraud. Fr. Luis of Granada wrote her biography.

first running it by him, without requesting his tangible presence, without receiving his stamp of approval. An angel whom she once saw in a vision, together with many saints and many angels, and regarding whom she knew immediately that he was her guardian angel. He reported to her the Lord's voice, the Holy Spirit's voice, the voice of the Mother of God and of certain saints. And he gave her encouragement and consolation at times when she was almost unable to go any farther. He also accepted her replies and her objections. She is very temperamental and impulsive; she does everything all the way. But he worked on her in such a visible way that she noticed and understood and approved this work. The angel brought about a "reservoir" in her life. When visions or insights were shared with her, when she received graces, then she recognized the correctness of these events in his presence. She did not reflect much; she did not look very much at herself; she did not ponder very long, whether this or that might be a deception: the angel's action always represented for her something like a mirror image of what she herself was called to do. The angel *arrondit ses angles* [rounds off her sharp edges], and that is why she remained perfectly faithful to everything she grasped and internalized. In her life, she was not able to wonder about many of the things that concerned her; but the angel always gave her the power to pray, to pray in just such a way, and thus she was always able to take his advice, so to speak, in order to do things the right way. She acted, lived, and prayed in a position of equilibrium, and this was not her own equilibrium but was communicated to her by the angel.

(*Her recantation?*) She did this more out of obedience than out of fear. With Joan of Arc, there was a lot of fear and uncertainty when she recanted. Here, it is more a sort of a "need of the moment". She also does not ask herself what consequences it will have, although she does have some idea about this. It is as if, out of the ascesis that the angel lent her, she received the doctrine she took to be true, a doctrine that "one" does not contradict, that "one" confesses; as if the position were prescribed in this way and no other. It is not a lie, not an untruth; it has nothing to do with all of this but is something much more direct: a response that comes out of obligation. A response that is perhaps difficult to defend with human argumentation but would be at the same time just as difficult to contradict ... There lies a certain objectivity in the question as it happens to be posed, and there is also an objectivity, perhaps even more so, in her recantation. She herself stands in a certain sense above it. There is also here something like a "for my part", ... but because she does not know very much about God's ever-greater nature and his mysteries.

JOHN OF THE CROSS (1542–1591)

He is, on the one hand, very devout and, on the other hand, very sensitive to beauty. Both at first on separate levels. Later, it is more and more as if his joy in the beautiful would disturb him in prayer. He prays in a way that has rarely been prayed in the Church: with an infinite surrender and a perfect self-forgetting. He disappears entirely into his prayer. He receives much vision, but also much "pre-vision"; this is in itself like a *Noli me tangere*, something that a person ought to leave alone, something one ought not oneself to make into a vision. Something that one ought simply to accept as a gateway, as a path, that leads somewhere, even if the path itself is not completely clear, even if only its origin and destination can be seen. A person has to be occupied also along the way entirely and exclusively with the goal to which God seeks to lead him. John dwells too long with the pre-vision; he describes it too much and is therefore compelled to give it the fullness of vision itself, and, in order to fill it up like this, he is forced to give it too much of his own substance. And thus, in what he leaves us, there is a lot that is ambiguous, because the objective is mingled with the subjective, and the objective at which God ultimately aims does not emerge with complete purity; rather, it is mixed with the subjective element of the states and the experiences of prayer.

What is positive is absolutely the general abundance of prayer, the humility, the way in which he takes the Cross upon himself and puts himself at the disposal of every suffering and darkness. He never tries to evade. And because he is so sensitive to everything of beauty, there are truly many things that are extremely repulsive to him in his mission of suffering. In spite of this, he takes it upon himself with an unbelievable availability. But then he tries, in all sincerity, something that is simply not proper: to make the grace of his vision accessible to others. He is not aware that one cannot administer mystical graces oneself. To be sure, one is allowed to report them, but not to dress them up in such a way that they seem, as it were, desirable. He thinks that he could make his personal graces useful for others by depicting them in such an ornate way. His contemplation is almost always connected with vision; it is exceedingly rich. In his own vision he always knows precisely what God wants from him. But he thinks that describing his path for everyone else could make others' path easier. He has more trouble with men than with women, because women are both more sensitive and at the same time more susceptible and more easily allow him to show them the path.

A. has not read his writings. But she thinks: When a person reads them, he would likely come upon pregnant passages at every turn in between other "decorative" passages. In order to figure it all out in reality, you would have to have a sort of key, in the sense that, for example, you would have to read every third word of an encoded text in order to decode it. When A. has a vision, she proceeds exclusively on the basis of the content of what she sees and reports what she has seen, what meaning it has, and what demands it entails. John, by contrast, proceeds on the basis of his state of mind and describes what effects the whole vision has on him. He believes that he is under obligation to do so, because he is of the opinion that *ecstasy* is man's *response* to the vision God gives. He thinks: The more sublime the object is, the more man must hand himself over, the more he must allow himself to be consumed. If a person is never worthy of an encounter with the Lord, nevertheless he owes it to the Lord to meet him in a state of ecstasy, in which I am in a certain sense the person I am meant to be, not the person I ordinarily am, that is, merely a common sinner. For him, ecstasy is, so to speak, the dress the soul dons for celebrations. Thus, he unwittingly exhibits a sort of cult or cultivation of ecstasy. When, for example, a young girl has an ecstasy (A. recounts her first vision of the Mother of God at fourteen years of age),[1] it would be easy for her to acquire the opinion that the sentimental enthusiasm that in a certain sense belongs to this age is a constitutive part of ecstasy. And then, when ecstasies come back years later, she would try to awaken this same enthusiasm once again ... There are moments in which John notices this slight excess and tries to correct it. But he knows no other means of doing so than by intensification. He thinks: once a person is able to leave this prior stage behind him, it will become easier. Once a person no longer has to "practice", everything comes more easily. And thus he has the tendency to "train" himself precisely to get beyond training. It is a little like an athlete who feels obliged to train in order to represent his nation worthily. He, John, knows that he has to be God's musical instrument and that every string in him must be able to reproduce a perfect tone. To a certain extent, he overlooks the fact that God is the one who makes the string resound and that, if God does not need to use a string in his instrument, it is not the string's business

[1] See PW 7.

to remind God that it is there. He also overlooks the fact that a person who has a mission, no matter how unique and lonely this mission may be, never possesses it in the same context as others. Of course, God needs perfect sanctity. But not in such a way that he requires every possible answer of sanctity in every single saint. What God does not ask, man does not need to answer of his own accord.

ALPHONSUS RODRIGUEZ, JESUIT LAY BROTHER (1531–1617)

His prayer comes in precisely at the place where St. Ignatius had the vision of the iridescent spheres of fire.[1] Originally, he had, as it were, naïve notions of good and evil; he sees them as self-enclosed contrasting spheres, which are precisely colored and determined in a way that makes error impossible: goodness is good, and evil is evil. There is no third thing, nothing indifferent. This original intellectual notion gives him a love that is ready and willing to offer its help, a love that comprehends everything and an incredibly strong and empathic capacity to make distinctions and to adapt himself to his fellowmen. He feels what they feel. Thus, he is able to get involved in anything in order to help them.

He prays in a naïve way, because he connects particular expectations with his prayer; he poses certain basic questions to God; he prays out of a need for love that he feels acutely but that is not in fact linked to his person and ought not to be used for himself. Instead, it arises from others' need for love, which he feels. This same need allows him to recognize God's need for love in relation to men, and his prayers are answers to God's questions of love. In the whole of his service and prayer, in his contemplation and in the things he does to help—it is as if in every case he received the question as something directly coming from God. He is somehow with his entire existence the possible perspectives of an answer, however insufficient it may be. If someone were to ask him what God demands or what he, the lay brother, is actually doing, he would very clearly explain, even if his words fell short, to which of God's needs he is now trying to respond. He has a lot of tact in his capacity for empathy.

He has very simple visions, the sort that shade off into the natural realm. There are moments—rare, to be sure—in which he experiences

[1] Ignatius sees, on the one hand, colored spheres, which slowly turn into eyes, the eyes of a snake, and, on the other hand, he sees something glowing, which unrolls and turns out to be a snake. Just as he sees evil as self-contained, so St. Alphonsus Rodriguez sees good and evil each as self-contained.

heavenly forms as standing apart and as characterized in that way; in general, they belong to his life in a way that would make it difficult for someone to specify where the dividing line lies.

ROBERT BELLARMINE (1542–1621)

I see him in the restlessness of prayer. For him, to pray means to seek. To seek God and to seek the path God intends for the person praying and, also, to seek whatever relationship is possible with God, from a personal perspective. But in general what one could say is that, for him, the things that affect him personally are not a primary concern, for he is very humble. He considers his task to consist in illuminating and clarifying, in defending and in obeying, so much so that he does not want to waste any time on himself. He sees himself as standing in a position from which he must take up his seeking, without making any strong reference to his personal desires. This seeking is not a fumbling in the dark, but rather an entry into the light, a light that is intended for men but that blinds them and is difficult to bear and to make sense of, because it is God's light and because God remains a mystery even in giving himself. He places his own intellectual and spiritual gifts entirely at God's service and, in fact, does so without sorting them out or tallying them, but rather offering them in their totality. This total offering and allowing to take effect is part of his efforts to avoid situating himself. When he enters the Society of Jesus, achieves honors, and accumulates experiences, then he always does so from this fixed point, which cannot be explained any further: that he stands before God and must do everything God shows him from this standpoint. He is neither vain nor vindictive, even when he undergoes difficult trials. And if he also seems to be predestined to suffer, because of a particular intellectual inclination typical of his time period and which clings to him as well, then he nevertheless does not suffer much, because he does not reflect on himself in his humble offering of himself. The blows that are intended for him, blows that would have been very difficult to bear if one wanted to imagine what they would be like in one's own soul in terms of their size, their number, and their possible effects, he does not feel them much because of his humility. Since he lacks self-awareness, because he does not *want* this, then the blows fail to achieve their effects. He is zealous; he is zealous in his seeking, and he has a nice way, when he has finished something, formulated something, or achieved something, of forgetting it immediately afterward, because it is now God's affair, and God gave him the requisite time and talent so that everything belongs to God anyhow.

I see his restlessness and his view of God and of faith. He knows God's "ever-greater" character and the distance that lies between God and man, and he wants to illustrate what he knows, what he sees, what he believes. He would like every painting to be a hundred times better than it is in order that it might radiate God's atmosphere and become a confession, which would not only attract, but would also broaden the image of the world, the way of seeing, and the faith of the person who contemplates the paintings. He is plagued by doubts, because he sees what is unfinished in every painting and would like to start over. And yet from the very beginning he knows: it cannot succeed. No talent can find its ultimate expression in art alone, if it is a gift of faith. And there are bitter moments, when he would rather be without faith, indeed, when he tries to be without faith, in order to work out a norm for the beautiful, in order to be able to find a "this is how it must be, and no other way", in order to paint human beings who are nothing other than human beings. In order to capture an expression in them that would be an earthly expression, in order to be able to bring out a finitude in their relationships, instead of having to achieve nothing but this openness to the Lord every time, this listening for a music that can be perceived only by believers. At these moments he is weary of the veiled vision of God in all things, because even his most pious angel, his purest figures do not express devotion *itself*, the devotion he knows the Son came to bring to the earth.

His prayer is sometimes a humble prayer; he confesses his deficiencies, the limitations of his abilities; then all of a sudden it turns into a proud prayer: he offered this work to God, and it would have been a proper work if God had allowed man to find his limits within the world. And then, when something succeeds, something that expresses genuine faith, then he prays *before* the painting; he adores with those who adore; he looks with those who look; he thanks God for allowing him to pray together with his beloved figures and to praise him. Then the depicted figure *has* more meaning than a living person, and what he wanted to put into the picture has more validity than his own ideas that he failed to realize.

Thus, over the course of his whole life, there is vacillation between humility and pride, between gratitude and rejection, between a child-like, wide-eyed faith and an inability to believe any more—or rather, a no longer wanting to believe. In the times of humility he is perfectly humble. And wants to stay that way at these moments. But he sees that he *has* to be different, that this being different is perhaps the cross

God lays upon him in order for the tension that is necessary for his work to remain alive in him, the sign that the Holy Spirit has taken possession of what belongs to him and that he acts in El Greco's work.

VERONICA GIULIANI (1660–1727)[1]

I see her prayer and her whole disposition. She is pervaded by the effective presence of God and she prays inside of this presence, insofar as she offers herself and the world to it, in a way that she leaves up to God. It is her custom to approach the Son in every prayer, just as a child does in relation to his mother, when he finds joy not simply in encountering his mother, but in seeing her, in feeling her, and contemplating her. When he takes pleasure not only in being in his mother's presence, but in having her just as she is. It is a childlike pleasure. When Veronica is clearly aware that Christ is there (and this does not have to be a visionary presence, it can also be the result of a seeking approach or of a confession or, outside of the sacraments, of a self-accusation or a fear of having provoked the Lord's dissatisfaction), then she knows that she will experience that atmosphere of God in abundance. It is only when she finds that certain individual points are confirmed or feels at home and a certainty that she stands before the Lord and no one else that she actually begins to pray and offers herself and the world inside of her prayer.

When something extraordinary occurs in her prayer, then she sees it as God's answer, but the form this answer takes is not the essential point for her; the main thing is that God ought to do what he deems right. What happens to her she always considers to be nothing more than starting points or signs. Starting points, because God could still bring a lot more out of her and do a lot more in her than now becomes visible; but they are signs that something has truly happened, that her request for self-gift was pleasing to God, and that he also involves other people; he is active in other places and does the same thing in other places. She feels herself to be a reactor; she reacts to what God also does somewhere else in the world; she is like a bodily instrument that registers what happens spiritually in God's mind in other places.

She is very humble; she never wants anything herself. She desires the gift of self, but not the signs. And she does not at all feel herself to be anything special. When she experiences uncertainty, feels herself to be tempted, or becomes restless, then she prays herself into a great

[1] A Capuchin nun. At the request of her spiritual director, she wrote extensive and vivid accounts of her visions. She was a stigmatic who was canonized by Gregory XVI.

peace, even when this equilibrium does not in fact lie in her own temperament.

When she is supposed to write down her experiences, she does so in a sort of objectivity; the ornamentations and flowery language that run through it are more something imposed on her from the outside. One cannot judge her on the basis of her style, which is more flowery than her soul. But her primary mission is nevertheless to be a sign of the presence of God and to be this more inside of her being and her body than through her writing, which as such is an expression of her time.

SHAKESPEARE (1564–1616)

A peculiar combination of caprice and humility; he is possessed by the idea of God's greatness, and yet at times he rears up against it. The revolt is not a rejection of God, but a demand to be allowed into the ultimate mysteries: to understand why the world is so wicked and devious. He also demands to be able to understand things, to unveil them himself in order to help. Then he comes to feel the fetters of human limitation once again; he becomes filled with humility, and he desires to perfect his work in a way that serves, to lend it an elevated style—in order suddenly to be overcome once again by powerful moods, in which he attempts to compare himself to God, to surprise him unawares and trick him out of his mysteries.

For him, the Bible is *the* book. He can never forget God. But there is little prayer in his life, more a birthing out of himself, which cannot exactly be called prayer. Nevertheless, sometimes a certain intention, sometimes the realization of something in his work can be considered a sort of outpouring of prayer. But he himself fluctuates between humility and arrogance, willingness and unwillingness. In this, he knows that God does not let him go, but occasionally he thinks that *he* does not let God go. He hates depravity, and yet he possesses a curiosity. In his bad times, he gives himself over to depravity, with the feeling that even thus he is doing something useful, a service to man, whom he can thus better understand. Then he comes to see that that cannot serve God and gives it up again; terrified and humble, he crawls toward the Cross, throws himself into his work, and seeks once again to make God's power and might known—until he ends up letting this go once again. He is convinced that God has placed an unconditional demand on him; sometimes, he thinks he understands it, then once again it seems to him that though the voice of God is near to him, he himself is so distant that his ear detects nothing.

(*And the Church?*) It has little to do per se with his interior life. He is disappointed in many ways; he sees in the Church the incarnation of a power that remains misunderstood and abused. A power that was good at the beginning and that people made evil and used in bad ways. He sees himself a little bit as a Catholic beyond the Church's borders . . .

MARY MAGDALEN DEI PAZZI (1566–1607)

I see her prayer and her vows, which are a devotion to the transcendent and which signify for her the perfect tension between her existence in the world and her existence in prayer. For these vows make the life of prayer free. So free that God truly speaks, and he does so with his creature, which as a creature no longer has any significance and also no longer wants to have any significance. The vows understood in the fullness of their strength and their totality, as truly a consecration to the transcendent, an acceptance of everything that happens, an availability, the will to live exclusively from God, promises that Magdalen knows only God, not she, can keep.

And now she has entered into the spirit of the vows, the spirit of obedience, with her own spirit, in such a way that the transposition becomes *visible*, that her body lags behind in a sort of abandonment, while her spirit is perfectly with God. Here it would have been the task of the sisters in her community and of Carmel to haul her in to a certain extent. In other words, the Order, the Rule, and the tradition ought to have bound her so much to the framework of the vows that it would have been possible to be at the same time obedient to the Order. Instead, there is a danger for her that she fails to come perfectly back into this bond but remains detached, so to speak. And this is not her fault, but it occurs because the religious life in the house is not strong enough to contain her to the extent necessary for the house itself. Thus, there ends up being certain derailments, which are not an objection to her, but rather to the Carmel in which she finds herself. She is the word that God speaks to this house, the word to which the house would have had to adapt itself, not in order externally to profit from her raptures, to make note of her words and wise sayings, and so on, but in order internally, in the reality of what the grace of the vows gives, to receive a share in Magdalen's grace. There is a division in the house, and this division becomes visible in her. The unity that Teresa of Avila embodies escapes her, though through no fault of her own. She is aware of this, even if she cannot find the words to express it; she feels that the discrepancy between her prayer and life in God and that which happens in the house is too great. She would like to return to a state that would be accessible to the others. But she is unable, and the others miss their chance.

As long as she is alone with God, her ecstasy is good and lies within a strict obedience and an openness for everything God gives. But the scraps that fall to the others from this are not gathered up; the cloister does not follow her, does not share in humility. Thus, the objectivity of her transmission is also impaired by the medium that receives it. When she admonishes and rejects, everything is not completely objective, because her discomfort mixes in with God's voice, even in the places where God did not demand it. The discrepancy she feels is so painful to her that she can find no way to get over it. What she lacks is an irreproachable superior and a completely objective confessor. Without them, she mixes what belongs to her into things; from her vision, which contains nothing of this, she brings her entire discomfort, her being misunderstood, or even more, the misunderstanding of God in the cloister, to expression, which is an expression of herself. Her vision is used in a way that it was not intended to be used.

MADAME ACARIE (1566–1618)

Her prayer is moody and erratic, but she makes an incredible *effort* to pray. She has an extremely personal way of effacing herself in prayer. When she resolves to pray about or contemplate a particular thing, then this intention is, as it were, bracketed out. God is then able to eliminate the brackets, so that the prayer in question can be set loose and her intention can be carried out, or he can leave the brackets in place, so that for the duration of the prayer she can feel, in a sense, that although she went into prayer with this particular intention, God now prefers something else. Then her contemplation is accompanied by the thought that has been bracketed out; she prays, as it were, "alongside", contemplating God's intervention or his will or the obstacle he left or the freedom he has to give prayer the shape he wishes—all the while not forgetting what it was she wanted to pray about. When such a deferral occurs, she recognizes how God's plans are created in relation to her and the person praying. But if God takes the thought away together with the brackets, then she prays, as it were, in the void. She sees no material for contemplation; she does not see God's will, nor does she see herself. It is then a sort of prayer of annihilation in the presence of God's majesty. Or God offers her other matter for contemplation, which she then embraces joyfully and contemplates just as God wishes her to. One of these four possibilities is constantly in play in one form or another, and this happens in such a way that every form of prayer leads her more deeply into the many different ways God relates to man. And she also experiences a certain enthusiastic love, a not inconsiderable ecstasy, and a benefit from God's grace. In addition to these, however, she also experiences a certain sobering dryness, which she takes into the bargain with a sense of humor. As moody as she might be, she is nevertheless unassuming with respect to God.

But things are more difficult with respect to other people. She is fairly extreme; she has exaggerated preferences, suddenly on fire for one person, but then someone else enters the picture. She also has a certain way of drinking people up and can be extremely indiscreet. It is as if she constantly had the desire to see people in prayer, not that people ought to pray all the time—although as far as she herself is concerned even the longest prayer always seems too short—but she would like to be allowed into their prayer herself. Just as she utilizes her own prayer with a practical sense, so too she would like to make use of the prayer of others.

In her marriage, she is both present and absent; she has a particular way of overlooking marriage. Because she is married, she accepts the duties that marriage brings, but she does so in a certain dryness and occasionally also with a certain indifference. It is a little like the way she later treats the tangible fruits of contemplation. She is often happy in marriage, but marriage is never something she fully acknowledges; it is as if her marriage meant a relationship to *this* man, but not in fact to the state of life of marriage per se. For her, children represent a part of marriage, but she lacks an enduring attachment; with all of her tenderness, she seems to be unable to understand complete possession. Mystical experiences are already present at the time of her marriage, more in the form of knowledge, as something conclusive. The great manifestations come only later, when she is in the cloister and, periodically, in the times in which she prays an especially large amount. In fact, her visionary experiences parallel in a sense the intensity and duration of prayer; this regularity is something one can trace. The reason is because she does not achieve a *disposition* of prayer. Something in her prayer remains to the end a function of her mood.

Carmel measures up to her conception of prayer and contemplative life. But if she experiences incredibly beautiful moments in Carmel as well, and her visions harmonize with the life of Carmel, she was nevertheless already too mature at the time of her entrance, too formed, to be able to play the role of a good nun. She is so closed up that she is no longer able to be fashioned. Of course, there is much renunciation in the step she takes; but she brings her original existence with her. It would be extraordinarily difficult for her to disappear altogether behind the partition. In some sense she knows that she will never be able to celebrate her final departure from the world.

FRANCIS DE SALES (1567–1622)

A. sees him at a large wooden desk, writing letters. The first impression is that he is overburdened. Too many people are waiting for a response from him. He is tired. He begins to write, not the most important letters at first, but the letters of fatigue, letters with this or that concern, which can be settled quickly and briefly. Then he passes gradually over from the business letters to the essential letters. The transition is carried out like a prayer. For now the concern is such that, in order for him to respond to it, it has to come to life in him. It is not given to him simply to toss off an answer; the answer does not lie right on the tip of his tongue; rather, it must be drawn up from the depths of his heart. Even when they often look, from the outside, like so many ready-made formulas, his responses are always for him a new experience. He undergoes something peculiar in all of this: in the personal experience he has to communicate, he enters into a new relationship, so to speak, with the person receiving the letter. In the moment of his response, this person becomes for him a new man; he becomes the man to whom he can entrust his mystery. He could no doubt go down other paths; he could write out the very best formulas, out of his own prior experience, or he could cite tried and true authors. And indeed he has also got the necessary documents. But he does not write anything he does not experience anew in that moment, in the very moment when he is speaking and writing. He does not fob anyone off with cheap fare. He will seek to be objective, but even more, to give something that comes from his innermost possessions. The recipient receives an insight into his innermost being, is, so to speak, brought into relation with him through the communication. But he is at the same time a person to whom Francis is grateful for having given him the opportunity to make contact with this mystery. He himself receives enrichment through the questions the letter writer raised; he himself would not otherwise have become acquainted with this possibility.

Only, he is not able to follow through with this completely. There is a fissure somewhere in his being. He would like to have the receiver feel how he gives himself, how he lays himself bare in such a personal way before him. But while he attempts to give of what most belongs to him, he does not succeed in taking the recipient in a wholly personal way. In a certain sense, it has become a habit for him to give himself. Everything crosses over a bit into a sphere of enjoyment: the pleasure of receiving, of responding, and of giving oneself. And thus there lies in this an extremely slight devaluing of the recipient. The self-gift has become in a certain sense too much a function of his job, just something he does, and the client, the person to whom he opens himself, is worse off for it. And thus he has to cover up this lack of an ultimate inner bond and balance it out with a coating of *douceur* [sweetness, kindness]; he covers up what is missing for the other person with this *douceur*. In the end, he is not obliged, in fact, to generate such a close, personal relationship; he could be more matter-of-fact without doing any damage to his mission. But this is what he has committed himself to, and he now tries to carry it out by these means.

This has an effect on his interior life. The Lord's earthly humanity seems to him to be something that can be brought closer to us and conveyed through the medium of superficial *douceur*. And because this *douceur* lacks an ultimate masculinity, it also takes away something of the masculinity of his relationship to the Lord. He himself feels this in his prayer. There are people who have to overcome an inhibition before they can express themselves and who have found a particular way of "warming themselves up" in order to come out of themselves. Francis uses *douceur* in his prayer in order to "warm himself up". He often has to overcome himself in order to love the Lord in a masculine way. This gives his prayer, like his letters, a somewhat "cliché" character. But the greatness and beauty of them remain that he himself experiences everything he writes about and in the way in which he writes about it. And in the fact that prayer and spiritual direction form a unity with him. The essential thing, that which is divine and corresponds to faith, is something he experiences.

A. then sees him traveling, with the difficulty he has in sticking it out. A part of his holiness lies in this, namely, that he never fails to push on. He constantly has to force himself back into service because of his own incapacity. He leans toward whatever is pleasant, but he restrains himself. It costs him something not to make the people to whom he has something to offer into instruments of his enjoyment. Even here something of his softness comes to the fore, which he must again and again overcome. Strangely, it is Chantal who gives him this masculine element. Chantal bears a great part of the responsibility for his truly having become a saint. She constantly "twists" him a bit so that he remains wholly in the proper direction; she does it very discreetly, full of love and often without knowing exactly what it is she is doing. She is like a screw on a tool that serves to regulate it. She creates opportunities to teach him something, almost without being aware of it. She does not do so in the same way he does, with many colors and circumlocutions, but rather in an extremely delicate and masculine way. She does not allow him to make any mistakes. She knows that she has a responsibility, and she is very aware of how she acts in relation to him. And although she feels he has already completed his most positive achievements, that he distances himself a bit, she nevertheless places the whole of her sanctity at his disposal. And it belongs to her renunciation that she does not require him to be the perfect saint. *She* is there to fill in the gaps. One could say that Francis was the holiest at the beginning of the trajectory, and Chantal is the holiest at the end; but she bears something of his shortcoming in her holiness. Their trajectories intersect at a certain central point. A part of her holiness lies in the fact that she takes the final breaking of his line upon herself and balances it out in herself.

JANE FRANCES DE CHANTAL (1572–1641)

She is pure, in the sense that the life she previously lived in the world did not affect her. But there is nothing seraphic about her. She is red-blooded and unvarnished. There is a tension between her life in the world and her interior being. Her life in the world demands of her a lot of elegance, but in spite of her nobility, she is quite rustic in her femininity. Her naturalness forbids her any form of exaggeration. It goes without saying for her that, if a person has a spouse, he must belong to that spouse. And of course a person has to speak the truth if he knows it. She has a sort of unproblematic character in her sensual life as well as in her intellect. And it "goes beyond" the whole finesse of her century and her milieu. But it does so in the sense that she is unable to take her entire task in the world with complete seriousness. She does what is demanded of her, with the whole of her being, and yet she retains a certain smile about everything. She does what is customary in her country, but she does not require that everything external form a perfect harmony with what lies most deeply within. She does not feel a need to understand everything. She lets external things be the way they are. And she knows, from the nuns she knows and from the books she reads, that there are other and greater missions. But, although the thought of the cloister was never completely foreign to her, she nevertheless does not stand in any immediate relationship to this "greater" mission. It would not have occurred to her to desire the death of her husband so that she could enter the cloister. Nevertheless, she has the rare gift of remaining open for other people in the things she does.

Then comes the new mission and, with it, many difficulties. And the more these increase, the more she is awakened to her mission. From out of the obstacles, she comes to see the need to respond to the new call that has come upon her. Finally, her encounter with Francis becomes a confirmation for her. Francis definitively awakens in her what has been asleep up to this point: the absoluteness of self-gift. The new is not simply an amplification of the old—namely, the gift of self to her husband and family—but a more serious form of gift. Something completely different awakens in her. She possesses in herself something like a sensorium for the most complete response to God possible, even before God's call presented itself clearly to her. Francis is the one who illuminates and sets in motion these possibilities of which she was not conscious. He impresses her; she recognizes his superiority; she sees the things with which she is not yet familiar in herself brought to reality in him. At the same time, he allows his favorite responses to God to become a question in her. He imposes the Christian form onto her natural form, and she begins to become aware of the discrepancy that lies between these two. Little by little he immerses her in a form. He expands her, allows everything in her to become an answer to God's call. For this, she will never forget him, even when she later in a certain sense outgrows him. And her gratitude consists in the fact that she takes over from him a lot of his burden. Francis achieves his contribution to her development with complete selflessness, without realizing that he is also working for himself.

At the beginning of her new path, her prayer has a little of the *douceur* that Francis infused into her. She has come to God so much with his help that at the beginning she takes a lot of things from him, even things that are not so recommendable. Then her path becomes more independent, and she advances, in a masculine and solitary way. Almost as if Francis led her in a beautiful bridal gown to God, and now she had to learn how to become entirely naked before God in solitude. Francis possesses from his youth a tenderness that becomes more noticeable later; he dresses Jane Frances up in order to lead her to God; he surrounds her with mysteries that are not always completely proper. The fact that she manages to find her way back to the naked truth will constitute the core of her holiness. As she does so, she understands that human beings are able to help one another all the way to the end, but only when each one is completely what God wants him to be and has the strength also to dispense with help from others, in gratitude, in order in this way to become a person who is genuinely helpful. Humility prevents her from seeing herself as someone who has attained maturity and someone who has grown independent. She will help Francis without feeling that she is entirely capable of doing so. But she has gone beyond the sphere of his "formulas" and entered into an immediate relationship to God; she has stripped off certain of the superficialities that Francis attached to her, often with the best of intentions.

As a superior, she once again becomes something new; this occurs in much prayer and in great goodness. Here too she had to free herself gradually from many of the things that Francis placed in her with this in mind. Indeed, she has to free herself from them precisely in order to become the person Francis in fact ultimately wanted her to be. He possesses a correct image of the true superior, but he does not see that his many instructions eclipse this image a bit. For her, the goal with which Francis presents her remains alive and unchanged, but she must separate herself from the path to it, because she comes to see that God's means and ways to this goal are more suitable. As a superior, she has certain difficulties that she also experienced when she was a wife. While she was a woman in the world, she thought the cloister could bring her the fulfillment of all she longed for in the world and would give back to her at a higher level the natural and care-free life she possessed in the world. The time of problems and difficulties seemed to be nothing more than a time of transition, nothing more than a time of adapting herself to the new situation in the cloister. She expected that the new tasks—like prayer, penance, and so forth—could be carried out unproblematically. What then happens in truth is that, on the one hand, she becomes for herself more and more natural in God's presence, but, on the other hand, her naturalness makes her increasingly more aware of and sensitive to the difficulties of the sisters with whom she has been entrusted. It is something completely different to be cheerful and happy with her maidservants than with women in the cloister. Moreover, she has to be careful: a number of her sisters have in fact entered the cloister more for her sake than for God's, compelled by the strength of her personality. She has to educate them away from her and toward God. She is not permitted to be a substitute for God in their regard and must nevertheless remain a mother to them. It is precisely here that she is not permitted to adopt the methods that Francis uses in relation to those entrusted to him, never permitted to put personal charm in the place of God's clear truth.

Her prayer is grasped in constant change, because it is full of the burdens she has taken over from other people. It becomes increasingly a prayer of substitution for those who are undergoing difficulties. She cannot simply dissolve these difficulties into her own naturalness. She must bear them just as they are.

She was not able to make the Visitation Order completely into what she had in mind. But she at least sent it in the proper direction. Because at the beginning a lot of sisters entered for her sake, and thus the Order turned into a sort of fashionable world; it then also remained so when she was no longer there, and those who entered were no longer able to model it in her spirit. Not because of her, but because of this fashionable character the Order retained a certain superficial flavor. But her spirit was nevertheless strong enough to keep away the principal dangers.

FIDELIS OF SIGMARINGEN (1577–1622)

I see his prayer; he is quite close to living in unceasing prayer. And prayer has long served him as a weapon against himself, against his shortcomings, against everything imperfect in himself he was able to uncover, because he always begged God with great zeal to take away his faults and because he forced penances on himself with great harshness, as punishment. He brought himself through prayer almost in a systematic way to holiness. In his great zeal for the salvation of the souls of all those he encounters, he never forgets that he has to remain an instrument, in a condition that can lighten God's work. Thus, he does not simply give an accounting before God every time, but he does penance, imposes a lot of prayer on himself as expiation, a lot of prayer for the souls that are entrusted to him, and finally a lot of prayer for the fruitfulness of each of his encounters. In this, he retains a cheerful attitude, which almost entirely hides the ascesis of his life, so that no one would guess how much he lives like a penitent. He is not especially gifted with words, but he makes every effort; and he is so convinced that the Holy Spirit ought to speak through him—in confession as much as in his preaching—that he also allows his prayer constantly to end up in a twofold request: that he might not be an obstacle to the Holy Spirit and that the Holy Spirit himself might act on men. He does not permit his thoughts to stray, at least when he is alone; they ought to dwell with God. When he relaxes among his brothers, often out of obligation, then he does so as much as possible in God's Spirit, in the joyfulness of God's children. And when his conversations do not revolve around God, then he tries afterward in prayer to give the things he said a new turn. He lies so much in God's hands that he has no concern about what will become of him; he has brought himself to complete indifference in his own regard.

In his martyr's death itself, he is already taken over by God, similar to the way in which Stephen was; but he saw the position come to a point beforehand. Indeed, as the thought arose that martyrdom might

137

be possible, he had dismissed it as much as possible with the thought that this is not his business. And where the flesh perhaps trembled, the spirit was completely determined, with a determination that neither found support nor saw a threat in the deed itself; he handed himself over once and for all. He did not trouble himself about himself or his death.

CONDREN (1588–1641)

I have to look around a bit to find him. There he is. He is zealous. He believes that, whatever he himself is not able to bring about can be taken up by others who in fact are capable of doing it.

His prayer is actually poorer than his conversation. He has such a clear knowledge of how one ought to help people, how one leads them, and what they ought to do in order to avoid constantly slipping back into lukewarmness. He knows this at the same time in terms of love of neighbor. In prayer, he is somewhat clumsy in relation to God. He believes strongly in a "personal sanctification", but a sanctification that is intended more for those whom he leads than for himself. He himself does it for others and knows it from their perspective rather than from his own. The lofty theories he constructs about God and prayer he receives from others; even for him they remain simply theories.

Once in his youth he experienced God. But this experience underwent a transformation, and he himself came off badly; he fell into a kind of idle running of his own prayer, less through a failure to will than through an exhaustion that he himself caused. First come the others, and, if there is anything else, he comes next. In a certain sense, he has more important things to do. He drags himself along, not in complete disorder, but nevertheless by letting things go in a certain sense. He did not manage to keep this great experience of his youth alive. Even the theories about the Lord's sacrifice arise more from the experience of others than from his own. To be sure, he is a leader for his age par excellence. But he has in fact read a great deal, spoken with a great number of interested people, who conveyed many things to him, without form, and he molded what was formless. In his religious life, the commandment to love one's neighbor is more important to him than the commandment to love God. Out of love for his neighbor, he makes use of his love of God for his neighbor's sake.

All of his followers have a fault: they look too much at one another. They act out a role, they know that they are doing so, and they hope that the others watch their acting and appreciate it. It was really a time period in which truly talented people did not shy away from studying

138

theology, people who would have done completely different things had they lived today. And what they placed in the scales was much more their gifts than their whole person.

PETER CLAVER (1581–1654)

He prays well. When he prays, God usually lifts him up into a heavenly vision, and in this vision—though he does not see with his own eyes here—he learns what God intended the Church to be, what she looks like in heaven. He does not see her as separate from the Church on earth, but rather he sees her as the fulfillment of the visible Church. What strikes him most of all, and every time anew, is that each individual soul comes to the fore, that each is shown his particular place, that God counts every individual and loves and needs every single individual. Claver possessed this vision even before he went off to the mission. He had seen long before then that each individual soul is important to God.

During his time in the mission, prayer always means for him a constantly renewed encouragement. When he prays, he no longer sees the tedium of the path; he sees, no longer the obstacles and the dangers, but solely the result that God awaits. And without being able to specify a particular moment of time for its realization, he knows with certainty: I have to finish it; that is how God wants it; and he turns from prayer with renewed strength and new insight back to his work. His exceedingly personal relationship to God is embedded within a vision of his mission: out of the grace that God shares with him, out of God's love, which is given to him to experience, he sees what God's grace and love in fact are. He does not see himself in this gift of grace as someone who has been chosen, a saint, but instead he thinks he is like the people who have been entrusted to him, and he thinks that a grace of this sort has been set aside for everyone. When he comes from prayer, he sees in his protégés people for whom God is waiting, those who are supposed to meet the quota. Then he is, however, very much with them in the midst of their difficulties, and also with those who cause them difficulties, and he suffers because of this. It is thus always hard for him in moments like these to harmonize the earthly reality with the reality of heaven.

His penance is, so to speak, a path from the earthly reality to the heavenly one. When he begins to do penances, it occurs in complete unity with his protégés. He carries it out as a complete sinner, as a person without a clue, perhaps even as a person who is overburdened. In the course of the act of penance, while he is still doing it, a transformation takes place, the same that God allows him to experience in prayer: it is like when he is with his followers and has an equality of rights with them, a unity of being with them, as if he had taken a step deeper into the grace of God. He is harsh with himself in penance, but God is gentle with him in receiving it.

MARIE DES VALLÉES (1590–1656)[1]

An incredible scope of vision. In her youth, there was a great naïveté and a shock every time she stood before the things she saw in the fullness of her visions. She is pious, but that is why she is shocked, because the sort of piety she has does not allow her to leave the things standing the way they are. She has fixed opinions: the life of prayer is for her a chain of tiny acts and accomplishments; the visions, by contrast, seem to her to be something whole and vast and, for precisely this reason, completely extraordinary. And she imagines that she is supposed to bring both of these things together, to tie together in herself the knot of unity. She would have done better to stay with her tiny prayer. Then she would have been humble, and the visions would have remained outside her own action and achievement. Thus, it cannot be excluded that she falsifies many things as time passes. She makes references to secondary, collateral aspects in her vision in order to depict it. She continues to recount things she has long ceased to see. She is convinced that she herself must be very important *because* she has visions and that the visions themselves must be something extremely important. For this reason, she feels obliged to "make" something out of the parts of the vision that remain unresolved, at first for herself, in order to justify her original opinion.

It would not be right to characterize her as a fraud. She remains pious. But she begins to project everything she experiences in her ordinary life onto the level of her visions. For example, she projects her bodily discomforts onto the Lord's Passion, so that she is convinced that she suffers horrible things together with the Lord. The heart, the center of her visions, is genuine and good. For this reason she does not risk herself further; for this reason the heart of her visions is preserved even through the falsifications, even in her reporting of them. But she grabs everything that is more marginal; she wants to explain it, to analyze it, and thus she falsifies it. Indeed, visions are always somehow embedded in a "landscape". In order to show something central, it is necessary to show the whole context. Whoever sees

[1] A mystic from Normandy. St. Jean Eudes was her confessor, and she was an advisor to him.

in a proper way looks at that which ought to be shown, and he perceives the marginal things only as "setting". If a person tries to interpret the background as something that exists in its own right, he is forced to project things into it.

With Marie des Vallées, there is something genuine in this falsification. She is convinced that she has to round out her sensations, until they become clear both to her and to others. And because the people around her quit reacting so long ago to her feelings and circumstances, she has to present them and fill them until they finally take notice. Then there always returns the initial naïveté, to think that, because she is pious, because she belongs to God, all her efforts and circumstances must come immediately from God. If her toothache or tummyache had no connection with the suffering of the Cross, then she would have the feeling that she was no longer in unity with God. This leads her to a form of self-divinization that is due to her complete naivëté.

Jean Eudes is so pure that he can abstract from everything that is muddy in her. He is at the same time not at all affected by it; he retains in every case the true center, which is intended for him: the beginning of the vision. For, the beginning is always correct, and afterward it goes increasingly astray. God's special patience can be seen in Marie des Vallées: he continued to give her genuine visions in spite of everything, probably for Jean Eudes' sake. He also allowed her her genuine little piety. This does not go away. It does not become false in its heart.

Every time *after* a vision, a completely strict obedience becomes necessary: this obedience provides the measure. A person ought to dwell with a vision he has experienced for as long as obedience requires, until everything that obedience sees as necessary is said, interpreted, and explained. Everything else comes from evil.

FRIEDRICH VON SPEE (1591–1635)

I see his prayer, which is very pious and warm and alive. He lives in the air of prayer. And if it is true that he has no visions, he is nevertheless very much at home close to the angels, to many saints, and to the Mother of God. He lives in a world that has eternal value and eternal meaning. He prays every type of prayer there is: liturgical prayer, prayer that just occurs to him, that pleases him and in which he dwells and which he continues early the next morning and once again the following evening, the evening after that, all through the day, from start to finish; it is also often the case that he afterward is not entirely sure what it was that occurred to him, or he does not realize that it does not need to be continued. He lives in the simplicity of a child of God, in a kind of contentedness, which rests on the matter-of-factness of his personal gift of self to God. It is easy for him to live in the Order, because he recognizes the Order's ideal as an excellent one, and because he is able to carry out what corresponds to this ideal. His problems are vital problems, the sort that lie very close to God; and if he throws himself into them, he does so with the whole strength of the personality he has received anew from God. What is remarkable about his attitude is that he lives in the sort of zeal a convert has with respect to God, a zeal that allows him to let himself be formed by God anew at every moment, and that he nevertheless pursues his tasks in a completeness and consistency, as if it were possible, and necessary, to arrange his life on the basis of his tasks, to weigh himself in a certainty that enabled him also to carry forward tasks planned with a view to the long term. He thinks of his poems as a testimony: not only point-ing to God, but also pointing *from* God. They ought to show in what world God allows believers to live. In their joyfulness and simplicity, in their seriousness, indeed, in their ultimate obligation to the truth, they ought to bear witness to one's belonging to God.

He is not anxious, and then he is anxious; he makes plans, and he comes before God totally without a plan. This is not a contradiction, but he does it in the knowledge that God's world is not this world and that it is also necessary always to allow God to intervene however he wishes and that a person cannot permit himself to be the obstacle that the world is for God. He wants to be what God wants. This deter-mines his prayer; it determines his attitude; it determines every single task he takes up and carries out. However, he would also prefer that others not be an obstacle but that all people would become witnesses of self-gift in the following of Christ.

LOUISE DE MARILLAC (1591–1660)[1]

I see her zeal and her prayer. Her prayer is sometimes stifled by out-ward activity; in periods of extreme busyness she almost forgets to pray and works for the sake of the work itself, until God always sends her a tangible warning, reminding her to return to prayer. But she is so active and so much caught up in her endeavors that prayer often seems heavy to her, or even more, she forgets it altogether. Those who stand closer to her know why this happens and thus take over a little of her prayer. They pray in her place, because they see an occasion for

[1] One of St. Vincent de Paul's co-workers. Canonized in 1934.

God's displeasure in this occasionally deficient prayer, and they are afraid that the work could degenerate into mere external organization. When she realizes her mistake, she once again prays piously and humbly, and she begs God to prevent her from falling back into her forgetfulness. In this, she is already aware that she exaggerates to a certain extent the importance of the work before God, or that she will exaggerate it, and that, when the problem arises once again, she all too easily gives into it. Thus, she vacillates a bit back and forth, and though she wills the good, she needs a steady hand. In relation to prayer, she is more like a climbing plant than a free-standing one, while in her works she is too much a free-standing plant, that is, she tends to forget that she depends on other people and that she ought to cling more to God and to the instructions she has received. But when she works, she does so fully conscious of her responsibility and involves herself for the sake of others. It is only that the balance between action and contemplation is skewed. Perhaps it would be good to see this as a warning about activism. For her, no abiding damage comes from this, because other people offer her support, because these others understand who are otherwise very much devoted to her activity. It is with her a kind of need to be right, which gets mixed up with her all-too-stubborn activity and which she can strip away in prayer only with difficulty. It is not easy to start over again *every day* in God's presence in the emptiness of the creature who lets things happen.

MARIE DE L'INCARNATION (1599–1672)

As a young girl, she takes everything very seriously. She prays abundantly and piously, and her prayer gives her a highly developed sense for ascesis. Whenever she prays, it strikes her that one ought not to pray without really surrendering oneself, and this means making sacrifices. She sacrifices a bunch of tiny things, things that would have given her joy but that she offers as a gift in the most natural way. And she does so always on the basis of prayer. She has an extremely practical mind and an extraordinary agility in grasping what God demands of her.

Later, she experiences all sorts of blows of fate; she sinks downward from her external position; she bears it with an incredible humility, a humility that is built entirely on sacrifice. Her humility stems not so much from a feeling of her own nothingness as it does from her sacrifice for the sake of others. And because she has now grown up and does not want to become bitter, but would rather stand firm, she perceives her external fate as the great opportunity that God gives her to

143

humble herself further and to sacrifice more. She does not content herself with offering God a one-time sacrifice, namely, the loss of her position; she constantly seeks other ways to surrender herself, to help, to make an offering of herself. And all of this occurs in prayer. Rarely has a human being prayed so much. In this period, she receives very few visions, but she seeks God everywhere and in all things. She does not seek to "realize God in herself", but rather she seeks the longing for God in all her sacrifices for others. If, for example, she sees a poor person, she thinks immediately of Christ's poverty. She serves him and helps him out of love for the Lord, without rushing on to the thought, in doing so, that she is thus doing the Lord himself a favor. In her humility, she experiences all her deeds solely as an act of adoration.

At the time she resolves to enter the cloister, she regularly experiences visions. They are demanding, urgent, and moreover in a certain sense they draw her. (A. says here: I believe I can see what she saw at one time:) She sees, for example, a poor young man on the street, completely empty-handed. And she petitions the Lord for this young man, who is as poor as the Lord ... Afterward, she falls into a vision and sees the same boy, but he has now become the Lord himself, and the demand grows stronger: the boy, to be sure, had many needs, but the Lord has needs in an urgent, irrevocable, and absolute way ... The urgency of this demand finally brings her to enter the cloister. She also has the feeling that she no longer is allowed to have control over her works and sacrifices. Instead, these deeds all persistently lead to a single, complete gift of herself, precisely in the manner of the self-gift involved in the religious state: all the individual deeds and sacrifices are merely an expression of the self-gift carried out once and for all. And it is not the individual, but the superior who has oversight over how one is to respond in every case to God's demand. Thus, she must transform herself now into a new form of gift, since God's demand cannot be satisfied simply through the increase of the sorts of self-gift she made before. She now understands that all the trees of her individual deeds have come together to form a *single* forest. This unity is given to her in prayer and in a vision.

In her previous life of visions she encountered a danger: when God's demands threatened her from every side, then she ultimately lost all idea how to protect herself. To which of these young people ought she to give her cloak, if she only has one? Thus, she is compelled to make a choice. But this unsettles her even further: she feels like she is a gourmand, looking for the thing that pleases her the most. She fully recognizes this danger and avoids it in the one way possible: through her entry into total monastic obedience. She avoids the danger before anything in her gets ruined. In her final decisions, she is admirably sure of herself; she has a completely simple and almost peasant-like certainty when it has to do with the whole. She is familiar with the fragmentation in her works and knows she will find unity in the cloister. She has a very deep insight into the essence of the religious life: that it is the life in which one acts the most for God and the Church, in which one has the greatest share in the salvation of the faith, that the vows are the lever.

After her entrance, she has a great impact on the cloister. And the visions become different: they are not so sharp, more balanced, and unified. She sees in them that she lives in God's obedience, that it was right to enter the cloister, to renounce individuality in order to be incorporated into anonymity. They are now visions for the cloister, for prayer and ascesis. The themes that are shown to her become greater, and the effects are increasingly to raise the level of the spirit of prayer in her followers. God's demands on her do not become any less, but she fares as one among many, among those who are the same, and she receives these demands and grace in the name of everyone else. This is not easier than her previous life. But she did not enter the cloister in order to stop feeling disquiet. At the same time, the disquiet in her changes in a sense into ultimate peace and certainty.

CALDERÓN (1600–1681)

The poetic element in him was strongest when he first began to write poetry, in the sense that he possessed a limitless love for the stuff of poetry, for the language, and for giving things form, and he recognized his own talent in the work, once it succeeded and was understood. Moreover, he was always able to draw the energy out of this work to apply himself to new tasks. But he did not grasp at success for its own sake—"success" here understood as the effect of his work on another's soul—but saw it rather as a result of God's task, as a grace, indeed, even as a permission: the permission to push things farther, beyond the success that had already been achieved. It is seldom the case that two or three matters impose themselves on him at once; rather, the new theme suddenly shows itself in the previous theme, which he has already developed to a certain extent. And through his own poetry, through his gifts and his achievement, he receives matter for contemplation, which leads him ever more deeply into prayer. He prays in fact about that which lies before him and is self-contained; it is less a request for new material, a request for the preservation of himself and his concerns, than it is a thanksgiving for what has taken shape and has become perfectly apparent to his vision. He himself is an instrument, and he is aware of his instrumentality. And he is increasingly convinced that God gave him this gift for the work, that therefore the work is something God wills. He is the craftsman for this particular work and no other. There is a great dissolution of his ego and his will in all of this. If he always grows stronger in God, it is primarily because of his work, but then also—especially in his later years—through all the discoveries that it is given to him to make in Christian matters. Brand new fundamental words and truths that had been unexplored until then constantly open themselves up to him, and his work becomes the way he can make these truths known. He makes discoveries. He is like a child who has been given a candle and who makes a voyage of discovery with this little light through a huge, unfamiliar forest at night and sees things in the half-dark that, with the approach of the candle, suddenly take on contours, unexpected forms, in order finally to become beautiful—so beautiful that the child remains standing for sheer joy in the middle of this miraculous wood with his candle and does not realize that it is not possible to live completely in the night in order to be able to wander around constantly with this light.

His prayer is simple, and ultimately all his works strive for simplicity of heart, even when they touch on the most varied of themes. The complicated theme he discovers provides him with simple novelty; the hidden truths provide him with the evident ones. And the entire unfolding of the game and his movement here and there is always a transformation into the true, into the good, into love. When he becomes a priest, he does so in order not to stand in any contradiction to the truth that is known, in fact, in order to support God in his design, to give his truth to the world through beauty and through his poetry. Remaining in the world, he would have been afraid of being led astray by many things that God rejects as distraction; for God's will went to the point of making him a visionary.

AGNES OF JESUS, O.P. (1602–1634)[1]

Hers is a life of pure service. She would have had a mission of coordination; the threads of various missions converged in her hand, and she would have had to facilitate the connections among the various impulses and orientations. She does this, and people even listen to her here and there, but one skims off the cream and leaves the rest and perhaps does not return to her at the right moment. And one recalls

[1] A stigmatic, and an advisor of Olier. Canonized in 1808.

146

certain words of reprimand that she uttered and would not like to run the danger of having the same thing happen again. She makes mystical "journeys" and appears to individuals; she watches them when they pray and when they carry out their tasks, in their rejections, and so forth. And she allows God to send her out again, sometimes night after night. She is a simple, good woman. Perhaps she has the fault that she does not see her own mission sufficiently and does not sufficiently devote herself to it. But it is not a deficient will. It is more a lack of knowledge and also a little failure through the lack of will of others.

She has a good prayer, a good contemplation, and many visions. She sees the Lord. Very often in her vision, she experiences her task as coming from the Lord's own hands. And she stands near the Mother of God. She is a proper saint, but surrounded by a bloated mass of religious, priests, and bishops who try to cloak her naked words with politeness in order to play them down.

OLIER (1608–1657)

I cannot see him; I have to look for him first. Maybe I do see him. I see a whole group of satisfied gentlemen; now I see him, I think. *Il faut vous démêler un peu, Messieurs . . .* [You'll have to separate yourselves out, gentlemen]. His prayer? *He* prays. He does not let prayer take place in him. He prays the way a person would read something out loud. He speaks in God's presence at certain times; he presents himself regularly for the roll-call, and then he tells a few nice things to the good Lord, *il fait la politesse au bon Dieu. Il a très bien appris son rôle* [he is polite to the good God, he has learned his role quite well]. A mission? Yes, . . . they all have a mission. Missions that are intended for each one and which nevertheless ought to communicate with one another in a sort of community or alliance. It is comparable to the way in which St. Joseph's mission went together with the Lord's Mother's mission and with the Lord's Incarnation and was dependent on all these. A mission of reform. But all of them together are incapable of letting their own ego disappear behind their mission. They are incapable of forgetting themselves. They believe that the most important thing is the individual and his realm, his sphere of duties, his share. The thing is not really taken in hand and worked out. While they speak about the state of the place in which they live, they ought to have picked up the broom and set to work. "Your room may be cleaner than mine, but on the other hand mine is really not that dirty when you look at it, although to be sure your things are to a certain extent more beautiful than mine . . ." On the whole, something tacky, plush furniture . . . , sweetened whipped cream . . .

I see her decision, which was not specifically a decision to enter Carmel, but rather a choice within God's own choice. It was to a certain extent accidental that she entered precisely the Carmelites, and it was not easy for her there. The piety that surrounded her horrified her; she had expected a superabundance and stood before an aridity that not only made itself known in her inner life but affected her externally as well and became a burden to her. A certain childishness reigned in the house, but above all a spirit of habit, of rigidity; the older nuns acted as if they were smarter than the younger ones, and there were even obstacles to confession. There was a formality and, thus, the danger of becoming formalistic oneself. The guidance consisted in few words, which, by the way in which they were spoken, were already robbed of their deeper meaning. Thus there was an entire period of time in which she always felt tired, in which she did not conform, in fact could not conform, in which she shocked the others through a certain guardedness, became a burden to herself. She sought God but could no longer find him; she sought her earlier devotion, which had disappeared; it was difficult for her even to continue to believe in the genuineness of her call.

Until she suddenly started all over again. And, indeed, she did so very spontaneously in a new turning of her attention to God, to which God responded with fullness and grace. He, who earlier seemed to have become unresponsive, now seemed not only to be present, but to desire to give himself in a fullness evident to her senses. She began, first, to have visions and, second, to discover a new devotion: no longer to contemplate the Christ Child through the lenses of habit, through the dead words of those around her, through the fundamental principles of the Order's traditions, but she looked on him with new eyes; she experienced him anew, prayed in a new way to him, and he became to her a brother, who awakened perfect hope in her. She was bound to him, surrendered to his destiny as a child. She recognized how necessary the surrender of a tiny child is. She remained for a long time at this stage of a childlike contemplation of the Child. She had the most stimulating insights in prayer, and in her visions she constantly received confirmations of this prayer. But because she did not change anything in the other aspects of her life and everything happened before her in the greatest matter-of-factness, those around her began to think that her experiences might not be genuine. They explained to her that such and such would have to happen if her visions were true. She would have to be taken up into ecstasy; she would have to become paralyzed under certain circumstances, to forget her surroundings; the world would have to fade away from her, to disappear. And thus she reproduced the states that they expected, not exactly in complete consciousness that she was doing so, but out of a falsely directed sense of obedience, and at the same time because the visions were in fact true and she knew that she had to save them. She truly did save them, but she paid the price of false guidance. It would not be at all correct to speak of deception; she did in fact have visions, and she continued to have them. She was like a cook who at the end perfectly prepares the food but, at the same time, starts out with all sorts of magic words and special tricks. If she had had an enlightened spiritual director or a reasonable, moderate superior, then two sentences would have been enough to take away her pretense, which she herself did not want but which she soon had integrated into the genuineness of her visions to such an extent that she acted it out for herself and her conscience every time she knew that a vision was coming. What she saw was nevertheless true, and so was her devotion, her faith, and her surrender.

ANGELUS SILESIUS (1624–1677)

I see his prayer, which *seeks* God. This seeking after God is like a desire to see from the highest peak, but not in the sense that one ascends the peak, but in the sense that one at first descends as deeply as possible, in order to be convinced of the height of the mountain. At the beginning, this prayer is almost a will to measure the distance. Then suddenly, as though in the middle of a conversion—which to be sure was prepared for over a long period of time and now nevertheless overwhelms a person with great force—his prayer becomes a prayer of jubilation, which senses the greatness to come. It can no longer be a matter of a will to measure, but now it has to be nothing but celebration in joy and gratitude. The whole of life is now lived in relation to prayer, and thus in God's presence and together with God, in a seriousness that binds Silesius to the highest self-gift. This obligation is not visible externally, in the sense that he, as it were, groans under its yoke or that he comes off as under stress in his actions. To the contrary, it is a dancing and singing, a joy, from which he is *permitted* to be unable to fall away any longer. What he prays and experiences and expresses is always experienced in the deepest sense, and at the same time the effect is always the same: it brings joy to the whole human being. Even when bitterness and criticism set in, he remains joyfully in God's hand; he is certain of doing what God demands from him, certain he is not doing it sufficiently, but that the direction in which he is moving is so completely the correct direction that distance and inadequacy should no longer grieve him. He is supposed to pray and love and remain present; he simply must never become unfaithful.

His prayer often consists in insights that strike him in the interim periods. He sees something; he makes an effort to find the connection between this something and God, to forge a relationship, which then acquires in his prayer a new aspect, and indeed an aspect that is for him definitive, one with which he remains. He regularly establishes something, but he also regularly recognizes that what he has established will possess its definitiveness only in heaven, not on earth, and that a person can always say things in a different way or grasp them in a different way, in order finally to confess that he in fact does not understand them at all. In his desire to understand and settle things, there is no presumption that he understands more than other people do, but rather a sort of humility, which does in obedience what is required of it. In the awareness of a mission, which never becomes completely transparent to him. Even when he eventually becomes a priest and has freed himself from everything else in order to be able to live henceforward for God alone, he knows that he remains behind his mission and his task, that everything he has achieved means nothing. And he wants ever and again to start anew, in order to be able to offer something new to God. And to do so in the joyfulness that never leaves him. His service is an explicitly joyful and grateful service. And when he also attempts to determine man's position in relation to God, then this never means that he is calculating his own progress and intends to measure off the number of steps. He remains in the attitude of a humble creature before his Creator and his infinity.

The paradoxes that he formulates are an attempt to take the incarnate God so seriously that man appears not only as redeemed by him, but also as freed from himself: an attempt to show Christ's deed as accomplished in every human being—even when one knows that, from an earthly perspective, it is not so. But he takes this out of the divine sphere, which for him acquires a more real aspect than the sphere of the world in which he has to live in the meantime. The paradox is that the truth of heaven for him replaces the truth of the earth. He draws his thoughts more from Christ's vision than from man's faith.

BOSSUET (1627–1704)

I see his devout prayer, which, for the first, long period, is a prayer he learned to say, a prayer of obligation, the Church's prayer that he adopts, a prayer of petition. While he is indeed entrusted with the ordinary thoughts and forms that belong to priestly and Christian prayer, he does not pray for the joy of it or because of need, but rather in order to fulfill his duty before God. Occasionally it happens that, while he is praying, prayer overtakes him, and he receives joy from it; he gets zeal from it; he promises to give himself; he desires to improve himself; he understands this improvement as a serious entry into the responsibilities of his office, to which he owes it to eliminate his faults.

He is governed by a form of love that expresses itself primarily as a deference before the mystery, fear before the greatness of God, modesty before his own incapacity. New aspects of life in God present themselves to him in prayer, aspects of the life of the triune God, of the life of the praying soul in God, of the life of the dead in God. And he perceives everything that does not live from faith as so offensive to God that he is often scarcely able to bring his prayer to an end. On the one hand, it compels him to get up and throw himself into the work of conversion; on the other hand, it compels him to hold fast to everything in prayer in order that it may penetrate him better and more richly. When he preaches or writes, then he slips out of prayer to a certain extent, as if his own powers were insufficient to do both at the same time. He himself perceives a certain emptiness in what he says or in what he intends to say or fashions at his desk; he feels that the words come too easily, that he has not given complete form to the ultimate reality he received from God, and he takes it as a humiliation that he cannot do it better, even more, that he typically fails because he allows himself to be caught up in the joy he takes in the beautiful turns of phrase, in the calculated unfolding of the insights, because he allows himself to be charmed by his own work. And he always resolves to do it differently tomorrow.

He enjoys preaching, just as he enjoys, more generally, giving advice to others; in the beginning, he does so as if it were a duty he had been charged with, but one that he was happy to undertake and that gave him pleasure. And once success arrives and his fame and people's respect for him grow, he becomes even more convinced of the necessity of his advice, and so sometimes he does things that it would have been God's business to do. He is then no longer simply the representative of the Word, but rather often one who himself speaks. And his prayer suffers because of it; it grows emptier. He had come to a certain understanding about his obligatory prayer and thus overcome his boredom in it. Now, this boredom somehow finds its way back; even in prayer, he confuses himself with the word that is spoken to God. But then—and this happens more because of understanding than because of faith—he comes to see that this cannot be the way; he collects himself, prays in a more deeply surrendered way, leaves his vanity aside, which nevertheless afflicts him again outside of prayer, so that he advocates things about whose justice he is not fully convinced but that, when they acquire the hoped-for use, always serve to increase his and the Church's good name—which he sees as reciprocally dependent on one another.

Mass is very much up and down. In solemn Masses, in the presence of the public display, he always feels as if he had the role of one who had been charged with the show. Then he becomes extremely attentive to the external, in the movements and in prayer. The spoken prayers are a sort of well-intended theater; the spectators are meant to be moved by his pious unction. When he celebrates Mass in private, it is much more inward, although not without some influence from the other style.

On a personal level, he is not able to deal very well with other people. In prayer, he can do something with them from the perspective of his preaching: he sees what sort of work he must do on them, where he has to start in order to improve them, in order to bring the Christian ideal closer to them. Here is where his best contact with people lies. But his vanity and his delight in the external always prevent him again from giving what he intends to give in direct relation with them.

With regard to the affairs of the Church and prayer, he remains the whole of his life similar to a child who suddenly grew up or came to think that he had to act like a grownup—even if this does not become visible in Bossuet's words and if his homilies exhibit a rather mediocre level. But there are brusque leaps in him, in his relationship to God, to the Church, to things, that he ventures for the sake of his office. Thus, his fight with Fénelon is half genuine and half distorted. The genuine part lies there, where he sincerely believes he has to proceed in a harsh manner, where he simply does not understand that the truth could possibly lie with his opponent. But he becomes insincere when he gets emotionally involved, and, when favorable opinions are voiced or he himself is overpowered by a truth, he fails to summon the courage to stand up for it, but instead he turns Fénelon into a personal opponent. What he lacks is paternal goodness, but also the paternal ability to be corrected, because he sees everything too much from the perspective of personal honor and ultimately wants to remain a winner. It is once again the same false identification of himself with the Church, since he believes in good faith that it will harm the Church if he does not come out of the fight as the one who was right.

I see him, and I see his twofold prayer. There is his Christian, personal prayer, which is not very different from that of a pious, educated person of that period: he is aware of his sinfulness and wants to improve himself; he sees his faults and wants to avoid them. And he knows about God's needs to have converts, to have voices on the earth that make him known, that do not keep the truth about him for themselves alone but welcome the task of increasing Christian truth and the Christian commandments. And in this first form of prayer, he feels he is being addressed; despite his feeling of his own unworthiness, he is ready to respond to God's ultimate plan for him, though it is not clear to him what this plan is. But he wants to try to fashion his contribution and his work in such a way that he pleases God, that he makes it possible for God to hear his divine voice on earth. This prayer does not distinguish itself in any essential way from the prayer of any worker who wants to work toward the increase of God's glory and who begs for the strength to do so and begs that the way to do so might be made visible.

Next to this is another prayer, which is much stormier, which carries him away and to which he is abandoned, a prayer that alienates him and that he almost would like to brace himself against, because its power is disconcerting. It is the prayer of inspiration, which God gives to him in the midst of his work. It may be that God wishes to lay hold of him with the words he is just now speaking and writing down, that his own voice suddenly becomes strange to him and strikes him as wild, pregnant with more responsibility than he can bear, or also that God pours into him things through the Holy Spirit that he absolutely must take into his work, so that afterward he scarcely recognizes the words he wrote as his own. Perhaps he recognizes the rhyme; but the inner meaning is greater than he thought and more foreign. The deeper meaning can be so great that he takes it for the work of someone wholly other than himself. He himself did not intend to say so much. He had not believed so much; God's severity cannot be so ruthless; his love cannot be so overwhelming; his order cannot be so clear! And if this insight is prayer, then afterward comes a prayer of peace, to which he must attune himself. Not as though he wanted to doubt the greatness of that which in the ultimate, perfect inspiration was prayer; rather, he says yes to this, and yes to this truth that he makes known. God chose him, and he desires to abide within the space of this choice.

And often he depicts sins, horrible sins, with harsh words. With Old Testament words that lie to a certain extent ready to hand for him, so that the might of the Old Covenant becomes visible therein, so that God, whom contemporary piety seeks to diminish, suddenly becomes present in his total inexorability. But then the space that opens itself up for Christian hope is all the greater and more beautiful.

The first person to be converted, over and over again, by his work is perhaps Racine himself. Others will follow, but he possesses a *primum jus*, a right that is so completely granted to him that he constantly draws new energy from it for the day to come, for the next project, even if he experiences lulls in the meantime and a fatigue or alienation from the work, which afflicts him occasionally with doubts. He is like a person who is allowed to drink from his own spring, because this spring ultimately does not belong to him but is his only because God has given it to him.

FRANCIS DE GIROLAMO, S.J. (1642–1716)

I see his confessional prayer. His primary concern is confession, in connection with prayer: the confession of sins, in order to be free to hear God's voice. And he can never see himself as an individual, but rather he always sees himself in the communion of saints and knows that the triune God would like to call the Church home to him as this communion of saints, that everyone ought to return to God together. The sole path of returning that he sees, however, is confession, the elimination of whatever it is that hinders one on the way to God, not merely because it obstructs the path, but because it makes man no longer able to recognize himself, makes him be, no longer God's creature, but the devil's. The thought of being one of Satan's creatures is for him the most horrifying thing there is; he is very much inclined to see the work of Satan everywhere and also to point it out in order that people might be converted and become free for God and his grace, which in his eyes is inexorable and which is able to bring about the conversion of all people through each individual.

He prays without ceasing, with strength, with surrender, with perseverance. And it is as if, already now in the midst of the confusion of his age, he had a share in God's joy, the joy he would have once all had turned back to God. Although he works a good deal and always undertakes new tasks, he nevertheless knows there is always just *one thing* to do and that this one thing is accomplished by God himself and not by him. Thus he strives to persevere in prayer, so that God can work in him according as he sees fit.

He is consumed by love. He loves God; he loves his fellowman, and there is no confusion in this love, because it is always purified through confession, because he always keeps his eyes fixed on the preparation for confession. Thus neither the individual whom he encounters nor the mass of people in general is absorbed into a vague love, but they are instead taken up into a transparent love that is to be attained through confession and absolution, a love to which one must conform oneself. He is happy when he becomes famous, not for his own sake, but because God's name will resound all the more on earth. He loves the Society of Jesus as a mission, but it does not play a very large role in his thinking. It formed him, and then he grew into his mission, which is the essential thing for him, though he does not distribute importance in his thinking.

MARGARET MARY ALACOQUE (1647–1690)[1]

She has a peculiar character. In a certain sense she is very humble, and in a certain sense she takes great pride in being humble. Moreover, she suffers in strange ways if people do not believe what she says. She has genuine visions and tasks. But if one does not believe her, the whole of her pride rears up. All the struggles that come from outside become an internal struggle within her, which plays itself out only rarely in the proper place, most often in a place that is too external, where what is good and what is distorted are mixed together. To be sure, those who are sent always face a struggle, an anxiety about their mission and about the truth of their mission. But when things go as they ought, the saint himself is not the one who has to fight through the struggle to the very end, because, no matter how holy he might be, the depths that God lays in him are never at his disposal; and thus God himself is the one who has to fight out the ultimate battle in him regarding his mission. In the most decisive respect, the battle is not a personal one that the saint has to wage against his own character, and it ought never to be attacked with weapons that, like pride, are in themselves objectionable.

She has difficulties in her cloister, chiefly with the superiors. She carries these into her prayer. But it is always as if her prayer were humble at first, in order afterward to revolt. Moreover, she struggles with her confessors until she finds the right one (Fr. Colombière). This one has a remarkable way of interacting with her, but one must admit that it is really not easy with her. On the one hand, he is convinced, indeed, absolutely convinced, that the thing is genuine, and he in part gives her the idea that she could be a saint. He warns her to give what she has; he demands that she see this person and that person,

[1] A. treats her several times.

and so on. On the other hand, he has a slightly uneasy feeling; not everything is transparent to him. And it is as if they both gave Margaret herself too much importance and her mission too little. In spite of this, she defends herself primarily for the sake of her mission and not for her own sake. She begins this mission in the midst of the greatest obstacles and difficulties and constantly has to improvise exits or alternate routes, in order to be able to keep moving forward. But in all of this her person always plays a role; she does everything in a sort of "personal union" with the Lord ...

If someone from her surroundings had recognized what was really missing—humility—then she would indeed have been capable of seeing it also for herself and of changing. "The better is the enemy of the good": this proverb was made for her. Of course, she prays a lot, and this prayer prepares her for vision. But there is a certain quality of hysteria in her contemplation. She is not able to rest in what she sees; she is not able to "do enough". She constantly breaks it off and passes over into something else. She enters into contemplation with preconceived ideas, because she is convinced that she is right and has to follow her own program. For the sake of her mission, God nevertheless sends her more visions. She ought to carry this task out for once, and, in order for it to be fulfilled, she ought not to fall out of her role. Insofar as the mission truly gets fulfilled in her—almost in spite of her—she is also holy.

FÉNELON (1651–1715)

I see his prayer, which is completely animated by the will to serve God. His prayer is meticulously designed and supported; it is artfully and often artificially composed. Especially in his younger years, he establishes a program for himself, which then has to be carried through. It is part of this program, in some sense, that a person simply hands himself over to grace, but he would nevertheless be quite shocked if God were to cast his entire program aside and proceed in a wholly different way. The program is designed outside of prayer, in a manner similar to the way in which a woman goes shopping for various vegetables for dinner: one for the soup, one for the salad, one for later, which is in the meantime "preserved"; while she is shopping, no one is able to figure out what she intends to do with what she buys. It is only when she sets to the preparation at home that it becomes evident. Thus, Fénelon too, for example, has a few great concerns, which he does not want to take up today, but which he "preserves", then a few questions for God, which he brings up as a petition, and finally a few thoughts, which are meant to serve him as spiritual nourishment. He becomes aware, for example, of certain faults and would like God to show him how to deal with them, and so forth. This is how the dinner is brought to the table: as a first course, a sort of polite presentation to God, with compliments: You are thus, and I am thus. Then his prayer follows the intended plan; the "courses" are brought out; but ultimately he never expects that God would ever set the table himself or mix all the food together—although Fénelon always intends something like this and in some sense desires it. As a fancy dessert, he presents his "amour pur", which however hovers in a sort of theoretical way over everything that came before, a little like the roof of a house that is not supported by any walls.

Thus the content he intends to pray about remains greater than the prayer itself; the words he says to God remain more convincing than the attitude of surrender. He constantly has the feeling that his prayer is like an article of clothing that is too big for him; he is ashamed that he does not fill it, that he promises more than he possesses. He makes an effort to grow into his prayer.

At first he thinks that one could allow oneself to be guided by prayer itself, that if one sincerely tried to pray, one could entrust oneself to it. He remains in this thought for many years, and he seeks to observe the progress he makes in the correspondence between prayer and life. Later, he will renounce this self-assessment, because the education he receives from prayer leads him beyond it. Now, he begins with words of adoration, which means that he presents himself to God, makes an examination of conscience, gives thanks, and says certain liturgical prayers. The subsequent part, which constantly grows in importance and extent, is governed by the thought of being in God and in God's presence, of abiding in a state of self-emptiness, in which he awaits God to fill him according to his own good pleasure. And if, as he does so, he thinks of the many people and affairs that have been entrusted to him, aware that he can deal with them only out of the power of prayer, then he takes this as an inspiration from God and allows himself in this case to be led by it as if in a free improvisation. He feels as though he is carried by prayer and thus never allows himself to be completely overwhelmed even by strong adversity. He also feels himself to be carried by the prayer of the woman who introduced him more deeply into contemplation, by the prayer of the many people for whom he is a spiritual director, and by the prayer of the Church. He lays a lot of importance on this being carried; prayer is for him a vast landscape in God in which he is rooted, both in what he does and in what is done to him.

What he calls "amour pur" is in essence correct enough, even if he exaggerates particular words or images. But this high, and for him to some extent lofty, ideal remains suspended above life, because he is never wholly free of certain faults, so that a complete unity between theory and praxis never comes about. On the whole, he is humble, but there are also prideful thoughts, inner rebellions, bad moods, and insufficient love of neighbor. Considering himself to a certain extent an intellectual, he takes certain freedoms here, out of a feeling that one ought not to exaggerate things. Within prayer, he aims at the highest point; outside of prayer he is more negligent; he does not summon the same strength in the practical sphere and perhaps does not want to summon it. But one cannot say for that reason that he is less holy than many of the people who have been canonized.

MADAME DE GUYON (1648–1717)

I see her prayer, which is constantly growing in devoutness. God seized her from a peculiar angle by revealing to her how necessary it is for him to be loved. She understood this necessity perfectly and knew that she was called to respond to it. But she had no idea how. To be sure, she was a believer and was clever, but she did not see any way to make her gift of self real. She saw herself put in a place that was the right one, humanly speaking, but one that nevertheless offered her little chance of following the path of perfection. It was the encounter with Fénelon that led her to understand that God now laid hold of her in a very serious way, and she was willing to respond. She thus allowed herself to be led like a little child. But she grew up very quickly under this guidance, insofar as God's word, which she perceived through Fénelon and which corresponded precisely to what she was able to expect (she immediately recognized the word) became itself her guidance. But she was also aware of a danger in God's word, because it brought her farther than she had initially intended to go. In her most sincere desire to respond, she at first erected for herself quite narrowly drawn boundaries, such as they were established above all by her milieu. But now she understood that she was henceforward permitted to entrust herself only to God's word for guidance, and all the limitations, all the obstacles within her, had to come down. In this quick maturation within guidance and prayer, she wanted for her part to share many things with Fénelon that were necessary for him; he learned things from her that she learned in prayer and in conversation with God. And thus it often turned into an exchange. In relation to him, she always remained the person who was being guided, but he was aware that he was responsible for her; that she was so faithfully handed over to the word that he spoke to her and accepted it so completely; that he found an echo in her answer, and words he at first perhaps had uttered to some extent by rote returned to him broadened, made more precise, imperative, indeed, commanding. In the precision that lay in her answer, he saw the correctness of her mission and entrusted himself to her in his masculine way. She was not shocked by this in fact; she understood that she had been placed in this position in order to serve him, in order to respond to his guidance to the extent that it corresponded to his mission: insofar as she was an echo, Fénelon's own mission grew. This, however, obliged her to more and more prayer. And since she had attained the prayer of peace, she was grateful to God that she was able to share her experiences with Fénelon just as they were. Had he prematurely retired, when she began for the first time to express her thoughts about the prayer of peace, then Mme. de Guyon would still have remained there, but he himself would not have entered in. It had to be that he remained in close contact with her for as long as it was possible for him. Even when he maintained a certain strictness with her, which lay in his mission, because he was supposed to understand as much and as clearly as possible; but this strictness was for her not entirely advantageous, because she did not always find what she expected in it. In spite of all the exchange, they were not sufficiently in harmony with one another.

The suspicions concerning her doctrines were ultimately irrelevant as far as she is concerned; they would have been themselves avoidable if Fénelon had been a little less rash in his behavior. He made many things public too quickly; she was not completely matured for this, insofar as, whenever she was harshly judged or explained to be in error, she took things too personally, absorbed them too little in her mission, ultimately did not find the harmony of a life that bore upon it the prayer of peace. For this reason, she also defended herself too sharply, with weapons that did not rise to the level of her mission. She possessed the prayer of peace and recommended it, but she did not have enough peace to fight out the external battle for this. If one were to take a careful look at the way she and Fénelon carried out their tasks, one would notice slight exaggerations. But one would also at the same time discover how much fruitful goodness there was in it, which has not yet been properly harvested, which perhaps also remains somewhat veiled by the time period's mores and manners of expression, but even so it contains genuine greatness.

COSTANTE MARIA CASTRECA (1670–1736)[1]

I see her praying. Twice, actually, and it is important to keep the two types of prayer distinct from one another. It is painful for her to pray, and the first type of prayer is given to her as the means of carrying on a very particular form of conversation with the Lord and leaving the efficacy to the Lord. It is as if he expected her to pray in precisely this way in order to share his grace: with a soul upon whom prayer has been imposed, a soul who has been called to pray as if it were a burdensome task. With a soul who sees the fruit of prayer as the fruit of the Cross and clearly understands that this fruit comes from the Cross and returns to the Cross. It is not at all the joyful acceptance of suffering or even simply a grateful or loving acceptance. It is the agony on the Mount of Olives: May this cup pass. And yet she understands that it must be so, and she prays with this painful understanding.

The other prayer is closely connected with this one: that she also experiences a craving for prayer; she absolutely wants to be together with the Lord and to bring everything to him. From this perspective, she is also familiar with all the transitions from willing to unwilling prayer. But the suffering that pervades the whole is nevertheless present here: it is a prayer from which she emerges as one spent and broken, and yet this prayer does not create an obstacle to the other type of prayer, a prayer that refreshes and energizes and brings her right up to the source of grace, from which she returns radiant and renewed in strength. But this prayer is intended only for herself, as the power of being spent, the power of knowing that one has been used up in the Lord. The people around her glimpse something of this radiant power, which flows from her and has its source in the Lord. Many feel its effect, and many know about its effectiveness, as it were, from a distance.

But then she once again has periods of anxious uncertainty, because she begins to believe that everything she has has been not only borrowed but in fact stolen from her. It now becomes so difficult to follow the path the Lord traced out for her that it seems to her that her anxiety, her fasting, her whole attitude of discipleship is henceforward allowed to appear for her only as something imposed upon her, something foreign, with an aspect one can never get used to. She can experience and undergo things of a supernatural sort in her own body, things that at the time mostly press upon her in such a way that they form a unity with her, and afterward everything appears to her so

---

[1] A Capuchin nun in Fabiano near Ancona. Cf. Herbert Thurston, *Die körperlichen Begleiterscheinungen der Mystik* (Lucerne, 1956), 136ff.

foreign, so impossible, that she is completely at a loss. Not like a dream; more like a nightmare. Something real, but the existence of which one cannot come to terms with. In spite of this, she is required to suffer through everything in a childlike way and to feel it and acknowledge it afterward as a part of her own life, something that completely fills it. It is as if the real experience were only a sketch, about which she later had to reflect and pray, just like a pupil who has to make a clean copy from a draft. In the same way, the things that remain to the end essentially foreign to her she must nevertheless appropriate as such.

BENEDICT XIV (1675–1758)

Yes, I see his prayer, which from the outside looks very dry but in fact is not dry at all. It looks this way because he gives it the imprint, the formulations, and the tone of legal documents. But when one looks more closely, one discovers he is obeying an inner necessity when he prays in this way. He would like to bring his entire life under the unity of the triune God. He would like, as an individual, to do nothing but the will of God. And because, as a result of his formation and actually also of his own taste, he possesses a clear way of thinking and is accustomed to order things, to arrange them, to weigh them, and to formulate them, he thus sees this as his mission and does not wish to separate himself from it even in prayer. He would often be inclined to let himself be carried away, this way and that, by the waves of prayer, to cultivate a sort of contemplation in which he gave himself over, without his will, to whatever it was that offered itself to him according to his inspiration. He would enjoy this sort of prayer; he would take pleasure in being permitted to pray this way. But he knows himself and avoids his weaknesses. He fears that afterward he would not be able to find his way back, that he would abide in the enjoyment; he would confuse the beyond with what is immediate, that, through an all-too-contemplative and surrendered prayer, he would forfeit the capacity to carry out his workload. Thus, he draws from his mission the right to interact with God in this sort of dryness. Not as if he wanted to impose limitations on God, the giver of all graces, in order that he himself might be what he wanted to be. Rather, he believes that he is justified in God's presence to save the more intimate, Father-child relationship for later. And he prays a lot and would never arrange anything or carry it out without having properly prayed over it, persistently, but in the aforementioned dryness. He is full of love and humor, but his humor finds no expression in his prayer. When he is with other people, his humor comes out in his quick observations, but not in his prayer. In prayer, he stands before God somewhat as a servant stands before his master, in order to receive commands, which he then carries out with the greatest care, as something holy that has been entrusted to him. He grows constantly into God's holiness; he understands more and more what is holy and what is human. And he does not allow himself to situate his own conduct, for it is neither human conduct that permits him to pray in this way, nor is it holy conduct; instead, it is the *conduct of unity* that stems from his mission. And he attempts to make particularly visible in his own person those very virtues that relate to his office: openness, justice, clarity, and the discernment of spirits.

It does not cause him problems to select saints. He allows himself to be advised extensively. But it is not the case that his piety gives him a particularly lively relationship to the saints. His having to select saints is something that results from his office. A person could say that his official interaction with the saints, his testing and weighing of them, sharpens his sense for holiness, not only the holiness of God's saints but of those belonging to the Church. But he does not simply let himself get carried away in all of this; he restrains his enthusiasm, because it is his task to remain objective. He cultivates the same objectivity in his judging of saints that he cultivates in his prayer life.

CRESCENTIA OF KAUFBEUREN (1682–1744)

She certainly does pray. But she is quite narrowminded, in a certain sense extremely dogmatic. And she is unable to allow herself to be broadened by the vastness of the Holy Spirit. She nurses a sort of inner fear that makes it impossible for her fully to give herself over. She prays vocally, but her mind does not really enter into the words she is speaking, because she shies away from understanding the fullness of the word. It is almost as if she were parroting the words. When she prays an Our Father, she does not trust herself actively to think through the "Thy will be done", to say nothing of truly praying the petitions that bear a spiritual content. The "Give us this day our daily bread" is for her fully clear and unequivocal, the same with the "Lead us not into temptation", but as soon as it concerns a demand made on the spirit, she draws back.

What is peculiar about her piety is that she always comes back to God, less in genuine prayer than in an effort not to forget God, to bring God into everything she does, and in everything she says to say something pious, something related to God. If she has a kind of heroism, it is above all in her disposition, for she understands above all that man is capable of nothing on his own and that he needs God; he needs a God who constantly accompanies him in order to be able to carry out what man is incapable of carrying out himself. But all of this happens with a narrowmindedness, with an unwillingness to go farther. The fact that she nevertheless has visions means that God is trying to bring her into his world, to reward her for her fidelity, which is not slight. Her disposition is similar to a being possessed by God; but in this, however, she does not cease to lend this God her own measure and to assign him her own limitations. It is not a falling into sin, but it is a narrow mind's falling into the vast love of God, of which she never becomes aware. And because she lacks an appropriate director, it does not become evident to her until the afterlife. She is praised on account of her readiness to help, her sensitivity to the needs of those around her, those who request her advice, for in fact she never grows tired of helping and of loving her neighbor as herself. In this context, her limitations are less visible than they are in prayer. Her prayer becomes repetitive, empty, and in any event she does not especially have a lot of time to pray, and thus it is above all in prayer that her weaknesses, her insufficiencies, perhaps even a certain arrogance in relation to God, become evident. She is like the little bourgeois woman who is unable to desire anything better for her children than what she herself experienced. But she does not reflect on her prayer at all, and it is no doubt better that way.

ALPHONSUS LIGUORI (1696–1787)

I see him praying, and his prayer is very dense and well provided for, and indeed more in terms of content than in terms of words. It is difficult to say when he begins praying and when he ceases, because he does two things: he not only begins and ends each of his works in prayer, but he carries it out with prayer. On the other hand, he takes quite a lot of his work with him into his prayer time and inserts breaks even into his prayer, in order to reflect, to rebuild, and to lay things out clearly. It is a contemplation that he introduces into his vocal prayer, and this contemplation always means the path from his work *to* God or *to* an event of the Lord's life on earth or *to* an event of the Old Covenant, an act of God's in heaven. Thus, there is a certain contemplation-shelter, which he attains through the interlacing of his work, his reflection, and his thoughts. And because this contemplation-shelter seems to him to be of the utmost importance and offers him also an assurance for the correctness of his work, he willingly allows himself to be driven from there into a more formless contemplation; he allows

God to produce in him whatever God deems necessary. He thus proceeds, to be sure, on the basis of the content of his work, whatever it happens to be, in order to be brought from there through all the digressions through which God wishes to carry him to completely different things, things that, because they are given to him in contemplation, do not however represent "achievements". But he then seeks, by means of more personal and earthly concepts, by means of his earthly methods of meandering and climbing up the steps, to reach the God-given ceiling of the contemplation-shelter. The one contemplation is thus from the beginning sustained by the content of his work, while the other contemplation is like a ceiling that spans too wide over a stair. And he constructs an access to this afterward, not by proceeding from the ceiling level and working downward, but by starting all over again from the cellar and ascending.

He is quite zealous when he begs for pure humility, when he endeavors to remain completely faithful to the truth. When at one point he becomes too severe, he feels as though he has been unfaithful to the truth, for the truth for him is ultimately Christ, with whom there is no room for a lack of love. He fears that he causes scandal to other people through his severity and thus casts them out of the way of truth. He prays quite willingly and also is happy to allow himself to be guided in prayer, insofar as everything he hears and recognizes, even what he learns from his visions, he takes hold of in order to provide new nourishment for his prayer. Translated into different words, this means that for him prayer is as important as a conversation with a friend can be for someone who is involved in a spiritual activity: he finds inspiration, judgment, and encouragement in it. He has a need to speak with God about his work, of course, in a Christian, pious measure. But in fact he receives stimulation. It is not only a being carried away and a letting happen; it is a joy and a need to be influenced by God's Supernature in his nature through the conversation with God.

His construction from below is for him also a way of making sure that he has heard everything properly. He seeks access, and he finds it. He secures the rungs in place in order that others might be able to climb up. For he does not assume that his own freedom from vertigo will be given to everyone.

His contemplation poured into him in a supernatural way. Whether he has genuine visions is difficult to say. It would be scholasticism to answer with yes or no. I would probably lean toward no: he advances all the way to the border of vision but does not make it to the vision itself;

what he receives is more the fact of having concepts poured in, which he provides with color and contour in his response to God in order to give them permanence.

The founding of the Order, considered in relation to him, is completely an act of obedience; to be sure, those who initially follow him introduce a little too much laziness and caprice. According to his own intention, the foundation would have been bigger, simpler, and closer to God.

His relationship to Maria Celeste Crostarosa is in order. But he surpasses her.

MARY FRANCES OF NAPLES (1715–1791)[1]

She remains in constant conversation with God, with the Mother of God, and with the saints. The daily events, in relation to which she takes, and must take, a position, are brought into this conversation. These are dialogues between God and her, and from the things discussed, there arises, somehow irrevocably, what she has to do, to think, and even to pray. But even the conversation itself is already a higher form of placing herself at God's disposal and of praying. It may be that people hear her speak. With an invisible partner, whose instructions she receives with precision. She no longer forgets these instructions, even when she only returns to them a great deal later. The divine partner's voice in her is so strong that it is difficult for her to tune back in to the voices around her. She can sometimes suddenly be overtaken by the feeling of shame that she was in God's presence, that he spoke to her and she did not fall down onto her knees, that she took it, as it were, in an all-too-human sort of way. Then she makes an offering of herself. Unreservedly. And if, in doing so, she says, "Take my hand!" then she might worry afterward that she ought to have said "Take the whole of me!" And she makes a new offering of herself, which includes ever-greater possibilities. She would like to give not only everything she has, but also the entire world. In God's taking, one ought to set no limits.

She is somehow neither cheerful nor sad, because she has handed over every mood, everything that belonged to her. She suffers if God suffers; she takes joy in God's celebrations, always in a relationship of response; she behaves in the manner she receives. She is sometimes understood by her fellowman, but more often misunderstood. If she

[1] A third order Franciscan, among the Tertiaries of St. Peter of Alcantara; a stigmatic who was canonized by Pius IX.

were to hold onto what the world offered her, then she would have many opportunities for worry, for personal injury, perhaps for dissatisfaction. But she simply lets everything happen. She possesses the resignation (*Gelassenheit*) of a child of God in a very great measure. And if things happen really to go too far, then she complains to God, not to people. And she also stops immediately when she does so, begs God to forgive her for her moaning, and is ready to withstand much more.

There is a lot in her experience that remains unexpressed, perhaps even ambiguous and dark, because she does not want to take the time to explore the things that have happened in her. She fears introducing her own measurements in an intrusive way into God's and then being found unworthy to bear something greater.

JOSEF HAYDN (1732–1809)

I see his prayer. He prays like a trusting child who awaits every piece of bread from his Father in heaven. For him, this implies simultaneously the guiding of his personality and the inspiration of his work. It takes a long time for him to identify himself with his work, for him truly to bring about in prayer the unity between what God demands from him as a Christian and what he demands from him as an artist. For a long time, he believes that God demands piety from him, while, on the other hand, it is his worldly profession to be a composer. Finally, he comes to see that God demands both in a unity. Then he increases his prayer, but he also increases his anxiety, insofar as he now has a deeper appreciation of the distance between God and man and, by the same token, the chasm between the way he envisions his work and the way he carries it out in reality. At bottom, there is one thing he desires: to be able to portray the voice of God in his creation, in his entire relationship to the world. And because he does not succeed in the way he had hoped, he finds refuge more and more in prayer, insofar as he would like to bring it to God from his prayer, but he applies too small a share of his "earnings", of his talent and genius. He is happy and gloomy at the same time. Happy because he is able to do in God's presence precisely what he feels called to do in the innermost part of his being. But gloomy insofar as he does not experience perfect success, because he in fact would like to invent a new kind of music, with new tones and new rhythms, a music that would be more suitable for praising God, and he is unable to do it in the way he wants. He dreams of a harmony that would in fact be impossible for any human being to achieve. His prayer is in part somewhat too close to the Old Testament, because he feels he has been brought before a strict God who

constantly measures and weighs the work in his justice; but then suddenly his prayer returns once again to the New Testament, and he
expects grace and fulfillment. But he is only rarely able to remain here,
because the demand always acquires harsh features again for him, even
if he loves it. He has days and weeks in which it is a sheer delight for
him to compose, but there are also times in which he has to wring out
every note, every melody, and every harmony with a torturous struggle. He would also like it to be that no one would feel called to music
in a human way unless he were called to it from above. He has an
incredibly lofty estimation of his art; it seems to him to be the expression of God's will, indeed, to some extent the re-presentation of paradise on earth. But perhaps his prayer occasionally comes at the cost of
intense seeking and at the cost of practice: he expects in fact to make
his way through difficulties more through prayer than through his own
efforts, through a truly *intimate* composition, because it always costs
him something to bring his way of life into perfect unity with prayer.

BENEDICT LABRE (1748–1783)

In God's presence, he is very straightforward and simple, somewhat *de
plein pied* [self–assured]. He has a sort of overflowing prayer and a longing for the vision of God, which eliminates every obstacle in prayer.
He prays in such a matter-of-fact and straightforward manner, just as a
healthy person sleeps or eats. He only has trouble with his fellowmen,
for he is not able to summon the simplicity he has in relation to God
when he is with them. He cannot approach them the way he approaches
God. And yet at the same time he feels approached by them as if by
God himself. To stand before God is no problem for him, any more
than it is that God gives *preference* to him in spite of his unworthiness.
Or any more than it is that God wants him to be with other people.
But it costs him a great deal of self-overcoming in order somehow to
forget how unworthy he is of the other people. He is so thoroughly
penetrated by the grace of God that his unworthiness in Holy Communion does not worry him any more. He knows it has been overcome in God. But in his interaction with other people it is not the
same. Nevertheless, he would like to bring them all to God; and if he
travels to so many holy sites with them, then it is because he would
like to give each person to God: and since he is not able to give the
person he possesses to God very well, since he is not sure how to
manage it, he tries to bring them closer to God in an acceptable way:
to transpose them into a state of more elevated joy of acceptance through
pilgrimage. It is as if he lifted people up and lowered God—not in an

objectionable sense, but in the sense of rapprochement, as he imagined it and as it flowed out immediately from his standing in God's presence.

GOETHE (1749–1832)

His relationship to God is expressed in his great wonder. He is a man who opens his mind to everything around him; he sees everything as a question addressed to him personally; he sees problems as much in things as in the people around him, in the figures of history, in the characters he himself fashions. And in doing so he constantly runs up against boundaries and understands how to push back these boundaries with his understanding and his genius and the work of his reason, in order to be able to move forward yet another couple of steps or even many more steps. But when he comes up against a boundary, or—to take a different case—does *not* come up against a boundary, but enters, so to speak, into an indeterminate region, which is allowed to continue as it were *ad libitum* but cannot be measured out in relation to his steps, then a question arises also in this region that lies beyond the boundaries. In his interest in people, in his need to justify himself in relation to their questions, he looks not only to something that comes from himself, but also to something that in part also comes to him from outside, which is mediated by the others, and even more to something higher, a power or energy, in any event something *given*, something intangible but whose existence is evident, which becomes evident in the things around him as a sort of "surplus". In the surroundings he sees, there lies something *more* than he had thought; man is determined by a power that means *more* than he knows.

But he does not achieve any relationship to God that would include prayer and being a child. He achieves a certain *awe* for the unknown, a deference toward that which is greater, indeed, often a rising up before that which possesses the power to govern human destinies, to interrupt paths that have already been begun and to forge new ones. Thus he is not without awe, but he is beset by a sort of curiosity that prevents him from submitting to faith or, for that matter, to love for God. He considers it proper to remain in expectation, and even to introduce obstacles, whenever his attitude seems to him to have become too easy.

When he reads the Bible, he marvels especially over the Old Testament and the figures it portrays, over the remarkable, over what they gave to their age, and it is for him as if the problems of humanity, both for individuals and for the race as a whole, always remained similar. But he thinks that it was an oversimplification of the whole question concerning the ultimate Power when the Old Testament men gave it the name God. The problem of Christ is for him a problem similar to the one concerning Muhammad. He does not want to establish a bond of faith, out of fear of losing the freedom of spirit, to take hold of the one and thereby to let go of everything else. Nevertheless, he would like, through a positive acceptance, to put an end to this posing of the question that more and more troubles him. But then he worries once again that he would be failing with respect to the unknown power if he did not preserve his spirit in a sort of openness in all directions; it would not be worthy of his mission if he were to recognize it as coming from God and recognized himself as having a responsibility to God.

CLEMENT HOFBAUER (1751–1820)

His is a very peaceful prayer, which unfolds slowly, practically motionless. There is security in this prayer. A lot of material for contemplation is missing, but everything is accepted in the greatest trust and most childlike straightforwardness. It is really more an attitude of prayer than an actual prayer. He prays a little like a model student: he has no distractions; he is happy that he is allowed to pray, and he does pray. Seen from the outside, it could seem a little monotonous, and it actually would be if his cheerfulness, his faith, and his childlikeness did not come to such powerful expression in it, if the fulfillment of his expectation, in spite of his knowledge that it was coming, was not constantly received as something completely new, with that childlike joy that chases away all boredom. His prayer also has a methodical character. And he prays in complete indifference to where he is. One could call it a temperamental prayer, if one meant by this his indefatigable childlike readiness and joy.

Among his fellowmen he is radiant, simple, and puts a good face on everything, insofar as he allows his prayerful attitude in some sense to become visible. This does not come off as indiscreet in his regard; it belongs to his mission not to strip himself of his character as a person who prays, even externally. The people who interact with him, who go to him for advice, find him in conversation just as he is in his preaching, and even as he is wherever they meet him: infinitely even-keeled, peacefully bathing in grace. For him, it is self-evident that happiness and peace and unquestionableness stem from God, so that even when people "revere" him, he does not allow himself to be taken out of his peace. Even when they see more in him than he would like, he nevertheless knows that he has to confess it to them, because he is one of those people who, by virtue of their mission, are a pathway to God.

He is also very humble. It almost seems as if he had no external personality, because he took everything in.

BEETHOVEN (1770–1827)

He is quite mercurial. His piety is not at all regular. He has periods of
ascesis, of deep prayer, of love for prayer, which are almost perfect; he
longs for genuine surrender; he wants to give himself over; he would
be ready to give up both himself and his work, if only God's grace
were assured to him. And then, mostly for some random external reason, he grows lukewarm once again; doubts assail him; he becomes
unhappy; he loses himself and his line; he becomes skeptical toward
the faith. To be sure, he is not capable of letting this faith go completely, but it nevertheless turns into a "concept" for him; he makes
faith and God's justice and love into an idea. Then the storms of faith
and humility return, followed however once again by rejection and
pride. When he experiences external humiliations or notices that his
energy is diminishing, he becomes humble again, but then he rebels
once more. And the same back and forth vacillation gets transposed to
another level, that of his work. His sudden doubting and his sudden
surrender are reflected again in his work, and they thus allow the equilibrium of genuine, natural faith to disappear. It is not as if the things
that spring from his deepest piety, that toss him about and come to
expression, fell out of the picture. But it is precisely the picture that is
missing, the picture that only daily prayer would be able to provide,
the domestication of the temperament through the consciousness of
God's presence, the elimination of success as much as the humiliations
in the knowledge of providence. The most extravagant things that he
composes or plays, the things that echo in his ears, make him happy, of
course; nevertheless, he is also the first person who understands that
an ultimate consistency is missing from his work and that this lack of
consistency has its basis in his personal character flaws.

Even in his great Masses he recognizes the weaknesses that arise from
himself. And yet it is precisely this work that brings God's presence to
him very often, that brings many *thoughts* about surrender, about the
Lord's presence, about transformation, about sacrifice. If he himself
had to talk about his work, he would point out both the high points
and the weak points and would explain the latter in relation to the
halfheartedness of his faith. Even when the great Mass arises wholly
from a period of seeking, of resoluteness, of being surrendered, the
inspiration does not hold out sufficiently, because even the Masses, as

much as the rest of his work, reflect the life he leads and whose pendulum swing they reveal all too clearly. He recognizes the decisive aspect of his energy in certain smaller parts. A part of his doubting, in fact, springs precisely from this knowledge about his own weakness and his personal inadequacy. Then, indeed, he forms a prayer from this doubt, but the totality of his prayer reflects both the doubting and halfheartedness, on the one hand, and the highest moments of inspiration, on the other.

J. ROOTHAAN (1785–1853)

He has perseverance in prayer and does not allow himself to be kept from praying, in spite of the fact that in prayer he is often overcome by an anxious feeling of enormous responsibility, which allows his prayer to become a sort of laborious mountain hike full of danger. This anxiety has absolutely nothing to do with his will; it is also something he is unable to anticipate. And when he emerges from an anxious prayer of this sort, then it is as if he had accomplished the most abstruse thing in fulfilling this obligation; he has done precisely that which contradicts his understanding, that for which outside of the state of prayer he is in the end scarcely able to answer anymore. The anxiety gives him two things: infallibility in doing his duty in spite of everything and a compulsion to act, which becomes the most torturous thing he can experience.

Then comes the peaceful, beautiful, and graceful prayer, which reassures—although with him in fact every prayer reassures, every type of prayer becomes for a him a sort of touchstone. He never acts except on the basis of prayer. The odd thing is that his trust and his readiness for prayer, his surrender in prayer is never affected by his extremely painful experiences in prayer. He will pray, now, immediately, but before he risks himself in prayer, he must each time utter an unconditional yes to it; he must perfectly accept the whole scope of the anxiety, all of the horror that goes with it and all the consequences that follow from it. First he must say yes to everything; then he can pray. Very often, then, nothing happens apart from a wholly peaceful confirmation of what he is doing, a guidance, an experience of God's nearness, a tangible help, a grace. But sometimes it is the prayer of anxiety.

When he recommends St. Ignatius' "meditations", it is like passing on the things he is able to share from his personal experiences in prayer: the meat of the nut without the "anxiety" shell, which is with him so much *ad personam* that it would be inappropriate to speak about it.

Because he leaves everything personal out of this transmission, what he recommends comes off as dry and rational. In his view, everything personal needs to be distilled out of it to the last drop, and thus what remains left over is something like a recipe in a cookbook, which no longer gives any hint of what one savors at the table. He himself has experienced the two things in prayer, both the wholly personal aspect of the experience and also the method. He is much less dry than his instructions. But, strangely, he is richest, fullest, and even noblest in the moments of anxiety.

MANNING (1808–1892)

I see his prayer, which is at once powerful and insipid. Powerful, because he collects himself in earnest in order to be able to come before God, for whose presence he possesses a sense. And at the same time his prayer is, so to speak, bereft of ideas. Whenever he begins to pray, a sort of emptiness befalls him. Beforehand, he pulls himself together; he also takes time for prayer; he collects himself in order to present himself to God, but then he immediately falls to pieces, as it were; actually, it is because he cannot bear God's presence. He would like to settle this or that with God, and yet he finds that it is not the right place. He always ends up creeping back when he prays.

Oddly, he is better as a human being and as a Christian when he does not pray than when he does. The reason is that he ultimately lacks humility. He is insufficiently childlike. He comes with full hands, but then the Lord empties his heart; he comes full of desire to do great things, with insights and goals, which all first need to be tested, but he is unable to stand before God with all these things because he does not want God to test them. Perhaps he is unable to allow God to do so, because action takes hold of him more and more insistently. His books also belong to this action, for ultimately they lack the contemplative dimension. They are deeds of his understanding, deeds of his intelligence, of his reason, his knowledge, his memory, but not of his humble conversation with God. He cannot allow himself to be corrected, even if it is by God.

Nevertheless, he has a particular sense for love in relation to his fellowmen; he respects them as creatures of God; he loves them as people who are unable to follow the right path; he pities them because things go hard for them; he desires to help them. But the boundary that passes directly through him in prayer also passes through this help: his Christianity is a sort of theory, and the praxis looks different. Despite this denial, which at bottom is an inward No that he utters in the

Lord's presence, he remains a militant Christian; he engages himself; he does not shrink from fatigue; he does not cease carrying forward the banner of God and the Church. He is a little like Peter when he fights for the Lord without wanting to listen to the Lord's voice.

SØREN KIERKEGAARD (1813–1855)

I see his prayer. It is good, and yet at the same time it is a lot like a madness. This happens because he sets up limitations for himself. He becomes the bearer of God's word, which he measures according to his own capacities. Not in the sense that he rejects the burden a priori as something too great, but rather in the sense that in the course of his prayer he allows whatever becomes too heavy to be stripped away: he draws certain lines and fixes them in place—and one cannot say that these lines are harmless—while he fails to draw out other lines, but allows them to merge into the ones he has drawn and thus robs them of their distinctive character. That is, he is held back by his own ego: not by an egotistical ego, but by an ego that can only do so much, an ego that reaches the boundaries of its own ability and has in fact fixed these boundaries in place, by an ego that clings to certain things, that is trapped within certain boundaries, and he is unable to free himself from the captivity to this ego. He can intuit the loftiest things about freedom and truth and surrender, but he is incapable of making them real, indeed, he is incapable of perfectly expressing them because their weight is not properly distributed, and he has to fall back into the center that he himself put into place.

Nevertheless, he prays, and indeed he prays a lot. He prays that he might experience the truth, that he might see things more clearly, that he might be capable of the mission he has been given, and that he might walk the path God has laid out for him; but it is as if a curse clung to his destiny, as if he were constantly drawn slightly in the false direction. His philosophy evinces the same deficiencies as his theology: he can invent extraordinary systems; he can inspect them in his prayer; he can spin them out, but always only to a certain point, which ultimately forms his *sick existence*, his concern for man as such, his concern for himself as man; he constantly reverts back to himself and his possibilities, and this reversion occludes his free vision of God. Even when he risks himself to a vast extent, he anxiously keeps his eye on the possibilities of going back; and if he ever happened not to look back in this sense, he would become so anxious that he would be incapable of any more work; his prayer would shrivel up; his theology would break off; and the work of his final years would be unable to broaden his philosophical system. He would have had to be transplanted, brought among normal, healthy, happy human beings, for the way he is robs him of a sense of humor, joy, and above all the knowledge of grace, such as it is made accessible in the sacraments. The sacramental bears a certain attraction for him, but he completely lacks the means of accepting it as an intrinsically perfect, given good— except perhaps for baptism. When he attempts to overcome himself, he cramps himself. Then his prayer turns into a child's anxious prayer, the prayer of a child who is scared that his mother's hand will let him go. And nevertheless this anxiety cannot be a purely Christian anxiety; it is far too personal, too calculating; it sees the anxiety of Christ, but not that this anxiety begins at the moment when Christ divests himself of every reassurance by the Father, in order to risk himself in the Father's venture and not his own venture.

WILLIAM FABER (1814–1863)

I see his pious prayer, which constantly grows in richness, consistency, and reality. It is not an abstract prayer, also not the sort of prayer in which he would have a lot of room himself, but rather a prayer that is guided and made for guidance. Guided: insofar as he forgets himself in prayer and allows God to work in him; and God works in him in fact in such a way that, through prayer, he learns to guide other people and, above all, to understand them. He receives the grace always to take up his place there where the decisions are made. He sees his fellowman as the brother who has been entrusted to him, the one who shows him who God is and, at the same time, discloses to him who man is; the one who reveals to him what grace is, who allows him, trembling, to see what sin means. If he is thus enabled by grace to see through sin, there is for him no uncertainty, no oscillation, that could interrupt his worship. Everything is balanced and good, growing and full.

He has a strong sense of responsibility; he is aware that he has his place in work and service and knows from experience what the fruitfulness of grace is. He does not calculate; it is repugnant to him to do so, because he understood so early on that the Lord expends himself without counting the cost. The love he feels for the Lord and his fellowmen has the character of service, the sort of service that ultimately does not seek to be understood or measured. And what he has gratuitously received, he gratuitously hands on and regrets only that grace is rejected by men, that he is unable to show to the person who hesitates, who doubts and does not yet believe, what God has shown to him in such a superabundant way. And although he is aware of their needs and shortcomings, he nevertheless believes he has not yet found the words that would really suffice to penetrate them in the way God has penetrated him.

He measures out neither his time nor his own person; he strives to hand himself over completely. And although he is not very significant intellectually, he nevertheless has a significant effect, because he bears things—which has Christian significance in the Lord. He bears things in order to pass them on. Moreover, he has a cheerful heart, which acknowledges in a childlike way every grace it receives. Everywhere he looks, he sees a reason to be thankful, but also a reason to renew his commitment.

DON BOSCO (1815–1888)

I see his prayer, which is essentially Johannine, full of love, affection, and astonishment for God. He does not have extensive knowledge about prayer. He does not have a very concrete picture of the triune God. He draws his nourishment from a few images from the Gospel and marvels at the Father, the Son, and the Spirit in Christ. He loves them and brings everything to them and takes everything upon himself out of love and above all out of wonder. His love for God is a bit *schwärmerisch*. It is not very easy for him to lead his fellowmen into the world of his prayer. What he lacks is distance: with respect to God and to the faith of the other and to his own faith. He lives in an immediacy, which is personally very beautiful and is of a Johannine purity; he desires nothing else than to be allowed to love and to marvel, and the fact that he and others are allowed to do so is a cause of his childlike joy.

In all the deeds he undertakes, he draws on the Lord's words: "Whatever you have done to the least of my brothers"; he lives in the immediacy of bringing things to the Lord, of seeking in the Lord's name. And if his helpers pray too little and take more joy in the action, in the undertakings, in the work, or in the outer shell than they do in God and in marveling at God, then he becomes sad and at the same time at a loss about what to do. He does not know how to convey his own enthusiasm to them. To be sure, there are a lot of things he could have left behind for them, but those who go back to him after his death will have to project him back more powerfully into the Gospel in order to gather more content than he himself was able to convey. His prayer lacked a certain depth, without this problem being an objection to him. Everything he does, he does in God's name, but he builds his work in a sense too little on the foundation of his prayer for this prayer to have been its true root. His intention is what is best, but the relationship between prayer and work remains a bit too simplistically conceived.

His mysticism always has an almost accidental character; it always elevates his marveling. But he lacks a certain capacity to appropriate, to construct, to build bridges. He is like a gardener who knows how to grow extraordinary flowers but who, when he picks them, is unable to weave them into a bouquet.

DOMINICA LAZZARI (1816–1848)[1]

She contemplates the Lord's suffering; as she prays, she feels somewhat like the Mother of God, who has knowledge of her Son's suffering. It is perfectly clear to her that she placed herself in the Mother's position through her own free will in order to contemplate the suffering of the Cross and, by being there, to help. Even after her contemplation has ended, she remains in a state of suffering and dread, perhaps even more in a state of anxiousness. Her anxiousness has two aspects. She fears that she has presumptuously put herself in the Mother of God's place, that this is not acceptable, not feasible, that she ought to have looked for some other way to draw near to the Cross. It is as if she suffered from a bad conscience. On the other hand, an anxiousness, indeed, a fear, has remained with her that does not belong to Mary and whose provenance she is unable to figure out. She is able to arrange her thoughts only concerning the first aspect, the presumptuousness. She sees the second aspect as a sort of punishment for her arrogance. And this second aspect remains and grows stronger, and she begins, while she undergoes this anxiety, to turn her gaze to the Son on the Cross, in his own anxiety. And now she suddenly understands that she has been given a share in the Cross itself. But in order to acquire this knowledge, a dread is necessary, which she for a long time considered something purely natural, but which was already secretly an anxiety of the Cross, which was administered to her, as it were, in small doses, so that she would not be too frightened and also so that, in relation to the Lord's suffering itself, she would not experience the same anxiety she has when she shares in Mary's suffering: it is arrogance to suffer it with her.

Everything else she experiences is a function of this anxiety. She is quite aware that she loves. And she desires to love. But she also hands

[1] A peasant girl in Capriana, Fleimsertal. A stigmatic who received many visits.

herself over to anxiety; she completely affirms it, because God has offered it to her and laid it upon her. At the same time, however, she has a terrible fear of this anxiety. Moreover, it is for her always quite difficult to turn back from God to the world, from prayer to her earthly task. It is also difficult because the anxiety, whatever may be its cause, accompanies her everywhere. Thus she begins to have the impression that she is extraordinarily shy, sensitive, and nervous. But perhaps it is in fact not at all demanded of her that she come out of herself as a "flag-bearer"; perhaps the anxiety occurs so strongly in order to deepen her humility, in order to allow her to live between suffering and humility. She makes nothing at all of herself; she considers herself to be completely unworthy to carry in her body the signs of God's presence, the stigmata. But even the fact that she "makes nothing of herself" tortures her, because everything she feels and experiences is laid upon her in such a way as to nourish her anxiety. She perseveres in this; she has no possibility of escape. The people around her see her as an anxious person and have no inkling of the enormity, the vastness of the genuine anxiety she undergoes in the following of Christ.

CONRAD OF PARZHAM (1818–1894)

I see his prayer and his attitude, both of which grow in simplicity and transparency. Everything he has to do, he does within the mystery, both of the Child Jesus and of the Mother's Yes—in a sort of simplicity, ease, and naturalness. The simplicity consists in the fact that he sets aside unnecessary questions. He said Yes, and that is the way it ought to stay. The ease is an external sort, because no one ought to be able to detect in him that he could be tired or frustrated or discontent. Indeed, he takes moods, which could be seen as frustration or discontent, as little needle pricks, which are necessary for him in order to purify his inner life, without his having to say anything to anyone else about it. And the naturalness means that he knows himself to be a child of God, that God has put him in this place in order to be the custodian of this little task, and he carries everything out in God's presence. God is absolutely present to him. There is no door that he opens, no answer that he gives, and no little difficulty that he takes upon himself that he does not do directly for the sake of the Lord who is present.

His prayer is a petitionary prayer. He asks God to make him right away the way he needs him to be, and then he asks for everyone he meets, those who are in his monastery, those who come from outside, those who have crossed his path even without having asked for anything from him. They are his neighbors, whom God himself has entrusted to him; indeed, they are God's images, placed upon his path, in order to remind him of God's presence. He also has a great prayer of thanksgiving. He is infinitely grateful that he is allowed to be there, that he is allowed to serve; also infinitely grateful that St. Francis is his holy father. And when he comes across imperfections in the Order, he does not dwell on them. He takes the view that it does not concern him; he needs only to convey it in a matter-of-fact sort of way to God and leave it to him, and, with the help of St. Francis, God will soon bring the matter to order. He has a boundless trust in prayer, in its power and effectiveness. If someone interrupts him while he is at prayer, it does not disturb him because he is always able to return to it as if the interruption never happened, by virtue of a sort of unceasing prayer. That proceeds without having to be forced, in gratitude and faith. What frailties he himself possesses, he bears and offers as the tiniest of crosses and does not make a big deal out of it. He does not allow the loftiness of prayer to be disturbed by the lowliness of little obstacles.

PALMA M. MATARRELLI (1825–1888)[1]

She loses those who were close to her after a life that was permeated by faith, a simple and straightforward faith; the loss affects her greatly in every case, but she submits to it. What was genuine in her faith life is at first little changed. She is unable to forge great insights about her loss; but she allows God the right to give and again to take back. "That is how it is"; she contents herself with it. Loneliness grows; at one point she feels the whole burden of abandonment, and then it is not hard for her to give God room, to pray more, to live more for others. But now it becomes difficult, very difficult. God draws her nearer to himself; he gives her the pains of his wounds and other signs of his intimacy. She does not understand it; the women around her who observe the things that happen to her, including the spiritual things, drive her away from her inner path; they show her that she has to play along. By telling her these things, they mean to help her. To fill in the miracles, to invent things that, in their opinion, would increase their effective power. Thus, they begin to cheat. Her path is a sign showing that man always remains free to turn away even when God gives him a superabundance of graces. The Mother of the Lord "could have" sinned ... could have ... ! Palma *can*.

[1] In Oria near Brindisi. She was widowed at twenty-eight years old. Cf. Herbert Thurston, *Die körperlichen Begleiterscheinungen der Mystik* (Lucerne, 1956), 107–12.

At first, it was more or less a harmless joke. But because the women and she notice that these become entangled, she becomes a helper, perhaps at first in good faith, in order gradually to substitute her own inventions for what God has given. Over and over again in prayer she makes up her mind to put an end to all this and, if not completely to become the woman God saw in her, at least to approach this image. As if it were possible to retrace the path step by step, first eliminating this lie and then the next, as if it were possible to grow, from the original white, which had now become completely black, gradually into gray, to get a handle on herself, once again primarily through her own effort. She does not cease praying, although she does play around with what she envisions. She defends herself in endless prayers and speeches before God; she argues with him; she often begs him to take what she does as his own work. Infidelity wins out, but she nevertheless goes on praying . . .

THEOPHANE VÉNARD (1829–1861)

I see his faithful, pious prayer, which perfectly nourishes and sustains him. He lives on prayer and in prayer. Moreover, he sees an abundance of things in prayer, although he never has the ultimate certainty that he is in fact doing exactly what it is that God requires of him. It is as if God left him in semi-darkness, which never got completely illuminated. He does not experience any sudden flash, any overwhelming clarity; he has a small path, which leads over little curves and little hills toward its goal, and he travels this path as carefully as he can, in order to keep from falling off, but he is accompanied by the genuine hope of never doing anything displeasing to God. Nevertheless, he remains aware that God could demand more, though he is not able to achieve this more; he understands very clearly that he has to manage the little he is able to do in relation to this insight into a possible "more". And thus he devotes himself. Not merely day by day, but hour by hour, minute by minute, in order to fulfill God's will, in an unfailing humility of heart. His prayer consists in adoration, surrender, promise, and in the great bearing of many concerns: concerns that are in part entirely foreign to him, but which come from people who are almost unknown to him, for whom he promised to pray, and he remains faithful to his promise. He loves the Church; he loves her feasts and celebrates them like a child in the simplicity of his heart, in a cheerfulness that seems to arise more from the essence of the celebration than from himself. He is happy if he is allowed to pray in this way; and if he tends to the tasks of a spiritual director or to missionary work, then he feels he always remains so much behind in his task that he is thankful for every moment of prayer or spiritual reading. Prayer is restorative for him and replenishes his energy. It gives the day-to-day life to him in a *small* dose—or at least that is how he experiences it—because he has the constant desire to flee to a monastic cell (although he knows he is not permitted to do so), only in order to avoid doing any damage to God's affairs through his clumsiness. He has surrendered his own destiny so completely into God's hands that he is indifferent to everything. His perfection consists in the fact that he does not concern himself with the things that affect himself but wants to do only what God's will is, in a today that promises more for tomorrow, in spite of the failure he experiences, in a fidelity and contentedness and, at the same time, anxiety, which allow him to give the affairs of day-to-day life a sort of indifferent importance. But, at the same time, one could not say that he is a mediocre Christian, because his surrender is genuine, and his absolute obedience is especially genuine.

PIUS X (1835–1914)

I hear his prayer. It is perhaps in the deepest sense a papal prayer. When he became pope, he was pious, very committed to the Church's well-being, a man with the simplicity of a heart that did not oppose itself to the intelligence. But all the things of which he was made did not blend into a unity. His attitude was Christian but, at the same time, permeated by weaknesses; his prayer sometimes tepid, sometimes borne by great warmth; his intentions were ecclesial, but he did not engage himself magnanimously in defending them. He possessed a certain love of neighbor, but of a sort that did not recognize the involvement of the spiritual advisor as the most urgent thing. When he became pope, he was deeply horrified. That is not something he wanted; he did not wish it for himself because he considered himself unworthy, and he also could not believe they were serious who elected him, that the election took place fairly. He feared there was an error, not one that perhaps he had committed, but one that he nevertheless aided insofar as he did not present himself exactly the way he was. He worried that he might have exhibited a false image of himself, that he played a part for others; he worried that his words were heard as having more significance than they actually had. When he realized that he had to assume the office irrevocably, he looked at it as the opportunity to turn his life around, to convert, to allow his gifts to be integrated into his task. The new task had to become one with what God had long ago commissioned from him. He saw that the way he himself imagined and wanted and honored a pope was a far cry from what he himself could present. He saw himself divided, full of shortcomings; the papal office should make something out of him that could be achieved only through a daily effort. He resolved to undertake and commit himself to this work. At first in the sense of "a creditable performance". Until it suddenly dawned upon him: the presence of Christ can achieve anything. The office of St. Peter, as Christ handed it over to him, must come once again in the relationship between Christ and Peter in Pius: a living, paternal office extending over the entire Church, which allowed him to be the father of the whole of Christianity, not in the sense that this title of father would be something earned once and for all, but in the sense that he arises from the Lord's presence renewed and full of life.

And now the Eucharist appears to him as the assurance of the Lord's presence, an assurance for the general establishment of what has to be established in himself, an assurance for the new revivification of the papacy as well. From this moment on, his prayer centers on communion; his supplication centers around this power of presence. There is much that he lays aside; there is also much about the external forms and demands of his earlier piety that he loses for the sake of his mission: to remain in Christ's presence, to strive anew to live in Christ through Christ; this demand increases in such a way that he henceforward sees the world, the Church, and those close to him in the light of the Eucharist, that he tests everything through the power of communion, and even *allows* it to be tested in view of this power. He seeks the Lord's presence everywhere. He had always been pervaded by the unconditional actuality of the eucharistic presence. But now this reality has become something so actual, so active, so deeply immersed in his mission that he becomes its apostle. And he endeavors to integrate everything into these ideas; he tries to love and to be loved; he grasps the power of love, not in the Johannine sense of personal, loving discipleship, but in the sense of a graceful sharing in the Most High; he sees it descending from above in a living stream, in which he is permitted to share and, therefore, which he must also share. His life becomes increasingly clearer and more transparent; he himself disappears in order to allow only what is of the Lord to be loved. To be sure, there are some things that he previously thought, tried, reflected on, and which now simply become a part, which disappear too, become unimportant to him, because the important thing must occupy the primary place, and it is clear that nothing secondary ought to enter into competition with it. And he manages to keep from falling out of his attitude of prayer anymore, to live in it as the Lord wills that he live in it. Here, without deliberately trying, he enters into the place of a John, who is the friend and the beloved. He is also one who realizes the Lord's love in himself and experiences it in a living way.

JEROME JAEGEN (1841–1919)[1]

I see his prayer, which possesses a remarkable importance for him. He is, of course, surrendered to God, but he surrounds his prayer with a solemnity; he honors the act of prayer as if he were an outsider, in order, that is, that he not neglect anything he believed he must do. It is not a prayer he says spontaneously, but primarily it has the character of something that was to a certain extent meant for the liturgy, to be carried out at particular times, which carries with it an a priori claim to be validated by God. It is perhaps very slightly vain, but with respect to the principal matter it is a responsibility to be fulfilled in relation to God, the Church, and the world. As a person who prays, *I* am not allowed to have a low estimation of my task!

Once he gets beyond this aspect, he enters into the interior dimension of prayer, and then comes, too, the forgetting of self; now he stands before God and wishes humbly to be filled by God. And God in fact fills him; God allows himself to be touched by this precision and painstakingness of a serious effort at love. God becomes present to him, and he allows God to dwell in him. It is just that this dwelling again becomes something too carefully observed; he keeps his eye on it step by step. Not only the divine that acts is contemplated, but also its reception, the human response. As if the creaturely conduct toward the most uncreaturely of all occupations, namely, prayer, were carried out professionally.

The people around him are narrow; he himself, however, is docile and follows exactly what is said to him; he keeps records, and he acts entirely in accord with the records he keeps, like an account book, in which no entry may be left out. What he records therein in terms of stages, degrees, and details ought to be taken much less seriously than his prayer. His prayer is really good, while some of the things he says about it are not, because in making his judgments he takes himself to be a measure of the thing, as an objective mirror, which registers things in a precise way, which confuses the free play of divine providence with "law-abidingness", which imposes the aspect of a humanly regulated process on God's "accidents". And nevertheless his work of prayer

[1] Unmarried layman. An engineer, bank director, and political representative of a Prussian province.

is not without significance, because he begins to pray in a place where otherwise little prayer is done. Moreover, his creaturely conduct and his relations to his fellowmen become better through the amount he prays; he becomes the Lord's apostle.

GERARD MANLEY HOPKINS (1844–1889)

His prayer vacillates a lot. It does so already in terms of frequency and density. There are times when he enjoys praying. Then he succumbs once again to the temptation to cease praying or to pray only a tiny bit. There are other times when he stands before prayer with a certain indifference; he prays as long as it lasts, but he quits praying when something else takes hold of him. He has the hardest time keeping a regular schedule. When he does not enjoy praying, then he becomes irritable and does not like it. He has the feeling that a veil lies over prayer itself; he looks at it, so to speak, obliquely, ceases for a moment to believe in the usefulness of prayer, in its necessity and effectiveness. At times, there are so many demands on him that he almost forgets to pray. Then there are again other times in which he prays with great surrender and begs God to forgive him his infidelity and neglect and the prevalence of things of lesser importance. Everything happens by fits and starts.

In the times when he prays and enjoys praying, he surrenders himself so completely that he thinks the danger has been removed, and now he abides in prayer; he also begs that indifference and fidelity be given to him. He has a delicate sense of temptation, of his own sins, of their sharpness, their regression; and when he turns himself right once again and is permitted to live in grace, then he detests himself; he detests the fact that he is unable to overcome himself when he is in danger.

Sometimes he prays in the same way he composes, and he sees a danger in this. Then he says the Church's prayers again and tries to be completely simple. And the more his prayer grows simpler and more straightforward, the happier he becomes, because it is no longer he himself who is praying, but rather prayer takes place in him [*es betet in ihm*]. He is thus permitted to use the words of Scripture, and he no longer depends on his own inspiration, which seems dangerous to him. For this inspiration puts him in a sort of trance, in which the beauty of the words and thoughts excites him; and it becomes more a hymn, a song, in which he himself is no longer wholly present. It is a sort of preliminary stage that prepares him for the composition of a poem. But he has a precise understanding of what is essential in prayer and what it is he must pray for, what he must deliver to the Father with the Son's word.

(*What significance does the Society of Jesus have for him?*) There are many days in which he knows he is out of sorts with the Society, and again many in which he loves and values it. But he sees its shortcomings with clear eyes. If he then thinks about Ignatius, he is overcome by an irrepressible love for the Society, and he stands before it more like a father before his child than a child before his father. He had once entered the Society full of enthusiasm and hope; it offered him the only place where his life was possible; and he constantly recalls that this is the case. But it does not happen without a struggle. One cannot say that his relationship to St. Ignatius is very animated. He admires him; he contemplated him and appropriated many things, but later represented them more as things he had earned ...

BERNADETTE (1844–1879)

A pure child, completely clueless, who suddenly, without any transition, receives a mission. It comes so much from out of the blue that she does not understand a thing. She does not even know what a mission is. She felt sheltered in the bosom of her father's house, in spite of all the poverty and frictions. Now something inconceivable presents itself to her: she saw Mary, she obeyed in her vision without knowing it, and now she has to live for this inconceivable, and yet simple and evident, thing. As simply as she saw it, that is how simply she recounts it. To be sure, she feels the mistrust that surrounds her, the web that is woven around her. But in the end it does not bother her; she always believes that this is somehow "life". Her mission is fulfilled; it lies somewhere behind her. The Church had drawn her to herself so quickly that she stands there as if robbed of her mission, a mission of which she was ultimately scarcely aware. She is placed in a cloister. Why should she not enter it? She is so childlike that it is no problem for her. She never sees the personal service that grows out of the mission—that in a sense her life in the cloister would be a consequence of her mission. A Mechtild, a Gertrude, and the two Teresas, see clearly the *task* and rise to it. Of course, they are unable to survey their task as a whole, but they nevertheless see its outlines, the cooperation it requires, the responsibility. Bernadette has no clue. She is terribly pestered in the cloister, but she bears it all in a sort of blind obedience; blind, not in the sense of St. Ignatius, but in the sense of pure unquestioning: she has always obeyed, and "one" simply bears it. This bearing of things makes her holy. It is as if she had always already received the whole gift of grace and now had afterward still to achieve what makes her "worthy" of having received the appearance. Most other missions have a prehistory: a person has to grow into it, to suffer into it. Here, the visible mission belongs to the past, and she has to pay the price for it afterward. In her prayer, Bernadette has a childlike simplicity. In the cloister, she might *once* have had the vision again, although it may in fact not really have been an original vision, but a reflection, a recurrence, of the previous one. Moreover, in her own life, the event that happened in the past in the grotto and the things she now experiences in the cloister blend together, and she always remains overwhelmed by everything and never entirely catches up to it. This utter simplicity, which never demands to understand anything, is what is great and unique in her. She does not know what she knows and also does not know what she does. Almost all the saints have a sphere of reflection in which God's events, which penetrate into them, become their own experiences. Bernadette remains without experience. A greater context of divine truth opens up to other saints through their vision. For Bernadette, nothing opens up. She is created so much for others, so perfectly expropriated, that she simply lets things pass through her; she transmits them, without having any idea that what she transmits could have become her own possession.

Before the appearance, her prayer to the Mother, her Ave Maria, was like that of a pure child. Since the appearance, she knows to whom she turns. She has seen the Lady. That is in fact the whole difference. Like a poor child who sews handkerchiefs for a rich lady: once the child has seen the lady, she then knows for whom she does the work. She does not reflect on it; she cannot imagine why the rich lady needs so many handkerchiefs. But now she knows who receives them, and she has been told that the lady needs her, although for all that the child does not have any better grasp of why. Bernadette continues to pray her Ave Marias to the Lady whom she has seen. And she tells her how beautiful she was to her and that she also is happy to suffer for her. This occurs in an absoluteness and unquestionableness that would almost reach the point of fanaticism if it were not the simple effect of grace, if it were not holiness.

TERESA HIGGINSON (1844–1905)[1]

I see her prayer, which is initially beset by a certain curiosity, a craving for knowledge, which is greater than her piety and surrender. She wants to know and to experience. This stems from a love that is not perfectly selfless but is love nevertheless. Then she gets *prise au propre piège*

---

[1] English teacher. Stigmatic. Cf. Lady Cecil Ken, *Teresa Helena Higginson* (1950).

[caught in her own trap], as it were; she experiences and sees more and more, without seeking it and bringing it about herself. And in the midst of this, she learns how to let things happen. From this point on, she lives within an infinite love, the waves of which she feels right away. She feels overwhelmed and carried away by this love, wherein she herself does not find her place (like the little Thérèse, when she decides to be a toy ball), but remains within the most complete anonymity. She is Bride, but she is also Church, when she experiences; she experiences for others; and her suffering, her pains, her mortal struggles and anxieties are appropriated by the Church. The Lord gives them in order that they might be used. Her soul becomes more and more transparent; she does not seek anything more, for she has been found. She is like someone who has learned something in order to reach a certain goal, and in the process of learning, a wholly new and completely unanticipated world revealed itself to him. What she receives by far exceeds what she has anticipated.

(*And her devotion to the Holy Face?*) Hard to evaluate. For her, this devotion has a completely objective character, of course. But it is nevertheless somehow too partial, too enthusiastic, to be something truly useful in this form in the Church in general. It is better for the Church to worship the heart; and it would be still better for the Church to worship the Lord. Teresa preaches what has become important for her. There was no particular task given by the Lord present for her to devote herself to. Her mission lies in suffering for the Church.

LUCIE CHRISTINE (1844–1908)

I see her prayer, which is pious, handed over, and slightly heated; prayer puts her in a state of excitement, which nevertheless leads back to calm, but not before she has come to understand what God wishes to show her. God shows things to her within herself and also in images, that is, what one might call "visions of feeling" (like when you hear a person you know doing something behind you: you do not need to turn around in order to perceive him), in various states of faith. She experiences faith as if it were a person who possessed influence and acted on the Lord's behalf. Her states excite her, to the point that she sees what produces them and comes to understand the path God thus points out to her. He uses her in order to achieve things here and there. She herself does not see what is achieved. She sees the Lord's suffering: here, he suffers ... there, he is humiliated ... here, faith has become tepid ... there, the Lord's will is not being done. And she has to confirm that she has seen these things; then peace comes over her, and she enters into the heart of letting-be.

In addition to this, there are periods of prayer during which she simply receives, as if these periods were basins for collecting God's graces, in order to pass what she received on into ordinary life in an inconspicuous way, so that it can be used by the people around her. There is a lot of love in her life. A supernatural love, which then gives the power to bring about love of neighbor as a commandment from the Lord. There are days in which she in fact never leaves prayer for a moment; all her thoughts then pass truly through the love she experiences. Her life is created in such a way that this is externally possible. If she were to lose the contours of her apostolate for a moment in the thick of her various occupations, then she would fly back into prayer as quickly as she could and link up the new prayer with the old. She always succeeds in making the bridge. She has also faced her shortcomings with great courage and has been serious in regard to God's demands. And she does not take delight in it for her own sake, even in the cases where many favorable things are said about her.

MARIA BAOUARDY
(MARY OF JESUS CRUCIFIED) (1846–1879)[1]

I see her prayer, which undergoes a thorough development. In the beginning, she has an extremely subjective understanding of Jesus' life, his suffering, and death. She desires to leap into it, to help; this desire rages in her uncontrollably. She scourges herself spiritually so as not to allow the desire to fade, so as to remain on the heights of availability, which ought not to lessen. She is raised up; she lends her own effort to this; she has no idea what humility, what obedience, is. But she wants to help.

Then God acts more and more within her, so that everything becomes genuine and good and true discipleship. Her prayer becomes correspondingly more and more humble. She becomes a real saint, but a saint who must never cease struggling. At the outset, her being possessed was not genuine but simply a transference from her feelings. But she took what is untrue as true, and then it was transformed into something true in her, and she became possessed and thus became a visionary and a stigmatic. There, where everything once seemed false, the genuine suddenly shines through. It is one of God's ways, which are inscrutable. Now

[1] From Syria. A lay sister who died in the Carmel of Bethlehem. Cf. Estrate, "Vie de S. Marie de Jésus-Crucifié" (1913).

she suffers for real and in a way that does indeed bring help, and love truly burns in her, and she lives in a perfect discipleship.

Her possession is at first like a concentration of evil in her. She imagines that she is possessed, because she is not in fact, because she is still willing to exaggerate. Then the possession becomes demonic: an offer to all evil powers to seduce her away from God. What had formerly deceived her becomes a reality; it turns into a function of her holiness. The devil acquires a circumscribed power over her; she can be "transported". But she does not do evil when she is possessed; rather evil accomplishes in her things that are contrary to what the superior and the Rule desire. It is part of her mission to be defenselessly handed over to it. God alone possesses the power, without any cooperation from the instrument, to expel this evil and to bring an end to these states.

LÉON BLOY (1846–1917)

I see his prayer. And his battle with himself and with God. With himself, because he would like to be the way he thinks God intended him to be. He sees himself as the Christian who is entrusted with a mission, the highest task of which is to remain true to this mission. And he engages in a twofold battle: he must keep the mission pure, fight for it, must be a beacon everywhere, represent Christianity, and draw people to it and its task with harsh words. But he must also fight for himself, insofar as he must attain the capacities to carry out the mission. That is the task, but in undertaking it he often fails, because when he defends himself (which to be sure he is called to do), he sometimes forgets to see himself as one sent and instead sees *himself*, with his wishes and desires. Then his mission gets somewhat eclipsed, because when he ought to speak about God, he speaks about himself, and he dwells too long on himself. He fights for the "daily bread", but in doing so he forgets to some extent the "thy kingdom come" and "thy will be done." The natural imposes itself, somewhat to the detriment of the supernatural. It happens in a sense completely in good faith, because he is equipped with all kinds of desires, which seem to be present as things to be satisfied ever anew in the need of the moment, and then he perhaps demands what he needs and receives it. But he easily forgets that it has to be immediately translated into what the mission requires. He has a thirst for the unconditional and would like to take this thirst for granted also in other people. When that does not happen, when people are halfhearted, he must always reawaken his awareness of his mission and become alert. At the same time, he may not himself ever become halfhearted in relation to the unconditional; he has to call up the strength in the quiet hours of prayer not simply to see himself as a sinner, but also to turn his attention away from himself as a sinner in order to gaze in childlike purity upon the Giver of all missions; he must become grateful, not only for the goods that he receives from friends, acquaintances, and admirers, but always for the mission that God has given to him. For the mission in its most active sense.

In his prayer and in his entire disposition, there is an aspect that he fulfills quite well, and that is the aspect of suffering: for he bears the humiliations, the pains, and the impotence truly just as they are given to him, in their entire fullness, and without making a tally. This not being permitted to reckon in suffering he feels to be a *necessary commandment* that is given by God; the only things he lacks are the bridges to pass from his own lack of reckoning to the reckoning other people make. He ought to bring them, too, to this freedom from reckoning. But he has no patience with them. He is like one who desired to bring someone who is seeking the truth of the Church immediately before the demand "to sell everything", with the warning that anything less "is worth nothing at all". While he understands himself in simplicity as suffering, he reads his own need for the unconditional into other people to such an extent that he would like to make them suffer in a divine sense; he admonishes them to *be* (and not merely to *become*) the way they ought to be. Here, he abridges his mission, because he takes upon himself the labor of accompanying and bearing others only begrudgingly; God's absoluteness is so primordially important for him, and he finds in this the whole of his Christian desire to such an extent, that the halfheartedness of his fellowmen becomes unbearable to him. He would like to select an elite, which is just what he cannot do, and it is difficult for him to find Christ present in the rest of the people who are slow and do not yet understand. It is difficult for him to content himself with this presence, which excludes no one, to come to see that the whole power of God is nevertheless there in this presence, which seems only weak and sparing, and that he too needs it for the fulfillment of his mission.

LOUISE LATEAU (1850–1883)

She does not have much explicit prayer, because it is not in fact she, but rather others, who are intended. And when she has visions and receives the stigmata, she is an instrument. And she lives in a certain detachment as much from herself as from the Church, insofar as she does not take sides in a strong sense. Without God's intervention in the stigmata and visions, without the explicit things he carries out in her for the sake of those around her, she would be a respectable, but rather average, Christian. God breaks through her mediocrity and her not very compelling prayer in order to take possession of her body and to do things that correspond to *his* will but that do not stand in any obvious relationship to her faith. In fact, he breaks his own law. She is to be sure not unbelieving; she moreover does not live in any estrangement from God; but neither is she very intelligent or particularly zealous in her faith. For this reason, she is unable to come to grips with what happens to her. And that is not required of her. But it is also not possible to say that she allows the things to happen in an Ignatian indifference; it is more a sort of apathy, for she does not take a strong position either with respect to herself or with respect to God's will. She very quickly reaches the point at which she no longer understands, but this place is inessential, because she herself is held so much aloft by God. She is like an experiment that God carries out, who shows through her: This is the way I do it, and there is no other way; indeed, it is immediate and that is all there is to say. The whole thing looks like a chess move that God makes against overrated reason, the rationalism of those around her, the "achievements of science". She does not undergo a conversion. In the things she sees, she remains naïve; it is in fact perfectly fine with her; here and there she experiences supernatural joy; here and there supernatural suffering, but always in the sphere of an objectivity that she does not personally develop any farther. In part, she articulates her visions; in part, she is, so to speak, neutralized; it is not something in which people are interested. She remains a bit of an enigma to the people who observe her.

MARIE JULIE JAHENNY (1850–1941)[1]

I see her, not as a stigmatic. I see her prayer, which is complete surrender, but also complete impatience. She wants to be used; she wants to be an instrument. And she expects that God will suddenly accomplish something remarkable in her, something that is remarkable *for her*, by converting her. But she also expects that he will set her apart. She acknowledges her shortcomings, but she knows the Lord can deal with them. It is just that she lacks patience. And instead of allowing herself to be overpowered by the Lord, she herself wants to overpower *him*. Thus, she makes use of certain changes in order to characterize herself as a stigmatic; she contributes an effort, she desires to be what she is not. But she desires it, not, in fact, out of a will to deceive, but

[1] A peasant girl from Bretagne. Cf. Antoine Imbert-Gourbeyre, *La Stigmatisation*, 2nd ed. (Clermont-Ferrand: L. Bellet, 1894).

rather out of an impatience finally to be permitted to accomplish something extraordinary. She has in mind a very precise sort of holiness, which would transmit a great reverence through it, in order to turn it into adoration in God's presence. She makes herself an instrument. And she no longer has the courage and the strength to stand apart from it. On the one hand, she is internally plagued to distraction by inauthenticity, which she almost manages to forget in the interim, but which she nevertheless remains aware of in the background, and she is also plagued by the devil himself. A devil that ultimately ought to be called bad conscience. And she makes use of her bad conscience to do battle, but in a way that already in advance gives the victory to her rather than to God. It is a willed imitation of a genuine state by one who is not called. She does not make it easy for herself, however, but rather very difficult, insofar as she, without sufficient support, struggles heroically against things that she herself brings about. It is a vacillation in her imagination, which is reflected in prayer and which is in turn nourished by prayer, because she works herself up into a state of things that are impossible and inconceivable but that she *almost* believes herself. And if someone were, at some point, to give her a little credence, then that would confirm her awareness of mission; she would then exaggerate even more and become even more presumptuous. There is in fact nothing in her life that she would not use to give herself validity, a validity she does not want simply to possess for her own sake but that she nevertheless insists on being hers.

MERCIER (1851–1926)

I see his prayer; it is in a way outwardly beautiful but impoverished in content. He fashions his personal prayer into a sort of liturgical act; he lends it a whole system, a rhythm, an edifice. He thus sees himself as a person interceding on behalf of an invisible community, but he is not humble; he does not focus on what he is praying. Instead, his attention is directed much more to *how* he prays, in a sort of attitude of external submissiveness. This is what he emphasizes. Nevertheless, he is inspired by the desire to please God. But he begins outside of himself. For this reason, he is also unable to find the right contact with people on the basis of humble love. At the same time he constructs a theory of Christianity, of its effective power and its results, and this theory comprehends everything—everything, that is, but himself. He experiences himself as the mediator of an energy that precisely does not make use of him in order to convey itself. The contact does not pass through him; the energy waves spread out, passing him by. And yet he is zealous; he attends to every new idea; he is a good conversation partner; he desires to serve the Church and God and works toward the unity of faith, which would at the same time be the unity of the Church. Of a Church, however, in which quite a bit would be form and in which the inner radiance would necessarily be missing, because he himself would be incapable of allowing it to burn in himself and thus to set others on fire.

He has a healthy human judgment for what is possible or impossible in the Church's situation. But his activity does not penetrate the depths, because he does not pray deeply. And when he constructs theories, it is for the most part out of ideas that have happened to float to him from somewhere, ideas that have enlightened him and to which he can lend a certain power thanks to his extensive influence, but without an ultimate and unconditional inward participation in them.

MARIE DE JÉSUS (1853–1916)[1]

I see her prayer, which is simultaneously very strong and very humble. Humble, for she considers herself nothing; strong, for she is convinced of the Lord's presence and perhaps even more convinced of the living presence of the Holy Spirit and that her house should be a house of the Spirit. She does not succeed in praying so strongly just like that; she has to struggle with herself quite a bit; a spirit of knowing better battles in her against the spirit of absolute truth in God. It was difficult to detach herself from this "knowing better" and, thus, to free up the whole space for the Lord and his Spirit. But then it became a victory that penetrated everything. She now knows perfectly what is at stake. She understands service in its integrity and has a precise sense of the Lord's demands on her cloister. The strength that expresses itself in her prayer is also given to her for everything she has to bring up in her conversations, always arising from a clear vision. And she walks on farther and unflinchingly ahead. To be sure, she is also aware of the human weaknesses, concerns, and the neediness of those under her charge, but she places these in the right light and allows God's light to flow over everything, in an attitude that is so upright that everyone knows: she desires nothing but to serve God. She knows the implications of her decisions, but she does not make them on her own behalf, but always at the same time on behalf of the hearts of those who have been entrusted to her.

[1] A Carmelite nun, prioress of the Carmel of Dijon. Cf. Marie de Jésus, *Gestalt und Leben* (Patmos, 1951).

She has a great respect for Mother Teresa of Avila, but she nevertheless refers less to her personally than she does to the spirit of Carmel, to the living Christ, whom the Carmel needs, just as the world needs him. In many things, she clothes her personal experience, the claim made on her person, with the experiences of the great Teresa. But it is the spirit of Carmel to which she entrusts herself, and she would be worried about giving this spirit the form of a person; she would rather avoid this. Finally, in her simple decisions, she goes back to what God originally demanded of the world, to the Father's demand for redemption from the Son, to the Spirit's demand on believers. And she lives with the Lord; she lives in the Eucharist, in God's presence, which she describes without any high-sounding words, for she finds her words and answers in humble, everyday service and knows how to offer them.

(*Her relationship to Elizabeth?*)[1] Hard to say whether there is any dependence here. They actually run parallel. The little Thérèse of course also influences her in some respect. But it is not clear that there is an immediate contact between the missions; we cannot really speak of a direct influence or even of a filial relationship.

(*Her relationship to P. Vallée?*) He was influential on her in one respect: he has an unbelievable internal consistency; there is no interruption or stopping in him. Whatever he recognizes in a clear way, he takes to be valid both for himself and for others. You cannot say that she receives her nourishment from his ideas or his mission. He carries out in her the duties of a good spiritual director, without any deeper osmosis being visible. He is like the gardener who cuts away the superfluous branches. No, more than that: he gives support to the necessary ones. The emphasis is on support. Very often he finds the words to express what she feels and knows in a way connected with the Church. His formulations encourage and confirm her, even if they are often merely the expression of her own world of prayer.

IRÉNÉE VALLÉE, O.P. (b. 1841)[1]

I see how he prays and works his way into prayer by begging for a better following of Christ for himself and for others. He would like to serve the Lord in a serious way, and he slowly recognizes that he must

---

[1] Elizabeth of the Trinity. On her, see below and vol. 2.

[1] A spiritual director in the Dijon Carmel and several other cloisters. Cf. R. P. Vallée, "La Volonté de Dieu, nourriture de l'âme" (texts collected by the Baroness Amélie de Pitteurs), 2nd printing (Paris, 1936).

strive as much as possible to awaken the spirit of others, other individuals, in the mind of Christ. In all of this, he does not have in mind a great reform of his own order's cloister, but he is thinking primarily of the individual followers who are in his care.

He thus immerses himself ever more deeply in the Lord's mysteries; he attempts to achieve a better understanding of how they fit into the Father's will, in order to be able to make it conceptually clear to the religious how they fit into the spirit of their Order: it is a conformity given by the Holy Spirit, which is altogether parallel to Christ's will, conforming to the will of the Father. There are two things he sees in this: the renunciation of his own shortcomings and weaknesses, of his own being, of nature's rights—and a constant strengthening of prayer. Prayer, not as closing oneself up in tiny forms of piety, which hinder great surrender, but as carried out in a complete surrender, with the fixed resolution never to seek himself but the Lord's will, in an openness of his own spirit to the Holy Spirit, wherein the will of the triune God can reveal itself. The spirit of the Orders always appears to him as a form adopted by Christ's Holy Spirit. He therefore does not stop at the spirit of the Order, but always points back to the Son himself. The advice he gives always bears the stamp of a reasonable surrender. He sees, and he also wills, that the other person see with him how straight and masculine the path is and that there is no room in it for anything unmanly, petty, or hesitating. He is quite intent upon eliminating everything petty from his life and the life of those entrusted to him. He is not a great intellect, but he is sincere and pious and trains himself to great regularity in the disciplines he lays upon himself.

(*Elizabeth of the Trinity?*) She has received a lot from him. She often adopts for herself his own words and teachings word for word. And it is only afterward that she completely grows into them. The fact that she does this is due to her obedience to her confessor and spiritual director. There are places in which she defends what is her own, but there is also a lot that she simply accepts, in a sort of blind obedience, wherein she no longer distinguishes between what is his and what is hers. She accepts many things that stem from him; but in such a way that the moment always arrives when she is able to consider what she has borrowed as her very own, because she lives according to it and provides the contents for the vessel. Her own mission lies more in living these things than in teaching. It does lie in teaching, however, insofar as P. Vallée's teaching would not be so accessible to the Carmel if it were not for her. It is scarcely possible to say in this context where the two sets of responsibilities and realms of mission are set off from one another.

RIMBAUD (1854–1891)

I see him at different times. Here and there he prays, but not much; there is prayer in his youth, which is connected with the attempt to fight against sin and its attraction. But he then reassesses this to such a degree that it no longer has anything to do with surrender to God; rather, it has to do with the contemplation of sin, the experience of being attracted to it, delight in its possibilities, until finally that which had initially been a sort of prayer disappears altogether. It does not exactly turn into blasphemy (it disappears too early for that), but he bathes in the thought and the imagination of sin. And then, in periods of great creativity, he is suddenly sought by God once again, and this becomes tangible for him. He knows that what he writes does not come from himself but that another inspires him; another gives him the words and the strength and the joy in form. And he would like to say something to this Other. It would have been much easier simply in the beginning to acknowledge this presence and attempt to abide in it; but in this altercation the state of grace is interpreted so much as a state of creativity, of inspiration, of receptivity to the beautiful that he himself and his desires once again become the object of contemplation, and God falls once again into oblivion on the other side. Between these periods, there are nonproductive periods, which are actually better for his soul because he no longer relies on himself; he no longer seeks himself and desires to assert himself in God's presence; he no longer desires to elevate the poet over God. And there is suffering and sickness, which again speak of God in a way to which he is receptive, in a way that brings a sort of prayer to his lips. But this prayer is like a final grace, which is given to him as the lights are beginning to dim. It is seldom that he is able to say the word "God" or risk a prayer in the clarity of his thoughts or in the will to surrender himself. He lives on what he accumulated as a young man, on the little prayer he possessed then and that is not yet altogether buried in spite of the years. It also includes (and this is perhaps its most important contents) the rejection of the rejection of God, the desire no longer to accept as true that a person could go so far. His work now seems to him for the most part something reprehensible. He knows that if he had been humble, if he had sought God rather than inspiration, then his work would have been different; it would have been a witness. This knowledge is hard to bear.

PIUS XI (1857–1939)

I see him at prayer, as a person who is convinced of his weakness, one who seeks to grow into his office but does not feel that he is growing. And because he is aware that he is not getting closer to being pope, he bears it as a cross that God has laid on him, and it is something he cannot get beyond, either in his prayer or in his personal disposition or in his thinking. It is the most difficult cross for him. He tries to bear this cross in a manly and Christian way, but this does not make it any easier for him. If he had prayed joyfully before he had entered into offices in the Church, if he had prayed in the surrender of a child of God, with a certain lightheartedness and trust, as pope he can do so no longer. Every time he prays, the first thing he sees is *his* cross. Not in the sense that he constantly dwells on himself and his unworthiness in his thoughts, but in the sense that he must take the burden upon himself each time as completely new. There is a certain resignation, which also becomes visible to those around him. He feels he is not capable of being the leader of Christianity, indeed, even of just the people around him. He attempts to engage the entire power of prayer and to do more in prayer than in the required action. It is his weakness, and he recognizes it, but he is not strong enough to overcome it. And nevertheless he knows in the end that God is able to work through whomever he wills. His greatest strength is perhaps his humility; but it is a humility that is accompanied by weakness, since he does not find in his humility the courage to stand up where he sees injustice being done, to do anything else but beg God to take the injustice away. He is good, and through his goodness and gentleness he becomes a father of Christianity. He tries to be friendly to every person he meets; he tries to pray for every person, for all of the needs of Christianity and the papacy; but he is nevertheless unable to achieve a full personal engagement. He thus does a certain damage to the greatness of his office insofar as he does not carry it out in a rounded-out way.

He faces the worldly realm with a certain anxiety; and when he sees catastrophes befalling the world, the apostasy of entire regions, this fills him with an extreme fear, which is to be sure in part a dread that participates in the dread of the Cross, but it is also in part a penetrating insight into his own weakness, and to that extent he is not capable of overcoming this weakness. But he remains pious and given over and is more and more filled with love for God and for others. Even a certain vehemence in his decisions is a sign of weakness in him; he is vehement in the same way all weak people are. He is also not able to improve his personal faults very much, because he is too convinced of his incapacity, his sinfulness stands too emphatically before his eyes, which is also what explains his grievances and misjudgments. Much in his reign is simply flight: flight from responsibility. It is as if he weighed the distance that separates men from Christ, indeed, the distance that separates the representative of Christ on earth from the Lord, in too one-sided a manner and for this reason gave up a lot of things in advance that in any case were no longer suitable for him.

His relationship to the little Thérèse is not very different from his respect for the other saints and especially for the Mother of God; people have made her into more of a "discovery" than she really was, and he was driven to this (or at least to his whole relationship to Lisieux) more by those around him. He respects her, in a childlike way, but when he speaks certain strong words, it is more because of outside influence. Perhaps the effectiveness of the little Thérèse, for example, in the missions, would have been greater if people had not forced her so much into rigid boxes.

COLUMBA MARMION (1858–1923)

He prays in a manner that is simultaneously childlike and cunning. Childlike, insofar as he prays in complete trust and asks for what he needs for his work. And cunning, because he ultimately knows that it will not be withheld from him, that he will receive it. This gives him a remarkable relationship to the Holy Spirit: that of a reciprocal arrangement. He prays to receive what is necessary, which allows him in turn to be able to pray even better and also allows him to lead others to prayer. His zeal in prayer is fostered by his zeal in the composition of his writings. Both form more or less a unity; he also attempts to live out his life in this unity, which does not permit the slightest fragmentation to creep in. He is in this perhaps not entirely disinterested, in the sense that he is quite careful not to let any of the things that occur to him in prayer fall out of his hands; rather, he uses them in his work; but he also carries whatever occurs to him in his work into prayer, in order to test it, to lay it before God, and to receive a judgment about its worthiness. In addition, he is really like a child who takes joy also in what he has constructed. It is not so good that he goes about his prayer like a work to be accomplished, almost like a business in fact. This sort of thriftiness—not to say spiritual stinginess—is however in part caused by a genuine lack of time. He attempts to compensate for this lack through an attitude of love for his fellow brothers and fellowmen, an attitude he finds difficult to maintain because he would like to stick more and more to solitude through his work. What he *needs* is God, not men, quiet work and not disturbance. But he does it as far as it goes and as best he can and is quite open and honest in relation to himself. He admits his mistakes, but also the "inevitability" of his mistakes; he regrets them; he promises himself or his confessor that he will improve, but he already knows that he will not free himself from them, because his work is more important to him than his fellowmen. He would prefer to leave the task of love of neighbor—for that is how he sees it—to others, in order to be able to devote himself better to his own tasks. On the other hand, he always makes tangible efforts to be available and understanding.

PAULINE MARTIN (1861–1951)

I see her prayer in various phases. As a young girl, before she enters the Carmel, she prays with great love, piety, and matter-of-factness, a little premeditated; it occurs without a struggle, easily, spontaneously. She does not need to turn away from the traditional piety of her parents but rather can quite simply cultivate what she has been taught. It is the same when she is first in the Carmel. But this changes the moment the little Thérèse enters. Now she feels herself charged with a boundless responsibility from one day to the next, a responsibility that exceeds everything she has ever previously imagined: she feels she herself is responsible, before her sisters and before God, for her sister's mission. And this feeling of responsibility does not let go of her as long as the little Thérèse lives. To be sure, it undergoes a weakening, because it begins to become clear to her that her sister is dealing with an extraordinary mission. At this point, she realizes she has to pray infinitely more in order to live up to her responsibility of initiating her sister *into* prayer; for it seems to her that this mission is too great for the child. Her prayer gets deepened by this; it acquires weight; and she herself attempts to efface herself more and more in order to make straight the path for the little one and to lighten her task.

After Thérèse's death, a new period begins. Her sense of responsibility does not sharpen at first but, to the contrary, recedes a bit into the background. Her prayer takes on the form almost of a challenge. She makes a bet with God, indeed ... almost against God, that she will manage to make her sister's mission known. And because everything goes well and Lisieux enjoys an ever-greater call, this weakens her own mission. No longer in the sense of the final years of Thérèse, when Pauline deferred her share in the little one's mission (or her own, which amounts to the same thing), so that the little one would shine all the more. Now it is more an entry into the "affairs of the Church", into the renown of the sisters, into the significance of her Carmel.

But once she has brought things so far, she experiences responsibility, with a new vigor, indeed, with a transparent clarity *that seeks its equal.* The sense of the little one's mission, the sense of holiness in the Church, the sense of correspondence. And thus she once again removes herself; she renounces everything that has to do with a too facile renown, in order to begin anew in an inward way as the last of the Carmelites. A new feeling of responsibility grows for the little Thérèse's mission: she worries that she has exaggerated or distorted something; she feels she may not have done enough penance or prayed enough, in order to help the little one to carry the burden that was laid upon her (in part by herself). She has the awareness that she perhaps demanded, and also received, many things too carelessly. The growing renown of her little sister and the miracles disturb her. It is not that she thinks they are exaggerated, but rather she feels that she herself did not bear enough; the people around her are enjoying the renown without devoting themselves sufficiently to penance and to helping carry the burden in God's presence. Her prayer now becomes a ceaseless contemplation. She no longer neglects the things of God; everything that shone onto her from the external radiance of the little Thérèse no longer touches her. What touches her is the essence of holiness, the essence of the Church's saints, the essence of religious life, the essence of the sense of responsibility that every believer has in God's presence.

ELISABETH LESEUR (1866–1913)[1]

I see her little piety and the lack of proper guidance. She remained on a preliminary level. On a level at which each person who seriously begins a life of faith thus has to deal with himself and necessarily has to examine his own conscience, in order to eliminate not only his big mistakes, but also the fundamental deficiencies of his entire engagement and, thus, to become free for God. But she is unable to risk this leap into freedom. She perseveres with herself, eternally scouring the same ground, *elle tourne en rond* [she spins in circles], and she remains the center of the circle. The center not simply of vanity, but nevertheless of a tentative surrender, in the looking back, the self-contemplation, the will to

[1] The wife of a French doctor who became a believer again after her death and entered the Dominicans when he was sixty. Cf. Elisabeth Leseur, *Journal et pensées de chaque jour,* ed. R. P. Janvier, O.P. (Paris: Félix Leseur, 1917).

make herself an instrument that works well. The instrument can never be properly employed because it is constantly being newly hewn, washed, and polished. The moment of employment keeps slipping by. What would be needed for this moment is something she is unable to manage. She trains with those around her, with her guests, the people she encounters; she contemplates them and deliberates what effect she might be able to have, but she never disappears in a way that would make the Lord's activity possible. A person who has healthy legs would not manage to walk in this case, because there is apparently no one in a position to show him that his legs are really instruments for walking. Thus, her prayer lacks the drive, just as her life lacks the conception of a mission, which, if it is present at all, has a silhouette that is difficult to make out. She continues praying, but without anything happening, because she is actually too afraid to let anything happen.

There would in fact be a mission there, but she never takes hold of it. From the moment she begins to have some sense of its presence, she prepares herself for a manifestation that, however, cannot emerge, because she sets her eyes, not on the mission, but rather on herself. Not on the Lord, but on his instrument. Thus, it is a *circulus vitiosus*, without exit. The shortcoming lies primarily in her guidance, but she is also to some extent at fault: she constantly pays attention to what might be said about her, and, even in God's presence, she contemplates herself and not him.

PÉGUY (1873–1914)

I see his mission and his prayer. His prayer is uneven. At times, he prays like a little child, perfectly surrendered, carried along by the words that make up the vocal prayer familiar to him, simple-hearted and at peace. Then suddenly he no longer sees anything, and he prays in a sort of despair. His trust has abandoned him; the words have lost their meaning; prayer as such has been robbed of its content. And he gropes forward, like one who goes through swimming motions on dry land, confused why he is not moving forward. Until he realizes that the supporting medium is missing, that is, that he has alienated himself, fallen into ideas that are difficult to reconcile with God's presence, that he has constructed a life that at times is not pure enough, that he demands things of those around him or even of God he has no business demanding, that he sets his eyes on paths that bring him into temptation and that are not his paths. Then, the trek back is difficult for him to make, because he sees the responsibility that he has in the meantime taken upon himself, and he no longer feels up to this responsibility. But he once again encounters grace and once again becomes a child who can pray and who takes joy in praying. Grace occasionally plays funny games with him, which you can see in his writings. He speaks and writes words of grace, of fullness, of knowledge, and of love in a genuine inspiration, the first fruit of which is that it carries him back into the childlike simplicity of prayer. His mission runs straighter than his prayer: even during those times in which he prays with difficulty or even not at all, he does not lose his knowledge about his mission and the responsibility he has for it before God. But there is no more striking proof of his mission than the conversion to prayer by the word he writes. In his internal struggles, which first acquire their proper interiority the moment he measures his path in the alienation from God, he can count only on God to show him the way back. Very often he distances himself already in the features of an idea that inspires him, the idea of a utopia, of a plan, whose difficulties he is perhaps aware of, but which attracts him precisely because of the difficulties and on account of the peculiarity of the insight. And before he has tested it in God's presence, before he has received in prayer the certainty of having made the correct choice, he gets lost. He lacks in part the discernment of spirits, and that is why insight becomes difficult for him. He begins things in good faith, which however cannot be brought to an end in good faith, because a person who has been sent can follow only the path God has shown to him. It can be that he sometimes confuses a certain enthusiasm, a desire to accompany others or to let them go on ahead, with the true interiority of others and with God's pointing finger. Nevertheless, the fewer the days there are left to him, the deeper grows his knowledge of God, the greater his surrender becomes. He is carried by prayer, but also by his work, to which he ultimately desired to give no other content but the fullness of the Word.

JOHN XXIII (1881–1963)

I see him at prayer. It is a childlike prayer. He would have been talented enough, and also knowledgeable enough, to pray like an adult, let us say, like an educated Christian. But he has deliberately maintained the childlike form. He is afraid of any form of superiority that could separate him from the Catholic people. He has also preserved his childlike faith; there were times in his youth when he looked upon precisely this, his faith, with critical eyes and asked himself whether all the propositions of the Creed struck him as credible. But he did not want to pursue these questions any further, because he had resolved to believe, and indeed to believe in a way that was close to the people, in relation to whom he could act in the *sensus Christi* on the people closer to or more distant from him.

When he became a bit of a *bonhomme* over time, that is the result of the position he took. It helped him to retain his whole humor. He tries to do good everywhere; to keep nothing for himself, to share with open hands whatever he has, whatever graces, truths of faith, or goods happened to fall to him. He is altogether without guile and without arrogance; he has no ambition. As one ecclesial honor after another fell to him, it was not entirely easy to keep himself free of every ambition. He seemed to himself like a sort of game, the rules of which made him curious, the winning of which appeared to him worth striving for. Even this was not without humor; it is as if he encountered something funny and wanted to play along. But the little stirrings of pride, when he felt like he had made something of himself, he always fought against in a manly way.

He prayed a lot, in a pious manner; he kept at bay everything that held him back from prayer. He loved his neighbor, how he was, and tried to be for the people the priest and the bishop they expected. In an altogether Pauline way, he wanted to be all things to all men, in a genuine, not a feigned, availability. He always wanted to understand and to help. And when he was tired or when he slept, then he always stayed close to the center, from which he did not want to stray. When the inspiration for the Council came, it seemed to him at first perhaps like a game; but he made up his mind to play this game all the way through and to meet the demands he saw placed upon himself as the Council founder. To be sure, he did not anticipate all of the difficulties, but he made a sincere effort.

When he then came to realize that he would not live to see the end of the Council, he simultaneously thanked God that he took this trial away from him and felt nevertheless very moved that he could not help and supervise and truly intervene all the way to the end, there where it seemed necessary to him.

In all his administrating he was good, and he really wanted to be the pope for everyone. And this was due, not at all to a desire for fame, but rather to a willing desire to help.

His journals? They are certainly not the most profound; they arose for him out of a need to give an account of himself, to mark points where it was necessary to correct himself, to establish the facts in such a way that they remained a lesson to him, even in his later years.

I see his prayer, which is something whole, into which he casts every-thing, all that he is and all he possesses. He possesses his judgment, his understanding, and his burning love for God, with a certain pride, but he also has his fits of rage, about all the things that are not the way they ought to be, though they do not get any better on account of his rage. Nevertheless, there is nothing else he can do, because for him his fits of rage are warning signs that serve to keep him from falling asleep. Instead, he has to point out in a careful way, in the highest righteousness and without letting up, what has become unjust and lukewarm and evil and indifferent. He feels possessed by God, truly a kind of possession, because it shakes him, and he must con-stantly give more and is never permitted to lay his head anywhere to rest. His external life, with all his changing situations, is in fact only a weak reflection of what transpires in his soul, and his writings and speeches are only a symbol for his prayer. For he drags people and things into his prayer, whatever has been achieved and what still has to be achieved, he drags it into his prayer in a sort of storm, and he echoes a storm with people and with God, and his prayer is this booming storm. But because he truly loves God and loves his saints and loves the Church, he would like to do everything for God that lies in his power. In doing so he constantly runs up against the limits of this power, the limitations of his abilities; he runs up against the limits of what is humanly possible in others, in the lukewarm and in the nay-sayers. He is unable to transplant himself into another person in order to give that person what he has. But in God's saints, he sees what they have suffered and desires in humility to be content and grateful, not only for his insight but also for his destiny. But his gratitude is shot through with ingratitude. He cannot be sufficiently grateful and persevere in gratitude because the "But!" that lies within him arises and defends itself. And thus it is rare that he ends a prayer in peace, for his entire prayer is almost always a struggle with God, often even a struggle against God, who permits this and that and lowers the bar because of man's imbecility. But then he begins again to make things better, he begins in humility; he regrets his obsti-nance and begs God to change him in such a way that he will be pleasing to him. But the inexorable "But!" never goes away, and it starts all over again. And then there are days when he grows tired and almost despairs that he cannot do any better. Nevertheless, this "not being able to do better" remains for him precisely the sign of his mission, the most personal response God has to give to him.

Whether he grows is difficult to say, because he passes through *trans-figurations* in his youth and later and again at the end, transfigurations that are never, however, for him the ultimate. Perhaps they were what was most worthy to be sought, but he always threw them away again and again, because he is unable to achieve any peace in his mission and indeed does not want any. The growth is perhaps clearest in the final months, when he knows he is already lost. Nevertheless, there were similar stages earlier as well.

MARIE–ANTOINETTE DE GEUSER
(CONSUMMATA) (1889–1918)

I see her good, pious prayer, but also a certain hindrance to complete surrender, which sneaks into her prayer, because limits are set to this prayer and this surrender from the outside. And, indeed, one first needs to draw a distinction between the limits that her health sets and the limits that the priests set, insofar as they overestimate the necessity of her task at home. She is born for contemplative life. She not only likes to contemplate, she does it well, for the decisive impulse does not come from her joy or her enjoyment of contemplation. Her contemplation is obedience. At times, she does it with extreme pleasure, but then it becomes again more difficult for her, since the impossibility of complete surrender (which she was not equipped to achieve, but which she knew, before God, she should have achieved) erects obstacles in her, most clearly in contemplation itself, where they constantly let their presence be known and draw attention to themselves. Outside of contemplation, she is somehow able to forget these detriments and immediately obtain surrender, insofar as she errs on the side of excess in what she does for those around her. In this, she attempts primarily to show them, through her disposition, the joy of being Christian.

She has a clear knowledge of the obstacles present. But she is not independent enough to make room for God's voice in opposition to those around her. She knows she has been called to enter Carmel, and she knows this best in God's presence; there it is solidified and true. But when she is together with her people, in the tiny tasks of everyday life, that which was solid liquefies again. Then she thinks it was an error; she follows her confessor, the people who advise her, not with a bad conscience, but with a secret fear that takes on a new form in prayer.

Perhaps it ultimately makes no difference one way or the other whether she entered or not; the fear would have remained even in Carmel, only it would have taken a different form and would then have become more fruitful. In Marie-Antoinette one sees a person who is overburdened by an immediate call when the Christian people around her are the sort who indeed praise total surrender but do not allow it in practice. The health reasons, which were not entirely without significance, were given too much weight and were used in an impure way to give support to the desires of those around her. This does not mean that the Carmel would necessarily have accepted her if her state of health had been accurately described. It simply means that she did not attain in this way to an ultimate transparency and clarity, because she herself was also a little too weak. One ought not to infer, however, that she was at fault for these weaknesses; one can suppose that they were permitted in order that others could see more compellingly what it would mean to leave all things behind.

Her childlikeness, her purity and love, her equanimity, which shows character, are exceptionally great and lead her more and more to God. She is Christian in a very unified way, and she never makes herself important. There is a great grace in the fact that she is not deterred by the obstacles and warnings that are placed in her path, but rather she meets the challenges in spite of everything, although the ultimate implications of her calling could not be followed out. A complete immersion both in joy and suffering as well as in knowledge thus remains difficult; a veil hangs over her; the ultimate contours do not come to light. At the time when she knows she is called and desires to enter the convent, and during the time when she does not yet see the obstacles, she has an incredible fullness of insights and inspirations, which later fade, because their radiance falls on her in a slightly oblique way. If she had been turned away from the cloister for perfectly objective reasons, then the veil and the restlessness would not have been there. The difficult thing for her is the fact that she is praised for something that is not entirely genuine. Hence the *mièvrerie* [preciousness] that is stamped on her from the outside, because she does not dare to plunge into the depths of the choice, of the decision, out of fear of disobedience. She cannot distinguish very well between what is a convention of her milieu and what is a necessity. The objection is not a serious one, but it explains why the scope of her radiance was not greater.

JOSEFA MENENDEZ (1890–1923)[1]

I see her prayer, which God, so to speak, takes over from her, while she gives herself and prays in an attitude of the greatest surrender. And

[1] A lay sister with the Dames du Sacré-Coeur. Cf. *Un Appel à l'Amour: Le message du Coeur de Jésus au monde et sa messagère Sr. Josefa Menendez*, ed. P. H. Monier-Vinard, S.J., and P. F. Charmot, S.J. (Toulouse, 1944).

this prayer, which contains everything that makes up her life, which is like a recapitulation of everything that happens and a testing of all these events in God's presence, an examination of conscience, a reception of God's instructions, so that everything is perfectly purified for him: this prayer changes with time, as the ordinary and small things slowly disappear into the realm of great love and she herself casts forth light toward God like a burning torch, immediately out of the love that God brings forth to her. And now the prayer becomes like a storm: it sweeps over her, over everything that was hers and not perfect, so that only what is worthy of God would be left behind. It is not reflections that purify her prayer, not the practice of virtue that brings her gradually to this purity, but it is God's grace, which burns and cleans and leads forth and carries away. This prayer is her ideal and rest, and out of it grows what she must do: her prayer must be as God expects it; it must radiate in the way God wishes; it must help in the way people require.

But in addition to this there is a sort of anxiety, which nearly takes the form of scruples. There are whole periods in which she feels herself to be so unworthy, in which she becomes so hesitant, so full of doubt—not about God's existence, not about the claim he has on her life, but about the way she responds. She is anxious that she entered the cloister out of pride, that she maintains her constant resolution to be pure out of pride, anxious that she is living too much closed up in God, that she accepts all the graces he gives her, the visions and voices she receives, in an all too personal sense, so that she now doubts their reality. On the one hand, she is convinced that everything is true, that she must remain in obedience, in order to please God. Indeed, even more: she does not *raise* the question of whether she pleases God in order that she might be even more obedient. On the other hand, she suddenly becomes anxious that she is exaggerating or that, by means of a power that is no longer a human power (neither is it the power of her sisters in the cloister nor that of her confessor), she sneaked in through a kind of training that perhaps makes real prayer impossible. She worries that her visions are figments of her imagination, that her voices are the sound of her own heart, that her prayer is a prayer full of pride. And now she attempts to take a step backward, in the midst of this anxiety, and here she plunges into the anxiety of the Cross, which is different from the initial anxiety. She shares the burden of human sin, the burden of the lukewarmness of the religious Orders, the burden of botched religious life, the burden of the Church as a whole. In this suffering, her images grow blurry, as it were; her entire prayer life up until now seems to her just a matter of feeling; she thinks she has put too much emphasis on experience, on seeing, on the subjective, and left too little place for God to place her where he himself chooses. But then the ardor and the simplicity and the life in God's childhood comes back to her, each time at a higher degree, as if God turned the screw of his hold on her one revolution tighter. And she sees the demand; she hears and experiences it ever more strongly, and even the words she uses to convey it have become better, purer, more detached, and she unveils God's pure gift from within their inner life. And thus she is at peace, without having sought it, and this calm suddenly comes over her, and she can pray further and continue to obey God, in order to encounter the Cross once again. But even when she is one who accompanies the Cross, and even when she is plagued by the doubts mentioned above concerning her righteousness, she remains at prayer. And indeed she prays as she is led, not only by her voices—as occurs primarily in the periods of ardor—but by God in such a strict discipleship that she is no longer able even to choose the words of her vocal prayer, but receives the content as a task given to her, along with everything she feels and says and hears and with the ways she is always brought back into the zeal of the days of light.

Her mission is one of renewal [*Belebung*]. Even in those times in which she participates a bit in the wasting of time at the Sacré-Coeur, she is meant to give new life to the pure mission, the joy in belonging to God. The fact that the language she uses to articulate things is closely bound to her Order does not affect their veracity in the least.

EDITH STEIN (TERESA BENEDICTA OF THE CROSS)
(1891–1942)

I see her groping, wonder-filled prayer, which in the beginning resembles a conversation she is conducting with herself and is very *managed*. It is half like a question she puts to herself without knowing exactly what she means; it may be that the step she takes does not need to be completed by her; the question does not need to be perfectly articulated; perhaps God would be able to intervene in the middle of her step, in order to make his presence known and answer her question in a much more profound way than she herself would have expected or even would have been capable of expecting. And God truly answers. She prays more and more and finally receives a victorious certainty and rejoices. From this moment of victorious certainty on, everything is perfectly simple and unambiguous. She will follow the path God shows to her; she belongs to him; she has rediscovered her childlike cheerfulness, which has increased and become clearly manifest through love and faith. It would be altogether false to infer that her philosophical knowledge helps her to struggle through to faith. That has an incidental role. There are certain things she must revise that provide stepping stones to the faith she has acquired, but she does not need to confuse them; she also does not need to test every definition and every formula in order to build a foundation for faith to a certain extent on the basis of philosophy.

Faith lays upon her the very conscious obligation to put her faults in order, to attend to a certain kind of holiness, and to keep it alive in herself; holiness stands before her as an unconditional demand, not in the sense of a personal mission, but rather in the sense of a gratitude toward God, who has called her. She attends to this holiness in order to receive, as it were, the senses that are needed in God's company, in order to allow herself to be formed by him in such a way that he can bear her presence. She prays a lot and enjoys it, and she becomes ever more humble and transparent. It is no sacrifice for her, not even an intellectual sacrifice, to renounce her previous vocation and to become what God requires of her.

Carmel represents for her obedience and poverty, contemplative life in anonymity, engagement in the Church, wherever this engagement is needed; it very powerfully represents the multiplication of the Church's treasury of prayer, an abode where one thinks only of God and lives only for him, where the personal element allows itself to be effaced, so that his Person may be alive and radiant.

Philosophizing means a lot less to her in the cloister than one might think; she is externally compelled to do it; she does her philosophical work in an obedience that she herself did not choose and in fact would not have chosen. And it makes her happy to think and to write; she is independent and well-trained, so that this task is easier for her than other external activities, and, indeed, she would like to carry out the task in the sense that she might thereby be able to awaken an awareness for religious questions among certain thinkers. But one could not say that this was her mission. Her mission is the *preference* of religious life over successes and battles and the noise in the world. But the external circumstances cover up in a certain sense this core of her mission. For her, it is not about an escape from human things; it is about an ultimate escape to God, the ultimate decision to live for him alone.

Martyrdom becomes the crowning of this mission; it becomes the entry into an even greater anonymity, as the bearing of Christ's presence into the ultimate place of suffering. And nevertheless it is almost as if the primary emphasis of her mission lay on her entry into the monastery rather than on her martyrdom.

THERESE VON KONNERSREUTH (1898–1964)

I see her ... with some difficulty. I see a peculiar life. A youthful striving after holiness, which means an effort to be good, to be Christian, in the striving to correspond entirely to the Lord's will. And an effort at prayer. And suddenly there is, as it were, a great deflection. She is praised and esteemed; she is taken seriously. In this sense: people think this is something she has been *given*; that she is good because she is not capable of being bad, that she desires the good because the bad is unbearable to her. She wants to follow in the Lord's footsteps because that is where perfection lies for her. Thus, already in her early years, people present her with an image of herself that is not far from being the image of "a saint". She is perhaps still too young really to be horrified. But she possesses a certain peasant cleverness, which plants in her the thought of corresponding to the adults' expectations. To act as if what they thought were the reality. To correspond to an image that for her is more the image of a good child than that of holiness and perfection. From this moment on, she is no longer able to give herself over to the provocations of evil, whatever they might be.

The role flatters her. The fact that it is a role is something she becomes aware of fairly early on; she does not want the good for the good's sake; she wants to be praised. She does not want to disappoint the parish priest. She wants the approval of the adults. Gradually, the human element enters more and more into her efforts; first, she owes it to others to be the person they hope she will be; later it is her own fault that she is unable to remove herself from the role. And half-consciously, half-unconsciously, she perseveres down the path of this presumed holiness, but she counts it bitter, because now really quite a lot of what she believed and sought as a child slips away from her. She is the person on this earth who points to heaven, who experiences things that other people do not experience, who has access to mysteries that are hidden from people. She herself becomes a symbol, but what lies behind this symbol becomes increasingly empty; her faith grows weaker and weaker; and if she corresponds to the image other people have of her, there is nevertheless no obedience in this, no genuine humility that outweighs the ego. An ego for which the people are admittedly responsible but that fits her, into which she slides in order to stay inside. This ego gets built up: more and more details accrue to it—they gild it, so to speak—that do not belong to her.

Had she at the right time received proper instruction, she would have remained a good, simple woman. Her parents have misgivings; they and the whole family thus become suspicious of her. Her own impatience, everything in her that has to do with original sin and other sin, is kept in reserve for her family. In this, she does not see that what she presents to the rest of the world becomes more and more a false image. She no longer sees the distortion, the role-playing aspect of her behavior. She thinks she is experiencing something, but what she is experiencing is ultimately just play-acting. A play-acting that seemed to be harmless for years and that perhaps even provoked the community and the broader surroundings to faith. She becomes a means of stirring faith in people, who find the ordinariness in the Church, community, and Christianity to be too little.

The bodily phenomena that she manifests are not proper. It is difficult to say whether they are entirely false, but in any event they are false for the most part. Therese is not humble enough to experience the things she displays. She counteracts genuine faith above all by dividing people into two groups: those who believe in her are the true believers; the others are one and all heretics. She also does not want her own case to be tested, for example, by doctors. She has certain capacities, which she allows to develop: she can go a long time without showing signs of kidney activity or digestion; she can fast for great stretches; she has a talent for hysteria, which allows her to produce the sorts of hemorrhages one usually finds only in the saints, and so on. Much of this rests on careful, often deliberate, but often also half-conscious practice. This falsifies her attitude in prayer, the way she stands before God. She becomes an actress. As a peasant woman, endowed with an average intelligence, she does not worry so much about this; she lets it lie there, in between knowledge and ignorance. Moreover, there is no way back, for she would have to let something go; she would no longer be the famous little Therese [Resl]; she would return to her earlier simple faith, and thus the chasm between the old and the new would be too great and too unbelievable. She has become proud and arrogant and now has to live out her conceit. Which does not exclude the fact that a certain goodness, a certain sharing in the fate of others, and a certain availability remain intact. She is perhaps in the end only a victim of the things that have befallen her and of her striving after the extraordinary. What is genuine in her is her first childhood and whatever has survived of it somehow unsullied, for example, the Our Father and her little children's prayers. No one asked her, for example, to pray the Our Father like a "saint", and thus this prayer retained something of the joy of faith she had when she was a child.

However, when she is given the task to pray for someone else's concern or for particular people, for a community, she becomes inauthentic, because then she places herself and her fame in the center of her prayer and requires the expectations of other people as a sort of stage.

She has only a few Aramaic words at her disposal; she overheard them once and always asked about them afterward here and there. She was clever enough to hold onto them for years before uttering them.

The parish priest believed in this, but there were times when he doubted and asked himself, and her, some questions. She knew how to ignore the meaning of his questions and to sway him to certainty, leaving his image of her intact.

SECOND SERIES

Portraits, most of which include answers to questions

I see him at prayer. He prays in such a way that, in every word and in every vision of his prayer, the Lord, the one he loves as friend, the one who is God, always stands in the center. This love provides his nourishment; it draws him up into divine love, and his love is transformed. Whenever he begins to pray, he wants to adore, to give thanks, and to make his petitions; he hands himself over; he offers himself up; he makes the whole of himself available. But the moment he begins, he is so seized by divine love that he no longer needs to do anything else: he is taken up; the Lord accepts his offer; and his sacrifice is confirmed. He no longer needs to make an effort; he no longer needs to will anything: God's will and his love fill him entirely. Everything becomes love, unity, and grace alone. And it seems to him that God needs exactly this prayer, that the Son was waiting for this in order to fill another with love, to give to another the complete gift of his grace. He is never so happy as when he is in this prayer, since grace enables him to share himself with everyone who is waiting for it.

(*And what is his love for the Mother of God like?*) He loves the Mother through the Son. He loves her initially because she is the one who, as the bearer of the Son, gave him the gift of this love. Then he loves her in a personal way and ever more strongly, and since the Lord ultimately gives his Mother to him on the Cross, the entire responsibility of divine love, from which he has learned so much in his love for the Lord and in his relationship to him, enters into his relationship to his Mother. Now he receives the Mother from the Son, just as he had received the Son from the Mother, and through the Mother he becomes newly aware how the whole Christian love radiates outward so eucharistically, how people can be entrusted to one another so that they love divine love more, that they grow in it and accomplish the Father's will in it. Such an accomplishment of God's task will never find satiety, however; their love will never find satiety among themselves alone, but their reciprocal love will want to share itself further in a constant superabundance. And thus Mary leads John to understand what was not so clear to him beforehand: that all generations will call both of them blessed and that everything they do together, everything they represent and are, will live on through generations, and that they are roots, founders, that through their Christian love they will possess not only an eternity in heaven, but are also meant to fulfill the ages on the earth, that they may not die; they have a task, which endures and remains until the end of the world and until the Son's return.

(*And when he is alone later?*) That changes nothing. He lives in the same love for the Mother and for the Lord, and his entire life is pure, divine, perfect love.

PAUL

I see his prayer. It is a little agitated, busy. Even a tiny bit forced. Strange, it is as if there were two people there praying, as if he were in contemplation but had taken the active Paul in there with him, so that the active Paul would not budge from his side and would have the contemplative Paul constantly introduce him to God ...

(*And his ecstasy?*) He is taken up, carried away into ecstasy. But this is then entirely objective. There is nothing "ecstatic" about it, if you mean by that a sort of enthusiasm. However restless his prayer otherwise may be, his ecstasies are completely peaceful. He is henceforth a mere instrument; as long as revelation is shown to him, there is henceforward nothing but mission and obedience. Here he possesses his most quiet contemplation.

(*What is shown to him?*) Heaven and the mysteries of heaven. He sees in his visions more and more the connections of the heavenly world, the connections between the Father, Son, and Spirit, and above all the connections between eternity and temporality.

(*What is the mystery he talks about?*) It is the mystery of obedience, that is, the mystery of there being one will in God. Maybe the best way to put it is: the mystery of unity in God in general, between Father, Son, and Spirit. It is as if he were permitted a glimpse into this mystery of unity as the *ultimate* mystery of God, so to speak, even into the ultimate mystery of the Triunity, there where only the one nature was visible, the one nature was so one that the distinction between the Persons did not come into view.

(*And when he is caught up into paradise?*) Then he sees the mysteries of paradise, which are at the same time the mysteries of heaven, the mysteries of the unity of God's creation, before it divides into two because of sin: heaven and earth.

(*What does he refer to as the seventh heaven?*) The unity between heaven and earth, but above all the unity of the Father, the resolution of all things in the Father, the primal mystery itself of the unity of God.

(*And why "seven" exactly?*) On account of the gifts of the Holy Spirit. But it is the place where nothing has yet been distinguished, where all seven are included in the highest, in the divine gift itself.

(*Is his vision different from John's?*) Yes. It is more goal-oriented, more bound to purpose, and also more active. It is more based on a formula of response.

(*But he says he is unable to express what he has seen?*) You have to distinguish. He receives the vision as a part of his mission; it serves to lend a greater importance to his words and his performance. Here they would thus have their goal in him himself. But he also discovers the more Johannine element of contemplation in his vision; and that is something he is not able to translate into his mission; it seems to him to be something that lies beyond his mission, something he cannot grasp in his mission. Thus he is also unable to put it into words.

(*And when he says: in the body or outside of the body?*) "In the body" is everything that is connected somehow with his mission, everything that can be translated, everything related to his task. "Outside of the body" means beyond his mission, as it were, beyond his personal activity, in a sort of communion of saints, which cannot be translated, in a surging toward the Father, which cannot be expressed in any description.

(*Has he always had visions?*) The most expressive came at the beginning, but he also has genuine visions later. The first were the most expressive, which clarified to him the content, the scope of his mission.

(*Does he also receive his theology from his visions?*) Yes, to a great extent.

(*What was the vision of the Lord in the temple like?*) Very similar to the vision in Damascus. Especially because the effect was the same: to be sure, the vision of Damascus was a conversion, but the one in the temple contains such an expansion of his mission, it is almost like a conversion. The effective consequences of the vision have more or less the same significance ...

STEPHEN

I see him at prayer. He prays in a completely transparent way, close to God and childlike and without any questions. The gift of faith is for him such a grace that he never forgets it. Almost as if believing and breathing were, for him, one and the same. He never needs to examine his faith, to test or weigh it: it is simply his. But he does not possess it like a rich man who has a treasure to protect; rather, it is like a person who gives, who constantly offers his treasure to his fellowmen and to God. When he learns something new in his faith, when he comes to an insight, he always takes it to be an expansion, a confirmation, which has given him *grace* and in relation to which he has no questions to ask. He accepts it, feels enriched by it, but not personally for his own sake; instead, it is for the sake of others and at the same time for the sake of making the Son's mission on earth visible.

(*What does the Church mean to him?*) The Church is for him the visible thing the Lord has left behind among men on earth. She is the Lord's work, the expression of the Lord among men, but also man's gift to the Bridegroom. He moves within the Church, just as he moves in faith and in prayer: among nothing but precious gifts.

(*And the disputation?*) When he disputes, he sees in his opponents much less sinners than those with a mission, who would have to be brought over by the Lord's grace, who have not yet grasped their mission. But when he is compelled to use harsh words, he speaks them as if they were "on loan", as if they had sprung from a mission that finds its key in heaven. When he has to do battle in order to bring others to faith, it is for him always like the time when his task stood before his eyes for a moment in heaven, and thus he can faithfully abide. For in himself he is pure goodness.

(*His martyrdom?*) It is hardly a problem for him, because he has given his life to God once and for all, and God has disposal over his body and his life, without his being able to do anything else but consent.

POLYCARP (d. 155)

He prays. He prays a prayer that is much greater than he can comprehend with his thoughts ... It is not an extravagant prayer, but a prayer that addresses itself to the whole triune God and enters into the whole of love and is seized by the whole of love. A prayer that grows quietly within him and comes to be and rejoices like a song and that fills all things. And he is nourished by this prayer, and many of the people close to him are nourished by this prayer. He is a little like St. Francis, when he includes both the tiniest thing and the greatest in his prayer and does not make distinctions between stages or ranks, does not separate the essential from the inessential, because he leaves all the measuring to God. And there is no contradiction between his life and his prayer. He is not so ... clever, not very well educated, and yet his prayer is somehow clever and educated, because he takes his entire humility, his entire being, his entire love, and he simply lays it out before God and hands it over to him. When he has prayed, he is not only spiritually refreshed, but his mind is full of new insights.

(*What is his relationship to other people?*) He loves people, but he loves them because of the Lord's instruction; he meditates constantly on this commandment; he loves people not only from his own resources, man to man; his love always also has the Lord as its object. It also serves to fulfill the word of the Lord, so that it never runs the danger of becoming selfish.

(*And his martyrdom?*) You have to distinguish different periods of time. Once he knows that his martyrdom is something that has been decided, he becomes frightened, but not in fact for himself. Rather, his fear is that he will not be able to serve God properly in his martyrdom, fear that he could begin to think of himself, to become weak at the last moment; he could say no, internally, or cry out ... And yet at the same time there is nothing he longs for so dearly as martyrdom, at least from the moment he sees there is no longer any way out. Now he begs God that he can approach martyrdom the way God requires of him. And that God might receive this martyrdom as a sign of his love for him. His martyrdom is itself a prayer.

(*What is his relationship to John like?*) He admires him. In love, he is completely his disciple. But there are differences. When John experienced the apocalypse, he was expanded by it, and he began to think at a deeper and more conscious level and, at the same time, to grasp the triune God more methodically. It would be possible on the basis of the apocalypse to sketch out a clear image of the Triunity, as John understood it. Polycarp, by contrast, understands very little in the end. For him, everything flows into love, without it taking on clear shape. He allows himself to be expanded by love, without his knowledge thereby being deepened in the sense of increased knowledge. It becomes deeper in the dimension of obedience.

(*Did he know John?*) Yes.

JUSTIN (d. 166)

He is not simple. He constantly stands within a tension between action and contemplation, between receiving and giving, between understanding and letting go. In itself, action is not very important to him. He would like to lead a peaceful life of prayer. He experiences such joy in prayer that he would like to remain in it: to stand before God, to hear every wisdom immediately from him, to receive everything God gives to his people. But that is not his path. He recognizes this quite perceptively, because he no longer manages his work well after a long time in prayer, and—as he clearly understands—he no longer fulfills the task God intended for him. And this is the case not only because when he prays for a long time he loses time for work, but because he thus falls into a sluggishness of spirit. At the beginning of his prayer, he grasps everything God shows him; toward the end, he loses the alertness and the readiness of spirit and is no longer able to grasp the significance of God's word, which ought to benefit his work. Thus, he once again attempts to pray less, to give up the joy of prayer, in order to avoid falling into that indulgent sluggishness, and thus the time of his contemplation, properly speaking, becomes brief. But the action, the open battle, like the work of writing, go against his grain; he must force himself to do it. He does so, because God so clearly asks him to. Nevertheless, when he has discussed things for a long time, when he has spent a long time thinking and formulating, his prayer turns into a prayer of exhaustion, in which he feels no refreshment. Which makes things really difficult for him. It is always as if his action spoiled his contemplation, and vice versa.

(*And the Church?*) He loves her. He loves her with a slight *agacement* (exasperation), but he does love her, for he knows that loving the Church is a task given by the Lord. He also knows he has to deny himself in loving the Church and to do things that do not suit him.

(*What bothers him about the Church?*) Apparently, at this period of time people wanted to give many things a settled form too quickly, things that happen to occur to people and they take to be true and, thus, establish as valid for the future. By contrast, he would prefer a Church that remained in a constant, living process of becoming, that retained her flexibility.

(*And other people?*) He loves them. When they share his opinion and his faith, then he loves them with an extraordinary humility. His love is humble in general, in spite of the polemical positions he constantly has to take.

CLEMENT OF ALEXANDRIA (150–217)

His disposition in God's presence is pure and good. He loves God and attempts to do his will. In small things, it is somehow very easy for him. When things become more difficult, he gives himself unbelievable pains trying to gain clarity. He worries about following himself rather than God and, to a certain extent, about inventing his own rules rather than working out God's rules. He is indefatigable in his striving to do God's will. In his prayer, too, he often asks for clarity. He has the feeling that it is absolutely crucial that he be clear. And, to be sure, this clarity lies less in the decisions he has to make as in his entire disposition toward God. He does not want to tolerate anything standing between him and God. He knows quite clearly that he can often go astray in his decisions, that he can occasionally do things that might not appear smart and good in God's eyes. But that is less important than that his most interior relationship to God be wholly in order.

He always stays right in the center in his prayer and, likewise, in his fulfillment of God's will.

(*And his scholarship?*) It is a great concern to him, because he sees in it the possibility of apostolic activity and of offering something. It is very important to him to have something to offer, and he believes that he is able to offer more in his scholarship than elsewhere, that he can *interest* people and through this interest lead them into love. Then he also worries that without exact scholarship, man's relationship to God would become blurry and that God could fade away in this vagueness.

(*And he also loves people?*) He loves God and loves others through God.

(*Does he have any ambition?*) No.

(*Is his image of the perfectly wise man not presumptuous?*) He is not presumptuous. It seems to him that nothing is good enough for God. Of course, he can be wrong about many things and get lost in the maze. But his relationship to God is not damaged by the fact that he follows complex paths. His intention is always good.

TERTULLIAN (160–220)

He loves God, but in a peculiar way. He would like to abstract from himself, but he cannot manage to. He believes he has to stand in the foremost place, as it were, in God's presence. When, in prayer, he feels he is able to encounter God or to be encountered by him, then he leaves something of himself, as it were, in this place, and then the further encounter with God effects a sort of espousal with him ... But the first steps of his prayer are always a self-willed, forced seeking, as if his faith lacked the necessary durability. He always counts on *discreet* prayers in order to draw near to God, not on the constant state of intimacy. He has moments in which God is completely foreign to him. And nevertheless God is the content of his life, his study, his thoughts, and his writing.

(*And the Church?*) His relationship to her goes through the same variations as his relationship to God. When he presents himself[1] to God as an individual, in a laborious way, suffering, making efforts, striving to overcome himself, and at the same time charging against surmountable obstacles, then he presents himself also at the same time to the Church; for, in many things, the Church and God form a unity for him, there where the Church is precisely wedded with God, where

---

[1] [The German reads "wenn er sie Gott vorstellt", that is, when he presents *her* (the Church) to God, but it seems more likely that *sich*, "himself", is meant.—TRANS.]

God is so much occupied with his Church that one can no longer separate them, so that a person cannot have one without accepting the other. And then he once again falls away, because at some point he meets himself again; he becomes important once again to himself and seeks himself again. (*A. sighs deeply.*) Then the Church becomes a stranger to him; he sees only her faults anymore, her inadequacies, and it is for him as if a harlot had sneaked into the Lord's chamber in place of the proper bride. And then he hates the Church, and even Christ becomes alien to him, because he allows such a thing. And then he pushes the whole thing away and tries to start over again, to see everything in a new way.

(*And other people?*) In relation to people, he is a person who takes an interest in them rather than one who loves. He immediately analyzes people; he moves them like chess pieces into his plans. He wants them to be perfect, in a perfect service and obedience to God. There are moments when he is the inspirational leader and displays a sort of perfect obedience. He then has to withdraw to a certain extent in order to keep from betraying the fact that he cannot sustain this gesture. And because he is never able to free himself completely from pride and self-love, these remain only moments. He falls back into himself.

(*After she awakens, A. is very tired; she feels, as it were, intellectually overworked and has a bad headache. She says:* it is like when you have put on a shoe that is too tight, and you can hardly get your foot in ...)

HIPPOLYTUS OF ROME (d. 235)

He loves God passionately. He wants to serve him; he offers himself; he wants to do everything God wills; and he would like to bring God to the world. He wants to bring about a sort of communion among men through his person, so that everyone who comes into contact with him would perceive something of the Lord.

(*Mary?*) He reveres her. But his relationship with her fluctuates. He tries again and again to reach the *pure* triune God, and in the interim there are times when he needs a mediator. And also the Mother. But there are also times when everything seems to him to get in the way; he would like to stand alone before God, and he would like for every believer to share in the same possibility, the possibility of being grasped immediately by God.

(*His prayer?*) He has different ways of praying. Just as he is ultimately disparate, impetuous, and rather unpredictable, so is his prayer. But even his peaceful prayer, even the prayer when he waits upon the inspirations God gives, is, with him, a prayer of passionate love.

(*And the Church?*) Yes ... he sees the Church in different ways. On occasion he sees her absolutely as the friend of God, the path that leads to God. But then again he gets stuck on the human element; he loses sight of her holiness and cannot believe that the Church, as she exists, is the one and only Bride of Christ. He always has the feeling that there was some mix-up. The Church, as he experiences her, in his view has no doubt received certain rules and forms from the real Church but, for everything else, has substituted her own sins, her own ambition, and her own desire to have things otherwise.

(*And he himself is not ambitious?*) Not in relation to the Church. In relation to God, he certainly is. He would like to be the one who approaches God in the most perfect way a man can approach God.

(*Does he love?*) He loves God.

(*And people?*) ... He would love them, if they were the way he wanted them to be. But he has a clear vision of their weaknesses and their hesitations, and that fills him with a displeasure, which eclipses his love, although that love is doubtless still present.

CYPRIAN (d. 258)

A peculiar prayer. It is as if he constantly wanted to mark out separate sections or parts, let us say three. Perhaps it is not always three, but in general we can say it is. One part is completely in order. Here he is indeed surrendered, in complete obedience, ready to do the whole of God's will. Then there is a second part, which is unclear. And he is quite ready to have God clarify this unclear part. He would like to receive clarity from God, and he makes an offering of himself, to do the whole of God's will, once he has recognized it. But then there is always another part, which he reserves for himself to a certain extent. Since he has his own opinion, and God ought to adjust himself as far as it is feasible to this opinion and ought to remain within the framework of what he desires. Here he says to God: "It is not possible that you think otherwise than I do. You only have to show me the way to let my intentions be realized! It has to turn out the way I have envisioned it myself, for in the end I have only arranged things with the understanding you gave to me. What am I to do other than make use of a gift that you personally gave to me?" Remarkably, it never occurs to him that this third part that he sets aside for himself encroaches upon the other two. He therefore also fails to grow in this relationship.

(*And how does he see the Church?*) Very much as a function of his own thoughts. In part, in a fine way; just as she really is and ought to be. In part a bit abstruse, wherever *he* is the one who determines how she has to be, where the third part of his prayer exerts an influence.

(*What is this abstruse image?*) He is very strongly tempted to construct an earthly Church, which would have to be ordered to a certain extent *solely* according to human reason and which God would then have to put up with, because he has given man an understanding fashioned in this particular way.

(*His love of neighbor?*) It is true that he loves people. He is a bit pitiless for those who are truly sinners, and, on the other hand, he charms his friends. On the whole, he loves people. But it is not his most outstanding quality.

(*Asceticism?*) Yes. Everything with a very personal stamp.

PACHOMIUS (d. 346)

He prays in a loving and fulfilling way; he is full of hope that he will be permitted to love forever, that his love will be fruitful, that God truly needs him. He takes people into his prayer; it is as though he did not want to end up standing before God by himself. He always takes people with him, those for whom he has intentions, but always also a few people unknown to him. And then he asks God to allow his love to be fruitful and also to make the love of those he takes into prayer with him fruitful, both those he knows and those he does not. When he takes strangers into prayer with him, then he knows: God knows them; God can choose them; God himself had placed them in his prayer. He also takes people into his contemplation as well as into his petitionary prayer. When he then learns something from God or sees something, he does not want to be the only one who learns and sees, and that is why he takes others in with him. And when he finds himself wholly penetrated by the rays of God's love, when he thus receives life and warmth and becomes more capable of obedience, then he would also like to give a share of all this to those he has brought with him, so that they might all feel God's presence and its effects.

(*And the people?*) He has a very loving attitude toward people; he is humble, peaceful, ready to help, open. He loves them so much that he renounces all the love he receives from them so that he can give it to God. He uses the dependence people have on him to encourage their dependence on God.

(*And his work?*) His work, his monastery, have grown out of his love for God. The goal he wishes to achieve in connection with his fellowmen is that they would be able to lead the same life he does, a life in God. He would like to help them, to serve them, to take away their fear of solitude, so that they might find the courage to begin, in order afterward to take upon themselves a new solitude in community.

ANTONY OF EGYPT (251–356)

He prays with an extraordinary love, a precious love. (*She smiles.*) With a love that undergoes a change during his prayer, as if this love took on a constantly new form over the course of the prayer, as if at the beginning of prayer Antony were there with his love, and afterward only God with his own words, with everything that belonged to God, as if Antony disappeared within his prayer, as if only love in love were left over and there were nothing that could present an obstacle to this love.

(*And other people in this prayer?*) He loves them and never loses sight of his apostolate. Even when he withdraws a great distance, he nevertheless never forgets that he takes people and their concerns and sins with him; he remains aware that his withdrawing, his being alone with God, is not an ultimate solitude but is being there for people and for God, and he asks God to accept the prayer of others in him and through him. He burns with a most holy love for God, but love for other people is contained in this love.

(*And his temptations?*) They are produced by his love. The devil takes a shot at him, but Antony emerges from this victorious, not with his own love, but with God's love.

(*What sort of temptations does he have to undergo?*) Temptations in the flesh, temptations in faith, temptations in love. In the temptations he faces, he is very similar to the Curé of Ars, just as they are generally related in a lot of things: in their love for people and also in the way they are able to see through people, and if the Curé listens to people especially in confession, Antony listens to them in a sort of totality and sees through them in their totality and brings them in their totality into God's presence.

(*Does he have visions?*) Yes. (*What sort?*) The primary thing is that he *sees*. He hears very little, but he sees a lot. And there are moments, especially in prayer, when all his words converge into a sort of vision, and everything God wants to teach him is shown to him in a visible way. They are visions that strengthen him in faith and unveil for him the mysteries of heaven. They are not prophetic visions, nor are they visions of mission in a broader sense. He is one of the greatest flames in the Church.

He loves God. He searches for his will the way a person might search for a pearl; praying is an inner necessity for him. He prays a lot, and he prays indeed with the desire that God might allow him more and more to fulfill his will, but he does this tangibly not for his own sake but for God. He is nothing in his own eyes but an instrument in God's hands; he desires to do nothing but what God wishes to have from him. And although his desire is his total personal concern, he treats it as though it were an absolutely objective desire. In a sense, he does not think about himself, his comfort, or his own possibility of obeying. He simply wills to be taken up without remainder by God's will, so that God might have in him as far as possible a person who follows him. Even in his homilies and writings, he seeks to reveal this beloved will of God everywhere, so that people might love him and follow him. He is not absolutely naïve, that is, he is familiar with evil; he suffers because of it; he is personally vulnerable, sensitive; but this is all the more why he earnestly tries to be wholly objective.

(*And his priests?*) He loves them; he respects them; he is like a father to them and sees them as people who have been sent by God. They represent for him people who fulfill God's will with him; they are like living signs of the living God. He would like to lead them more and more to fulfill God's will, just as the Son fulfilled it, so that God might see them as brothers of his Son and so that they themselves might experience more and more that God is their Father, just as he is Christ's Father.

MARTIN OF TOURS (316–400)

His soul is childlike and good and has something so immediately genuine about it, above all something so unspoiled, it is as if he had preserved the faith he had as a child, as if he had never had any bad experiences at all in his life. To be sure, he has experience with sin; he knows how bad people are, but he sees them so much in the light of the Lord's offer of grace that grace is more visible to him than sin is, and he is moved more profoundly by grace than by the possibility of sin. He is like the child in the fairytale who can see only the good fairies and overlooks everything threatening. Like a child who wants to share everything with others and does not even consider the possibility that someone might refuse his offer to share. Like a child who plays around with someone, tells him stories, and is certain his stories will delight his hearer as much as they delighted him. Thus, he brings all his concerns before God with the awareness that God will hear them. And God constantly hears him, because Christ regards him as one of the little ones whom he invites and calls to himself. He cannot turn down a single request of his. His prayer is good and full of love, and he does not have to lead himself into prayer or be led; his entire life is prayer. His vocal prayer and his contemplation are only sections of this life, which as a whole is a prayer. When he pauses in his work and prays, then it is as if he wanted to rest for a bit and gather a few directions for the next section of life. Even his work in the Church is a labor of love, of love for God and for his neighbor. He occasionally suffers because of the Church, but almost in an impersonal way, that is, not in the sense that certain particular occasions cause it, but from the outset within the Lord's suffering. And he always imagines that the Lord suffers much more from the thing than Martin himself suffers at the moment.

(*And what is his death like?*) I see anxieties regarding death. And afterward, in the midst of dying, perfect surrender. Perhaps it is also the case that these anxieties in part are a substitute for the anxieties of which he otherwise had so little experience in his life.

SIMEON STYLITES (d. 459)

He is quite remarkable, that is for sure ... he is good; he prays with great love. But he spends a large part of his love, as it were, in order simply to be able to remain on the pillar. In the beginning, there is a sort of training for this pillar. Later, he becomes so accustomed to it that it would be a penance for him to come down. In fact, that would have been the proper moment to leave it. Initially, the whole thing had something forced about it; toward the end, something easy, practically self-evident, which runs counter to the difficulty of the sacrifice. He himself is unaware of this. He is too convinced that he ought to serve God in precisely this way. On the other hand, he has no one who could break the matter down a bit for him.

(*Did he have any guidance at all?*) Yes, before he climbed up the pillar. Afterward, not. And then he succumbs to precisely that danger to which almost everyone succumbs who lacks guidance. Then it is almost as if the thing itself, the standing, were more important than God's will and, in any event, were the only proper thing.

(*Was it a call from God?*) It was indeed a call from God. Absolutely.

(*Is he still able to love other people?*) With time, they begin to disappear from his field of vision. They are like far off creatures, perhaps even like far off angels; he no longer remembers exactly what human beings were; he sees them truly a little the way a person sees angels.

(*And his prayer?*) It is great; but it is too much pervaded by what *he* is doing. There are moments when there is something like a self-evaluation with God in prayer, he measures perseverance against perseverance, service against service, love against love . . .

(*Does he have some sense of apostolate?*) In the beginning, he certainly does. At that time he wanted to have an apostolic effect from the pillar. As time passes, though, he finally forgets it . . . But one ought not to hold it against him, because his intentions are so good and because he really has no one who could have guided his love onto more human tracks.

LEO THE GREAT (d. 461)

His prayer is . . . full of anxiety and full of love at the same time. And the love is great and glorious, and the anxiety is small and personal. In the same prayer there is an enormous back and forth swing. He is worried about remaining the person he was before he became pope; he is worried that he may have become pope through a misunderstanding, that he is hardly sufficient for normal priesthood and was only chosen to be pope through a chain of unbelievable circumstances. He is anxious about having to represent the epitome of Christianity and not being himself a good Christian. He has a constant anxiety about doing something that would be against God, something that could seriously damage his Church. He has a sort of personal pusillanimity, about which he never spoke openly, which he experienced from his youth on but which became more pronounced than ever once he became pope.

And at the same time he has a wealth of love and humility. And each prayer is an approach of God's glory and his perfection. But then something occurs to him: "It is too beautiful! . . . And I cannot be the person who has to embody all this in the name of the Church, so that the priests and the believers receive instructions from this person and see him as the one whom the Lord placed before them." He is courageous when it has to do with action. God bears him then, insofar as he knows his own weaknesses and confesses them again and again to God and sees his anxiety as the sign of his weakness. His weakness is not exactly humility; rather it is an enlargement of his faults in this petty anxiety. His external courage, in his homilies and instructions and deeds, stands in stark contradiction to his innate timidity and cowardice. Even his contemplation is constantly interrupted by his glance falling back to himself in his fear.

(*And his relation to people?*) He loves them, but he is a little afraid of them. He lives in the constant fear that people will see through him and that he will thus damage his office; he always thinks he possesses something that has to be kept hidden.

(*Why is he called "the Great"?*) He is great in everything he does for the Church. And he can do it because he truly loves. The other thing is only an accompanying weakness. And because, even when he constantly turns back to himself, he at least nevertheless always goes beyond himself.

PATRICK (d. 461)

His prayer is very close to God. It is completely one with his being and with every moment of his life. His times of prayer are like moments of rest that a traveler takes, in which he simply stands still for a moment in order to see where he is and then continues on. It is not very different from the times when he ostensibly is not praying. He has many periods of time that are devoted to pure prayer, but the other times of his daily life are in fact also times of prayer. His entire life is *one whole* prayer. And this prayer is very pure, almost angelic; it finds its way immediately to God and is fulfilled and carries this fulfillment also into the outside world. What he brings to people is nothing other than his prayer, and when he reflects on his tasks or otherwise on some other problem, whatever it might be, all of this is always prayer. It is as if he were to sit constantly together with God and arrange all his affairs with him.

(*What does he see in this prayer?*) That is difficult to describe. It is not really something one can grasp. Every time he enters into such an intimacy with God that he is always filled to overflowing again and again by him, but what he receives is not very different from what he already possessed. He is like a plaything in God's hands that constantly has to be wound up. And he always gets wound up again before he has run down; thus, he has no experience of weariness.

(*And his penance?*) He regards his life as something God has given to him *in order that* he might always have something to bring to him. But also the sufferings and the self-denials he takes upon himself never enable his inner life to change. In the acts of penance he carries out, it is as if spirit and body stood over and against each other in a reciprocal challenge. And everything has significance for others, as much the penances of his body as the consolations of his spirit. He wants nothing for himself. He loves other people, for they are the creatures of his God. And when they do not believe, he pities them terribly; he has infinite compassion for them.

(*And his external prayer practices?*) They are what prevent him from losing himself in prayer. He needs them in a sense as navigational aids.

In fact, he also needs this body and this tiredness and this other position, and so forth, in order constantly to stand before God in a sort of attitude of sacrifice. This also corresponds to his character. Both the quality as well as the quantity of his prayer would be exaggerated for anyone else and not something that could be imitated. But it is apparently just right for him. He also would not be stubborn if someone could reasonably show him that God expected something different; he would grasp it immediately and adapt himself.

MAXIMUS THE CONFESSOR (580–662)

I see him at prayer. He asks God to purify him. He sees a great task lying before him, and he does not feel the strength to carry it out. He believes he lacks this strength because his faith is too small, because he is not pure enough. He has firmly resolved to attempt everything God asks of him, and he believes God's will is absolutely determined. He believes that what he has to do cannot be done by anyone else, because God has given this task to him personally and not to anyone else, because God has chosen him, and it would be a genuine disappointment for God (and for him, Maximus, the occasion for the most profound human disappointment) if he were to fail. In this situation, it is as if he considered his relationship to the Church something secondary, that is, something that completely flowed out of his relationship to God. He has to get things in order with God so that the Church can receive something from him. And he cannot get things in order with God if God does not purify him himself for his task. He wants to be rid of absolutely anything that would prevent him from doing everything God demands of him. It occurs to him, however, that his will may run ahead of his capacity. He is already willing to do what he needs to do. Whether he will also be capable of doing it, that is something that depends on his being purified by God. This is his opinion: the fact that he is determined is a small beginning, and God will then bring about his intention either with him or against him; he will have his will achieved in an actual deed. Maximus has to present himself to God as a shell. Everything that is demanded of him in this prayer is that he open the shell and remain in the place near God that is intended for him. And that he not recoil in horror if the divine procedure is painful. That is how I see him in his prayer.

(*Did he also have visions?*) Yes.

(*What sort?*) That is hard to describe, because they are like instruments.

(*What does that mean?*) They are tools with a meaning that has to be discovered. He prays: "I am weak; you are my strength", and in the same moment he sees the weapons that come from God and express God's strength ... And he sees them as offered to him by God ... His visions lie at the same time inside his theology. They often give him the precise expressions, the analogies, he needs, but also the certainty and the promise. The fact that he sees the tools of God's power gives him a wholly different conviction in comparison to the sentence he believes and understands: "I am weak; you are my strength."

(*What is his martyrdom like?*) It is handed over, like his prayer. He attempts in his martyrdom to be the way God wishes him to be, not to shrink from his presence and to receive martyrdom as the ultimate purification that God gives to him in his grace.

(*What is his piety like?*) It changes. Christ, the Trinity ... Like Ignatius, he has times when he occupies himself more with one thing and then again with something else. Moreover, his theological work and his piety always form a unity. If he is dealing with questions about the Trinity, then he prays in a more trinitarian way; if he deals with questions about the Incarnation, then the Lord takes a more prominent place in his prayer. If he is describing some virtue, then he attempts to practice it and to beg for it in prayer.

(*What is the relationship between action and contemplation in him?*) Contemplation stands in a sense in the service of his theological work. He has little time for pure contemplation. Also, the visions are for him like an indication, a recollection, of his contemplation. If he had more time for contemplation, or if he could give himself over more deeply to it, then he believes his visions also would have become more independent. He would indeed like to enter into it, but because contemplation involves a long process for him, the time to stop always comes before he gets very deeply into it.

BONIFACE (675–754)

His prayer is quick, penetrating. He prays the way a person swims: he jumps in headfirst, and then he prays and prays and prays, to a certain extent without seeing the other shore. It is as if God himself had to give him the sign: now the shore is here, and there is the earth under your feet; now it is time to continue on by foot, my son. It is as if God himself were a stopwatch, because he, for his part, would never know when to end. In the beginning, he throws himself in; he leaves everything behind that would burden him, the world and its sin and the completely ordinary air and atmosphere. Then there is an allowing himself to be taken up into God's prayer, into his heavenly air, into his will, which grows visible. He is fashioned anew in this prayer, as it were; he is newly filled with powers and ideas and newly bound to divine obedience and equipped for the coming tasks. And he is unburdened of all that could not be achieved, of all that lies behind him once and for all. Many of the things he sees as holding his fellowmen back—their sins, their unwillingness—are laid bare for him in prayer. God desires to present even his neighbor anew to him in prayer, to inspire him with insights into how to encounter people and how he can make this water, through which one has to swim, desirable to them.

(*And his apostolate?*) It is nourished by his prayer, it is filled by it and flows immediately from it. It would be a burden to him if he could not find the strength and the confirmation for his apostolate in prayer. He is not a man of action by nature. He is actually a contemplative with certain massive interruptions in the middle of his contemplation.

(*And his neighbor?*) That is difficult to sum up in a word ... He loves him, because he wants to follow God's commandment, he wants to do it all the way, and nevertheless his neighbor goes, so to speak, against his grain in this love. It would be nicer to be alone with God and not let himself be irritated by these troublesome people. And nevertheless it is right for him to have precisely *these* neighbors: he has to win them for God, and he cannot win them in any other way than by bringing them the divine love that he has to make into his own love.

MEINRAD (d. 861)

He prays in a very solitary manner, and prays well, because his entire prayer is supported from first to last by his faith. And in a very solitary manner, because he has to present himself before God at the outset of his prayer, as it were, in complete nakedness and solitude, as though he would be able to stand before God as a representative of the world only if he completely forgot himself. He not only has to sever the ties that bind him to the world, but he has to forget the world itself that he represents in order to be able to represent it. This is a complete adventure every time. It is as if God demanded of him that he take off all his clothes ... and yet, on the other hand, he nevertheless had these clothes on again, and he was not naked ... and the world clothes him, and he is not alone. It is just that he has to feel *as though* he were naked and *as though* he were alone when he accompanies the world and actually keeps his clothes on. He has to forget. And this forgetting implies that he must, so to speak, take the world *into himself* and keep it enclosed within his inward being, so much so that no memory of the external world remains left over in any sense. It is only when he has finished his prayer that he finds the external world again. He then finds the world that he abandoned out of love for the Lord, so that the Lord might find a better entry into it, with his help, or even without him.

In prayer, he experiences an incredible intimacy with God—he draws close to him, to his concerns, and to the Church. It is an objective recognition of God and his demands.

(*Does he also have visions?*) Yes.

(*And what is he like outside of prayer?*) More complicated than inside prayer, more worried. He has adopted something in his being that feels Franciscan but is something he has just adopted. He has trouble comporting himself in this way; by nature he has a fiery temper.

(*Does he think of himself as being the start of something?*) There are moments when he does. But more often he sees himself as an end. The end of many things that he wanted. And he is constantly worried that an end is coming; that the Church and prayer will no longer be able to hold out, that God will turn away once and for all from the world that does not want him, and that the world will turn away from the God it does not want to have any more to do with . . .

(*After awaking:*) *A. had a hard time doing this saint. She says:* It was like a thick or dried-out layer of skin. *She could not penetrate him, as it were; the shape of their souls was too different; she compares it to an encounter with a person whom one thinks is nice enough in himself but with whom one scarcely has any point of contact.*

SIMEON THE NEW THEOLOGIAN (d. 1022)

It is as if the approaching ecstasy always drove him into prayer. Like when a person is hungry and this tells him that the time for eating is here, so he recognizes a sort of pre-ecstasy, which pushes him into prayer. No matter how irregular its arrival, it announces the time for prayer. In this pre-ecstasy, he is restless and searching; it is always for him a period of time when it seems as though he did not know what it was he was looking for. He knows that the restlessness comes from God and leads him to God, and yet an uncertainty comes over him, as though he had no idea what he was looking for or what he had to find. As though he were helpless. As though this restlessness were not the sign that God was expecting him. Suddenly it becomes clear to him: it is time for prayer. Then he begins to pray, with words and thoughts that suit him, in peaceful security. He gives an account to the Father, and immediately the Father's answer comes; he is taken up into the whirlwind of ecstasy; he sees, he hears, he feels, he obeys, he is carried away; he thereby loses every contact with what has gone before, with the ordinary, with the surrounding world. And nevertheless he is charged with a mission to the world, and the world acquires a new aspect, that of being the object of his mission.

He learns many things about God's power and glory and light; he learns it in such a way that he at first must let it simply pass through him. His initial prayer was like a confession; it gave him the capacity to receive as much as God wanted to allot to him. Then he allows himself to sink ever deeper into ecstasy. He is from this point on only obedient. In this obedience, God's power and grandeur take possession of him, as it were. And most often the ecstasy quite suddenly comes to an end, and he finds himself standing there, unsteady on his earthly feet. Everything he experienced swims around his head, and he sets to work translating everything.

(*And is he successful in this translation?*) It is almost successful, not completely, because he was too badly shaken up, and he suffers from the aftereffects of this disturbance and likewise has trouble recovering a calm balance.

(*And what does his mission to the world consist in?*) To convey new images of God's love. To be a witness to God's eternal life. To bring this life out of dusty storage bins.

(*Does he have experience of love, of substitution?*) He knows both. He knows love because he experiences it many times a day and is indeed shaken by his experience. And he knows substitution, because it is the price of love and because he experiences in his body and in his soul the mission to suffer in compassion. This compassion is both a compassion for all the people in whom Christ lives, as well as a compassion for Christ, in whom once again all people are represented.

(*What is his relationship to ecstasy?*) He seeks it, but only when he is driven by pre-ecstasy. And this is indeed the right way, the way God wills it. He seeks ecstasy because he has to seek it, with a certain reluctance, because ecstasy is also in some ways very painful and exhausting for him. And he tries to bridge over his reluctance through a readiness that may be a bit exaggerated, a readiness that bears certain signs of self-will.

(*And what significance does confession have for him?*) He does not see the office; he sees it too much in a personal sense, as an I-Thou relationship. He is so much caught up in his own light, he is influenced so much by his own disturbances, that he does not grasp the objectivity of the office.

(*He is able to obey in spite of this?*) It is not his strongest feature ... but his more essential mission lies really in a direct experience of God's light and power, his immediate presence in every moment.

234

I see how he prays and how he frets while in prayer. He prays in close proximity to the Cross. He prays in such a way that he sees how the Son suffers; he does not see it in a vision; he sees it in his own prayer. He prays in the suffering Son, who reveals himself in this prayer, and the more deeply he prays to him, the more he himself feels the Son's suffering overcome his own and take hold of him. On the basis of this suffering, he begins to understand why the three years of Jesus' action led again into a contemplation of suffering. Why the contemplation of the thirty years bridges over the three years of action in order then to continue in the Passion. Thus he understands that there are believers who have to devote themselves totally to contemplation, a contemplation that does not exclude suffering, perhaps is even built on suffering, aims at suffering, leads through suffering. In any event, they accept suffering as a constitutive element of contemplation. And insofar as he prays thus in suffering and understands thus in suffering, the idea of his foundation grows in him.

(*And can he carry it through?*) Everything presents difficulties. But he accepts the difficulties as a part of suffering. It is worth noting that he understands this suffering outside of prayer differently from the way he understands it inside prayer, that the power of understanding in non-prayer, however, stems from the power of understanding in prayer. In prayer, his suffering is always a part of the Lord's suffering. Outside of prayer, he grasps it in a much more practical, limited, human, and manageable way.

(*What is his relationship to people like?*) It is true that he loves them. But he remains a little distant. He has a little trouble interacting with people who do not share his aspirations. Even when he interacts with his like-minded fellows, he always feels a distance. He would like to bring them into the same strength of prayer that he himself possesses. But that is hard to do.

(*Does he have someone to guide him?*) No. He has friends with whom he discusses a lot of things. But he does not have guidance in the strict sense. Nevertheless, he is led by God in his prayer along very strict lines, and indeed by the suffering God.

(*And his mysticism?*) It is in order. Only, it costs him a lot to separate himself from ecstasy. The ecstasy comes to an end when his prayer does, when his time for prayer is over, and it is always painful for him to return to ordinary life afterward.

(*What is the nature of his ecstasies?*) They are above all ecstatic states. He feels himself led to a place where God reveals himself to him in another way than he does in normal life. He is encircled by some mystery of God, which is then suddenly transposed into his own center and compels him from this center to some consequence: to more asceticism in his life, a stricter time of prayer, more obedience ...

(*Does he have visions?*) A bit. He feels more than he sees.

(*And did he understand obedience?*) Yes.

ELIZABETH OF SCHÖNAU (d. 1165)

(*Do you see the Elizabeth of Schönau?*) Yes.

(*What is her prayer like?*) (*A. sighs.*) I do not see any real prayer ...

(*Then what do you see?*) (*A. sighs.*) I see a sort of restlessness, a sort ... of preoccupation with thoughts about holiness. She elicits things from herself. Like a sort of quiet time, during which a person assesses himself and makes plans.

(*And visions?*) I do not see any visions; I see a sort of continuation of this preoccupation ... (*A. becomes restless.*) ... Like when a person entertains something in his imagination and in fact envisions it more in the outcome than in the act itself.

(*Does she have love for God?*) I see only ... love for herself.

(*And for her neighbor?*) I do not see any love. I see only busyness.

(*Her relationship to priests, to spiritual directors?*) It is part of this busyness. It is as if she were possessed by a single idea, which everything else had to serve.

(*And what is that idea?*) Self-love.

HILDEGARD (1098–1179)

I see her in prayer. It is a very powerful prayer. She expends in fact an enormous amount of energy to pray. In this, it is difficult to say how much she throws herself in and how much she is drawn into it. But she has a powerful drive. The longer her prayer lasts, the more she is drawn into it and the more peaceful she becomes. She has a peculiar way of looking at things: She is convinced that if she did not throw herself into it with all her might, the Lord would have too much difficulty drawing her in.

When she throws herself in in this way, she leaves her whole sinful ego behind her; it is as if she stepped out of her last layer of skin in order to present herself to God in complete nakedness. This skin is a mixture of sin, of dependence on the earth, and of worldly ballast, from which she would like to free herself, and she gets free of it in prayer only with the most extreme effort. She throws herself in almost like a person who is stumbling, a person who has struggled through barbed wire and falls head first into freedom. Her feet were tangled up in a net, and now, since she managed to get them free, she needs the last of her strength, as it were, not to take the step into freedom, but to let it occur by leaping and plunging into it.

The moment the step occurs, she becomes completely calm. In ecstasy, she is peace itself, waiting for what will be shown to her and demanding nothing.

(*And she takes it all in?*) With the means that are at her disposal. With her intelligence and her acquired faculties.

(*Even in the vision itself?*) Yes, even in the vision itself. After she has taken the image in during her ecstasy, she begins consciously to translate it.

(*And does she do so correctly?*) That is part of her mission.

(*And her infused Latin?*) It is correct.

(*And the other things she claims to have been inspired in her?*) They are correct. Of course, they were inspired and acquired at the same time. She possesses an incredible memory. She retains everything she has seen and heard. But the very things she acquires are also given to her again always anew by God and expanded.

(*Does she dictate from memory or in ecstasy?*) Both.

(*And does she remember things correctly?*) Not everything. But when she afterward sees what she dictated, then she recalls things again and fills in the gaps. These supplements are not false, because what she had dictated during her ecstasy was often too condensed.

(*And what is the purpose of her whole cosmology?*) She believes she has to lay it out. Many things were shown to her that go in this direction, and she believes she has to ground it to a certain extent scientifically, to give the whole a scientific appearance, so that it will have an impact on the unbelievers who have the knowledge.

THOMAS BECKET (1117–1170)

... He is difficult to describe ...

(*What is his prayer like?*) It is here and there childlike, naïve, spontaneous, the expression of a need, a striving after God, a seeking that is very important to him ... (*She sighs.*) And when he then comes out of prayer, he is sometimes completely radiant with the experience he had in prayer. But it is often the case that he is unable to bring the experience of prayer into harmony, so to speak, with the experience of the time afterward. Then it is as if his faith faltered. Before, everything was so simple and close and warm and good, and now everything is cold and alien and repulsive. And when this mood of being rejected and living in coldness gets the upper hand, then he has to force himself to pray; he does it out of a need for order in relation to God, because of a sort of rule. His prayer sounds like something forced. He takes the coldness with him into prayer and thus becomes himself so cold that he is no longer able to feel God's warmth. Then he reckons with God. His prayer turns into a strangely led conversation, in which the partners do not understand one another and do not want to understand and cannot find harmony, because neither will budge from his position. And thus the alienation after prayer becomes even greater than before. Often it is a friend's word that gives him the occasion to find his way back to God, some sort of encouragement from outside; then he feels like he is loved again and dives back into it.

(*And the Church?*) He can scarcely bring the Church, such as he experiences her, into harmony with the Church as she ought to be. But at the same time he decides once and for all to see the Church as she ought to be, and he tries to refer everything back to this "way the Church ought to be", to love her and to defend and serve her.

In his childlike prayer, he is honest; in the other one he is not. He is constantly pulled back and forth between honesty and dishonesty. But he is above all arrogant. And only love can disarm his arrogance. Nevertheless, he constantly makes what one might call a demand of God: God ought to show him (he owes it to him), through the love and respect of others, that he is loved.

(*And what does his full mission consist in?*) God wanted to make a saint out of him, who was above all to act in the Church of his age in the way suited for that particular time. He was supposed to be a sort of counter movement; he should have undertaken a purification of the Church, above all on the basis of his position. He should have been an island: an island of courage, of firm belief, of conviction, which perseveres in its work. And in part this is just what he did. But he was also partly unable to do this because of his arrogance, which always interfered. Thus, he fell into entangled relationships, which his moments of arrogance had some responsibility for bringing about.

ANTONY OF PADUA (1195–1231)

He prays with a lot of love, and he takes other people into his prayer with him. He expects a fruit from his prayer that he can then bring back to the people. He does not want to hold onto a single thing for himself. All the words that he brings to people, all his sermons, consolations, and encouragements, he draws from his prayer. He allows himself to be led completely by his prayer, allows everything to ripen in it that he has to carry out apostoloically. His love for God is childlike, simple, without reservation; he does not want to hide anything, and whenever he realizes that he did not entirely correspond in a certain point or did not hand everything over to the very end, then he is incredibly ardent in presenting everything to God and apologizing to God for having hesitated for so long and asking God to make him so that God can use him to bring to completion everything he has at his disposal.

(*Visions?*) He does have some, but for the most part it is more feeling than seeing, more knowing than hearing; it is a being guided by God. If he does something that does not absolutely please God, then he feels it immediately. He lives in a perfect harmony with God.

(*And his relationship to Francis?*) It is the relationship a son has to his father. He tries to love all things in the same way Francis loved them; he sees Francis as the model of perfect human love. And his poverty, his simplicity, and his primitiveness attract him.

(*His writing?*) He tries to let God guide him and inspire him.

(*Why is it often so abstruse?*) Because writing is not his gift. He writes only with reluctance. He is at bottom too simple to be able to write. Twenty sentences would be enough for him to complete his entire apostolate.

(*And the visions with the Child Jesus?*) Yes, all of that is proper.

BONAVENTURE (1221–1274)

I see him at prayer. It is a stormy prayer, suffused with love, without equilibrium, moody; he drags everything on his mind into prayer with him. But not sorted out, not reflected on and clarified beforehand, but like the way a person empties out drawers, in order to get things in order, the important things and those that are unimportant, things a person absolutely wanted to hold onto, other things he forgot about, and the things he cannot even use for anything anymore—and suddenly he finds the essential thing. Everything randomly tangled up with everything else. For it is only in prayer that he collects himself, his petitions, and his worship.

(*What does God do in this prayer?*) He shows him what is essential. Bonaventure has moments when he is ashamed at dragging so many inessential things around. But he always falls back again into the same routine.

(*And does he take his studies into prayer?*) Yes, very much so. Everything he is writing, everything he is pursuing, everything he preaches. All a bit too quickly, like a student who brings to his teacher not only his final version but also his rough draft. Nevertheless, he is filled with great love and with much humility. And suddenly he breaks out in

239

laughter in the middle of prayer when something turns out well, when God is happy. And then he becomes sad once again, when he sees he brought along so much that was unnecessary.

(*Is there any ecstasy?*) Yes, something like it ... but ecstasies that are actually only an intensification of the need for love and the experience of love in prayer.

(*Do his theories about prayer express that?*) No, because they abstract more from the man as he lives.

(*In his theories, he lays out many stages and regions.*) That is true, but he does not know these regions from his own experiences. He only thinks they could be useful: that they might prevent a person from coming to God with a heap of trash.

(*And is he able to bring his study and his prayer into unity?*) Yes, for moments at a time. A unifying thread runs through everything. Next to this there is much that is initiated but not brought to conclusion, many fragments, fits and starts. He has too strong a character; he is in certain respects insufficiently docile, too fervent.

(*His love of neighbor?*) That always tends to go astray. He loves passionately, and he passionately breaks love off. Then he tries once again to rekindle what was broken off. His character constantly gives him trouble. But he wants to love, and indeed he has become what he is through love.

(*How is he as a superior?*) Also uneven. But humble.

(*And competent?*) At times; not in everything. There is nothing a person could say he is completely. For this passionate taking up and throwing away, this disorderedness, clings to many things. But, nevertheless, in the end this is a disorder due to love, a love that simply is not sufficiently able to measure and sort.

THOMAS AQUINAS (1225–1274)

(*A. is silent for a long time.*) (*I ask: How does he pray?*) ... He kneels down ... his hands are folded ... over a book ... (*She groans.*) But when he calls to God at the start and then remains in the position of one who is calling out, then it is like a disputation with God or like a scholarly conversation with him. As if he, Thomas, were responsible for making the whole *frais de la conversation* himself [for keeping the whole conversation going himself]. He lays out theoretical problems before God; he shows him the fruit of his recent thoughts. As he stands before God, he formulates the new insights that are the most recent results of his study. But he does not let God speak. It remains a monologue. And when he suddenly experiences an uneasiness and gets the feeling that he ought to proceed differently, that he ought to wait, perhaps even stand before God in humility, and humbly receive something from him, then he abruptly leaps over this experience as if it were simply out of the question that he could really be wrong. As if he possessed, once and for all, the most adequate way of serving God, the chosen way, at least for himself. And as if the most important thing were that he never distance himself from his conceptual constructions.

(*Is there another way that he loves God?*) I do not see any. It is as if love got stuck by the busyness of thinking. As if it were taken for granted that he had once and for all settled the question of how to live for God and to serve him, as if he were always able to justify his behavior to himself, since it was accepted on the basis of this will to serve and of love for God, and he now moves within the framework of this service and has no time to lose with unnecessary considerations. He is not a Christian who daily begins anew.

(*But at the end of his life?*) When the intellectual power weakens, then something does emerge that is more like love. His meticulousness loses strength, so that a kind of goodnaturedness comes out that was basically missing beforehand.

(*He does not have any visions?*) No. He *cannot* have any.

(*And what was he like in his youth?*) There was an experience of God's intimate presence in his youth, which was objective and which he later sustained subjectively, in order thereby to justify his behavior to himself. He tries to keep something of his earlier experience alive in himself in order not to allow the growing distance to be so tangible.

(*And within his thinking?*) God is a concept for him, something to analyze, to take apart and put back together. But the Spirit, who makes this operation possible, Love, is not there. Everything remains intellectual, according to the understanding.

(*Does he love his fellowmen?*) He sees people in relation to his task. When he speaks with them, it is mostly with the hope that he might acquire something from the conversation, he might catch a word that could be incorporated in order to get a proper understanding of a notion that might otherwise have escaped him, to see an approach he might otherwise have overlooked ...

DUNS SCOTUS (1215–1308)

His prayer is tentative, but it is full of love, a love that is itself cautious and that is almost afraid of having come at an inappropriate time. He is always a little worried about inconveniencing God. But he nevertheless loves him and prays in a very loving way. And he prays a lot.

When the time he has set aside for prayer comes to an end, then he takes his prayer with him into his work. He brings prayer into work much more than he brings his work into prayer. When he mortifies himself, keeps vigil, deprives himself of sleep, skips meals, it is not in order to work more but in order to pray more. The time he saves belongs to God, but to God in prayer.

(*Mysticism?*) He *feels* God very powerfully. He feels him constantly and does not lose this feeling of God's presence even when he is at work. When he writes something, discharges a task, it all takes place inside God's tangible presence; if this feeling of presence were to come to an end, then his soul would immediately dry up and he would be incapable of writing any more. His work is constantly generated out of his prayer.

(*And other people?*) At the very beginning, he had love for his fellowmen; he always saw the good in them. The longer he lives, the more he sees how much distance there is between men and God, not because God is so great, but because people are so sinful and indifferent. Then a great struggle arises in him. (*A. suffers.*) He begins to worry that his work alienates him too much from people. Seeing this distance grow through his work causes him to suffer. On the other hand, however, it is as if seeing people's sins were necessary for his education, as if there were many things, even completely theoretical things, that he could share in only through interaction with people, as if he had to come into contact with the guilt of others in a totally concrete way, to be stained by it, in order to be able to grasp it also intellectually.

DANTE (1265–1321)

(*Do you see him praying?*) (*A. smiles.*) Yes, I do ... with him, there is little vocal prayer, but everywhere a seeking after God. Within this seeking, there is an adoration, an astonishment, and next to this astonishment, perhaps even closely connected to it, the obligation to praise, to sing, and to tell of his experiences every time in such a way that you can feel the adoration and the astonishment that lies within.

When he sees something—an evening sky, a star, a forest—and is filled with the thought that it comes from God, that it has its source in God, he experiences in himself a sort of danger. He would like to come to rest there, to become a pantheist. But then he steps back and recalls that God gave the commandment to love one's neighbor and that therefore man is more important than the rest of creation, and he turns back to human beings. He believes that he has to convey to them all the beauty he experiences, so that they can come closer to

God. He has a very clear sense of mission, and that comes to expression everywhere in his adoration. His personal relationship to God is always pervaded by this mission; when he prays, it is not so much himself as it is his work that he places before God.

(*Does he have a vision of the afterworld?*) Yes, he has a vision of it. A vision that is not visionary but is nevertheless a vision in the true sense. The vision of the afterworld appears to him in an ideal form, but it also appears experientially in his heart, in his prayer, in his intuition of God, a vision that holds him captive and in a certain sense takes possession of him, but that he has to translate in order for it to become completely accessible to the senses.

(*And the Mother of God?*) He does see her; in fact, he sees her just as God sees her: from the perspective of an ascending hierarchy of creatures. Just as he must start from man in order to attain an idea of God, so too he must start from woman in order to reach the Mother of God.

(*Does he have a love of neighbor?*) Yes, he does, but it is very strongly contained within his concept of beauty. He loves his neighbor in God, and what he loves in all things is whatever belongs to the image-character of creation as well as whatever is necessary for him in order to fulfill the commandment to love one's neighbor. He loves all the neighbors he sees as images in a spontaneous way. But an individual who is not an image for him he is able to love only by virtue of the commandment.

(*And his condemning people to hell?*) He does it in order to show more clearly the power of sin. At bottom, his hell has nothing to do with love or non-love. He damns in order to frighten.

(*So he does not hate?*) He hates sin. But he does not hate the person, the sinner.

(*Is he humble?*) Pride and humility exist side by side in him, and they grate roughly against one another. Pride takes hold of him sometimes like a temptation. There are moments in which he compares himself a bit with God in his pride. After such moments have passed, he has to laugh about it himself. First he laughs, in order then to humble himself.

CHRISTINE EBNER (d. 1365)

(*What is her love for God like?*) It is genuine and good and simple.

(*And her vision?*) It happens for the most part during prayer; every once in a while she suddenly has a vision even outside of prayer. She sees many things, and she also sees properly. But she has difficulty taking in what she sees. Her focus on what she sees immediately dissipates the moment she has to report it. She reports the things much more weakly and anxiously than she experiences them. More weakly, because the essential aspect often does not come to light, and more anxiously, because she never manages to be absolutely natural.

(*Why is that?*) Perhaps above all because she is never guided calmly enough. She knows that the visions always mean something very great, but she is unable to leave this greatness simply in God's hands. She is unable to have the knowledge of this greatness in her soul without involving herself in it; she cannot simply contemplate it as a mystery of God, which he *incidentally*, so to speak, left with her, but she thinks that this too has to be part of her account of the vision.

(*Do you mean the fact that she was chosen?*) It is not quite so simple as that. But the fact that she is not permitted to lay aside this greatness that comes to pass in her.

(*Is it her confessor who makes too much out of it?*) Not just him, but *also* him.

(*But she is correct inside the vision?*) Yes she is, and in love too. There is very little keeping her from being altogether correct. At bottom, she *is* correct, and there is very little keeping this correctness from show-ing itself everywhere.

(*Did God say and show important things to her?*) Everything the Lord says is important. There was not perhaps anything that would turn the Church over on her head. But good, useful things ... The mystery in her makes her in some sense uncertain, and thus she is also no longer, as it were, completely ready for anything. That is a consequence of her imperfect translation, the lack of peace.

RUYSBROEK (1294–1381)

He prays like a whirlwind. He is seized by prayer and, as it were, beaten and scourged by it. He is spun faster and faster, more and more breathlessly whirled into the mysteries of God. He pants; he cannot keep up; he loses his breath ... , and then suddenly he is sheer vision. And he falls back onto his feet; he prays peacefully for a moment; he prays even without energy, because he is almost at the end of his strength, for the whole thing is unbelievably demanding. But scarcely has he come to himself and thinks he is able to catch his breath a bit, scarcely has his prayer acquired certain manageable forms, and he is once again mercilessly taken up into the whirling. One vision follows another, one inspiration after another, one ecstasy after another. There are also moments in which he does not want to pray, because he is afraid of being seized again, and yet even in this fear he betrays the fact that he takes delight in it, that he cannot wait to be taken into it again. And thus these experiences are colored by his person: insofar as the ecstasies lie very much at his command, insofar as he abhors them and wishes them away and thus does not sufficiently leave their measure to God. But God himself is complete generosity in his regard. He always immediately holds the gate of ecstasy open for him, and one prayer is enough, the simplest prayer, the first words of the Our Father, to carry him through these open doors, at first very gently, and then immediately the whirlwind. And yet he keeps close to the wall when he dances in the ecstasy so that there is always a door nearby that he can open when it becomes too much for him, when he cannot go on any longer. And thus his vision loses an ultimate depth in spite of its intensity and frequency. As vision, it is completely genuine, but he adds a little too much of himself.

(*And his translation?*) The translation is in part very good and very clear, but it is also in part incoherent, in the places where the greatest depths begin, where he himself no longer gives his complete consent, where the ultimate mysteries lie, as it were, behind a veil and he does not trust himself in the ecstasy to allow himself to be whirled through the veil. Above all into the trinitarian mysteries. Therefore the vision of the Triunity, for him, is deprived of essentially new aspects. They are informative for his mode of seeing, but rather poor in insight for the mysteries that God wanted to have him see with new eyes in the ecstasy.

(*And the rest of his life?*) It is in part a proper life of penance, in part a simple life without any particular penance. In part also a sort of indulging in the visionary possibilities. He is in a certain sense always underway with his spirit.

(*Does he translate his visions correctly?*) Yes, but with a strong inclusion of his personality. He cannot leave himself out of it.

(*After she wakes up*): *A. has the impression of endless dancing figures, rolled up into many veils and garments and rolled back out of them. But the entire vision, the entire experience remains somehow too much within perceptive experiences, almost (but not entirely) within an enjoyment, a certain excitement, in which to be sure the limitations have fallen away, but still an ultimate self-control has remained, which makes it possible to call out: Enough!*

JULIAN OF NORWICH (1342–ca. 1442)

Quite often, prayer and vision form for her a single thing. Vision takes charge of her prayer and dictates her words and her states. She often sees very simple things that lead to a very simple prayer. Then she suddenly sees things that are so great and sublime and complex that the subsequent prayer taken up into this vision is scarcely intelligible anymore, even for her. Her visions embrace many things from her daily life, but also many mysteries that are barely accessible to her.

(*Is she able to express them?*) When it is simple, she can express it very well. When it becomes complicated, she is mostly able to get down the essential things. But she knows that her visions extend *farther* than the words of her prayer and her expression of them. It is for her always as if heaven descended over the earth and completely enveloped it. Thus, she is consoled, even though she does not understand everything. She knows that the life in her vision is greater than the life on earth and that this life here is embraced and supported by that one. Even when she is not able to translate everything for herself or find an expression for everything, she is content; indeed, it is a good thing when a little room is left over to play in.

(*What does she understand the best?*) Maybe love, maybe love of neighbor. And surrender, the readiness that lies within love. Also many things from the life of the Lord, which are not contained within his earthly life but are offered to us as commandments, pointings, and indicators. There are also things connected to the Mother of God . . .

(*Is she properly guided?*) Sometimes . . .

(*Is she correct on the whole?*) Yes, she is. She is very childlike in her vision. She accepts things just as they are offered to her, and she carries them around with her. She does not separate herself from her experiences, but she does not at the same time accord them an undue importance. She is humble.

BERNARDINO OF SIENA (1380–1444)

His prayer is so incredibly inspired. God always draws him into things while he is at prayer. Even when he intends to pray, now for this, and now for that reason, he is nevertheless taken over by God the moment he begins, so that prayer acquires the form God gives to it. And then in the midst of his prayer he receives insights for his activity, and in his action he is perfectly led on the basis of his prayer. He possesses the perfect certainty of being properly led. And even certainty concerning the fact that what he is now doing is precisely what God asks of him. Sometimes he does not know what decision he ought to make at the moment: whether he ought to preach at this moment and about what topic. Then he prays, and, in doing so, he becomes entirely certain and at peace. Often, through prayer, the whole course of a conversation he will have to have, with all its arguments, becomes present to him, or, on the other hand, he sees the whole of an undertaking in all its parts. He may not know the details in a material sense, but in a spiritual sense he does. God himself is at work in him when he prays. While he preaches, in his action, he follows the guiding thread he received in prayer.

(*And his fellowmen?*) He loves them, but he does so completely on the basis of prayer. He has an understanding for simple people. Whenever they close themselves off and he cannot see through them, by nature he would be inclined to become severe, dismissive, disinterested. But prayer always tempers his anger. After every prayer he is the same way he is after every confession: clean and bright, and he desires to follow what was suggested to him and to improve himself.

(*His image of God?*) More than anything else, he sees what he saw in his childhood: the goodness of the Lord. His simplicity, his human life among us, his love. That is the basic line, which he never loses. Then comes the Mother of God. And only then there are the abstractions pertaining to God: his omnipotence, his Trinity, his eternity, and so forth; even these are taken up into the simplicity. He has the powerful need always to translate what he knows into something useful, something that can be shared, and to give it to the people.

(*The Church?*) He tends to see her from the perspective of his Order, and life in the Order is for him a conformity to the Lord's laws. He would like to have every Franciscan be an immediate follower of the Lord, in an altogether primary and primitive sense, like the apostles in the earlier times, who had nothing standing between themselves and the Lord.

SAVONAROLA (1452–1498)

His prayer varies a lot. There are times when he prays like a child: very matter-of-factly, trustingly, naïvely. And then suddenly it all changes, and his prayer becomes harsh, bitter, and demanding. At bottom, he always returns to the desire for whatever God wills, and whenever he does so he collides with everything that is not good and hurts himself. And he would like to turn around precisely that which is against God. But he desires this with a sort of rage, an ultimate bitterness and narrowmindedness. And thus he hits his head against everything. This tires him out, and in this fatigue he becomes humble and begs God for forgiveness for having wanted to make these demands on him. And he begins once again to pray in simplicity and humility. But it always happens that his prayer becomes, as it were, a part of his struggle. He gets his weapons from prayer. It is almost like a dual with God, and he measures himself against God. It is only when he is exhausted that he surrenders as one defeated and acknowledges that God is the one who is right, not him. But he loves God, loves him with a fiery love. And he *knows* who God is. He knows what it means to be a Christian. And he has moments of the loftiest knowledge and the greatest intimacy.

(*Does he have revelations?*) Yes ... in a certain sense, anyway. He suddenly realizes that things are the way they are and that is all there is to it. They are like very general revelations, like general propositions, which are, as it were, suddenly directed solely at him, are shown to him, so that *he* may defend them and stand for their truth.

(*And his fellowmen?*) He loves them more the more they are believers, the closer they stand to the Lord. But once a great mercy takes hold of him, he also loves his enemies and would like to make them friends. Nevertheless, he never loves them in peace, but it is always a struggle. He loves them as people who have been entrusted to his care, people whom he is supposed to lead to God. He loves them, not with a love that seeks what is good for them as human beings, but with the sort of love that is perhaps the most intense love a human being can have: with the love that constantly seeks to enkindle its own fire by the heat of God's love.

(*And his relationship to the pope?*) I also see the two extreme points in this relationship. He wants to obey and yet has to rely on himself; he wants to rely on himself, and yet he has to obey.

(*And what is his death like?*) It costs him a bitter struggle. He is horrified when he realizes there is no way out other than death. And yet his final hours are wonderful, since he is personally led by the Lord. Since all that remains for him is personal love.

(*Is it right to say that he was proud?*) Yes, you could certainly say that.

(*How does his pride go together with his love?*) The pride lies perhaps in the moments of conversion, in the times when his struggle for humility ceases. And also in the struggle there is something that is truly proud. But the love that stands next to this pride is genuine. The pride is the human element in which he is caught up, but it is not strong enough to do any serious harm to his love.

JOHN OF GOD (1495–1550)

I see him in prayer, how he grapples with knowledge and obedience and love. Knowledge, in order to have a clearer vision of the path he must travel, because he does not want to travel blindly, but rather he wishes to follow a clearly marked-out path, since he has to make decisions all the time and needs to have his entire understanding present when he makes them. He begs for knowledge from God, a sharpening of his understanding. But he also asks for obedience; he would like to request of God the certainty that, if God shows him something, he might recognize it and, when he recognizes it, also that he might be obedient. And he asks for love. His way is a way of love. He feels that he is loving, and he—John of God—loves God and would like to offer his love out of love. But each time he undertakes something, he is troubled by the fear that he is following his own lights and forgetting his obedience to God.

And his way is a way of discipleship: he ought to take up the Son's task, which has been laid upon him, of gathering people around himself and undertaking tasks of neighborly love. He is not permitted to discharge these tasks on his own in an intellectual and theoretical sense. Rather, he knows he must love and show mercy in deed and in truth and, at the same time, be kind and obedient and, at the same time, recognize and know himself that he knows only because of God; he must decide and, in doing so, know that it is not he but God who decided, and he simply inserted himself into God's decision.

He manages to do this, but it is a constant fight. His times of prayer are like battles in which he struggles with God, the way lovers struggle with one another, but while he fights, he begs for his own defeat, as he gathers all of his strength together in order to be able to fight better and as he begs in this merciless battle that God might remain the victor and eliminate whatever stands against him.

(*And as a founder?*) He is both well and poorly suited to be a founder. Well suited, because he is obedient to God, because he strives to the end to do God's will, because he loves God with an extraordinary power of love. Poorly suited, because it is difficult for him to bear the weaknesses of others, to be the strong one among those who are weak, to deal with the mistakes of his fellowmen. He cannot, and is not permitted to, come to terms with them, but he ought to acknowledge the weakness in love and attempt to improve it in love. On the other hand, he demands from his followers immediately the same seriousness, the same surrender, the same love that inspires him and that he nevertheless considers imperfect. He demands too much at once, and thus his brothers have difficulty keeping up with him, and he has trouble forgiving them their weaknesses and hesitations. He is convinced that God demands everything from him, but he believes that God does not require any less from other people.

249

(*Is that not correct?*) It may be correct. But in order for it to remain correct, a person has to have a lot of patience. And one needs patience not only in order to bear the weaknesses of others, but also to support these people themselves, to allow them to pass through one in order better to be able to offer them to God.

(*And his relationship to the mentally ill?*) It is one of mercy and love. He sees there an area in which up to that point too little has been done by Christians. They are, in his eyes, the plagued, the misunderstood, the abandoned, just as he also sees the Lord on the Cross as one who is plagued, misunderstood, and abandoned. He constantly encounters this resemblance. And for himself he chooses the humiliation of the Cross. He understands it well: the humility of suffering, the humiliations of being misunderstood, and the discouragement that comes with abandonment.

CHARLES BORROMEO (1538–1584)

His love is good, simple, and at the same time intense. He loves God like a child, and he takes it for granted that one ought to bring everything to God. But then he has a certain system of love, which is certainly beautiful but also a bit complicated. He brings all his worries and everything that others have presented to him, everything that occupies him, and lays it before God. And he often commends it to him with vehemence. He also often simply allows it to ripen under God's gaze. And at first he leaves it to his own intuition how he ought to treat the things he has brought before God in order for God to accept them.

(*Why does he do that?*) It is his way of handing things over. It is not bad at all. On the contrary, it is so remarkably colored by his personality . . .

(*His prayer is mostly petitionary prayer?*) Very much so. Indeed, more than anything else. But in a good and broad sense. He tries not to leave any of the things that occupy him outside of God's direction. He is very consistent in this.

(*And what does his greatness consist in?*) Perhaps in the fact that he never leaves prayer, insofar as he does not want to withdraw anything from prayer and from God. At bottom, the whole of his day is a prayer. He stands very close to the Son in this attitude, in the way in which the Son stands before the Father.

(*And his love of neighbor?*) It involves a lot of struggle, but it is there. He derives it entirely from the Son, for on his own he would be rather distant, and he has to work sternly on himself in order to make room for love.

(*His reforms?*) They are very good. Truly everything is set on God. You cannot say that God is reflected with the same brilliance in all his works, but he seriously tries to let God be seen in everything.

(*His love for the Church?*) Good.

(*Does he receive particular graces in prayer?*) Yes, above all God's presence and encouragement. He feels perfectly guided by God.

(*Visions too?*) Actually, he stands on the border of vision. He knows that he stands immediately before the Thou of God and feels the heat of love that is given to him in an immediate way.

(*His penance?*) It is also very good.

CAMILLUS DE LELLIS (1550–1614)

He prays humbly and well and at length. And very slowly. Prayer is his restoration; prayer is his strength; prayer is his life. And it costs him a lot to tear himself from the exclusiveness of prayer in order to enter into active life. His prayer is an offering. He offers up himself; he offers up the whole of suffering humanity. He also worships, in a universal sort of worship in which all take part. He draws into the Spirit with him all the people he commends to God. There is very little petitionary prayer in all this; instead, there is much more general worship. Rather than saying to people, "I will pray for you", he says, "I will pray *with* you." He consecrates them into the mysteries of his God and presents them to God as his brothers who are praying along with him. He also has ecstasies, but they are once again like a sort of carrying others along with him: he is immediately transported from where he stands, so that others can take his place; he must ascend more deeply into God's mysteries so that others may enter into his previous knowledge of God.

(*His love for his fellowmen?*) It is immense. There is an excellent balance between his love of God and his love of neighbor. He loves people in order to bring them to God, and he loves God and brings him to the people.

(*And his founding?*) It is proper. He is good to the people he takes with him. For him it is always a matter of taking people *with* him. He could never imagine doing something simply by himself. He has a vivid vision of the fact that the Son is with the Father on the Cross and with the Spirit and with the whole of suffering humanity, and he sees in this something that was given to everyone and must find its continuation everywhere.

(*Why did he choose specifically those who were sick?*) Because they are sufferers. He himself experienced sickness. And he knows that the sick are especially receptive to the gospel. He is simple, well-rounded.

VINCENT DE PAUL (1576–1660)

(*What is his love for God like?*) Complicated. It is like an onion with many layers ... It is as if he were required again and again to hand himself over in his innermost core, and he was unable to summon the courage to allow the ultimate unity to be realized between this innermost core and his ordinary life. He loves God, and in God he loves the poor. But he still makes too sharp a separation. He is slightly afraid of God's burning love, and thus the poor every once in a while become a substitute for ... fire.

(*And his huge apostolate?*) It is to the poor, as I just said. Even among the like-minded he is always a little bit mixed. It is as if he had a chapel for himself, in which he encountered God but did not trust himself to tear down the walls in order to expand the chapel and allow other people into the worship, to participate in the worship. He is a little like Francis de Sales. He sort of forms a shell around himself ... security. He is afraid of the unfamiliar, of debris, ruins, crumbling walls. It is as if he constantly had to live within a determined order, an order he himself approved.

(*Humiliation?*) In God's presence, he bears it well, inside the realm of fire. In relation to other people, he bears it quite poorly, both in their presence and when it comes from them. He is like iron that has been heated to glowing on only one side.

(*And his foundations?*) They were always committed in their innermost core but ultimately did not draw enough from the fire.

(*Is this perceptible in them?*) A little bit, sure.

(*Does the founder's attitude remain so important, then, for all the time that follows?*) Yes, it does, *if* the foundations truly try to acquaint themselves with the founder's spirit and to work in this spirit and not to distance themselves more and more from it by putting up new walls and fortifications. There is in every founding a humble attitude toward the founder, which can assure stability to the foundation on the basis of the spirit and goodness that come from the founder.

(*So do founders have a great responsibility?*) Yes.

(*Or does God simply allow his grace to pass through them?*) No. They remain personalities. God does give grace through them, but they must seek and claim the personal character of their mission.

DENIS PETAU (PETAVIUS) (1583–1652)

I see his prayer. It is good and simple. What is remarkable is that he never comes into God's presence alone; he always stands before the triune God and with the entire Church. He thinks of himself so much as a person with a task that, when he prays, he always takes the Church, the religious Orders, his neighbors, and all men with him. He comes before the Lord with this whole community of people praying along with him, and the moment he stands in his presence, he sees in him also the Father and the Spirit. Because the thought of the triune God never leaves him, his prayer acquires a very universal character. Its scope is vast; even when he comes before God during his meditation with a mystery that he has selected, a particular word from the Gospel, he does not forget that the answer, the vision, the resolution of this mystery lies in the triune God. He is unable to contemplate any of the mysteries of the Son without at the same time being convinced of the truth of the Father and of the Spirit in this same mystery. He certainly makes a distinction between the three Persons in his prayer, but he sees their unity once again so clearly that he always finds all three Persons in a single mystery.

(*How does the Church fit into his prayer?*) He sees her always absolutely as the Lord's Bride, who does not trouble herself to get to know her Bridegroom enough. And he sees her as a task, not merely as an institution; he experiences her as an obligation that falls to him and to all believers, an inescapable obligation, precisely because she does not exactly demonstrate the features the Lord envisions in his bride.

(*And what does his work mean to him?*) A great joy, a joy in God. Everything he wants, everything he achieves and formulates, he sees in the great context of a mission rooted in God. Even when he is tired, when the strength leaves him, when he has trouble giving form to things, when the mystery seems opaque, he is never abandoned by a secret, inner joy. This joy, however, does not come to the surface, but it remains evident to him in the depths. It is for him an unbelievable opportunity to be allowed to be a child of God and as such to be able to sound the mysteries of the Father in his mission.

(*What significance do other people have for him?*) They often present him with hard nuts to crack. But he tries to see them as included within his divine mission. And he is grateful for the provocations they give him and also for the fact that they ultimately help him carry out his task, insofar as he is able to lead a life that is adapted to this mission. And he has a strong sense that he belongs to them; he is a believer with them; he is Church with them; he stands with them in community in a relationship to God that cannot be taken away.

His prayer is holy, fervent, pure. He actually prays without ceasing. But he does not have enough guidance. Therefore he cannot always return to normal life. His ecstasies are certainly correct, but he has no one to bring him back. The everyday world with its obligations, being a human being among others, the fulfillment of his task, the smallest action, all of this remains at a distance; it never gets inside him. He follows the good Lord in ecstasy, but it is as if God always gave the task of concluding the ecstasy to something other than him—in the form of a particular rule, a spiritual instruction, a word of encouragement in confession, and so forth. God himself does not dismiss him. And yet at the same time the man in ecstasy has to be sent away, because he lives on earth, and the call that summons him back must come from the side of the earth. Because Cupertino never hears the command to "go back", or does not hear it clearly enough, his mission remains somehow imperfect, less fruitful than it could have been.

(*The superiors do not call him back?*) No, they do nothing but watch. They are interested in the phenomenon, and in their curiosity they allow themselves to be attracted by the peculiarities and take pleasure in them, until it ceases to be appropriate. The whole thing seems like a show for them. They neglect their duties.

(*And the flying and levitation?*) It happens completely in the ecstasy. It would be less explicit, much less frequent, if there had been some success in binding him back to the earthly world. Because no one calls him back, it is as if he fulfilled only the commandment to love God and gave no attention to the commandment to love his neighbor.

(*What would his mission among people have been like?*) It would also have been a contemplative mission, of course. But he should have spent more time among people, working among them. Thus he almost does not see anyone anymore, and his earthly mission comes up short.

(*But is it not the case that God himself brings the ecstasy to an end through a mission?*) Certainly, if the mission is understood. But God can also allow the ecstasy to go on so that the confessor and spiritual director might learn something from it. So that they might recognize that even this sort of interaction with God can lead to a certain sterility, as for example the mere observation of the commandment to love one's neighbor becomes sterile if one does not make contact with God. God always desires to create situations in which both commandments are carried out.

(*Was he also taught humility?*) Yes, he was, but this humility only strengthened his ecstatic life.

Her prayer is radiant. It is full of surrender and full of ecstasy. And she suffers in prayer. It is sometimes for her as if she were no longer able to find the strength to pray. For the moment she begins to pray, her suffering starts. It is as if God made her prayer into the harshest penance. She suffers in her body and in her soul. And the essential thing in this is that her prayer is the sort of penance whose measure and extent remains entirely up to God, while she in the meantime, in the periods between prayers, practices penances that she has devised herself. And these are also proper.

(*Not exaggerated?*) Well, yes, they are . . .

(*But?*) Because they are exaggerated, they take away from her a share of the fruitfulness that she also would have had externally. She has quite a lot of visions, but they are often distorted, almost absorbed, by her penances. She then no longer has the strength to translate her visions. She is a sort of slave to her penance.

(*Why does she do this?*) Out of love for God, out of pure love. There is not a trace of self-consciousness in her, no self-love. Although it might seem like she sometimes was trying to break a record in the practice of penance, it simply is not true; it is just that she would like to give more and more and sees penance as almost the only way to do so.

(*What is the content of her visions?*) Hard to say. It is multifaceted. There is much that comes from the Lord's Cross and from his path of suffering. Much from the Church and world. Some has to do with the Mother and the saints. The whole is quite variegated. Often it is sin and God's offer of mercy.

(*Does she develop?*) That is not the right way to put it. She does die more and more to herself, though. Her visions remain more or less the same.

(*Does she know how to translate them?*) Not very well. She is also not aware that it could be important for other people.

JOHN FRANCIS REGIS (1597–1640)

His prayer is strong and good. It is a prayer that God always very quickly receives and fulfills. He recovers the whole of his strength for his deeds in this prayer. He possesses an incredible concern for individual souls, an almost boundless love for individual souls. And at the same time he always sees them in the context of their surroundings, among other souls, in the sense that one can never separate the region of one soul from that of others without always having to run up against them. He sees the coexistence, the "with" that binds one soul to another; indeed, he grasps each soul inside this "with". This increases his responsibility and his burden. He is unable to take care of an individual without seeing all the other souls at the same time, and in turn he is never able to deal with the many souls without the awareness that this multitude consists of individuals. And he suffers from their sins, from their unbelief, from their unwillingness; he suffers in such a way that much of his strength is spent in this suffering; it is swallowed up by it. Then he recovers in prayer. He bears everything like a single whole in God's presence; he casts it all at God's feet. And God lifts him up with all of his burden to himself, and he himself carries some of this burden. In such a way that when he returns to action, he can return light, peaceful, at one with himself, each time renewed by the Lord's grace as if from the bottom up. He is aware of this, but he does not abuse this possibility of restoration. When he prays while hearing confession, when he prays as he preaches, he always does so in such a way that he experiences the burden, desires to experience it, allows it to weigh upon him; it is only when he once again has the entire burden on his shoulders that he brings it once more in an almost conscious way before God, which does not mean that he otherwise constantly lays out before God everything that people lay before him.

(*And his brothers?*) Yes, he has many difficulties with them. He is respected by certain individuals, but they are in the minority. Many cause him great vexations. People doubt his methods; they even doubt his orthodoxy.

(*And what significance does Ignatius have for him?*) His relationship to him seems to me to be very clear and simple. He sees him as fiery saint, the saint who desires with the whole of his soul what the Lord desires, so that Ignatius is constantly a mediator for him. He does not know a lot about him, but what he knows gives him a lot of strength. It is as if Ignatius were giving him a hand.

(*A lot of penance?*) Yes. And occasionally the same temptation to escape as the Curé of Ars experienced, even if it is not as pronounced.

(*Does he receive consolation from people?*) Yes, if they are in God. The people who truly believe and the people who genuinely seek are a consolation to him. He has a share in their belief; he is enriched by their obedience. He experiences people in a very natural way, without much intrusion from his office ...

GRIGNON DE MONTFORT (1673–1716)

His mission lies very close to the place at which the Son becomes man. The mystery of the Incarnation forms the mystery of his mission.

But not where God the Father resolves upon the Incarnation with the Son and the Spirit, but where the Annunciation is made to the Mother, where she receives God's seed so that the Son might become man. His love for the Mother grows more and more out of this mystery; he sees the humbling of the Son, who entrusts his emerging body to the Mother's human body, gives her body power over his own, allows himself to be formed by her, grows in her, receives everything necessary for a human body from her human substance. For Grignon, our spiritual obedience to the Mother grows out of the Son of God's bodily obedience to her. If the Lord has become what all of us are, then we must stand in an obedience toward the Mother that subordinates itself to his own obedience: keeping our eyes always on *him*, we have to be obedient to *her*.

(*This means that his love for the Mother is correct?*) Yes. He possesses a love that is constantly renewed by the Son's love for her and nourished by it. It is a living, Christian love for Mary.

(*And he correctly carried out his mission?*) Yes. All sorts of human aspects cling to it, but the core of his mission is correct.

(*And the way he expressed it?*) It is bound too much to the human, too strongly dependent on his own personality. But in itself it is correct as it is.

(*And his work, his founding?*) It is like his mission. Good in its core, good in its obedience, but less good in all its human dimensions. It is as if his personal shortcomings affected his work too much.

(*What are his shortcomings?*) There is a certain vanity, which is unable completely to forget itself; there is a certain pride concerning his mission. He speaks the *Dominus non sum dignus* more with his lips than with his heart.

(*And it is nevertheless possible to harmonize this with his love?*) Yes ... it is, so to speak, something essentially marginal, which is not completely taken up into love, like the final residue of an insufficient humanity.

PAUL OF THE CROSS (1694–1775)

(*What is his love for God like?*) I see his love for the loving God. I see his mercy with the Lord, and I see how he begins in prayer, filled with mercy with the Lord, to understand God's mercy. It is as if this mercy initially sprang from himself, as if it embraced God, so far as it is possible to do so, in order then to allow itself to be embraced by God and to be taken up in God's ever-greater mercy. And I see how, out of mercy for God and inside of God's mercy for sinners, he desires to accomplish a service that arises from this passion. And I see how it becomes difficult for him to provide a foundation to this service, because he himself still feels resistence; he himself does not yet understand that there is only one thing a person can do in relation to God: namely, to follow him. In particular moments, it crosses his mind to gather around himself men who are meant to live on the basis of mercy, but he thinks of this mercy as being limited, so to speak, to people. By his own efforts, he would have done things this way; he would have helped in a human sense whenever any opportunity might have arisen for him and his followers. But now he understands that he has to do everything inside of God's mercy, which means from out of the place of the Passion, which he himself does not comprehend, which is only distantly related to his own mercy. And he has to forget the pity he once had for people in order to be taken up into God's pity and from this pity to relearn his own pity for human beings *and* for God.

The institution already began with the initial idea of a founding, but it was then brought to completion only with the new, deeper knowledge.

(*Did this founding succeed in the way God wanted?*) Half and half. He had a lot of trouble carrying his point personally with his followers. There must have been people among them who from the beginning were, to be sure, influenced by his original idea, who took it as their point of departure and for whom the love for people stood nearer and appeared almost more certain than the love of Christ. He himself possessed a wholly pure attitude; it was perhaps among the purest imaginable. And his word had a certain power because of its purity, its sincerity, and its goodness, which he was unable to pass on to his people, so that they did not entirely continue the work in his manner. The gap between him and his followers quickly increased, and one cannot say that it was his fault. There must have been a countercurrent in his founding from the beginning, a tendency to flatten things, which did not allow him to shine forth in the way God had intended.

(*But there were also saints in this Order?*) Yes, there were. But it was from the beginning something basically just thrown together. Perhaps he was too naïve in his acceptance of people, perhaps he always saw too much only the good in people. He came to believe the bad only when it was already too late.

(*Did he have visions?*) Prayer visions, which are often difficult to distinguish from especially pronounced consolations.

(*And his prayer is good and correct?*) Yes. He is good. He is above all very good when he is turned to God. With people, things go a little astray, because he does not possess sufficient discernment of spirits. His primary feature remains his God-given mercy.

MOZART (1756–1791)

(*Do you see Mozart?*) Yes, I see him. (*She smiles.*)

(*Does he have a prayer?*) Yes, I see him praying. I see him praying something, perhaps an Our Father. Simple words that he learned as a child and that he prays knowing that he is speaking with God. For in relation to God he is like a child who brings everything to his father: the stones from the street and peculiar sticks and little plants and even once a ladybug; and with him all of these things are melodies, melodies that he brings to God, melodies that he suddenly *knows* when he is inside of prayer. And when he has finished praying, and he is no longer on his knees and no longer has his hands folded, then he sits there at the piano, or he sings with an incredible childlikeness, and in doing so he no longer has any idea whether he is playing something for God or whether it is God who is using him to play something at once for himself and for Mozart. There is a great conversation between Mozart and God that is the purest prayer, and this entire conversation is nothing but music.

(*And what place do people have in this?*) He loves people. He shrinks from them and loves them at the same time. He shrinks from them somewhat in the way children shy away from other, rough children who might break their toy; but Mozart is actually more afraid that God's toy might get ruined than he is thinking about himself. And he loves people because they are God's creatures, and it makes him happy to be able to delight them with his music. And he would like to present them with the question of God in his own way, even in the comic pieces he writes.

(*He does not distance himself from God in his art?*) No. Of course there are moments in which art takes precedence in a certain sense, but it remains included in God. It is as if he had made an enduring pact with God.

(*And the sadness?*) All of that goes into it. For he knows that God also concerns himself with people who are sad and have a longing and that it is difficult to bear the heaviness of the world, and there are moments when he feels something like a mighty weight on his soul; but then he has to take all of it up into his music; he has to draw attention, through his music, to everything that concerns God and man.

(*And Don Giovanni?*) When he depicts pride, he does not himself go along with it; he does not take part in it. When he depicts sensuality, then he does go along with it to some extent, because sensuality is obviously close to him. But even his sensuality is so childlike that it never actually becomes bad.

PIUS IX (1792–1878)

His prayer is unstable, just as he himself is unstable. When he submits to God and desires to do God's will, then his prayer is rich and good and simple and full of inspirations in spite of his simplicity. Or: precisely in simplicity the simplest holy things are shown to him, which he also receives in a holy way. But then there are also moments, days, weeks, when he is seized by a sort of ambition and is not really able to pray. I do not know whether ambition is the right word ... but it is a sort of exhibition of prayer, which corresponds to an exhibition of his own papal position. The rhythm resembles that of a manic-depressive: there are very good times and very bad times.

(*And his love of neighbor?*) It undergoes the same vacillations. And the peculiar thing is that in the good times, God gives him his grace in an incredible abundance, because God and the saints do their utmost so that the world might have a saint in their pope. So that genuine sanctity would shine forth from Rome. In these times, when grace is able to reach him, he also loves people.

(*And what significance does the Church have for him?*) In the good times she is what God has entrusted to him, whom he must lead to God, whom he has to bring into unity with the heavenly Church. In the bad times, she is for him the instrument that provides him with the means of being pope. In these times, those around him take him to be depressed, but that is more a game he plays in order to hide what is really going on in him.

(*And the Mother of God?*) He loves her and has a real sense for her. In the bad times, she is in fact the only one to whom he can still turn.

VINCENT PALLOTTI (1795–1850)

A peculiar prayer. Humble, unforced. He has certain unique intentions, which he takes with him into prayer and which in themselves are quite beautiful. He would like to send priests more emphatically into the world and at the same time protect them more strongly from the world by means of a Rule. He would like to renew the apostolate in a certain sense, and indeed less in its forms than in its apostles themselves. He sees every priest as an apostle, in somewhat the way they were at the time of the Lord, with the same inner drive, the same restlessness, the same "incompetence", insofar as the apostle appropriates a truth that is for him never entirely graspable and appropriates it in such a way that it forms his sole sustenance. And thus he begs for apostles of this sort, for each individual one, and less for the form of the apostolate in them than for their simply being apostles. He is, as it were, possessed by this idea of being an apostle. There is hardly any room in him for anything else, to such an extent that his prayer is, so to speak, burdened by it, and his contemplation is in some ways obstructed. But nevertheless it is correct this way, at least because he has no one to show him any other way and also because the path he sees stretched out before him was in fact once given to him by God in order to be followed. Admittedly, God expected that he himself would cooperate in fashioning it more and more strongly. And here he fails a bit: he allows himself, as it were, to be driven from the path. But he prays a lot, in a dryness that demands much energy. When in interim periods he possesses genuine consolations, an incredible feeling of God's presence, then he becomes afraid that something is not right. And he prefers to remain with the earlier experience, with the dryness, with the burden, which is more familiar to him and thus seems safer.

(*And what did he give to his congregation?*) The example of an apostle, who strives to bring office and love into unity. Who truly loves the people, insofar as he sees in them the "People of Christ". He is deeply convinced that the people are hungry, that they expect nourishment, and he would like to bring them this nourishment. He would like to hand this nourishment over to his congregation. He also gives them the example of serious self-surrender.

What he is unable to pass on to them is the vision of triune love. He gives more a love that does not know what it is needed for, a sort of following that is born out of the impulse of an inner need but that does not trust itself to ask, not even really to open its eyes, that instead renews itself from day to day. Although the self-surrender is valid for the whole of one's life, he does not throw this "whole life" in fact onto the scale; he does not form any plan. For he always begins with the apostles' human connection to the Lord, an all-too-human connection that does not have a sufficiently careful or attentive view of the further path that would be determined by the Son's love for the Father and for the Spirit.

(*Does he understand obedience?*) Yes, but in a broad and loose sense. He understands it more the more he realizes that there must ultimately be an order here, someone has to be the superior to whom one submits. The deep, trinitarian sense of obedience escapes him.

NEWMAN (1801–1890)

I see him in prayer. He prays so carefully, with a fastidious, good love, a love that has no patience for anything that is not entirely pure and entirely *righteous* [*rechtschaffen*]. He brings everything that is troubling and occupying him into prayer with him. At first, it is all unsorted; he sorts it out in prayer. And in prayer, he receives a certainty concerning whether what he brought is really worthwhile, whether God can use it, whether God can bless it. If God blesses it, he contemplates it once again in prayer and looks to see whether God's light is now reflecting from it. His thoughts, his concerns, his recommendations are like diamonds that were not initially polished, stones he was not entirely sure were in fact really diamonds. Then the expert, that is, God, inspects them and gives them a true polish, and in the end Newman also sees that they were in fact precious stones. But one would have to say that almost everything he brings to God is really a diamond and that he already made the selection in a holy way.

And then he denied himself, threw himself into God's hands, handed himself over, as if he were a monk. His ascesis, his idea of obedience to God, his idea of chastity, of poverty, of love, are absolutely worthy of a monk and, indeed, of a well-formed monk. It is as if, at the time of his conversion, he had the whole life of a monk poured into him in a concentrated form. He possesses a rule that lies in God.

(*And his work?*) He loves it. He loves it, because it is God's work. There are things in it that he is happy to do, and other things he finds difficult; but even these he loves with a fastidious love, because he wants the work to belong wholly to God. It is often the case that he writes, as it were, with his blood and attains to insights with the last of his strength. There is much that is demanded of him personally. In fact, he stands in relation to his work the way the founder of an Order stands in relation to that which he founds.

(*And people?*) He loves them. It is a bit odd. He sees them as God's creatures, but in a way that somewhat resembles an entomologist who loves his insects. He often has difficulty making the first human contact. He receives it first through the translation in God.

(*Visions?*) None. Inspirations here and there. Sudden certainties, but they are rare.

(*How does he develop?*) Very, very slowly. For a long time, it looks as if there were not any progress at all, then out of the blue he takes three steps. And then he does not move again, and suddenly ten more steps. But his entire life is an ongoing development.

(*And those of other faiths, what is his relationship to them?*) There is love, understanding, and hope that they will come in. But he has a lot of understanding for their hesitations.

(*And the Church?*) He loves her. Nevertheless, he has some difficulty getting used to her. He always hopes he can restore to her some of her divine dimensions. He suffers a lot from the fact that she exhibits so much that is human. He loves her a bit in the way a person loves a child who did not turn out the way one hoped, but one does not give up hope that he might still come around . . .

(*After waking up, A. says:*) Newman is certainly a great saint. He reminds me in a lot of ways of Ignatius, especially in his fastidiousness.

LEO XIII (1810–1903)

His prayer is above all humble. Here, he strips off his papal dignity and all of his externalities. And he stands before God like a little boy. In part, he does this consciously, for he recalls his childhood with joy, the way he opened himself up like a child to everything beautiful and was receptive to anything. He lives to a certain extent on his memories, in order to adore God, to petition him, to contemplate his mysteries. He is like a child who wonders at the fact that so much beauty is possible. Doing so, he completely forgets who he is. His prayers also have something very personal about them. He truly loves God's mysteries. He also has a great love for the Mother of God. He knows a lot about her way of praying, her way of standing before God, and he is happy to associate himself with her in prayer.

(*And the Church?*) He loves her too. But he is quite scandalized by her. He always sees the great discrepancy between office and love. And he also sees Rome's falling asleep, with its many offices and its "life-long appointments". The many things that obstruct it. Also the things that obstruct people's involvement and their prayer and bind them back to the earth, instead of giving them a great push into heaven. He does try to counteract this, but his primary aim is to allow God to act. And when he speaks with people with whom he can speak without being disturbed, he always attempts to shift the conversation to the effectiveness of God's love.

He understands that he has to be the highest shepherd for the Church; he understands this above all in relation to people and to individual groups of people or individuals. On the other hand, he has great difficulty representing the hierarchy. It would be a great relief to him not to have this crowd of dignitaries around him.

(*His love of neighbor?*) It is not a love that would be capable of a great sacrifice, but an attitude of complete benevolence and understanding.

MARIE LATASTE (1822–1847)[1]

(*Her prayer?*) It is very good. She is quite ready to sacrifice. She is little.

(*In what sense?*) She is not very advanced, not very widely opened, not very progressive. She moves about on a tiny spot. But in this place she tries to give everything.

(*Is she properly guided?*) No. She is guided in a far too *little* way ... although I do not know whether God really had any great plans with her.

(*And what is little about the way she is guided?*) Everything turns around the same point ... it is as if a great field were available, and only a tiny little garden was built, but this garden was built with great care.

(*And the stigmata are authentic?*) Yes.

(*And also borne properly?*) More or less. She takes a certain pride in them, but a pride that is ashamed, which is difficult to explain. It is a little like a peasant woman in relation to her money. She reminds me of Marguerite Bays.[2] She wants both to show and to hide her stigmata. She is happy to be permitted to share in one of the Lord's great mysteries, but as time goes on a little self-contentedness gets mixed in with this joy. Of course, if the whole huge field had been plowed, it could have been a "proper field" [*ordentliches Feld*]. But because only a tiny garden came out of it, it is precisely an "extraordinary garden" [*außerordentlicher Garten*].

(*And her visions?*) Good. A bit small in the translation. She does not have a complete grasp of the essential, more the branches than the trunk.

[1] A lay sister, member of the Dames du Sacré-Coeur in Rennes. A stigmatic.
[2] A Swiss stigmatic.

THIRD SERIES

Inner attitude, confessional attitude, prayer attitude

Inner attitude. Great zeal. He constantly wants to do what the Lord wills. But he cannot do it properly. His is one of those temperaments that desire a lot and yet acquire a new anxiety every time they take on a new responsibility. An anxiety that is not a little bit physical. Peter would be happy if the Lord's teaching and the following of him were something clearly demarcated, so that one would know what to adhere to, so that one would not always end up on impracticable terrain and have to live, as it were, a marginal existence, human speaking. When he denies the Lord, he does so above all out of physical anxiety; he fears for himself. Moreover, he does not see his office properly; he always has the feeling he ought to grasp something with regard to his office that evades him. Every time he confronts a test, he becomes inwardly despondent. He secretly hopes that the Lord will bear the weight in such a way that a sort of minimum will remain left over for him. He is willing to do everything for the Lord and to love him, but he would like to have a certain assurance that he will be *protected*. It is as if, prior to the Cross, he still did not bear a total Yes beyond himself. Afterward, when he has experienced the grace of the Cross, it will be different.

He sees the Lord's countless miracles and feels surpassed in every respect. But at the same time he constantly has the feeling that no one can demand any more from him, Peter, than that he stand next to the Lord in awe and love and support him a little. With the miracle of the 153 fish, he understands quite well that he is personally intended, that the Cross has more of an effect than sanctifying the whole band of apostles and making them followers of Christ, but also that he must assume a wholly personal discipleship and that from now on no failure is allowed.

Already during the Passion, he feels that the fearful instinct of self-protection that he has had up to this point is no longer permitted. This occurs because he also experiences something of the genuine anxiety that the Lord undergoes. Not like John, who participates in the love of friendship, but in an entirely objective way. And if he afterward sees his own death coming (he now knows that he will be crucified), then he understands that he is thus allowed not only to serve the Lord as a martyr, but also to atone for all of his previous false anxiety, in a genuine "excess" [*Darüberhinaus*] that characterizes the Christian life. He also knows that he is sharing in the atonement for the whole Church.

With the 153 fish, what he understands best is that he was personally intended; and with the promise of the Cross, he understands that the Church was intended in his person: he is inseparable from her, so that, in atoning for himself, he atones into the Church, and he cannot "afford" to commit sins anymore personally, because the ecclesial office would thereby suffer injury.

Confessional attitude. Peter's denial became known among the apostles and everywhere among Christians. This guilt, as it were, strips him of all his clothes before them. For him, when he stands before them, it is as if they all knew exactly what sort of sinner they were dealing with. Thus, he made a compulsory confession in the Church's name. Confession is, so to speak, introduced into the Church through his attitude. When the cock crows for the third time and he realizes that his love has failed, he is made to confess in a passive way. He is converted, so converted in front of everyone that a confession is unnecessary. It is as if the Lord had already drawn the confession from him through his prophecy and as if all the apostles who witnessed it were his confessors. Thus, it is no longer difficult for him later to enter into a confessional attitude. Even if he no longer committed any sins and did not need to confess anything, his sin became so well known that he lived in a constant attitude of confession. He became an example of confession. And his sin is not a mysterious, opaque reality; it lies open to the light of day in the Lord's word and is unambiguously related to it.

Prayer: With him, it can be summed up in a word: "Lord, you know that I love you." That is, at bottom, his whole prayer. Of course, he also has the Our Father, which the Lord gave to him; he has an attitude of prayer. But the prayer that is proper to him is precisely this manner in which he brings himself to the Lord and, through his official existence, brings the Church. He brings the entire Church with him to the Lord, and there is always a sort of tremor in his prayer: there is in fact no prayer in which he does not recall his denial. He knows: once he intended to love, and it came to nothing. He also has a sense of how much the Lord has to take over on his behalf in order that his love be correct.

JAMES, SON OF ZEBEDEE

Inner attitude. He lives in John's shadow, so as to set John's love in relief, to give his attitude its contours. He is very humble but also filled with love. In a certain sense, he is not capable of stepping forward and accepting a great role. And yet he *has to* be absolutely present. He is like a presupposition for John's existence. He himself is unaware of this, both in thought and in words, but he lives in the attitude of one who loves and serves, who allows his service and his love to act in the background. He is supported by John's love, and yet for his part he is a silent presupposition for that love. He would not be able to be so quiet in the background if John did not stand so radiant in the foreground. There is a reciprocal bond between the two of them that enables each to serve. He has the same fidelity as John, the same infallible lines. But, among the group of apostles, he is certainly one of those who are holy through mediation, those who walk their own path through the mediation of another. He loves the Lord and gave his life for the Lord; but he did so in the shadow of his brother. To be sure, each of them received his own call. But the endurance of his answer, its constancy, is a function of John's call. For John, it is a sort of lightening: he is able to carry out his greater service even more infallibly because his brother, who has the smaller service, is faithful. John is the one who is exposed, but one cannot say that James is less necessary. And just as the "thunder" shakes and splits everything open, so has Zebedee given everything he possesses: the great son and the one who stays very quiet. Admittedly, this is a Zebedee who has been elevated by grace, whose quality becomes visible only in his effects and his fruit. James is taken along with Peter and John; in their group, he also represents the anonymous one, but the one who remains unconditionally faithful. He is simply the one who accompanies, the reliable servant.

His *confessional attitude* is a completely natural attitude for him. Here, too, he does not make a spectacle of himself. He simply stands constantly ready to show whatever is asked of him. At the same time, he strives so much and so constantly to do the Lord's will, to remain within his influence, that he does not run the danger of going astray or alienating himself. Of all the apostles, he is perhaps the one who has most renounced a private life. This could be the reason he remains so constantly in the confessional attitude. He is so anonymous that he can constantly remain the support, the resting place, the assurance, for the others.

His *prayer* is excellent. It is a prayer that accompanies him in all that he does and in all his work. He remains constantly in a state of response and readiness. He is very close to living in unceasing prayer.

For John, everything has its basis in love. His *inner attitude* never falters; it always stands centrally within love. And his love grows with increasing insight into love. He loves in an undivided way, in a way that always corresponds to his internal state. He goes along with love from the very first moment of his call. And the more he is *permitted* to love, the more he opens himself to love. More and more, things are illuminated by God's love in him and unfold in this light. And thus love expands him farther and farther. Love becomes more and more obvious to him, but it never becomes something settled and taken for granted. Instead, it remains an ever more perfect gift of self. He was prepared for the vision of the apocalypse from the very beginning; nevertheless, the Lord wanted to allow his love and readiness to grow and develop until it reached the fullness of this vision.

The confessional attitude is very important to him, because it makes clear again and again the distance between himself and the Lord. On the basis of this attitude, he is able to avoid ever going astray or getting too close to the Lord, becoming too familiar with him. If he did not have this humility, which lies in the background of every confessional attitude, then it would have been possible for him to become spoiled by love. But his confessional attitude is so intrinsically connected with his love that he never falters. He knows none of the moodiness of the enthusiast but is perfectly in balance. His confessional attitude makes him like a woman who is aware of her subordination to her husband and relates herself to him with perfect constancy—without always having to allude to that fact.

He learns his *prayer* directly from the Lord. He prays to the Father, but he does so through the Son and together with him. He is a model for Christian prayer, because he receives Jesus' words with so much love that he accepts them as if they were the words of prayer. He understands that the Son is constantly held in conversation by the Father and that, if Jesus speaks with him, he invites him, through his words, to participate in his prayer and conversation. And also when Jesus is not there, he is nevertheless present through the word that remains in him and does not lose its content. On the basis of this enduring prayer, which comes about by virtue of his personal relation of love to the Lord, he finds access to a state of contemplation. Moreover, the Son also gives him a share in his own contemplation of the Father. And thus it is not difficult to show him the apocalypse, because, with the help of Christ, whom he knows as God and as man, he has become accustomed to finding God in man and to seeing the leap made from heaven to earth in the God-man. The indifference of his vision has its foundation in the center of Christ. When he rests his gaze on him, when he speaks with him or sits with him at table, then he knows that he possesses no standard of measure that would be able to limit the Son in his human form. Thus he is also not surprised when the apocalypse is given to him, which provides him with a new participation in the Son's vision. It is not hard for him to see things that he has previously believed, things of which he had no concept or representation but about which he nevertheless knew, just as he knew about the Son's heavenly world, in faith.

ANDREW

Inner attitude. The feature of the Lord he understands above all is his goodness, his gentleness. He is different from John, whom love has so powerfully seized that he never has enough of loving and being loved, a person who makes demands in love. Andrew is constancy, gentleness in love. He responded to the Lord and entrusted himself to him in peace; he remains with him; he does his will and carries all of it out in perfect equanimity, in certainty and the greatest conciliatory spirit. He does not perform any great feats of love, like John, but does have proportionate achievements, which does not mean that he holds himself to the most minimal standard. Instead, his program is the following: to make accessible the most he is able to grasp—which in his eyes is little. To establish a *beginning* is the most he is able to grasp. He is completely aware of the fact that it is just a beginning. He remains the one who seeks in peace, who does not need to find the ultimate; he is not at all looking for an absolute discovery; that is, in a certain sense, not on his mind. He remains in a constant openness to everything that occurs, without making demands. Indeed, he would be happy if everyone were at least to begin to believe and, in particular, if everyone could get along with one another. For what he has grasped has a strong effect on the way people live together. His inner attitude is perhaps best described in terms of this demand, which elevates his behavior toward his fellowmen. He desires to love them but not to overwhelm them. He desires to clean the air between people.

His *confessional attitude* is very clearly influenced by this. He sees it as an attunement that makes harmony between people easier. If a person who has made a mistake regrets it in humility, it encourages others to do the same. If, by contrast, one person is proud and closes himself, then he becomes an obstacle for other people on the path of repentance. But this has nothing "Oxfordian" about it; for him it is simple and genuine. Perhaps the apostles in fact confessed their faults to one another. But already by the fact that Andrew confesses even just to one person or another, he gives to them all a greater share in his truth, his attitude. He feels very clearly that if he did not confess, he would not be able to interact with people in unsullied truth and to speak with them of love.[1]

PHILIP

The wise one. He has a gift for understanding. He is skillful, inventive. This is the perspective from which to grasp his *inner attitude*. When he hears a word from the Lord's mouth, he inwardly mulls it over thoroughly, and he carries out a great purification in his heart. He is the man of constant revolution but completely reasonable. And he works out to completion, in a certain sense, what he has understood. Nothing gets lost. But he does not construct any theories that get more and more refined; instead, he translates into the practical sphere. He does not understand every one of Jesus' words, but once he does understand a word, then it becomes clear to him that it has to be transposed into reality. If he has thus "finished" with an insight, then no problem arises for him; he waits in peace. He is not anxious about what will come next, he manages his energies wisely. He is faithful, devoted, and courageous. He is not one to overwhelm the Lord with questions; when he has something to ask, he does it in an unimposing way. And when he teaches the other disciples, he tries to make it practical, but nevertheless in line with the Lord's intentions. His own opinion concerns him only insofar as it is an expression of the Lord's opinion. He endures the Passion in a sense through the words the Lord left behind for him. But, come Easter, he is still far from having finished his translation of these words. He is also the one who is concerned about little things in the Lord's presence for the regulation of a crowd. The answer the Lord gives to him before the multiplication of the loaves is for him very characteristic. He is also never the person one has to reel in; he does not lose himself in speculations; he never takes things "tragically" and does not need to be appeased. Everything with him moves at the same prudent level.

[1] A. did not do the prayer attitude for Andrew.

272

Even *confession* is something quite practical for him. He has a solid grasp of the effectiveness of the confessional attitude. The examination of conscience does not present any problems for him: where his sin begins and where it ends ... ; he simply desires to lay aside whatever was not good. And because he nevertheless wants to serve and does not want to occupy his mind with things that are injurious to service. Whenever a thing has been spoken, it then lies definitively behind him. Then he is free to pursue his "affairs" further. He immediately repents after the fact when something was not entirely in order. Faith and peace are for him one and the same thing; everything that throws him off track makes him restless; he repents of it immediately and works his way back onto the track. And in his practical way, he promptly looks around for ways to avoid committing the mistake again. He also is aware of his weaknesses and knows what one does better to avoid.

His *prayer* is indeed good, but it has a strong practical orientation. He prays a lot for insight about how to translate and use the teaching the Lord gives him. He does not ascend to an adoration of God, who for him dwells in the heaven beyond his vision; he prays instead to the Lord, for he always also has something to give to him. He will never contemplate the triune God in prayer, but rather he contemplates the Lord with his earthly needs during the time when he was man and how these needs, which he did not have in heaven, were given to him, as to us, for many reasons, not the least of which being that we might learn how to order our needs according to the way he orders his, that we might not accord them more weight than he does, and so forth.

BARTHOLOMEW (NATHANAEL)

His *inner attitude* is characterized by a very great certainty in the Lord, and if he happens to need proof, then he conforms himself completely to the Lord's answer. His certainty pervades everything. He never wavers, but he also does not hold onto this certainty for his own sake; he knows that he must translate it into an apostolate. For his part, he needs no proof or strengthening. For he knows that his own certainty is a grace and that he may not take the same grace for granted in everyone. He is like a person who completely masters a language but who studies its grammatical rules in order to be able to teach others. He has the certainty of contact, of prayer, of discipleship. He recognizes that his personal certainty is a tiny certainty embraced within the great, comprehensive certainty of God. He does not presume to ascertain constantly where he stands; it is enough for him to know that it is the path of discipleship. He is, as it were, the opposite of an inspired person. This latter receives the truth as something poured out all at once without any rational proof, and if he happens to need a proof outside of his inspired activity, then he must seek it himself and build the bridge between inspiration and ordinary life. For Bartholomew, by contrast, these two are intrinsically connected to one another. He forms proofs inside of his grace-laden certainty. He would say, for example, "I have received such and such from the Lord; I did not trust my ears, because it seemed unbelievable to me, so I asked the Lord whether it really was so, and he confirmed it. Thus I came to see how it was to be understood . . ."

He is well aware how much his entire life has to be conformed to grace. He cannot bear the contradiction between the greatness of truth and a tepid, inadequate discipleship. He tries to carry everything out in the Lord's truth, so that every one of his movements will be true. In his understanding of truth and in the edification of his certainty, he may be compared to John. Or more precisely: the truth and its prov-ability is for him what love is for John. But in such a way that the proof is truly valid. In relation to every truth, he even entertains doubts in a pedantic way in order to see them both in confrontation with each other and to bring them together. Already in the scene with the fig tree, he sees two possible paths: he believes for himself even before he asks. But he asks because the others need a proof. If he afterward affirms his belief, then he does so on the basis of a certainty that may not become explicit before it is achieved for others as well.

His *confessional attitude* stands in the same certainty. Once again, he resembles John: this latter holds himself in his confessional attitude out of pure love, while Bartholomew does so out of pure truth. He must confess, demonstrate, what is not proper in himself, so that he might become all the more capable of grasping truth and being in the truth. He sees every inclination to sin as a denial of God's truth and thus as an unbearable contradiction. There is a slight bit of intellectualism in this. Arrogance would be the wrong word for it. But he has a remark-ably precise understanding of sin and falsehood. He repents almost more strongly for having lived in a way that was no longer absolutely in unity with the truth than for having fallen out of God's love. His intel-lectual precision thus also gives him an exactness in confession.

His *prayer* is plentiful and abundant, because it partakes of the certainty that he needs for others' sake. He has no problem with scruples, but he is very precise in prayer. He does not let anything lie in confusion.

And he prays a lot and, in prayer, sees his concerns and also his worship completely in the light of truth. He worships the Lord above all as truth. He is, as it were, happy to have in Christ the end of all questioning, the definitive answer, once and for all. The three attitudes completely penetrate one another in him. Everything converges in his person, which has little extensions or possibilities in various directions.

MATTHEW

Inner attitude. He is the one who has been called, the one snatched away, who had no question beforehand and then suddenly perceived the call. He abides for a long time afterward in the suddenness of this call. Everything he encounters in his life—and it will continue for a very long time, until he writes the Gospel—calls him farther. For the change was so precipitous that he remains with the belief that the first step he took was the first of many, the many steps that would come later. He awaits another reversal and then another . . . and all of these reversals were indicated by external signs. It takes a long time for him to realize that the furthers steps are spiritual ones. He constantly has the feeling that he stands within a trajectory and that that is more or less sufficient; and if he had acquired sufficient capacities and knowledge on this path, then the Lord would continue farther on—or rather, no longer the Lord, but perhaps the Father, the Spirit . . . It is only when he has composed his Gospel that he will finally understand what Christianity is. Until that time, he is docile, loving to a certain extent, but the boundaries he unconsciously fixes still have to be taken away from him.

The Gospel is given to him in inspiration. But as he writes it, he follows along; he clearly registers what he is writing. He is in this respect best compared to Luke. When it concerns external events, an inner voice says to him: "Yes, yes, that is how it was! . . ." And as for what concerns interior mysteries, it occurs to him at once that the meaning of Christianity is now presented to him and to others in a new totality. That he has indeed up until now traveled a Christian path in relation to which no other paths of the same sort will follow; that, instead, the whole of life is *one* path, to which one must always conform oneself.

To help the writing of his Gospel, he has documents, recorded reminders, notes. Some of these things he possessed prior to his inspiration, when he did not yet know that he would have to write. He holds on to them, mostly in order simply to fill things out. He takes notes like one who does not know yet what purpose they will later serve. What he does have is less a preliminary basis than a subsequent confirmation for the accuracy of the inspiration. But because the things that are shown to him connect with his memories, they are more present to him than they would have been if they had simply been experienced only once, especially with the way his mind works. He was, indeed, called before he had a chance to prepare himself, and now he prepares himself in a certain sense so that he will not be completely surprised by yet another unsuspected call. In a sense, his presentiment is correct: the new call will make him into an evangelist and, indeed, will claim not only his human way of being, but also his memory and his work. God's providence prepares him ahead of time insofar as it allows him already beforehand to be occupied with Jesus' life, which does not in any respect weaken the power of the subsequent inspiration. One ought not to take the concept "inspiration" in too narrow a sense: the voice, which will soon give "dictation", can already be awakened in the mind of a person before it begins to speak. Thus, the angel's voice is already alive in Mary before she conceives. God's call similarly lives in many of the elect before they are aware of it and hear it. The writing down, properly speaking, occurs under the "dictation" of inspiration. Afterward, making use of his notes, he can fill out this or that aspect. But not change; rather, only carry to term what was already latent within the inspiration. Because the whole of life is enveloped in an objective inspiration, such as that of the evangelists, subsequent additions can also be parts of inspiration. Insofar as inspiration, as an act of God, is greater than what a human being can indicate, it challenges him to place everything that belongs to him mentally at the disposal of inspiration, in order to build it up or allow it to be built up. Even the logic and the inner disposition of Matthew's Gospel was essentially included within the dictation, but it was included as something "jotted down", so that a lot of space remained for the apostle to expand and complete. This disposition is the very place in which Matthew anticipated the largest part of the coming Gospel in his prior plan. But one cannot say he had sketched out the entire plan beforehand, only that inspiration takes over the beginnings of his plan. And it reaches back to what was already there only because the person had already beforehand conformed himself to the coming demand in unconscious obedience.

Once Matthew has finished his book, he lives, no longer in anticipation of a turning point, but rather in the ever-greater character of the Lord, knowing that he must respond better and better and that all his personal expectations have their place only within God's expectation.

His *confessional attitude* is completely in keeping with his expectation. Because he predominantly experiences external things, he confesses

276

more the external. But he is convinced that one must confess and live in openness. He simply does not yet see what ought to be open here. He thinks it will be shown to him one of these days. Thus, he does not occupy himself much with it inwardly. He recognizes what is not correct in himself and does not want to keep anything secret; but he is occupied with other things so much that he also does not deal with this that much. His community lives perhaps most strongly in his confessional attitude as the community of believers. He has an inchoate feeling that the love of neighbor is mostly cultivated and made known in the confessional attitude. But he saves the confirmation of this in a certain sense for the time of the coming turning point.

His *prayer* is naïve and good. The level of his prayer, as it were, lies for him much higher than the level of his life. In life, he always oversees what he is doing; in prayer, he feels himself drawn toward something mysterious in the Son, toward the Son's divinity, toward the Father and the Spirit. And he always believes that the turning point in his life will one day bring a confirmation of his prayer. He sees too little that he has to bring his life into correspondence with his way of praying already today. His prayer is a bit isolated. He is like a person who might say, "Every morning I pray for an hour. It's wonderful! It is the highpoint of my day! If I didn't have this time, I wouldn't know how to bear the boredom of the rest of the time!"

He expects the great turning point, not only for his own sake, but also for the Lord. He thinks that God's Son took on the restricted form of earthly life but that he will soon leave it for the sake of another, better form and then call him to participate in this better form, just as the Lord once called him away from the tax collector's coffers. His expectation is not false, but it is too naïve, it is the subjective translation of a great, inner expectation of grace in him. The joy of this expectation is absolutely present, and the Lord gradually expands this joy into the great Christian joy. He constantly builds bridges with his apostle's human notions. But occasionally he also allows them to have their own translation as a reference point: *their* expectation is clear to them; thus they translate the Lord's greater expectation more or less into the form of the expectation that they are able to imagine according to their own lights. And it is precisely also by means of such translations that the Gospel shares in the ever-greater truth of God and allows his absoluteness to be reflected in our relativity.

Bernadette, who did not understand Mary's word, had to repeat over and over to herself: "I am the Immaculate Conception." The first time, she would not have been able to retain it. Nothing is repeated to the apostles. They themselves have to express the concept, which is inconceivable for them, in such a way that it becomes something they can retain. And precisely because the inspiration refers to things that are already present in their minds, the human element also comes to expression as the substrate for the inspiration. They cannot of course simply let go of everything human and leap over it, because in that case there would no longer be any foothold or point of comparison.

JUDE THADDEUS

His *inner attitude* is impeccable. But he possesses the same name as the betrayer and has to carry the consequences of this name. The moment people begin to notice that something is not right with Judas, he feels like he himself is implicated. There is a certain malaise among the apostles, even before the actual betrayal. When they ask, "Who is it, Lord?" then they do not dare to believe that the betrayer has already been so clearly marked. At the same time, there is a sort of dark zone that surrounds him. Thaddeus feels as though he has been confused with someone else. He knows there is no suspicion about his being the betrayer. Nevertheless, when the others have an intimation, he experiences it as if he were its object. While he knows that it is not he, he also knows that it is *also* he. That ultimately it is everyone, but it is he above all . . . He has a very deep sense for human weaknesses, and he is always ready to bear them.

Initially, he also has the reaction: "Thank God it isn't me!" Then he learns more and more how to bear things with others; he learns how to desire to compensate for others, how to bridge distances. With everyone who makes a mistake, he knows: I am there with you. And he becomes more and more humble. It is a humility that never disappears, because it *wants* to bear things. There are also moments when he wonders whether the other Judas, the betrayer, shares some of his own betrayal and whether he took over what would have been his, that is, Thaddeus', role. And thus he prays for the betrayer. He mercilessly contemplates his own guilt in the act. Peter's denial, too, makes a profound impression on him. No other disciple was more powerfully struck by it. For he knows the path that leads from denial to betrayal. And because he himself feels that he has been pushed into a doubtful light, he investigates, more perspicaciously than the others, what his own failures are, what beginnings there are in him that could grow into something bad. And he willingly accepts this fate of standing in the betrayer's shadow in order to bear a part of the Lord's burden. He experiences it this way, too, although objectively speaking no glimmer of a suspicion ever in fact fell upon him.

278

The inner attitude is at bottom already a *confessional attitude*. His "bad conscience", that is, his experience of sharing in guilt, is tangible. When *we* have a bad conscience, then we try to free ourselves from it as quickly as possible. He, by contrast, knows that he has to bear it. And in his supernatural faith he recalls his nature in a particularly powerful way. He knows he would be capable of committing any sin. And he has a feeling for every sin. But he never expresses this, though it allows him to take everything in. He sees everywhere the threads that bind him to the individual sins of the world. This whole thing is not a terrible suffering; it is more an awareness that accompanies him wherever he goes.

He is also the one who understands others, a person to whom they are able to go. He is like a confessor for all of them.

He *prays* well and a lot, especially petitionary prayer. And if someone makes a mistake, then he is the one who prays most for him and petitions in his name for forgiveness. His prayer is much more one that goes from below to heaven rather than the reverse. He is a beast of burden, who loads burdens upon himself and carries them to God.

JAMES, SON OF ALPHAEUS

He is responsible for the Catholic letter. His *inner attitude* is very precise and not subject very much to fluctuations. And if he ever comes across a weakness, a human failure, then he immediately needs to straighten it out, to keep it from being forgotten, to incorporate it into his doctrine, in order thereby to teach people better. He possesses an astonishing dexterity in the grasping of human deficiencies. He does not deceive himself about anything. He contemplates what he did, both good and evil, not with self-contentedness, but with the objectivity of an examiner. He presents to himself a great, Christian experience: it is as though he *felt* his entire human being constantly under the workings of grace. It is his sense of responsibility that allows him to feel this way. There is a piece of truth here that ought to be acknowledged. He grasps the paths he takes, his actions and reactions, by continually referring back from the end of the deed to his point of departure, in order to measure the distance; he oscillates back and forth, although he does so less in himself than in the vastness of God, in order to get a better understanding, both for his own sake and for the sake of other people. But this examination occurs entirely inside of God's love and allows him constantly to experience God's presence. He never forgets, and he never wants to forget, that he stands within the radius of God's action.

In the sphere of God's illuminating light, he never places himself in the light. This is what distinguishes him from Paul. Paul steps forward out of God's light and illuminates his personality. James never for a moment thinks that he ought to expose or transpose himself, that he ought to point to his own personality, in order to return to God's objectivity afterward. Paul often takes this step: "Look at what I am if you wish to understand what God is." James always points exclusively to God: "Look at God; I am in him, and everything he does in me remains visible in me." He does not by any stretch have the greatness of a Paul; he does not have the love of a John, who gives everything he experiences immediately to the Lord—in his neighbor—and who is never alone because he always fulfills the commandment of love. James is a solitary, because he always resolves to remain within his relationship to God and because his neighbor never represents as immediate an access to God as he does with John.

The Old Testament is important for him. He does not want to demonstrate his theories about being in God simply in relation to himself. He stands entirely in the transition between the two testaments. He must constantly look back at what has been in order to assure himself that he dwells in God. He relates his position more to the past, while Paul looks ahead and John looks into the expanse of his fellowmen. Moreover, James does not risk any leap. The Lord himself was circumcised! His fidelity to the Lord has little capacity for transformation and adaptation. His sole development turns on his increasing understanding of his position. He is like an artist who produced *one* beautiful work and who spends the rest of his life touching it up here and there. Or like a researcher who made a particular discovery and attempts to make it better and better. His own being never turns into a sheer springboard. He moves, so to speak, along a single line, indeed, he is himself this line and must grow in his understanding of its position and length in God. Disciples become enthusiastic about something and then move on. James never "gets over it". Whatever he has known, apart from sin, whatever he has loved, he wants to *prove*. Others have a freedom with respect to their own possibilities: a person does one thing, does not worry about the others, perhaps he comes back to what he did later, perhaps not. Such a relationship to things is completely foreign to James. Moreover, his gaze is so objective that he cannot transfigure things by looking at them. If he looked at a kitschy painting, he would not be able to have a direct perception of the love of the person who painted it or to see both at the same time. For this reason, he is unable to be everything for everyone. This is the point he cannot keep up with. Therefore, he has a consistency that extends to the farthest extreme, to the limit of rigidity. He is reliability itself, fidelity, comprehensibility (in contrast to Paul); there is no arrogance or self-aggrandizement in him.

His *confessional attitude* lies in his great openness. It is one with his inner attitude; more precisely: it determines his inner attitude. It is the more important of the two. For it is essential for him to contemplate himself in God. He considers sin, in a sense, as inherent in his given human nature, as a deeply rooted inclination. And he thinks, if he thus suspends himself in God, this inclination will wear down in time. In spite of his theory about service, he knows no other way of fighting than placing himself more determinedly in the light of grace. He would like to let his sinful nature be consumed in grace.

His *prayer* is fidelity. He keeps from letting himself get carried away in prayer. He thus takes himself in hand; he observes himself in such a way—he thinks this is due both to himself and to God—that his prayer loses its simple immediacy. It remains an explicit service but does not have much radiance or any great intensity. He prays a lot, but always under his supervision. And when the Lord would like to take him a little farther, he becomes perhaps a bit mistrustful, because he no longer knows how everything transpires.

THOMAS

In his *inner attitude*, he is one of those who have composure, not least of all because they are not challenged. He follows the Lord; he has faith; he experiences no internal conflicts. He believes, but his faith does not extend *over and above* all things; instead, it moves *into* all things, whatever is provable, whatever can be clearly demonstrated. He has no reason not to believe, no reason to make himself an exception, to reject obedience. He is like the novices who, so to speak, follow a call, submit themselves to a Rule, do what others do, and avoid any major conflicts, because each day has challenges sufficient for them. He is one of those who build a sort of house ultimately on the foundation of the Rule and the demands made, first walls, and then doors and windows, and they fail to notice that they themselves are directing things and that they are limiting their faith and obedience. They have never felt an inner impulse to throw themselves into their faith. The Lord said: Love your neighbor. Good, then I'll love my neighbor, the person whom I am encountering just now. But I do not have to make any special effort of my own to broaden this small circle.

After the Resurrection, Thomas is suddenly faced with the demand for absolute faith. But because he is unaccustomed to allowing himself to be stretched, he cannot risk the leap, cannot suddenly affirm what he has not seen beforehand. (When he said to the Lord before the Passion: We want to die with you, then he was speaking out of the constancy of his accompaniment of the Lord. He did not have any concrete image of what dying meant. For he also did not know what the Lord's *life* was. He said it out of a kind of certainty that lacked a sufficient foundation, almost within a schema that he had previously seen and a conceivable further development.) Now he is incapable of believing, because, without really noticing it, he refuses to accept the faith that is ever-greater. The fact that the supernatural laws now leap over the natural laws seems to him unacceptable. Previously, there was an apparently determinate relationship between nature and the supernatural. Even in the Lord's miracles there were always two evident points that bore scrutiny: at first the man was blind, and now he sees; before he was dead, and now he is alive. Thus, no doubt was possible. But Thomas believed the miracle only once he had a chance to check it. Ultimately, he believes his evidence rather than the Lord.

It is the encounter after Easter that first throws him from the saddle. Soon after he will receive the Holy Spirit and become a saint. But in his previous unbelief he represents many people, many Christians, many religious: people who believe they have made a big decision and yet do not yet know what it all means.

Confessional attitude. As long as he has not been cast to the ground and learned to believe anew, he adapts his faith to himself, and in his attitude, he does not get beyond a confession of accommodation. He will be ready to acknowledge this or that as a sin within a narrowly circumscribed region. In order to pray the right way, he first has to break out of the whole circle he walks around, for example, insofar as he begins to understand that guilt exists for him precisely because he is more profoundly responsible as an apostle, that he has to help others carry their own guilt, and so forth. Otherwise, he would remain the chosen person who follows the call externally but remains inwardly the same as one who was not called. He is the model who demonstrates that responsibility increases with one's mission.

His *prayer* corresponds to what has been said. But after he has dared to make the breakthrough, it overflows on every side in him; now he cannot pray enough. He always takes his point of departure from the miracle *that* the Lord exists and that he really breaks open all laws. His prayer has its point of entry in the infinitely greater being, the infinite possibility, of God. It is a prayer of love, but in a very different sense from John's prayer. John leads a dialogue; Thomas is simply inundated. With him, one can scarcely speak of an answer, although his attitude is also more than an answer.

SIMON THE ZEALOT

He is the most unbalanced in his *inner attitude*. He struggles and strains himself and then goes limp once again. He always pushes one step farther, but he never makes it through. From the first moment on, he is very much present, but like someone who is off the mark, as it were. He has "understood" everything so much that he almost knows better than the Lord does. But at the very moment when he ought to deepen in peace, he collapses. He has trouble entering into contemplation. When he has put enough energy and effort into it, he cannot find his way back; he no longer knows what to do. He draws his strength from his own deeds rather than from the Lord. In the moment when he folds, he has the clear insight that he cannot get out of this by his own efforts but needs grace to do so. However, he is not able to manage what a person has to contribute in order to enter into contemplation. Even so, the Lord's pure grace has such an effect on him that he does not in fact founder in his depression. He recognizes this grace and also tangibly feels it. Then he plunges once again into his activities.

This picture lasts, not just until the Cross, but until Pentecost. He thinks that one can *also* overcome the Cross with one's zeal. But a transformation occurs at Pentecost. The Spirit's grace gives him peace and a sort of contemplation. Nevertheless, he retains his restlessness at a natural level; he does not achieve a proper attitude of contemplation. Contemplation is given to him from above without a corresponding human foundation, which apparently runs contrary to every theory. There is in Simon in fact no correspondence between his human attitude and the contemplation he receives from above. He is too unsteady for that. There always has to be something going on. The other apostles gave him the name "the Zealot". They hold him in high esteem. Whenever there is a need for a "great achievement", *he* is the one to carry it out.

Confessional attitude. He approaches the attitude, but he never really grasps it. At the moment when it ought to occur, his zeal overtakes him again; he overlooks the decisive thing; he passes over it. There is a sort of vacuum in him, a place he cannot reach, a point at which things become strange for him. He feels he is not listening totally and completely to the Lord, even though he would like to. But he cannot discover the reason for his failure.

His *attitude of prayer* is like his confessional attitude. He wants to pray. But scarcely has he begun to do so when he turns his mind already again to his activities. In this, he is full of practical techniques. He certainly knows the sorts of things a person could do in order to avoid distractions in prayer, but while he reflects on this, he fails to realize that this is already a distraction. Later, when he has become more tranquil, he suffers a bit from this peace. He would ultimately rather be engaged with something ...

JUDAS ISCARIOT

Inner attitude. He is chosen by Jesus, and he lets himself be called. And Jesus knows who it is he is calling. Nevertheless, he wills to act as a man—it is a part of the Cross that he bears in advance—in spite of his divine knowledge with respect to Judas. He knows that Judas will betray him. But he does not make use of this knowledge. He lays it aside. He relates to Judas as if he had no knowledge. He calls him, because Judas is on the path of vocation, because God is the one who determined that Judas would be one of those who could be chosen. One who possesses particular prerequisites for the acceptance and the fulfillment of a vocation. Already prior to the call itself the Lord conceals his foreknowledge about him. And thus, they stand before one another as a superior and a subordinate, and the call of the latter is arranged and worked out within the context of human judgments and intentions. The Lord does not *want* to know anymore than a superior knows, who lacks any access to knowledge beyond the ordinary. In this respect, Jesus' relationship to his supernatural capacities for knowledge becomes especially clear. He has free disposal over what he wants to know and what he does not want to know. Moreover, he does not want to take from the future superiors in the Church the possibility of guiltless error, of believing in good faith that something will happen that turns out not to happen. The Lord wanted to feel this experience of the Church in his own body.

Judas' attitude is that of standing in a growing contradiction to the Lord. And it is uncomfortable for him. But above all Jesus feels an unease in relation to Judas. He allows this unease to occur precisely within the sphere of his human nature. He does not allow it to grow or diminish through his divine knowledge; he does not hate Judas as the betrayer. But he is also incapable of simply setting aside his unease and ignoring it until the time of the Passion. He allows it to follow its human laws and development. Judas has a certain share in this discomfort, with increasing rancor. He sees more and more that something is not right. Why does the Lord not intervene, since he in fact sees that it is not right this way? And because he does not do anything about it, perhaps he is not the Messiah. But Jesus does not make an exception for Judas. He gives him the entire lesson of Christianity, just as he gives it to the others—no more and no less. Judas does not receive any "private lessons". Jesus cannot make any *special* efforts in order to convert him, for these would have had their ground purely in his divine and supernatural knowledge, not in his human knowledge. But he cannot use his divine knowledge against his human knowledge; he would be able to justify an extraordinary effort only on the basis of the whole of his knowledge, which includes the human. Occasionally he does make use of the higher knowledge, for example, in his prediction of Peter's denial. But what he does in relation to Peter he does not do in relation to Judas. He does not give him any predictions; he does not warn him. In relation to Peter he lives his divine nature and his human nature in unity. Thus, he makes use of his divine knowledge in order to warn him. In relation to Judas, he fundamentally avoids doing this. He turns only his human knowledge toward him. It is almost as if it were necessary to avoid forcing Judas' guilt too far, almost as if Judas already had enough to bear, without awakening in him an extraordinary faith through extraordinary graces, which would only burden his betrayal more deeply. By keeping silent, the Lord protects Judas. To be sure, an abyss opens up here for us: we are unable to see what law the Son of God is following in administering his divine knowledge, when he uses it and when he does not.

Judas becomes inwardly more and more alienated and stubborn. He plays in a sense with his inner attitude: he clings to the fact that the Lord called him in spite of everything and, then, again to the fact that the whole thing is not possible; everything he picks up from the Lord's teaching makes it possible to deny it even more. And nevertheless he is involved. He is like the religious who has taken vows and can no longer undo them. Ultimately, he has no faith. He acts as if he were trying to decide between belief and unbelief. He weighs what it would be like to believe ... But the most important thing is: he has no hope. And, therefore, no love and, therefore, no faith. He does not *hope* that he could become someone else through his calling, that God would root him in himself, that he could accept Jesus' teaching. He does not hope because he thinks he knows himself.

There is no *confessional attitude*. He does not believe in any forgiveness, because he ultimately does not believe in any sin. When he lies, for example, he is completely aware of the fact that he does not speak the truth. In fact, he knows this quite clearly. Indeed, it would be desirable for the majority of Christians to have such a clear understanding of their sin! But Judas recognizes them, not as sins, but only as facts, which are arranged somehow in his life's system, in the system of his self-justification.

Prayer is foreign to him. When the others pray, he blasphemes God inwardly.

In the moment when he betrayed the Lord, there is the glimmer of a possibility of hope in him. It is the first time he reflects: "Perhaps he truly was the Lord!" Something like hope is born out of despair: "If it is the Lord, then he belongs to God, and then the truth is in him and not in me." This could have been hope; this could have been liberation from the ego, the recognition that God is the one who is right. One cannot say that Judas did not know this "hope". Nevertheless, he does hang himself. This situation, in any event, is too monstrous, too brutal for him to be able to find a solution *for himself*. But he sees that there may perhaps be a solution *for the Lord*. Because his betrayal would not be able to thwart the Lord if he comes from God. And it may be that he turned to his Lord for just this reason, ... like the evil tenders of the vineyard, who say: he is the Son, and *therefore* we want to kill him ... And the hope for Jesus, for the possibility that he could really be the one, is somehow so powerful in Judas that it does not leave any room in him, as it were, for any hope for himself ... The "regret", which causes him to bring the money back to the temple, is a fruit of his hope; he would not have been able to achieve this if he did not have this hope. And if he does hang himself, then it is because he is no longer *able* to live anymore, because he betrayed *the Lord!* If hope—a single hope—had arisen before the betrayal, then it would have been available for himself as well. He is like an Abraham who really *did* kill his son Isaac and now realizes the angel was in fact present to keep him from doing it ... And thus Judas murders his whole negating subject; his deed appears to him so deserving of destruction that he destroys himself. He knows no other way of undoing what was done.

MARY MAGDALEN

Inner attitude. She has sinned; the Lord has raised her up again; but he actually took her sins into himself. And this increases: the more she is liberated, the more he bears, and she is also aware of this. She grows into the Lord, as it were, because he has taken over everything she previously was, and he gives her everything she will be. Thus, a peculiar humility comes about in her: she can no longer meet the Lord without at the same time meeting her sin in him, and her sin in him has merged with the guilt of all people. For her, the Lord is now the one who bears her guilt, insofar as he at the same time bears the sin of the world. She confessed one time, repented one time. But there remains a fundamental confession in her: what belongs to her expands in love into something that concerns all people. She will no longer be able to encounter the Lord without praying for all sinners. Without being reminded that it is now her turn to forgive others. For he has shown her how one goes about bearing the sins of others.

And since everyone knows what the Lord has accomplished in her, she becomes a sort of apostle. She is a living parable, a memorial. She now truly has to lead the life the Lord demands of her and that he has made possible by forgiving her sins. The excess of grace has to be legible in her. And it will be, because she does not for a moment ascribe anything to herself: she wants only to show what *he* is, what *he* can do. Her inner attitude results from the fact that she is not asked whether she wants to follow the Lord. In the moment when she is liberated from her sins, every problem comes to an end: now she *has to* follow. What happened is so much a miracle that no other call is necessary. The call is included in the Lord's deed. Everyone in whom a miracle has been performed has received this sort of call.

Confessional attitude. Mary Magdalen confesses continuously. The Lord indeed posited a single act, but from then on she makes herself available, so to speak, so that confession may pass through her, so that the others may see the Lord's absolution in her and may thus be prompted to repent and confess. So that the Lord might be able to take them all up and redeem them. She becomes someone put on display. But the mystery of the demonstration lies entirely in the Lord, not in her. That distinguishes her from the bottom up from all of the "converted" in the sects. Her active contribution in relation to the Lord is limited to her not withdrawing herself.

Her *prayer* is part of her mission. She attempts by means of her prayer to win other sinners for the Lord. And she knows that no prayer is ever lost. She is perhaps the first one in the Church who prays *ad intentionem*. When the Son prays: Thy will be done on earth as it is in heaven, then that includes every one of the Father's wills. When Mary

Magdalen thus prays, then she says it *ad intentionem* of the sinners, whom she would like to bring to God. But she says clearly: Thy will be done. She has a very good conception of the essence of Christian prayer. Most people who prayed at that time for a particular intention had something individual or concrete in mind, for example, a healing or a miracle. With Mary, the intention is spiritual; she already takes the miracle for granted.

MATTHIAS

He is the one who substitutes. He comes to a position that was lost; now it is his job to fill this position. He cannot do this with the naïveté that the other apostles had at the time of their calling. He is a late-comer, and if he now begins as the thirteenth, he nevertheless feels as though he were taking the place of the twelfth: he must atone for the evil the betrayer committed. Thus, he is the first one who is unable to build any relationship at all on his own strength. The others who had come in order to follow in a certain kind of love and to correspond to a call were without presuppositions and could reflect: "The Lord will certainly make it happen." But he sees what Judas made out of his calling; he already has to ask the Lord upon his initial entry to make something out of him and his deficiencies that can fill the empty place. His *inner attitude* is therefore from the outset that of a child who renounces everything, who desires nothing but what the Lord desires. He even surrenders his own being accepted by the apostles. The others did not yet know what they were called to do. They lived in the following of a man whom they at first did not know. Thus, at the beginning a two-sided relationship developed: between them and the Lord. If a person has to come after a person who has failed, and this is common knowledge, that person is much more profoundly afraid, prepared for much more. He has the humility of one who knows what it means to fail at such a post. A new sort of humility. He is a person like Judas; he stands where he stood, ... no one would "settle into" a position like this. Matthias is perhaps the first person who experienced the precariousness of Christianity most profoundly. He has to pray from one moment to the next: "Strengthen me, that I may remain faithful!" He does not have the "once-and-for-all" experience the others had.

Confessional attitude. If the Lord did not have such a firm hold on him, he would come close to becoming a scrupulous person. He is so thoroughly permeated by his unworthiness, so convinced that Jesus tried everything to support Judas in his struggle with his own will that he

288

believes he sees the beginning of sin everywhere: "Isn't that already a sin? Isn't that already the beginning of a denial? ..." He is one of those Christians who would prefer to confess their sins twice.

His *prayer* is very faithful and kind. In prayer, he makes every effort to avoid being a person capable of betrayal. He also has the experience of looking over his own shoulder, but one could not say that he is too preoccupied with himself. It is the grace of a person who has just been called, who constantly worries about the many things God has to accomplish in him so that he may suffice. But he will give it a try; he has a tangible love for the Lord. His conception of God's greatness is infinite. He is like a little child who is afraid of stumbling, who smells danger everywhere, but who is mightily proud of the strength of his father, to whom he gives his hand and who can hold it. His love is completely different from that of John; it is not an eye-to-eye relationship with the Lord, but it looks up to the Lord entirely from below. He would never dare to rest his head upon the Lord's breast. That is not something everyone is allowed to do. He is happy if he is permitted to do the lowliest thing; why should he worry about anything else?

PAUL

Prayer attitude. In prayer, he is good, simple, and surrendered; the only thing lacking is that he never loses himself entirely. Even when he feels closest to God, he does not lose himself or his task. It is almost as if he had given everything to God except for the awareness of his mission, the awareness of the work that was waiting for him, the awareness of all of those things he still had to carry out. That is something of which he never lets go. Even in pure contemplation, he still desires to feel the mantle of mission on his shoulders. And thus, in whatever it is that God shows to him in contemplation, he constantly looks for a way to turn it to a practical result. It would seem futile to him, as it were, to want to give his mission back to God in order to allow himself to be guided henceforward wholly and completely by God, with the risk of never receiving it back from him. He is so convinced that his mission constitutes his life and that God never separates it from his life that it would be ridiculous for him to call this mission into question, for example, by his placing it once again at God's disposal.

This has the effect of producing in the whole *inner attitude* a certain rigidity in his mission. He has to pursue his mission not only inwardly, but practically externally also. Each person who encounters him, no matter who it is, becomes aware of his mission. We would be happy if our reflection of God caught people's attention and would accept it if that happened in a detour around our mission. But Paul, by contrast, insists that everything be led through his mission. Even when he glorifies the Father and the Son, when he proclaims the pure Christian teaching, he nevertheless points at the same time to his own service, his position within the truth that he is proclaiming. If the words were not too strong, I would say: Just as Christ is God become man, so Paul is mission become man. Everything heavenly, mysterious, sublime that can have any connection with a Christian mission comes to bear on this mission.

And therefore it would be very tedious for him to stand in a *confessional attitude* before a mediator between God and him. In relation to God he is constantly ready to acknowledge his faults and confess them. But it would be difficult for him to do that in relation to a man, because the importance of his mission does not give him license to be weighed down by faults, to be a sinner, to make a judgment today about what he did yesterday. Because, as a matter of fact, he was already yesterday a Christian and one who was sent. He thus also divulges very little about what he did yesterday, about his previous unrighteousness, because it lies behind him and now is the time of grace and mission. At most, he mentions his past in order to shed light on his present mission. What ought to become visible in him is grace and not whatever distance or alienation might separate him from God. In relation to God, he does indeed possess an awareness of sin or at least an awareness of omission, but in relation to other people he does not think this is something he can achieve.

MARK

He is the disciple in whom the difference between the *inner attitude* and the *attitude of prayer* is perhaps greatest. In prayer, he allows himself to be guided; he is very powerfully led and does not need to deal with himself on his own. Every time he withdraws in order to pray, it is as if he were freed from all his concerns, almost from his entire being. He does not need to struggle to find and defend a position; his prayer is free, pure, a gift. And he prays a good deal. He prays like a child, in complete simplicity and single-heartedness, without reflecting at length on what words he wants to use or for what exactly he wants to pray. But it is also the case that there are many things that are not given to him in prayer; everything happens on a very straightforward level.

On the other hand, when he is not in prayer, then he constantly has to fight with himself; he has to concern himself step by step with his own attitude, to assure himself that he believes, that he truly wants to follow, that he loves. And that ultimately everything will turn out right. It is not given to him to hand himself wholly over to the Lord once and for all and to entrust the Lord a priori with all his difficulties. He has to fight for his trust; and, for the most part, also for his love. And because there exists such a tension between his attitude of prayer and the rest of his inner attitude, he would be happy if he could pray twice as long or longer. The very fact that he cannot and that the Lord demands something else from him already represents one of his difficulties.

The *confessional attitude* is good, because he sees his weaknesses and faults without difficulty. Indeed, he feels that if he could persist in the confessional attitude—and perhaps his inner attitude is not to be distinguished too much from a confessional attitude—he would overcome his difficulties with time, not he himself, but the Lord in him. If he could do this, he would abandon true confession. For he often grows tired of himself.

The inspiration for the Gospel. He was afraid of this. He is the only one who really knew ahead of time that he would have to write. He resisted it, because he thought he would have to write in an ordinary time or that he would not be docile to the Spirit's guidance. And then it actually went very well. As the inspiration came, it brought about in him much of what he had long wished for. Some things were clarified for him in his writing down of the Gospel; some of the things that were questionable beforehand now became unquestionably good, filled out, brought to closure.

Concerning the type of inspiration he received: At first, it is as if he himself chose his starting point. On the basis of his knowledge. Then this point was overtaken and advanced. Everything uncertain he had contributed out of his own resources disappears. He finds obedience in relation to inspiration much easier than he imagined it beforehand. He esteems it a particular gift of grace, which gives him clarity. Before, he was like a person who was afraid of an upcoming interview: perhaps his partner would demand more precise things from him than he would be able to provide. And then the conversation is conducted in such a way by the other person that he himself receives more clarity and a wider view.

In relation to his fellowmen, things are not easy for him. He is difficult, burly. One cannot say that he lacks humility; rather, he lacks a certain objective clarity of spirit. He is not as capable of overcoming himself or becoming simple in his interaction with others as he is under inspiration.

The simplicity of his Gospel is like an "accommodation" that the Holy Spirit makes in his regard: so that everything might be very clear and sharply defined, so that nothing might be lost in reflection and interpretation.

LUKE

His *internal attitude* is essentially shaped by the fact that he gave up his profession in order to allow himself to be taken up into the new life, without any assurances. Of course, he brings his previous understanding and his previous capacities with him. But he submits them altogether to testing in the faith. It is as if he constantly wanted to distinguish between what he had learned and was able to do and what he was now compelled to do. He is set apart from the other disciples of the Lord by his capacities. He is more educated, more differentiated from them. For his part, this does not make any impression on him. He is completely humble; he wills only what belongs to the Lord, and he seeks constantly to lose his knowledge and capacities in the Lord. And this is not because of some uncertainty or lack of understanding; instead, it occurs in the certainty of one who has chosen. Everything beforehand remains inessential; the essential thing comes now, and everything that came before must arrange itself accordingly.

In his relation to Paul and to the other apostles, it is touching how he sees everywhere the goodness in what they do. He has a particular form of love that does not have any sudden upswings; it is not that he is incapable of such a thing, but he walks, so to speak, the "little way" (like the little Thérèse), in order to be completely at the service of others, so that they might be better able to carry out their service of the Lord. He gives up the things that touch him personally. Among the apostles, he is the one who best embodies the discipleship of discipleship. He also has a certain dependence on the others. That is something that characterizes his confessional attitude to one degree or another.

He stands in a humble *confessional attitude* toward the Lord. But also toward the others, whom he serves as one who confesses. Insofar as he makes an effort to lighten their service, he also tries to do whatever it is they wish; he never puts his own deeds in the limelight. He learns from the others. If he were to commit sin, he would be afraid, not only of harming the Lord, but also of harming the others. He never closes himself off and thus remains continually open to confession.

Confession in the proper sense is somewhat less significant. His greatness lies in his availability for confession. He is so convinced of his inner sinfulness that he constantly strives to remain in an availability for confession.

He *prays* quite a bit. And in a very small way. His prayer is very precise, very much tied to what it is he is saying. He prays a bit in the way a person carries out scholarly work, like a doctor. There is system in his prayer. It develops like a medical history, from the onset of the symptoms to the diagnosis to the treatment. Everything he sees is for him an opportunity to pray. He is perhaps the disciple who prays most for the apostolate and for the apostles and also the one who takes their private concerns and desires and requests into his prayer. He is also a bit the one who admonishes the others, but in an infinitely humble way and never without first having reflected over everything in God's presence.

He is very dependent upon Paul; but he never thinks his personal relationship to the apostles through to the end. It is perhaps not something that is particularly enjoyable for him, but he does not reflect on it. He has been assigned to Paul; he is subordinate to him; he makes a note of everything and does everything that needs to be done *ad majorem gloriam Pauli*. He always bases himself on the Lord in his contemplation, to the extent that he knows him. Some bit of knowledge that he has, something that occupies him, something that can be useful to him: he starts with this. And from there he enters into contemplation. Even his contemplation has something very ordered, even scientific about it. Just like his inspiration. A great similarity exists between the two. It is as if his inspiration were something that incorporated itself into what he already knew. He is almost able to write his Gospel from memory. But at the moment when he is capable of doing so, everything gets taken over by inspiration and broadened, so that he must do it, and must do it in a greater way than he would have been capable of on his own. But he is not bound to any particular state when he writes. His inspiration has something altogether peaceful about it; he enters straightforwardly into it as if he were entering into obedience.

JOHN CHRYSOSTOM (344–407)

His *inner attitude* is good and very good. He wants to do everything God wills. The only thing missing is self-criticism. The feedback he receives from his affairs is either immeasurably affirmative or so limited in its criticism—at least for him, he is unable to come to any understanding with his critics or to find any basis for conversation—that he is always referred back to himself alone in the end. And he acquires the impression that what he says and does is very important. Perhaps this attitude would have led any other person to a culpable sense of self-importance. With him, it is in a certain sense unavoidable, because he has no external reference points. His friends praise him in general without restraint, and no one takes the trouble to speak a genuinely critical word to him. Apparently, people gave him the idea that the Holy Spirit speaks through him. But he himself did not trust himself to fasten reins on the Holy Spirit. He is so convinced that he has to do what he is doing, that one has to do it in this particular way, and that there is hardly anything in it that anyone could change. In all of this, his inner disposition is blameless. He is humble before God. It is only in relation to men that he is lacking a confessor, an advisor, precisely also for his work. He formed his insights into the Church's affairs for the most part on his own. For example, concerning monastic life and priesthood. He actually does not listen when others speak. But why should one if a person is indeed God's mouthpiece . . .

His *confessional attitude* is not bad, but too flat. He has a certain shyness about exposing himself. It is as if he did not trust himself "already now" to penetrate so deeply into himself, because he had not yet come "far enough" in his work, his writings. It is as if, were he to strip himself now and bring this or that to light, he would inflict damage on the Holy Spirit in him; for the Spirit has not yet expressed himself on this point to him; he has not yet prompted him to speak on such things; it has not yet passed through his writings.

(Even if it is true that people did not confess in Chrysostom's time the way we do today, there nevertheless were times of opening up, of speaking out, of giving an account of oneself before God and men. An indubitable sin is not something one kept to oneself. The educated people, the priests and the monks, have a particular person to whom they open themselves. Even if they have already made amends for their mistake, a person knows he is obligated to give an account of it afterward. And one also knows at the same time that the one who receives this account is a certain means of God's grace and forgiveness. But the reflection at that time went no farther. One sees the person to whom one discloses oneself as a friend of the Lord; this man achieves a service of friendship for the sinner by listening to him and thereby bringing him back into friendship with the Lord.)

His *prayer* is good, but it is extremely simple. It lags, as it were, behind his knowledge. And it does so, not because it gets caught in formulas, but because he has the distinct feeling that this is the proper way to pray: a clear distance has to be preserved between work and prayer. It would not occur to him to take into prayer what he acquired through his work. And, moreover, he has the feeling that God already knows, better than he, the insights he has achieved in his work, so that it would be superfluous to lay it all before him. He remains somehow stuck in contemplative prayer; he always moves at the same level. He does not wish to go farther; it may even be that he does not see the good in doing so. He makes an effort to grow more and more in readiness and purity. But not to draw nearer to the greater and deeper mysteries in contemplation. He is of the opinion that, in prayer, the childlike images are the best, because otherwise one runs the danger of going astray and inventing things of one's own.

EVAGRIUS PONTICUS (346–399)

Inner attitude. He is like Bérulle in the sense that he does not stay near the trunk, but ventures out onto subtle branches. He is very occupied with himself in the sense that he makes himself the object of study. This is initially not at all in an objectional sense. He simply wants to learn in himself what doctrine is able to offer to a person such as himself and to what extent he is capable of truly understanding it, appropriating it, and passing it on. He opens up the Gospel, places himself before it, and begins to meditate, though all the while never forgetting that it is he who is meditating. Afterward, he puts in his place a broader circle, people of his formation, with his goals: What does the Gospel have to offer them? And finally, he does the same for the broadest circle, the Church as a whole. Thus, three concentric circles arise, as it were: he himself, the narrower circle, and then the Church.

Then there is, moreover, a study of doctrine for its own sake, without regard for his person. For example, the commandment to love one's neighbor, without any regard at all for the persons one has to love. Here, he becomes extremely abstract and often abstruse, and he ascends into punditry. But even here he recalls that he was supposed to measure the basic features against himself, against the circle, and against the Church, and he therefore afterward acknowledges human beings once again in his propositions: their spirit, their motives, their intentions and goals . . .

This is of course in some sense very interesting. Whenever he measured himself, he did so with great objectivity. But it is nevertheless dangerous. For here he comes very close to arrogance and ambitiousness. However, he is smart enough to know when he begins to become arrogant. He has analyzed himself; he knows himself. Nevertheless, in doing so he has not eliminated his arrogance; he has let it be, and even cultivated it, because he needs it for his studies. In order to understand the discernment of spirits better, he has to know what it feels like to be haughty and ambitious. He has, so to speak, inflated his own facilities in order to be able to get a better view of them. He possesses good characteristics, insofar as he has given them over to God and allowed God to increase them. But the bad characteristics he has kept for himself for the sake of his studies. He needs them in order to clarify the teachings and dogma concerning them. It is like an exaggeration of the discernment of spirits, which is ultimately not very useful theoretically, because he makes himself into *the* Christian and thus forgets that he is only *a* Christian. It is also not very useful practically, because the individuals whom he wants thus to address and illuminate are far fewer in number than he realizes. He himself is precisely a sort of isolated phenomenon in his talents and his abilities to respond. Ignatius will be clearer, more objective and transparent in his rules for the discernment of spirits than he is. His intuition is always to some extent fancified: the backgrounds, the presuppositions of his speculation are not simple enough. They are in a certain sense mounted on a pedestal.

But he *confesses* in a proper way. What he says is true. But he cannot keep himself from taking even confession as a kind of experiment. To be sure, he did not have anyone to tell him that this was enough of self-knowledge. He was lacking a second person, who would have relativized and reversed his standard. What he achieves is ingenious and interesting, but far off course.

His *prayer* is good. With time, it becomes a little too brief. But he has exact knowledge of grace and the necessity of prayer. He is like a Protestant who has no restraint on his speculation because he does not have any objective norms, because there is no Church standing behind him trimming back the wild branches. The Church is for Evagrius like a thousandfold multiplication of himself, of his own experiences in other people. She contains something invented, something constructed. He has many consolations in prayer but no visions. He has a peculiar way of projecting the things he feels: his prayer and his contemplation are so real that they reach the very threshold of vision. He is able, as it were, to compensate from his own resources for what he is unable to see. In prayer, he observes himself less than otherwise. He would ultimately be a visionary if he had not observed himself so much.

And if he had not been of the opinion that vision was a stage of prayer that a person could reach by virtue of his own persistent effort and strategies. Thus, he achieves an inner knowledge, feeling, and illumination. The light of which he speaks is not a visible light.

On the whole, he is not objectionable, only complicated. What he lacks is guidance, but he desires to place his experience at the disposal of all.

CYRIL OF ALEXANDRIA (d. 444)

It is difficult to describe his *inner attitude* in relation to a central point. He is constantly passing through one stage after another. He has a certain keenness. He is incapable of carrying anything out in a neutral way, of doing anything in a purely matter-of-fact way: he throws himself into it. And he always attacks things head on. Afterward, he comes to see at what place be began to become subjective and filled with passion; he makes plans to do it better—and everything begins again at the next opportunity. If someone points out to him that this has once already been the case, then he does not learn the lesson. He is convinced of his inner progress, with a sort of vanity. He is strongly convinced that he desires the good and that the good has to make itself visible in him, in his life and in his deeds.

In his own opinion, he is pious; but the object of his piety changes. He prays; he would like to do what God wills. Then he begins to reflect on something, to write and to preach, and the moment comes when he is no longer able to distinguish between God, the focus of his reflection, and himself. He himself has become unattuned to the object of his piety. Then the moment he finishes with this occupation or things reach a boiling point in the matter he was reflecting on, ... then he enters into himself and begins anew with a genuine sort of piety. On the whole, he is much too preoccupied with himself.

The impersonal tone he often acquires, the particular dryness he has, ought really to hide the fact that *he* is the subject with which his prayer is concerned. He has an art of covering himself up; he can develop entire theories in order to lay a veil over everything he does. Not out of humility, but out of a particular form of vanity. It gives him comfort to veil himself in this way. He does not do this only with his faults, but also with the positive element that lies in him. He thinks of himself, so to speak, as too good to be poured into his reader's food trough.

A *confessional attitude* in this strict sense is not possible. He goes so far as to think, when he has sinned, that his experience has enriched him.

To be sure, he confesses his sins. But in doing so he explains: "God allowed it to happen, indeed, he has more or less demanded it from me so that I do not forget that I am a man. For he has otherwise granted me such graces that, if I did not fall, I would run the risk of expecting too much from my fellowmen! ..."

One cannot deny that he has a certain holiness. He wants to serve. But he serves along a side track, which he himself laid, and in fact he does so always by jumping again and again off of God's track. He is like a person who ought to enter the monastery, and even wants to enter, but who then suddenly gets engaged and thinks he is doing the right thing. The moment he gets married, he immediately realizes that it does not work, and once again he seeks something else. In this way, his entire life disintegrates into false starts, attempts, and fragments, because he missed the main track.

Prayer. He wants to pray and, indeed, he does in fact pray. But even here he hides himself in a certain sense from God. He thinks one has to separate one's external life from one's internal life. Externally, he does much more than he does internally. He does not realize that he would be able to act in a genuinely fruitful way only on the basis of the unity between them.

RAYMUND LULL (1235–1315)

His *inner attitude* is very consistent, perfectly unbiased; in his actions, in his work, his course runs straight. When he stumbles upon obstacles and cannot get past them, he returns back to his starting point and checks once again to see whether everything was correct. He has no preconceptions. He is totally impartial with respect to his own thoughts; he tests his opponent's arguments and his own with the same objectivity. In this respect, he is completely humble.

His way of loving God is perfectly correct. He experiences an extraordinary awareness of God's presence. The only thing is that, in a certain respect, the experience itself is more correct than what he makes of it, than his articulation of it. In a sense, he is timid and awkward; he has difficulty explaining himself clearly. He also feels hindered by what he knows of other people. On the other hand, he feels the uniqueness of his experiences, and he thinks he has to express them in a correspondingly unique manner. He thinks he has to distinguish between various forms of expression, and even of experience, as they are known to him from the tradition. And his career path has taught him quite a bit about mystical experiences. But he confuses the genuine and required subsumption of the mystic into the Church, into the community of believers, with a nesting into certain mystical categories. This is the dilemma in which he finds himself: his experience has caused him to feel alienated from the general run of people, and, on the other hand, his experience of others has made him feel a part of them.

His experiences are correct. But when a person reads them, one begins to wonder whether they are in some sense incomplete. An unease seems to persist. But it is the unease that Lull himself has, insofar as he is unable to integrate himself. And there is no one around to do this for him. He knows that what is special about him leads somehow to a general principle, but he does not have anyone to show him the way.

His *confession* is excellent. Precisely the discomfort that he carries around in himself because of his mystical experience helps him here. He has a very profound knowledge of his sinfulness. He prays within a context, within the community with other sinners. He is very open in confession.

His *prayer* is not very focused, but quite correct. It is like a slow prayer, which gradually covers everything over. His mystical experiences shake him powerfully. Then he needs to recover to a certain extent. God knows this and therefore leads him to stroll around slowly in prayer. And he allows it to happen. Not a lot occurs in this prayer. The mystical states, of course, happen for the most part (but not always) in prayer, but they do so suddenly; they overtake him; they carry him away and a long aftershock follows. Details and specifications of the ecstasies often come only afterward in this time of subsequent prayer. It is like what happens in an earthquake: a sudden shock, a great jolt, and then the person walks through the house and looks around to see what happened: there is a leak here, a broken vase there, an undamaged room there, and so forth.

Above all, he sees Christ the Lord, and he sees him as one who has become a man among men. And then, as if at a certain distance away from this image and not completely united with it, he sees the Father through Christ, as the Father of the Son, and the Spirit as the one who accompanies him. Further, he sees the power of God, of the Creator, who is in heaven and is so great that it is impossible to conceive him. And on the basis of this power he sees the consequences, as it were, the extensions of this power in hearts, in prayers, in conversions, and in the things that happen to human beings. All of these individual facts can be conceived in their unity only if one sees God's unity; but he does not look directly into this unity; instead, he grasps it, so to speak, on the basis of its *properties*, which lie scattered about it. The moment he distances himself from the concrete image of the Son, everything then becomes immense but, at the same time, quite vague. They are erratic blocs.

His studies do not hinder his prayer. His recuperation from study is always prayer. In his heart of hearts, he feels he would be unable to work if everything were not in order with God. Being in order with God for him means: praying. He is pure and naïve. God's gift is received in him by an ever new heart. He is not one to take things for granted. And this is because of his nature, for his formation in the monastery did not change much in him. This is *not* a Franciscan element in him.

ECKHART (ca. 1260–1327)

His *inner attitude* is very good and, at bottom, very simple. The one thing he is constantly concerned with is the realization of experience. He is always a whole, never divided. Whatever he receives, he immediately translates into action. And he is very humble. He never deceives himself, and he does not wish to deceive others. He desires only to echo precisely what he has received and to understand precisely what he has been shown. What sounds somewhat exaggerated in his theories is merely the helplessness of his means of expression. He is not eloquent enough to say it plainly. But he never works himself up into something. He has genuine ecstasies, which he is never completely able to translate. But when he reads himself over, he nevertheless has the feeling that he has expressed what he felt, because for him the words truly acquire and preserve the content he gives to them. A person could understand him completely if he had lived with him and seen him.

The *confessional attitude* is likewise genuine and good. He has certain faults and difficulties: he is impatient, flares up quickly. But he is not at all a dissembler and would not want for anything in the world to be taken for something other than what he is. He does not embellish his faults, but he also does not make them more important than they are. He tells them as he feels them.

He does indeed talk about his mystical life to his father confessor, but a proper guidance does not exist. Things work anyway, because he is simple. And he does not make it into a big deal. He has more people to whom he recounts things, who accept what he tells them matter-of-factly and in a fitting way. He also here and there takes himself as an example in his instructions, but in a completely objective way. Like someone who is naked, but without any shame, in complete naturalness.

His *prayer* is the most difficult. For its part, the ecstatic prayer is in order, including the visionary prayer. On the other hand, he has great difficulty getting through the periods of dryness. Then he possesses a sort of impatience. As natural as the ecstasies are to him, to the same extent their absence is unnatural. And then he forces it a bit, so that they return. He is like one who always offers himself to God, asking whether he would like to send him or not send him, but is somehow used to being sent. If he happens not to be sent at some point, then he experiences a slight impatience. Thus, there arises within the dryness that is laid upon him his own sort of dryness. As if he actively compelled himself to become dry. Then he lacks to some extent a simple openness. Like in a conversation, when the partner ceases to respond. One thinks: There is no point in talking anymore; you are not answering.

HENRY SUSO (1295–1366)

Inner attitude. He does not follow as straight a course as Eckhart. This latter is wholly pure, simple, and transparent. Suso is a bit hidden precisely where he seems to be most transparent. He has certain danger zones. His mystical task would have been suited for showing the entire breadth of what he learns, without adding his own emphases of whatever sort. But he constructs his own kind of theory of his experiences and states. In his ecstasy, he looks with open eyes at what is shown him, but it is, as it were, in order to work out this or that chapter of his own experience more clearly. He makes a selection. And precisely because he himself decides where the accents go, he is convinced that much of it is quite transparent. He can also present it in a transparent way, but at the cost of the whole truth and of simplicity. What suffers is the directness of his intercourse with God. He is too influenced by his situation. If, in order to put things in imaginative terms, the visions were distributed among the hours of a day, then Suso would always describe, almost automatically, what went on in this particular hour, between eleven and twelve. He does this, as it were, with the best of intentions. He has picked up the notion that, if he had a complete understanding of the hour from eleven to twelve, everything else could be explained. It is as if certain questions imposed themselves on him more strongly than others. What he says is not false, but it does not represent the whole.

In *confession* one sees the same thing. To be sure, he acknowledges his failings. But even here he insists on preserving his own order. He does so in the way he opens himself. He prepares his confession of sins. He is indeed ready to say everything, but his readiness does not "go beyond" this. With a certain impatience, he confesses: This is what I have done. And one should not ask him: And that is all? Do you have anything else to accuse yourself of? He rejects such a further examination. For he has already fashioned his confession. He is in a certain sense his own teacher. And he braces himself against being forced open. He feels that what he presents is perfect and complete. He is not dishonest, but a bit too organized.

His *prayer* is good, but it also possesses to a certain extent the character of being finished. He bears the dryness after his ecstasies well. He knows that a person has to be thrown hither and yon. That a person becomes a bit shell-shocked from having been shaken up so much. But he does a little of the leading in prayer, in relation to God. He comes with a certain program. He allows God to carry out what he has in mind. But the moment it is his turn to speak, he places boundaries around himself.

He loves the Mother of God and is greatly devoted to her. But precisely here, although he sees her as great, he does not have an eye for the unlimited breadth of her consent. For him, she gives her Yes to *this* path, to *this* Son, to *this* sacrifice . . .

PETER FABER (1506–1546)

His *inner attitude* is very respectful and good. He is a little like Peter; he struggles internally until he has brought himself to do something, until he has properly assimilated something complicated. But once he has come to believe something, he believes it completely. He has to be led a bit by the hand in order for things to go smoothly. But once he has come to understand, then it is so obvious to him that he can scarcely understand anymore his prior hesitations. This tends to happen again and again. But he perseveres in readiness. He has a certain capacity to adapt when a person introduces something new to him; thus he had less difficulties than Ignatius with his studies. But when it is a matter subsequently of drawing the conclusion in relation to himself personally, of seeing the implications, then it is easier for Ignatius than for him. One cannot say that his will is lacking, but rather his understanding, once things become personal. On the whole, in spite of this need to catch up, he is very straightforward and good. And it would have been impossible to make anything else out of him than something quite simple.

(*Why did he understand the Exercises so well?*) Because he possesses a certain nobility of soul and because he masters whatever he has come to understand with his entire soul unto its farthest reaches. There is nothing wound up or tangled in his soul; his surrender is exact and complete. Because of this, he understands the basic lines of the Exercises. He translates them immediately in this life. He is one of those who are pure and simple in spirit and who therefore live happily with the angels.

His *confession* is simple and good. He is so pure that he himself has little to confess. His confession, moreover, is not very extensive; but he does not make a big deal out of the fact that he finishes so quickly. Moreover, in contrast to Ignatius, he does not need to confess very often. He lives in a sort of unproblematic way. Confession does not have a particular relevance for him.

His *prayer* is very pious but very slow. The angels who surround him do not offer him anything for his prayer, but rather they only guide him. He has a strong sense of the angels' presence. But he does not really have any explicit visions. He looks at them in a certain sense without seeing them. And he does not make a distinction, in his case, between the moment in which he feels surrounded by them and the other times when he is occupied with other things. At those moments, too, he knows he is living in their midst.

SUAREZ (1546–1617)

His *inner attitude* is unambiguous and unified but also very much hard won. To such an extent that it becomes, in part, a little cramped. In the things he writes, he is often guided, as it were, either by God himself or by the compulsion of his thoughts. Then suddenly he breaks off and asks himself whether he is able to realize inwardly the things he is writing. Here is a particular proposition. He can justify it with logical precision. But a fear overtakes him: Is this also true—in reality? Can I make this my own in a personal way? Then he has to go through an internal process before he has found the proof of correctness also to his own satisfaction. In order to speculate or to work out purely objective, historical matters, he needs to have a certain sobriety, which he is able to achieve. But afterward, he changes the measure and makes himself the measure. It is as if a person were writing a novel and suddenly had to ask himself whether his hero were truly capable of falling into such a blind rage. This is the element in him that is hard won: he has to struggle to achieve an inner attitude that corresponds to his writing. But this lies on a different page from what was said before. When he praises a virtue, he must be capable in his own eyes of possessing it and practicing it.

His *confessional attitude* is somewhat complicated, because he refers above all to himself in his work and in the way he reconciles his work and his attitude; he has to be able to manage his standards and proofs in an accentuated independence. From this perspective, he always becomes completely uncertain in confession, as if he no longer knew what he was doing. He would like to entrust himself and surrender himself to his confessor like a child. He would like terribly much to do it properly and just does not know exactly how. He has scruples of a sort. He would like to ask: How should I confess this? Is it an exaggeration to confess this? ... His confession is ultimately not bad; it is only fearful.

His *prayer* vacillates between great fearfulness and perfect security. His piety is genuine; he prays a lot, and his prayer pours out; it gushes forth. Often, he begins nervously: Should I pray now, and what and how should I pray? Then he begins at once to gush forth. And he is very grateful to God that he does not have to go through any thought processes in prayer. He also perceives many things in prayer; he receives a particular knowledge that is granted to him; he feels taken up or abandoned or accompanied or carried off. It is in this sense that he "perceives"; not in a mystical way, properly speaking. Of course, he also perceives things that possess an importance for his work. But he does not pray, as Thomas does, with a view to his work. He does not seek to profit from his prayer.

BÉRULLE (1575–1629)

Inner attitude. With Bérulle, you cannot talk about *a single* inner attitude or about *a* confessional or prayer attitude. You cannot even say a unity exists between these three attitudes in the various periods of his life. There are times when his inner attitude is in order. But in a particular moment, like when he becomes sick, it has to be put thus in order. Like when he suddenly no longer possesses enough tension. It becomes too unambiguous for him, too monotone. Thus, he begins to create problems, to analyze them, to mull over them, to construct new questions and new theories around them. In these moments, he distances himself from his inner attitude. He enters to a certain extent into someone else's skin, which he himself has fashioned, in order to live there.

He was fairly differentiated from the beginning, but he wanted what was right. Then he begins to distance himself, as it were, from the trunk and move out onto the branches; he chooses a side branch, in order to turn it into a new trunk, and then from there to create a new attitude. The trunk was simple obedience in his profession, just as it was; he would then have been able to fashion his prayer, his instructions, his sermons, and so forth, from the perspective of where he stood personally. But insofar as he turns off onto a side branch, his new position becomes abstract, and on the basis of this abstraction he seeks to create for himself a new concrete foundation for life and—although at bottom it does not exist—to recommend it to others. Even in the things that remain correct and concrete in him, there is also a little difference from reality. It is as if he were to say to his audience: "Take heed, after a half hour of contemplation, the moment can come, etc . . .", and he describes something to them that is so concrete that everyone is compelled to think it corresponds to a concrete experience, and it would never occur to anyone that it was only an abstract possibility. Thus what is often missing in his writings are the reflections that bind the trunk together with the farthest branches. It is impossible to identify the moment when he leapt from the thickest trunk to the most fragile twig with an unlikely agility. Therefore, his inner attitude ultimately contains an element of eclecticism. It would be an exaggeration to say that he has *no* attitude, for even from an eccentric position he attempts to gather what is best. It is just that he forgets that God wanted to keep him for the most part on the central trunk and perhaps later would have led him farther, but perhaps not. The branches seem more interesting to him, because they are more differentiated. He can come up with truths from these branches that do not sound so ordinary. Once he sits upon his branch, he records the tiniest reflections in an almost scrupulous way, as if to keep a balance that way.

Confession is, for him, a little labored, petty, hesitating, and detailed. He sees the trunk to a certain extent: the basic sins. But then immediately all the tiny branches that shoot off from it. He accuses himself of the most trivial details and overlooks the supporting connections, the middle position. He feels this and is therefore happy to confuse his being a sinner a bit with his being human. He believes, in a sense, that the uncertainty he feels is the uncertainty a creature always has in God's presence. And because the branch beneath him cannot bear his weight, he feels an internal threat; he feels like he is floating over an abyss and that an "annihilation" is imminent. He does not know whether God has already rejected the main branch on which he ought to sit. The person who claims the main trunk already sees where he has to come to rest. But at the farthest branch, one cannot see it any longer. Perhaps this inability to see any farther can be justified at some point. But one needs to have come to that point by following the authorized path.

His *prayer attitude* results from this: he prays a lot, and it is not bad. But he distances himself from what is central in a peripheral prayer. He can dwell on a single point for days, especially in his contemplation, a point that, to be sure, originally had something to do with the central matter, but then became so subtly differentiated that it finally lost its substance. He then becomes abstract and "adventurous". He pursues his speculations and forgets the simple "seeking of a fruit" in prayer. In the proper prayer, one somehow begins on one's feet and ends up when the prayer is over back on one's feet. He, by contrast, scrambles upward and prefers to start the next day with the "lofty" peak where he had stopped the day before.

PASCAL (1623–1662)

His *inner attitude* is characterized above all by the fact that he never lets go of himself. To be sure, he is possessed by the idea of God, by the idea of his power and grandeur. But all of this is contained within a clear juxtaposition of God and man. He never forgets, when he thinks of God, that he is man. And, starting from this point, he then draws two concentric circles. In one circle, he places all men, and thus he too is there. Inside of this circle, there is a second, smaller one, the circle of the elect, among whom he also stands. Being thus elected is a grace, which falls straight down from above. But the moment a person has received it and has become aware of it, it turns into an obligation. It is not possible to remain in it in the sense of coming to rest in it, so to speak; it requires an effort to know and also, again, a continual act of will. A person must achieve something in order to remain, and every effort a person exerts can be ultimately explained only on the basis of this will to abide within the circle. It is as if a person had the security beforehand of being allowed into the final match in a particular sport. But how much extra training this demands from him! A person is indeed predestined, but for that very reason he has to strive to his utmost. In this way, every childlikeness, every naïve spontaneity is destroyed. The knowledge of his being chosen also leads to a certain kind of new ambition: to justify this election.

Pascal is, as it were, broken by this knowledge. His "knowledge" stems from particular experiences in prayer: God has granted him a certain consolation in prayer. But he runs everything through the same ringer; he relates everything—even this consolation—to his predestination. Admittedly, he does experience this as grace, but he does not simply allow it to be grace. A saint, whom God would call holy, would not have to deal with the temptation of comparing himself with other saints, of considering them as being on a par with himself, of pondering over his own holiness day and night. Pascal runs this danger: the pseudo-feeling of election. He does not understand that God can entrust certain truths to a man for whatever reason, truths that later, as the mission continues on, may and ought to fall peacefully out of sight once again, because the other thing, which comes afterward, now becomes more important than one's own ego. And if one's own ego happens in fact to be unveiled and displayed in prayer, this is not meant *ad hominem* by God, but rather *ad Ecclesiam*. Pascal relates the grace to himself.

If a confessor says to him at some point that he is arrogant, then he does in fact recognize this: he may then perhaps become less arrogant at that point in time. But the possibility that his entire attitude is characterized by this arrogance is something of which no one can convince him. What another person calls arrogance seems to him to be a certain obligation: to distinguish himself from the masses, from those who have been less called. He also counts the confessor himself among these latter; the confessor is there in order to hear his confession and to absolve him, but not to penetrate his innermost sphere. For no one knows better than he what path he has to trod. To be sure, he makes use of the Church, her means of grace, and so forth. He can also in fact humble himself in confession; but he is nevertheless the one who has matters in hand. He thinks often about himself: it would be much simpler to be nothing more than a child of God, like the others. But he cannot get rid of the feeling, which he experiences as an obligation, that he has to raise himself up. To take rest in God seems to him something dangerous, forbidden.

This attitude is there from the beginning; it belongs to his *tournure d'esprit* [cast of mind]. In his old age, he does indeed achieve a certain insight, but it does not lead to a breakthrough properly speaking. The memorial is an instantaneous conversion, but it does not go all the way through. He ought to have put on a new robe. To be sure, he cries out: Fire! But he protects himself from being destroyed by this fire. He always spares his innermost being. For he observes himself; he keeps an eye on himself; he also thinks about the impression he will make on posterity. Because he is a chosen one, this is important.

(*Is his battle against the Jesuits serious?*) That is hard to say. *He* is serious. He writes in the heat of the moment, in the context of a mission, but that is above all in order to see what *he* is capable of achieving. What he himself happens to be doing always seems to him to be the right thing, because he enjoys being in the vanguard in this way. He may obey well, but before he does what he is told, he always nevertheless reflects that, *if* he were to do the opposite, he would also do it with the justification of his election.

Confessional attitude. He prepares himself very carefully; he is totally willing to say all the improper things he has done, and he confesses them. At the same time, however, he never wholly acknowledges them again; he never loses the feeling that they nevertheless had some kind of justification. There is no way it could have been so badly intended at the time, because after all he is Pascal.

If there is something annoying about this attitude, one nevertheless has to say that it is not pleasant to live this way, to meet oneself wherever one goes and to drag oneself around like this. But precisely this is what he thinks he owes himself and the world. And, moreover, he was the *Wunderkind* who was gaped at everywhere, even in the Church, and who was reinforced in this attitude by many people. He was told he was the only one who could do it, who could reason and pierce through the argument, the only one who moreover would have the stylistic capacities to deliver the crushing blow, and so forth. And he believes it.

(*And his Jansenism?*) He is very attracted by it, more than he himself realizes. Even when he does not inwardly consent completely, he is nevertheless drawn into the fight by obligation. And he thinks he has to keep up the fight, to provide new arguments. There are moments when he regrets it and is sorry that his entire path does not lead in a different direction. But then the other thought crosses his mind: it was nevertheless Pascal who did this.

Prayer. His prayer is utterly without regularity. He often prays very much, but then later very little. He has the feeling that regularity in prayer is something he is unable to achieve. And the same is perhaps true for most people. They are not sufficiently detached from their earthly sinful state to be able to place themselves completely in God's spiritual world. He is also afraid of growing dull to a certain extent: it would bore him, somehow, to pray a lot, and he would no longer be able to engage the problem of prayer in a sufficiently alert way. This too comes up again, the fact that he thinks he is the one who has to give it form. When the desire overtakes him, he can pray for eternity. But if the desire disappears, then his prayer almost entirely runs dry.

The prayer during the time of desire is in a certain respect artful. He begins with the greatest warmth, but he secretly controls himself: How warm should he be? . . . Then it is God who outwits him, insofar as he carries him away, as it were, for God is merciful with him and sees his good will. And at certain moments God grants him his absolute presence, in those times when he takes control away from him. But when Pascal wakes up once again and comes to himself, he has nothing more urgent to do than take the reins into his own hands once again and reflect over everything.

He certainly feels his own wretchedness. But he infers from this: How great, then, must be the wretchedness of those who have not been chosen! So that his descriptions of human misery are not altogether free from such background thoughts, not altogether true. It is only toward the end that true wretchedness breaks through and, with it, great knowledge and the insight that much of what he had previously done was not real. What he previously recognized more in other people, without really thinking of himself as one of them, from now on he is able to see in himself as well. The anxiety about failing to achieve, the anxiety about standing before God, the anxiety about the great shadow that he sees over his life, overtakes him. And he would like to entrust himself entirely to the grace of God. But his habit prevents him from doing so completely. He was so accustomed to accompanying himself that he is unable completely to forego this accompaniment even in the final minutes.

MARIA CELESTE CROSTAROSA (1696–1755)[1]

Her *inner attitude* follows a curve. It is essentially better at the beginning than it is afterward. She was genuinely pious, surrendered to God, and she prayed a lot. She is not a great visionary. Initially, she sees without having a mission; her prayers are conversations. She perceives answers, hears voices, knows about things, and has visions. The mission ought to have followed the same lines as it in fact did. But everything got a bit rushed. God would have liked to work longer on her. She should have suffered more and longer for Alphonsus' work. The preparation was interrupted too soon. All of a sudden, one wants to draw fruit from her. She has to translate every vision, every voice, and every prayer; she has to cash it all out. Where she can do no more than stammer, she is required to utter complete verses. Her piety does not allow her to resist; to satisfy her confessor, she has to take the

---

[1] In Foggia. Co-foundress of the Redemptorists.

things she has perhaps only seen and transpose them into words; she has to put words in the Lord's mouth, and so forth. And her confessor tells her in advance what is coming—"If the Lord said this to you today, then tomorrow he will certainly move things in *this* direction, take heed ... !"—in order that she not remain in a position of pure passive reception, in order that she no longer be a pure recording plate, but rather (because this is what people tell her) in order to proceed to the vision with certain preconceptions.

Alphonsus uses her too much. And he thus strikes a tone that continues in his Order. The Redemptorists ought to have developed more slowly. They would then have become more "gentlemanly" and not so "instrumentalist". More depth, more restraint.

Celeste has visions until the end; but on occasion she must have seen things she did not see in truth. She has to comply with an expectation that is no longer in sync with the expectation God gives her. The instructions for the formation of the Order were not intended with much detail but, for that very reason, were greater.

Her *confessional attitude* is initially very good. Celeste is ready for anything. Later she is no longer able to show her confessor what is not going right with her. Her readiness in relation to God has fallen out of harmony with her readiness in relation to the priest. And that is something she cannot show. Her confession exhibits the character that corresponds to her confessor's expectation. It is good that this state of affairs causes her so much pain; she compensates constantly through suffering the things that are not correct. On the other hand, she is perhaps also not altogether smart enough to grasp the thing as a whole. And then it is also the case that when she attempts at one point to bring the hidden discomfort into the light, it grows in a frightening way before her eyes and practically crushes her. And she does not completely understand where so much harm is coming from. For she still has the feeling that she has been obedient all the while; she herself would in fact prefer to remain in the background. But she is pushed forward; people tell her: No, precisely that would be disobedience. And because she herself cannot make the decision, she leaves it to her confessor. She thinks it would be due to her "sins" if something did not work somewhere. She thus lost the perfect certainty and peace she had at the beginning, though she did not lose her willingness.

Her *prayer* is in itself good. She prays in a pious and nice way and has a great need for a life of prayer. But distortions nevertheless creep in. The moment she folds her hands to pray, she is no longer sure she is doing the right thing. It seems to her that she is casting a false light and that everything has somehow changed.

MARIA THERESIA VON MÖRL (1812–1863)[1]

Inner attitude. A certain cleverness. In some corner of her soul, there is a childlike faith, but one that almost seems like superstition. She does not have the strength to order her life according to this faith. In herself, she would have the possibilities for a mission. At one point, she experiences something of the power that she *would have* if she were completely obedient. Then she transforms everything into a sort of game and lets herself get caught up in this game. It begins almost with an accident, and now she herself is seized by it: "What if it were true? ... Is it not true? ... It is true!" And she installs herself in her own words, to such an extent that they make her invulnerable. And because she sees how she has "done" it, she is of the opinion that other people also "do" it like she does. And it may therefore be the case that, where she seems most trusting, she is in fact the farthest removed from faith. Faith is for her like a trick; a person simply has to remain within this trick in order to be able to do many amazing things. What is important is only that one not get caught. In all of this, she is pious and allows herself to get trapped constantly by her own piety, which is, however, like a façade that hides her lack of living faith.

In God's presence she is afraid, because she is clearly aware that she is not doing his will. That she has made a false bed for herself. But you cannot say that she knows she is being deceptive. At times, perhaps. But the moments when she seems to dissemble most, she is least aware of it, because she always lets herself fall into her own trap. She is like an artist who paints a horrid picture, but not without traces of good taste. He sees what he has turned out and is horrified. He knows what the painting ought to look like at bottom. Then a person comes along and begins to sing its praises and to find it authentic and original. And the artist says to himself: Ultimately ... maybe it is not so bad after all, perhaps the fundamentals of the whole are good, even if the details would have to be improved ... This is how Maria feels when she has an admirer or a guide who believes her, who elevates her, and she plays along naïvely. She is happy if other people believe her and thus adopt responsibility for her, and she simply has to stay within her own lines. She has in a certain sense a peasant wisdom:

[1] From Kaltern, South Tirol. Visited by many people throughout Europe (Görres, Brentano, and so on).

"He's an expert, he's the one who ought to know! ..." Although she is smart enough, on the other hand, to understand how much her game has shaken her entire faith.

It is difficult to say anything about her *confession*. She confesses her failures. Her main sin, that she stands apart from truth, is something she cannot confess. Otherwise the whole building would collapse. Her role demands that she sin very little. She cannot afford to sin. She stands apart from truth and yet, at the same time, not actually in false-hood. She first established a fact that was true in itself, even if it did not correspond to her, and then she arranged everything else accordingly.

There is a lot of *prayer* there, pious and simple prayer. But in addition to this she traps herself in her own words. And then she enters so completely into them that she is ultimately unable to do anything other than believe her visions. Along with this, she ultimately does not have any special ambition to be a visionary; it is simply that she cannot take it back. If she were to take it all back, she would do so much damage, cause so much offense and harm ... In a sense, she is magnanimous. But there are also moments when she is truly convinced that this is the way things must be. If the people around her find the image so beautiful, then there must in fact be something in it. At other moments she is worried about the state of her soul. But then she calms herself again.

Very often, a proper mission lies right next to a false one. It is as if God tossed missions like so many rings in the air. A few are there who catch them; some do things wrongly, and one of them does it correctly. Apparently, by tossing out missions, God seems to want to give a series of people an opportunity. God determines part of the mission according to the age, so that when the mission arrives, floating through the air, it may be experienced as timely. Humanly speaking, as it were, God thinks: It is too much for a single saint; a few more people ought to bear the yoke of this task. Thus, there may happen to be seven or three founders called to establish an Order. But it can be the case that only a few respond, and the others do not. Of course, this is not how every mission is. But here in Mörl that is how it was. The people from the surrounding area were familiar with another mission, and this one was correct. If a person had inquired about it at that time, he could have experienced it ... There is even the crazy possibility that a false saint may happen to stand right next to a proper one, and if the false saint performs miracles, then it occurs because God hears the prayer of the proper saint. Such things do happen.

PETER LIPPERT (1879–1936)

His *inner attitude* is perfectly upright, solid, without fluctuations. An enormous goodness, a little bit of impatience, and no looking back at himself at all. Nothing in the whole is false, and his inner attitude is quite differentiated. But this inner attitude does not pass over into a *confessional attitude.* Confession takes place within a schema, just as he always becomes a bit schematic whenever it concerns his person, his faith, or his development. Because the circles of these two attitudes do not perfectly coincide, the fruitfulness of his work suffers. In the things he says, does, and writes, it is as if he had to check to see whether it belonged to the narrower circle within him. The confessional attitude becomes a standard to measure things. His inner attitude could be much greater. This does not mean that he does not also give himself in a "liberal" and "magnanimous" way. But form and depth are lacking in this attitude. And scope. "The mirror of confession". It is as if his sins were so much like everyone else's sins that there was no point in seeking out new paths for himself. In his guidance of those who are seeking, those who have converted or who are looking for advice, he is much more personal than in his guiding people to confession. His inner attitude has something very personal, very distinctive, while his confessional attitude adheres more to the general framework of the Church and thus—in his eyes—does not concern him as much. To put it crudely, it is as if it would already have been enough for him simply to have brought the sinner into the confessional, and whatever happened from that point on did not concern him personally anymore.

His *prayer* is multifaceted. He stands before the Father like a child. Very often, he puts order into things before he prays; he begs for forgiveness; he is aware that a person can begin a conversation only once everything has been made clean. He can pray in a very plain way, a simple Our Father, without distraction, and then immediately return to lyrical ecstasies. He has no mystical experience in the strict sense. He is too much of an "ale-brewer" for that. In any event, it is not something that interests him much. He leaves it be, as it were. Even his proper contemplation does not rise very high. If something good occurs to him, he makes a note of it for his work, for his spiritual direction. Everything is too quickly transposed into his writings, and so on. Even his writing itself comes too quickly to a conclusion. He builds his prayer up a bit too much for his praxis, although, on the other hand, he is very precise in what concerns prayer. But because he always immediately converts his capital, he does not have much in reserve, and also he does not deepen things enough for his own sake.

313

There is a slight ingratitude toward God in all this: one accepts the contributions that God makes, to the extent that they benefit one's own work.

He does not understand much about Ignatius; in this case, too, he does not store up many provisions for himself. He had a better understanding of how the Ignatian style could be useful than he had of Ignatius himself. His prescriptions are often a bit too simple. He had hoped a bit to receive more finished formulae from the Order. He explicitly looks upon his studies as a sort of treasure, which a person gets to take with him, a reserve set aside, which a person can dip into later, but about which in the meantime a person does not have to worry himself too much.

LOUISA JACQUES (1901–1942)[1]

Her *inner attitude* is, as it were, divided in two. On the one hand, she is truly inspired by a desire to understand, to believe, and to serve; on the other hand, she constructs and makes her own contribution, insofar as she imagines her experiences in part and, in part, exaggerates them. Nevertheless, she does this with a sort of selflessness and genuineness. She is in fact convinced that a person can really serve only if he stands at a certain level of self-denial, and this has to be identical with higher, mystical experience. She therefore contributes her own effort. She also exaggerates her illness and its symptoms quite a bit. To be sure, she was bleeding; but she somehow knows for certain that it was not actually bleeding of the lungs. And nevertheless, she had to believe it was for the sake of the image that she had of her mission. In this, there lay less for her in her image than in her service. Even when she had genuine mystical experiences, she at the same time "stretched" them. It is only in her last years that she ceases to do this. When she writes her autobiography, she no longer knows what it was like before. She is so much possessed by the will to serve that the personal element becomes entirely a function of this will.

She converted because of the feeling that a person can achieve more as a Catholic even on the human level. Her way of thinking was not false, but she saw things at that time too much from the outside. She "stretched" her own inner attitude, so that she would seem greater to others—for the sake of the truth of Catholicism. "I don't lie anymore

---

[1] A convert. Poor Clare in Jerusalem. Cf. Sr. Marie de la Trinité, *Conversion, Vocation, Carnets* (Beyrouth, 1943). A. was in Leysin with her.

314

so that those on the outside might not have the impression that Catholicism is a deceptive religion . . ." She thus does it sometimes more for the creature's sake than for God's.

But because she never ceases looking for the Lord, it is given to her genuinely to feel his presence. She feels him very powerfully, but she does not see or hear him. He speaks to her in a prayerful attunement. But in order for her to play her role better as a Catholic—and not at all for the sake of her own reputation and not out of self-love and vanity—she supplements it and interprets it. There are certain things she would never have written if she had not been aware of the fact that they would be read. She is like an actress who loves the part she plays and desires to bring prestige to it.

Confessional attitude. She is educated in a decisive way by confession, because she is very humble in confession. For her, confession is always an overwhelming experience, an astonishment. She confesses very well the things that lie outside of her exaggerations. Because, however, the exaggerations themselves are not transparent to her, she thus runs up against a wall. If she happens to receive a truly good piece of advice, then she immediately strives—to the extent that she understands it—in the given direction.

In a true saint, the *inner attitude* and the *confessional attitude* converge more and more into a unity. He is able to confess at any moment and is able to do it with a complete naturalness. In relation to God and the confessor, who represents the Church, he has nothing to hide. With Louisa, confession at first includes only certain regions, certain fields of grace; but these fields have the tendency to extend themselves and thus to influence the inner attitude more and more.

Prayer attitude. It took a long time for her to come to understand proper prayer. During her conversion, she prays a lot, but she is caught up in a sort of formalism. Nevertheless, she does not have a genuine experience of the soul's humble kneeling. She has to grope around for a long time before she finds access to contemplation. In the cloister, she frequently has to fill up the time of contemplation with vocal prayer, with a sort of spiritual intensity and strongheaded zeal, in order to avoid dispersion. Later, she grows more and more into a true contemplative.

God takes her away very soon after her best time, also in order that she not discover how she was at an earlier time.

FOURTH SERIES

Saints engaged in their characteristic prayers

It goes without saying that A. formulated the prayers in the following series in her own language and her own vocabulary, with the intention of reproducing their spiritual content, their favorite ideas, and the particular saint's general attitudes. However, she also heard verbatim individual sentences and often entire prayers, too, and partly in their original languages.

IGNATIUS OF ANTIOCH (d. 109)

A. sees him at prayer, very simple, very close to the Lord. And at the same time very close to the Church. With an awareness of the relationship between the Church and the Lord, as it will later scarcely ever be achieved again. He cannot pray for himself without praying for the Church, and he cannot utter the word "Church" without seeing the Lord. He feels himself to be a member in the Church, but the Lord is her head, in indissoluble unity with her, which is, however, not in any sense a melting into one another. He sees them as two, who are, however, so inwardly bound together that it is impossible to see one without seeing the other. For him, it is unthinkable to worship the Lord without bringing the worship of the entire Church before him and to express in himself something of the Church's essence.

His prayer is not contemplation. It is simple, but very deliberate. He feels that what he *sees* clearly in the Church and in the Lord needs to be brought to expression again and again in each prayer. He would be afraid of surrendering himself to a sort of contemplation. For one thing, there is no one to guide him and to show him what to do, and, moreover, he is afraid of getting lost in a dreamworld. His determinative and formative mission seems so strong that he places himself entirely at its disposal even in prayer.

Prayer is not only a need for him, but also a duty and obligation. When a problem occupies him, he takes it with him into prayer. He does not pray for the clarity of knowledge. But rather he prays while he thinks and reflects. At the same time, he also does not treat prayer simply as a means to better knowledge. It is for him the highest thing into which he places his reflection and examination. He would not know any other way to seek and to act other than as embraced within prayer.

First prayer: Lord, I stand here as your servant in your Church, with the will to serve you in this Church. To serve in such a way that I not only maintain the title of servant but also receive it anew every day.

You see how faith in you and faith in your Church fill me so full that I have no desire to do anything anymore that did not belong to you. However, I know myself, and I know how weak I am. And I also know that your Church does not yet grasp your love entirely, that there is still so much in her that is adapted to us as human beings and sinners and that can be transformed into your purity and goodness only with difficulty. I see your love, Lord, in the fact that you permit me to work in your Church, to give her the form you desire, that you show me this form so that I can help bring it about in reality. And I also know that, in order that the task be carried out in a way that brings you joy, you must first of all transform me myself; you must make your faith effective in me, so that, with the power of your grace, which is love and which dwells in me because you give it to me, I may pass everything on to the Church just as you give it to me, so that the Church can mold herself into the form of your Bride. I beg you, Lord: Bless your Church; bless me in your Church, and bless all those who enter into the Church through the Church, who, through us, your servants, are called to be Church. Allow that the work you have accomplished in your apostles be continued in us and flourish, so that your faith and your presence may become ever more alive among us. Amen.

Afterward, A. sees him with an incredible longing to serve the Lord by his death. It is a burning thirst for death, and it is so in spite of the fact that he loves life. Actually, he is far removed from indifference. He desires death almost as a proof that God takes him completely seriously. In death itself, he will have the joy of being certain in this regard. If God had not accepted his sacrifice, he would have thought: God thinks I am lukewarm! His attitude is very attractive; but it has a certain primitiveness that is no longer permitted. That is precisely because indifference has not yet come to be understood. But that is no matter; he gives to his age the best he has to give. He is very intelligent; but his understanding transposed into our own age would prove to be the religion of a person who has not been formed or guided. His simple, passionate, masculine love, when you see it, immediately awakens the desire to die with him! Everything in him is straightforward; there is nothing reflected, nothing affected. It is a sudden, mighty experience of being overpowered by the will to sacrifice oneself. But wholly out of love.

He has a deep knowledge of the Eucharist, of the true presence of Christ in it within the Church.

Second prayer: Lord, it is not possible for your entire Church to die a martyr's death, for believers must remain to carry your faith forward and to pass it on, just as you give it to us, not a dead faith, but a living one, as you give it to us again and again in your Eucharist. But there also have to be some among your servants who die for you, whose martyrdom bears fruit in the Church. The Church is still so weak, so human, that she has constant need of death in order to draw new life from it. You have given us the new life of the Eucharist out of your death. Allow us to give the Church and you the new life of our blood out of our death. Do not reject our petition! Grant us this death! Grant it to us also so that we may know we are allowed to be yours. So that we may have the certainty that you have heard the prayer we have been making all these years as well as the certainty that it will be fruitful in your Church by the power of your grace. Grant that not only what has been, but what is to come, namely, our death, which ought to be a prayer, show you that there is nothing in our possession that we love more than you and your Church. Preserve all those who are weak, who might become unfaithful in the last moment. Grant us, in spite of our knowledge that there is a risk in our request—the risk of the faithfulness we must keep—to die in the way that you expect from those who belong to you, with love in our hearts, with faith and hope in your eternal life. Amen.

IRENAEUS (d. 202)

A lot of faith, a lot of work and prayer. In work, he always runs up against the core questions, but he constantly faces the temptation to digress and to set out on side paths. Then prayer compels him to get back in line again. The side path leads him away, even his prayer; but then he notices that he has to retrace his steps. He does not grow tired of seeing falsehood anew each time, and his energy for getting back in line does not lessen. The return happens, not primarily out of humility, but rather out of the deepest obedience of prayer. He comes upon evidence that shows him there is no path leading forward in this direction.

He possesses what one might call a knack for contemplation: he places himself abruptly in the center of faith before he begins to contemplate. With his innermost being, he feels out this center, and, taking this center as a point of departure, he begins to think through the new thing that occupies him. He then sees that it may not altogether fit, and he must therefore revise things from this center. That is something one ought to be able to sense in his work.

Of course, he never affirms heresy. But when he studies systems, there may be moments when he asks himself: Is there not a certain truth here, which a person could use and build up? But then he measures the idea against the Whole that the Catholic faith represents, and he returns to this Whole without the slightest concession. The passage through the false doctrine enriches him; he knows much more about the truth at the end than he knew at the start. He establishes his central path by means of his interaction with the periphery. He now understands much better why the Catholic is the way it is. It is his contemplation that conveys the measure to him. It itself contains this measure; it is what stimulates him, almost from the outside, so to speak, like an example, like a friend on whom one calls.

Each time, his return from the external branches to the center also means a clear act of his intellect. Outside he distances and alienates himself; he runs the risk of losing God himself. He returns then in order to give his assent to the greater evidence. It is not simply out of humility in the presence of the God who remains greater than he. When he moves outward, it is like a sort of stubborn insistence on his being right, but then when his thinking needs to be bound back again, he allows himself to be bound back.

He knows about God's silence. When he begins to pray, there is at first a silence. But then something in him rears up to a certain extent against this silence: namely, his joy in knowledge. It is as if he were to say each time: Lord, you know I desire what you will. I absolutely want to remain in the center of your Church. And I know that your Church exists in order to give you glory, and I want to give my entire life to you and to your Church, above all because you have entrusted me with the task of keeping watch over your doctrine and her form and purity. I also know how the path from your doctrine runs to you and, even better, how you yourself hold your doctrine in your hands. Each time you entrust it to us it is as if you grasped it firmly in your hands and held it tight. Nevertheless, you also allow my hands access. If you called me and gave me the task to devote myself to your work of clarifying your concepts and setting your dogma into relief, I must nevertheless add my own knowledge to it. Today, I bring to you what I have discovered since the last time, but it does not yet allow itself to be integrated. At the beginning of my prayer, I actually thought I brought back to you only what already belonged to you, but it is only now that I see that it does not allow itself to be incorporated. For I feel you immediately more distant, as if this new idea stood between you and me like a fault. Therefore I know: there is nothing left for me but to return back along the path to the trunk, which is more secure, and to stay at the place that is formed according to your measure. I must do it against my own will, because I had previously gone outside of my own accord. Of my own accord and, nevertheless, also together

322

with the spirit you ultimately gave to me. I feel that I must now receive your Spirit anew, that I must return against my will and yet at the same time consciously and willingly. Allow me to build up each sentence and each word anew in the unity of your concepts. Grant me, too, the fighting strength to accomplish it again and again, so that in the end nothing else remains but your doctrine in its purity.

At the conclusion of the prayer, there is a surrender to God of everything that was not entirely in order in him, of the things that he simply must leave to God, though it is something he is not able to manage completely. And when what he considers to be his alienation, his sin, is settled, then everything ends with a radiant prayer for the Church. It is as though he had to intone a hymn of gratitude for the path that is newly given to him, the path he does not yet see (work is what will reveal it to him). And God truly gives to him in the end the strength to start his work over again.

CECILIA (d. ca. 250)

She is the woman of small prayers but of a great prayerful disposition. She has no conception of contemplation in the strict sense; no one has formed her in this. But she has a powerful inner guide. And she has this to such an extent that she is not even shown in what direction the path leads; she sees only the general Christian life in front of her. Step by step, she does what she ought to do; she does it without an overview of the whole. She has no contemplation that stretches out over her daily work.

If she does not live from within contemplation, she nevertheless does live from within vision. There is in fact nothing extraordinary for her about visions. And vision always determines whatever it is that comes next, so that she simply has to obey. She does not constantly have to direct her senses back to the Lord, for she looks in his direction without having to make an effort. She is gentle, amiability itself, and these properties are the expression of her entire being. But this basic feature has more the character of "expectation" than of "fulfillment". As a contemplative, she would have been constantly "fulfilled"; as a visionary, she is wholly a person who waits expectantly, ready to be directed farther at every moment. She sees a lot of angels, and always the sort that are entrusted with a task, just as she herself is constantly one who has been commissioned. It is not individual words and deeds from the Lord that are present to her, but rather the Lord in general and her mission. She is incapable of any movement by herself. If she sees a task, then she is not able to work it out, interpret it, and understand it in contemplation. She is directed to beg the Lord: "Send me your angel, so that he might explain it to me." She does not demand to see God in prayer; it is enough for her that God exists and that she is permitted to love him and to stand constantly at his disposal. If God wants something from her, she is there. It is as if she stood in the room next door. God needs only to come over. And precisely because she loves God so much, she does not demand to know what he is doing or what he is thinking. She is certain that he will let it be known when he needs her. Something therefore remains, as it were, incomplete; but at the same time very beautiful, because it is very childlike. And because she has recognized that martyrdom is coming, she is wholly surrendered, without fear; because God has said it to her through his angel, everything is in order for her, and she will bear it as a witness to love.

The first prayer comes from this period, because she does not yet have a complete understanding of the essence of virginity. To be sure, she is already someone who has been set apart, but she does not yet know for what purpose. She says Yes to everything God desires and, in doing so, does not know what she is promising. God gives virginity to her, so to speak, in a sealed letter, which she is able to open only when she enters into marriage. In the meantime, it is as if she has received something through the Church that was so intangible that she herself did not grasp exactly what it was. Something so pure that she was able to receive it only in the most perfect surrender and handing over of herself.

First prayer: Our Father! I am more and more filled by your goodness and your grace every day. I want to belong entirely to you, so that you can make whatever you want out of me. I have uttered the required vow in the hope that you would accept it as what it ought to be: a sign of my love for you, a sign of my readiness to receive from you what you desire to give to me, to remain ready for you, and in this constant readiness to renounce what women call marital bliss. I renounce children, and I renounce a husband, so that you can do with me what you will. Lord, I feel that this vow, which I do not entirely understand, gives me strength, the strength to promise still more to you. And thus I desire to devote every moment of my life to you and to receive from you the death that you have resolved to grant to me. I beg you to dispose of me and not to allow me to be unworthy of your promises. Amen.

At the time of this prayer, she thought that every believer is inwardly called to something special, that she is simply doing what every believer does. She will broaden the vow. Then she will have an even better understanding of the interconnectedness of all believers, of the Church. Up until this point, she saw almost only the individual paths to God. Now she begins to pray for others and for the Church.

Second prayer: Lord, death is near. It is the death you grant me to die. The death into which I am permitted to enter for you, for the other believers, for so many who ought still to come to faith. I thank you for this grace, for I know that a death like this is a grace for the entire Church. It exists, not in isolation, but in connection with the death of all the martyrs who joyfully gave their lives for you. For you, for your Church, for all believers, for all those to come. I cannot thank you enough for this grace. But you see that I am a weak woman and that I will perhaps not be spared anxiety in the end. But I beg you, and I beg you with the power that the promises I have made to you lends me in your regard: allow me to die truly in accord with your will, and grant that I may be allowed to show to your Church unto the final moment how much I love you and that I receive death in no other way than in love for you and in readiness to do your will. Lend me the assistance I need; let me suffer together with you; and give your grace to all those who will have to travel down the same path of death as I do. Bless those who follow me, who do not yet believe, the people close to me who already believe; bless all the believers who have become mine through you; bless your entire Church, and receive, finally, from me my gratitude for being permitted to understand now in truth how great the grace is to be permitted to die for you. Amen.

ORIGEN (ca. 185–254)

His work. He is very dependent upon his circumstances when he works. He makes no progress for days and extended periods of time. Then suddenly it bursts through. The things that shoot up are intellectually very rich, but the things that are won slowly and through hard work have a better foundation. He ought to test the work that shoots up during the time that passes more slowly. But this is not something he likes to do. Despite the sharp differences in the modes of working, he is absolutely even-keeled in prayer. It is a consistency in endurance, in intensity, in the will to pray, which is extraordinary. Prayer soaks through him in a constant flow. He also prays a lot for clarity and for his work. But he often does not have the time to test the work he has accomplished within the mind-set he has in prayer.—In work he mostly leans on himself. To be sure, he has read a lot; he is abreast of all the current ideas, is very educated. But things acquire value for him only when he has digested and assimilated them. Thus, for example, he is not able to criticize a thinker right away. He first has to take him into himself, and this is how he takes a position. He is not polemical by nature; he is also not able to attack others from the outside. He has to appropriate what is alien and then to see what value it has. The things he receives from outside are at bottom stimulations for his own reflection, on the basis of which he then comes to a reaction. The polemical thinker counters claims with other claims, truths with other truths. But Origen discusses everything within the one common truth, of which every true claim is a reflection.

The *personal*. Whether he is in a productive phase or he is working at a slow pace, his days are filled, filled to the utmost. He tackles a host of things all at the same time; but in his own estimation there are always a lot of things in his work that are left unfinished. If he writes ten sentences about a particular thing, then perhaps two of them would be complete, while a few others would be flashes of insight in need of revision. But if a person were to go after him and attack him for the unfinished sentences in need of a reworking, then he becomes merciless. But he is driven to do this, not out of anxiety, but rather out of a certain humor. He is not one to hold a grudge and has no problem with *ressentiment*. If he shuts a door, then he knows it will no doubt open up again at some point. But contradiction bothers him. And he knows: if a quarter of what he has said were not true, that still means that three-fourths of it is true. With this persistence, he has a peculiar feeling for his own worth. Things he simply jotted down begin to become interesting for him once they are attacked. He is now able to get excited about them and defend them, not without wit. And then, in his zeal, he comes up with such glorious and witty arguments that he himself becomes convinced of how right he must be. Even his strayings occasion genuine insights in him or, in any event, interesting intellectual positions. If he had had a single true friend with whom he could relax, then he would have taken back many of his stray ideas. For though the defense of these things often struck him as so amusing, he would nevertheless have been willing to retract them in love. If only he had known in relation to whom. Somehow, he is a child. If someone had spoken to him in love, he would have understood most of it and given preference to the greater service of God. For in his prayer, he offers up everything he has, and if there is anything lacking in his offer, it is perhaps only because he does not understand it all. If a person wanted to study him seriously, he would come across the most beautiful truths at every turn, which were neglected in the periods of time that followed.

His *fellowmen*. When he looks on them during his preaching and addresses them, then he is full of love for them. When he succeeds in abstracting from the real human beings, such as they are, he thinks: "Here before me is a community of seekers", and he is then inspired to reach the loftiest tones. But when he then looks at them individually—the way they sit there and fail to understand anything—he feels sick. The same is true at the workplace; where he works, the relationships between the teachers and students are very much regulated. If he looks only at these relationships, then they appear to him as something holy, divine, liturgical. But if he then considers the concrete situation, the men themselves, it drives him up a wall. That does not prevent him from maintaining contact with many significant people. In relation to a man whom he recognizes as significant—and this adjective is very important to him; it is a standard for him—he can be very warm and genuinely humble. He appreciates people without ulterior motives. But with insignificant people, he is only very kind when they represent for him the anonymous masses. If they stand before him as petty individuals, then he becomes enraged. He hates all things petty. But he knows his faults and ultimately does penance for his failures in the constancy of love.

Hell. He once had an experience of hell, which is reflected in his prayer. On the one hand, he would like to remove the fear of hell from people, but, on the other hand, he would like to increase the objective truth of hell so much that no living human being could have in fact any place in it anymore. Precisely because he does not see anyone in it, hell is for him a much greater and more important reality than it is for those who fill it so full of people. He sees it as something so horrible that it surpasses any creature's capacity to bear it. Man has room in grace, although this too also infinitely surpasses him; but he has no room in hell. Origen sees it as the inelimnable remainder of God's wrath. And he cannot avoid seeing something good in every human being, some sort of good impulse or deed at some moment in his life. And he transposes this way of seeing, multiplied to an infinite degree, onto God. He has the feeling that, if *we* are able to find a tiny hint of goodness in what is evil, then God will be even more able to do so.

Trinitarian unity. He never gets tired of trying to sketch out images of the Trinity, to distinguish the Persons in such a way that it is accessible to the intuition. He sees the Son's mediation, his reconciliation, his

327

life in the world as a totality, a huge sum, of personal paths of suffering, purgatories, because he has left the Father's "heaven". The Son bears our sins and, in doing so, has a perfect understanding of them because he is pure. And each one of us who is purified in the purgatorial fires of the world receives a share in the understanding of his own sins, just as the Son possesses it. Origen is admittedly unable to carry his schema any farther. He made the attempt conceptually to join together the Holy Spirit and hell, but that is something that cannot be carried farther.

He always tries to *hierarchize* things. He hierarchizes the Trinity, purgatory and its path of purification, the Lord's life in the world, and even the lives of individual Christians. And at the same time he relates the things to one another: for example, the Father with youth, the Son with middle age, and the Spirit with old age, and so forth. The levels are banisters or scaffolding upon which he can try to come to a rest, because the upswings of his thinking are so overwhelming that he otherwise would get lost. He is absolutely not the inventor of "systematic progress". Many of his insights were discovered in the moments of "outburst". But because much of this was too risky, he later weakened it and settled it down in moments of peace. It is often as if his spirit carried him so far forward that his own strength no longer sufficed to call back what was said. He prefers to think in trilogies. The part that stands in the light concerns the Son. But he knows that this is only a third of a trilogy, and this is something he has not brought to completion. He also lacked the support of the tradition in this regard.

He sees God's "ever-more" character as an advance, not strictly speaking as a leap or even a reversal, a turning around. It is the constantly developing, the continual opening of new perspectives, which he would like to follow out to the end as far as possible. But at the same time he knows that this cannot happen. He knows this with a sort of frustration. If he is "in good shape", like an acrobat, then "he'll accomplish the trick." If he is not, then it seems to him to be "too dangerous". He hopes at some point to reach the divine limits. He learns God in the way a person learns grammar. He still cannot manage to master it, but if only a person could make the right effort ... ! This attitude is somewhat childlike; it belongs to the Church's first years. He is very much attached to the idea that God is the grown-up, who has the full knowledge, while man is the one who must learn, the child, the image, the one who strives more and more to correspond to the original.

First prayer. He starts out for the most part in a personal manner in prayer by introducing himself. He is childlike before God, in the same way that he is humble in the presence of people he admires. And he prays:

Father, I come before you, your Son, and your Spirit, as I do every day. As always, it is with the request for knowledge and for help. You know that I do not pray in order to give my work more glory, in order to increase the fame that surrounds me. My request is part of my worship. I desire to glorify you. I desire to serve you. And the more time passes, and the more I think I have grasped something of your mysteries, the more profoundly and strongly I know that your mysteries become greater with every approach and that everything I think I have understood always remains nothing more than a beginning. Nevertheless, I desire to persist, for I know that this beginning is necessary and that you yourself desire this beginning. Often, because I take so much delight in this beginning, in this work, because I feel myself so enriched by everything I am permitted to do for you, I become afraid that I do too much by my own means and leave too little of the choice to you. However, Lord, I know no other way to do your will in a serious manner than to ask you: Show it to me, and have me do it. Then I see again that my fears are idle, because the beginning is always in any event a beginning in you. But, Father, this beginning drives me toward the center, and in this center I take up for myself too great a place, with my own insights and my pleasure in work. And it is always too late before I come to see it. I am unable to come back, and I cannot move ahead: If I break things off, then your task is not carried out; and if I move ahead in the knowledge that I was seeking myself too much, then there is a disagreeable interruption, a break; the thought process is, so to speak, cut short—in the hope that your own may come back! Just as you stood at the beginning, so should you stand every time at the end; it is only the center that has trouble holding you, because I myself am in this center. And not only I, with my ideas, but the ideas themselves, and the people who are working on the same thing or who have an opinion on it. Lord, if I knew the way to allow you to be both beginning and end and to allow this center, which I myself am—I and the imperfect Church, I and the imperfect people that surround me—to disappear, then I would be greatly in your debt. For I know that you truly are the beginning and end in all things, and I do not want to remove my activity from all these things. Father, accompany my work today and allow it to have a genuine beginning and end. Allow me to disappear; do it out of love for your Son, who teaches us what it means to disappear. Have mercy on all my sins, on all my imperfection, both my sluggishness and my impulsiveness, and allow what is mine to become yours. I ask you in the name of your eternal life; for your eternal life is you, your Son, and the Holy Spirit. Amen.

Second prayer. Father, you know that today I want to speak about you, together with the Son and the Spirit, to speak about your triune light. I have announced it, and everyone expects it. And it is indeed also the logical continuation of what I have begun. Father, it was admittedly a lack of respect, but I thought that I possessed the power and the insight to grasp your triune essence in such a way that I would also be able to describe it. And above all also that I would be able to awaken a need for this knowledge in your community. And now I see that my longing for you is indeed too small and that my longing for knowledge is too intellectual, too problem-oriented. Not simple and not pure enough. Father, you see that the intention was good, and now I do not know how to carry it out. Now everything I have to say sounds hollow to me. The reason is that I myself stand in the way, because too much of what I have used for my research and understanding came from myself. Father, you must help me, I beg you: Do this just this once for me so that your community does not grow angry with me, so that they do not believe that everything is so small, so limited, as I see things now, but that they instead understand that each of your truths is infinitely greater than my impoverished conception, interpretation, and preaching. Father, I promise you from now on to put myself more and better at the disposal of your Trinity, to be less and less occupied with myself and my comfort, and to try to serve you, the Son, and the Spirit. But guide me, Father, and turn everything to the Good that threatens to turn bad through my own fault and carelessness. Amen.

ATHANASIUS (295–373)

A. first sees him in the way he works. Some word, some theme, greatly occupies his attention. But it is as if he did not have the strength to attend to a single theme; he splits things up, and he uses this fragmentation to find the theme's center. His entire aim is to preserve the purity of doctrine: as much inwardly in its foundation as externally with the rebuttal of whatever opposes it. This great framework has a very clear tension. But in its inner sphere, there remain constant new beginnings; he tries out one thing at one point, another thing at another. In the very same day, he tries out things that contradict each other because he seeks a rest from one thing in the other. There is something erratic in his work. The same is true for his prayer. He can say the strangest prayers. He begins with praise and thanksgiving and then ends the prayer with a terrible begging for mercy. Or he contemplates the mystery of Christmas and right in the middle of it engages in a great meditation on the Cross. It is as if he would founder on the catholicity of the faith: it is too vast to comprehend; he cannot cope with it. He sees not only the dogmatic connections, for example, between Christmas and Good Friday, but passes immediately from the mood of the one world to the other. He is, in prayer, like the eternal Jew. That does not prevent him from being the pillar of the Church, which he has become through his openness and the final sum of his work and his immeasurable love for the Church.

He needs respite from his work, and he seeks it in things that provide relaxation, such as in music. But something forces him mercilessly out of this respite and back to work: he cannot free himself from associations, and now he begins, by negating the accident, as it were, to take these associations as necessary, and he incorporates the things his recreation time provided into his principal work. Because many of the things that befall him during the day are full of meaning, he likes to turn everything that happens to him into a "fate". Thus, accident and necessity, what is central and what is peripheral, end up falling along a single line.

In all this, he constantly forces himself to obey God better. He avoids everything that might distract him from his task. He makes an incredible effort to triumph over the natural man. He is a great ascetic; in his asceticism, he does many things that are perhaps not given to him to do, but he does them anyway in order to be an example for other people, for whom such things might be more given than they are for him. In every counsel he gives, in everything that could have importance for the Church or for monasteries, he would like to be able to give exemplary advice. And he treats himself like a guinea pig; he does not spare himself the utmost trouble if he sees significance in it for others. He knows, both for himself and for others, how necessary ascesis is, and he leaves a lot of extra room for the "for others" aspect in his personal ascesis in addition to the "for himself" dimension. But not in the sense that, every time he finishes with the "for himself" aspect, there is still something left to do "for others", but rather he begins again from the beginning for the others. He possesses a tough-minded magnanimity, insofar as he sees himself so much as an instrument and object for the Church that he uses himself as if he were an instrument, while someone else in his place would leave things to God—presumably without fault.

He is intelligent, but he would like to be even smarter than he is, in order to serve better. He thus often fails to have a precise sense of his

331

limitations. In his belief that he needs to be able to do everything, he often goes a little too far. Because he thinks that every event is fated, he expects too much of himself. He prays a lot; indeed, constantly. He carries it out on the basis of an insight that the Church needs prayer, that the individual needs to pray, that also the ancient Jews prayed, that no obedience to God would be possible without prayer. But his prayer rests, as it were, on an intellectual foundation. It is only when he is persecuted, when he is in prison, and so forth, that his prayer becomes *free*, that it becomes a cry or something else personal. Before this, his prayer was not exactly forced, but there was something too official about it. The harder he is persecuted, the simpler everything becomes. He first comes to a deep understanding of the perfect freedom of the children of God in his later years. It would also be difficult for him to remain within the obedient bond that his obedience to God would form. He would not understand what that was; he is too dependent on his own judgment of what is important.

First prayer. Triune Father, since you have given the Holy Spirit to your Son in his Incarnation in such a way that the Word that was in you became man—and yet still remained Word—so that your Word could dwell among us and show us your will, I thus ask you: Give me your Spirit, so that I, who resist you, may become your servant, whom you need for your Church. Daily, in every moment, I see the task; but I am inadequate to it; I do not even know how much you demand from me and what the most important thing is that you need in order to establish your Church. Thus, I desire to ask you: Give me your Spirit of Illumination; give him to me in such a way that he might make this useless instrument a serviceable one. In such a way that he might take from me my own disposal over myself in order to place me more and more in your hand. But grant me your Spirit, not in a way that would benefit me alone; lend him my words, my writings, my intentions; give him also those who engage with my work, those who allow themselves to be strengthened by this work, which ought to be your work, and also especially those whom this work ought to dissuade from their false doctrines. Father, share your triune Spirit; give him to your entire Church; lend him to every believer and also to those who do not yet believe but who, through your grace and through the grace of your Son, could become believers. Grant that I may lay my entire life in your hand, renewed, that I may hand over to you my work, my prayer, my penance, everything I do, so that you might use it as you see fit. Amen.

Second prayer. When you were small, Lord, in order to avoid persecutions, you had to flee from one country to another. You were a child; you handed yourself over completely to the Father, who fashioned your flight. No one asked you; you had nothing to say. And you participated in this flight, without care, just like a little child, because everything was thus preordained in the Father's knowledge. Lord, I beg you, allow me to share in the childlikeness of your suffering of persecution. Grant that I might undergo this flight that wears me out, this imprisonment I do not like, in your Spirit of childhood in relation to God. Grant me the capacity to bear everything disagreeable in the way you bore it, without asking why at every step; but rather by trusting in the Father. By leaving my will to you alone. I know that he knows the reasons for everything and that all the persecutions to which I am exposed represent, indeed, only a tiny portion of the persecutions of all Christians. And I wish to learn how to accept everything in your Spirit. I wish to let it happen and not always to be provoked to raise questions that come from my person, questions that are superfluous and that could even hinder the ripening of the fruit of persecution. I want to leave this fruit with you, and the bearing of it, and everything else along with it. Only give me the Spirit of your childlikeness, for I know that you were persecuted in your childhood and that you thus did not serve the Father less than when you died for us on the Cross. Bless these persecutions; make of them what you need; bless all those who believe in you; bless the truth of your Church, so that her truth may become more and more manifest; and bless, too, those who are persecuted. Amen.

HILARY OF POITIERS (320–367)

He makes a clean cut in his religious life between prayer and work. There is a certain modesty in this: he does not want to burden God in his work as well. He is constantly aware of the fact that he works for God and that God is the one who makes his work possible. But he does not allow his work to flow together with his prayer. If he has greater inner difficulties—and these are not spared him—then he needs a longer time for prayer in order to become completely pure once again in God's presence. He has a strong need for confession—in the form it had back then—and indeed everything has to be expressed precisely and thoroughly. Even the things he has already settled he brings up again, in order that he not give the impression he has always stood where he is standing today. According to his feeling, this too demands the *opus operatum* of absolution: that everything be laid out as

333

perfectly as possible and that it would be an obstacle to the perfection of the absolution if the "father confessor" did not have a completely clear view of everything.

He experiences something similar in prayer. Perhaps he stands in a difficult place in his work and cannot make progress. Suddenly, he discovers the reason: he himself is standing in the way. Now he takes a lot of time until he has brought everything into good standing with God. If he comes across a coarser mistake, which would otherwise not fall in his line, then this disturbs him for a long time. And when he has distanced himself from God in prayer for a period of time and returns to nearness and intimacy with God, then he puts the whole of his work from the preceding days to a precise test, in order to discover whether it has perhaps been infected somehow by his alienation. Even in this, he remains strong, though there may seem to be nothing noticeable externally. He is like a person who knows when he is in a state of grace and who uses this awareness in order to be able to work peacefully. Then he does not actually need to interrupt his work in order to pray, and at the same time he does not need to come to God with questions for every tiny little thing.

First prayer, in the time of inner order: I thank you, God, for having allowed me to serve you. I thank you for giving me the strength to use my understanding and my knowledge in accordance with your will. Never allow me to fall outside your grace, so that I may carry out, with your help and in your service, whatever it is that corresponds to your expectation. You see that the work I undertake is difficult, and you also see how subtle the objections are that I have to counter. I want to understand everything more profoundly in order better to fight in your name and to be better able to formulate the positive things you show me. Give me the strength and grace for this. And I ask you especially to give your grace to those who are meant to use my work, which ought to be yours, in such a way that they learn to serve you more and more. Amen.

Second prayer, in alienation: Father, I call to you as if I were still your son, as I was before. I beg you, turn your eyes to me as if I had not alienated myself from you. But you know that in the last days I have not remained in your presence, I have turned myself to things that grab me inwardly and that are nevertheless not things that belong to you. I have once again succumbed to the temptation to seek my own and to neglect what is yours. Looking back on these days, it is now clear to me that every step of mine carried me farther from you. Once again, I stand before you, in contrition, and I do not dare to take your work again into my hands until you have forgiven me. Accept my contrition, my penance, my prayers, and take everything my weakness offers you as a sign that I no longer want to think of myself as lying in my own hands but desire to try in the future to serve you more faithfully. Allow your grace to shine out of my deeds, so that I may experience again that you do not hate me and that I am permitted to continue to do your work. Give it the power you wanted to lend to it, without attending to the fact that I, an unworthy sinner, am the instrument that carries it out. Rather, I ask you instead for a share in your Spirit in this work and that my share in it might be embraced wholly within your will, so that everywhere the work takes me something can happen for you. Amen.

A. says: This second prayer ought in fact to be formulated with still more pathos—with many interjections, and so forth.

In relation to other people, Hilary is very warm. And he does a lot of penance. His tendency toward a great care and conscientiousness develops in such a way that he experiences nights full of dread at the end of his life. He cries out with anxiety and seeks for a long time what could be false in him and in his life. And he always finds something. But in all this it is not the case that he "gives himself a good conscience", in order that he might work well the next day. It is a sort of illness that he has, but which becomes for him an occasion to refine his conscience. It is a particular "night program" from God that does not belong to the "day program". He must allow God to "take the ground out" from under him, and not only does he not reject it, but he himself does what he can to push himself into anxiety and emptiness.

GREGORY NAZIANZEN (330–389)

It is the age of great heresies. There are endless disputes over half a word. He has to do theological work, explain concepts. He fights, and he nevertheless finds himself again and again attracted to the contrary opinion, in spite of everything. He has an incredible temper. He would prefer to defend his truth with an axe—and he has to focus his energy on the apparent splitting of hairs! Nevertheless, he does it with delight and elegance. As long as the discussions are Christian, everything goes well. But the moment they become personal, it becomes more difficult. It is most difficult when he is dealing with people who used to be adepts but who have fallen away, those on whom he realizes he can no longer rely. Then he makes himself an enemy and drives them away, when he could have guided them with a good personal word. When he has the time to reflect, to read over what he has written, that which was initially violent becomes tender. He understands that he wounded his opponent too quickly. He ought to have behaved differently with him. He thus now engages things seriously. He distills out what was merely temperament, what was hard and explosive, and what neither helped nor harmed the truth of dogma, because it does not belong to the matter at hand. He becomes objective and allows himself and the impression that the matter makes on him to fade into the background. As a writer, he is elegant and subtle.

His prayer does not occur without mighty inner struggles, which derive from his temper, which so easily forces open doors. His prayer has something of this vehemence, but also something of his humility and refinement. Then, he wants to correspond to God's will, even if the others are against him. If he was objectively right in a particular dispute, but his opponent was right at least in a formal sense, then it demands from him a very particular surrender to God's will in order to acknowledge this will also in the opponent. His passion is not without vanity. The opponent's resistance offers him a not unwelcome opportunity to pour an entire Suada[1] onto the proposition he must defend, and this is what internally reconciles him to a certain extent with his opponent.

Every time he provided proof that he can do more than people thought he could, and indeed even more than he himself suspected in his humility, he uses the new opening as space in which to linger indulgently. But his faith is completely genuine. And although certain false doctrines hold an attraction for him, he nevertheless inclines toward the truth with the whole of his soul. On the other hand, he is grateful to the truth, that he himself is able to shine in its light. But he also likes the intellectual competition; he takes a little pleasure in dazzling the simple citizens, and if he can do it within the truth, he is content. It costs him a struggle now and again not to slide to the edge of heresy in order to shine even more. A characteristic temptation for him: "If I actually became heretical under certain circumstances, then perhaps I would appear even more interesting. But posterity would discover it, and thus it is better for my reputation if I remain in the truth." His vanity is often naïve. He can thank God that he is permitted to bask in God's truth in this way.

With his fellowmen, whenever he finds his way back, he is always good again. In letters, for example, he can be very warm.

[1] ["Suada" is the Roman name of Peitho, the Greek goddess of persuasion and charming speech.—TRANS.]

Prayer: I stand again before you, Father, and know that your Son and your Holy Spirit are together with you and that all three look down upon me in the unity of the triune essence, that you too were witnesses of the battle that I waged in your name. You saw how a holy zeal once again took hold of me, because your doctrine was not able to shine out in its full radiance in my opponent's words. I sinned to the extent that I let myself get carried away more than righteous anger would have allowed. I was untrue to myself and have once again shown myself for who I am: impetuous and rash in the assault directed at my opponent. And yet, Father, when I contemplate how lofty you are, how inscrutable in your triune essence, how unfathomable in your hidden being, how poor the concepts we are able to form of you are, then I am often no longer able to restrain myself when a person deals with you in such a way. I beg you, accept my anger as a sign of my love for you, a sign of my impatience when one offends you by seeing you as less than or different from what you are. And I thank you for the mission you have given me, namely, the mission to fight for your glory on the front lines, even if a bit of the light from your glory does not fail to fall on your servant, who is permitted to fight on your behalf. Amen.

MONICA (331–387)

She is the unflagging prayer, the piety that does not fall asleep. She knows no great fluctuations in prayer. She is very much surrendered to God and also to the Church. The intensive dimension of her prayer lies above all in its perseverance. She is able to repeat one and the same prayer for the longest time with the same energy. Vocal prayer, for her, never becomes merely something mouthed with the lips. She possesses in fact the prayer of children, those who are able to pray in a very intensive way, but without knowing an answer will come from God, without even expecting such an answer, but also without at all thinking that no answer will come. One simply brings before God what one has to say to him, with the greatest possible love. There is not much more to it than this.

She is a strong and intelligent woman. Her life is full of trouble and frustration. She would like to help, but with what means? All she has is prayer. So she prays in the way she knows how: a uniform, almost monotone prayer. She cannot conceive of God's help in any other way than as the granting of prayers or of God's will for her in any other way than in the form of prayer. She admittedly lacks a helper, who could have given this uniformity a certain shape. She lacks the breadth that another person might have had to take things in hand. Because her concerns are serious and righteous ones, she is also unable to imagine that God would desire anything else. Thus, God will be prevailed upon; and he will *allow* himself to be prevailed upon.

She has no one to guide her in contemplative prayer, to clarify for her that it is not necessary to talk incessantly to God in order for him to receive it as a prayer. That there is such a thing as an attitude of prayer, which embraces the whole day's work, a state from which the individual act of prayer arises, not as something new, but rather as the expression of something that is always the case. This is something she does not know; therefore, a certain anxiety dwells in her, the constant feeling: I need to pray again, to cast myself into prayer again. Thus, her confession of sin has something anxious about it: she thinks she has to express everything in words in order for God to receive it as a confession. But it is also, once again, a mark of her particular humility and surrender that she utters constantly the same prayers, tirelessly the same appeals. She suffers a lot; but she thinks this suffering will be meaningful and effective only if it is incorporated into her vocal prayer and in this way is presented to God. The wordless groaning of suffering she translates immediately into a vocal prayer.

Her contemplation is actually limited to her availability, which lies in the spaces between the individual vocal prayers and which constructs a bridge from one prayer to the other: namely, her enduring surrender. It is a particular form of surrender, which embodies something entirely essential in the Church: a foundation that supports other things. Her son's mission will be much more differentiated, but it would be unthinkable without her own. Their missions pass over into one another. Once he has had his conversion, his mother will experience a certain fatigue. Like with a person who has an enormous effort behind him and who afterward, once he has rested, is no longer able to rise to the same level of achievement.

She is very warm in relation to her fellowmen. There, too, she tries to take everything up again into her prayer. She distributes it: one prayer for this person, one for that one. She does not have a good understanding of how graces flow into one another, the one grace that bears all things and arises for everything, the grace in which one cannot count up every single individual detail. But she takes *every* individual she encounters seriously, not only her son. Nevertheless, because she lacks proper guidance, she gives prayer preference over active love: she believes she is able to give the most through her prayer. And it is for her not altogether easy to pray so much. It costs her some overcoming of self.

A. first sees him in his youth. He is in great straits regarding his faith. He is very preoccupied with faith, with individual propositions of the faith, with the order among them and their interrelations, but without ever being able to work it all out in a human sense. He is like the student who says during instruction: yes, he has understood everything; but the moment he finds himself alone, everything becomes foreign to him and impossible to assimilate. He is unable to pray over it. The things he is able to understand to a certain extent do not converge into a unity in prayer. Afterward, he becomes accustomed to praying an Our Father, and perhaps several of them; but it takes place without any inwardness. At the same time, one could not say that this is a dryness that has been laid upon him; it is instead an inability to conceive, an inability to enter into things. It is as if his theology were purely a theoretical matter and his prayer were something completely different from and juxtaposed to it. He makes a false move every time he tries to confect a unity. He is also unable to ask God to fashion this unity, because he has too strong a feeling that it is something he himself has to achieve.

Later, a crisis occurs; apparently it is not long before Augustine's entry. It is a period of success, of conversions. But even this activity does not integrate into the rest: one part of his soul prays; another part reads and studies; and a third part speaks and convinces people with success. He is fully aware himself that all of this ought to form a unity. It is no longer the painful separation that it was in his youth; he has made a sort of habit out of it. It is only with his success that the crisis comes to expression. In this success, he comes to understand how much he has to accompany in prayer the people who have been drawn to him through his words and writings. The crisis is unleashed by the fact that his study and prayer suddenly seem to lose their value, that only the success is still there, incontrovertible, and yet unintelligible, meaningless without the other things. For a brief period, perhaps a few days, perhaps a night, he is overwhelmed by a great temptation: arrogance. But he does not succumb to it. Previously, success appeared to him as something ridiculous. Then suddenly the possibility arises: it would be possible to take control of this success oneself. But in the same moment he turns away from it. Not like this! And then he carries out a renunciation of success and asks God, for the first time in a long time, to give him prayer. A prayer for its own sake, pure, anonymous adoration. He denied himself, and God hears his prayer: he gives him what he asks for. And indeed he gives him precisely the anonymous prayer he intended in his request. It will never be a very rich prayer, but a humble and pure one. He will completely forget in prayer that it is *he* who prays.

For a time, the Church plays a wholly subordinate role for him; she is almost a necessary evil. He does not yet have a full understanding of her. Then suddenly he sees her in need; he becomes inspired; he would like to help her. He sees her as an indeterminate mass, without precision and structure, like something one has to work on. For him, the Church is this and that and then something else, and all of the facets seem to develop in different directions; there is no unity in her. But he would like to bring about precisely this unity of the Church. A comprehensive unity. It is from this perspective that one can understand his position in relation to worldly rulers. There are many passages in the Bible that he interprets in this direction, namely, that even worldly power ought to be taken up into the kingdom of God. When Christ says: My kingdom is not of his world, then Ambrose sees this as a resignation, the expression of a fact but not of a necessity. If Caesar would freely contribute his kingdom, then this would enrich the Lord's kingdom; his perfect sovereignty over the world would then express itself even better.

In his youth he is strict with himself for many reasons, not the least of which is because of the disquiet between prayer and research. In the period of his first success, he transposes the strictness into his preaching. It is only after his "conversion" that he becomes much stricter with himself, and his strictness with respect to other people evinces more love than it did earlier.

Prayer: He always begins with the Our Father. Afterward, a long transition period often transpires before he enters into proper prayer. He often practices penances in the meantime, though these penances stand on their own and are not actually a part of his prayer. Or he reflects and makes a decision about how he will fast in the coming time. A. hears what follows in Latin, and she has to translate it mentally:

God, grant that everything that our people do might happen more and more in your name, that everything might exist in the unity you determine. You see that it continues to be difficult for me to carry out my deeds in your name. I try again and again to place my entire day's work and my office at your disposal to such an extent that I do not forget you for a moment and so that you might be constantly present in my soul. However, I now feel again and again as though my intention to carry something to completion is always connected with you but that, when I carry it out, I completely forget that I am doing it for

340

you. It is as though I remained stuck on my words and deeds, as though I recalled my original intention to serve you only after I carried the deed out, so that the realization that occurred in the meantime from that point on seems foreign to me. Father, this alienation is not good for me. It abandons me too much to myself, and the less I think of you as I am carrying out your task, the more I think of myself. It is not the case that the task wholly occupied me for periods and that for this reason I forgot you. Rather, the truth is that I am looking at myself and listening to myself . . . Father, I beg you, take this away from me; it could also become a scandal for my listeners if they were to notice that I do not live the way my words say one ought to live. Over and over again I preach to them that they ought to behave as if you were present everywhere; and you are indeed present in truth. And I myself forget your presence! . . . Father, I desire to recommend to you my office, my work, and everything, every day, indeed, to place them entirely into your hands, so that you would rather take it away from me than allow me to become a greater sinner. Father, accept this imperfect prayer! Hear it; I desire to have spoken it in the Spirit of your Son. You know that I love him; I love your Spirit, and through your Son I also learn to love you more and more. Grant that something of this love might also be contained in my prayer, and allow me, great sinner though I be, to pray together with him: Our Father. . . . Amen.

AUGUSTINE (354–430)

A. sees him first in the time of his initial zeal, the time of his conversion. His entire soul is seized by the novelty. He places himself entirely at God's disposal; he desires everything that God wills. It is the zeal proper to conversion, which takes hold of his innermost being. And everything in great humility: he simply cannot grasp that he really believes! That grace is so great! He constantly returns to his faith and contemplates it, as a mother approaches the crib of her first child in a state of pure wonder, astonishment, and gratitude, unable to understand how it could be possible. He feels the uniqueness of faith with an extraordinary power; he contemplates other believers and sees: it is the same faith. And very soon he begins to suffer from the fact that the others do not feel everything and experience everything the way he does, that they are not seized by it as much as he is, that they do not experience the same inner energy and surrender that he does.

Prayer from the early period: Father, when I stand before you and am permitted to give you the name Father, then every time I cannot help feeling it is scarcely possible that you have truly given to me this entire fullness of faith, which accompanies me day and night and shows to me everything I encounter in a new light. It often seems to me that I am scarcely allowed to look upon the truths of your faith; they are so huge and, because of their size, still so foreign to me—even though they fill me and surpass all my expectations—that I am constantly afraid they could burst before my eyes like soap bubbles; they could be meant some other way than the way I imagined and above all that they are not really meant for me. And then I nevertheless know each time that it is truly your gift, that you have truly given me the fullness of belief, and that this fullness will be filled out more and more, with growing knowledge, as the years go on. So many years went by when I knew nothing of you, and I have been a stranger to you for so long! And now you have forgotten everything and made a believer out of me, whom you strengthen anew every day! Father, I want to thank you, but not without begging you at the same time: Let this knowledge pass through me to everyone you wish. Grant that I not diminish your words and that I not sully your truths. Allow me to pass on in truth what I have received. Allow me, too, to persist in the disposition of one who worships and who awaits, and if it pleases you to spread your faith through me, then let this faith be alive, and let the experience I have undergone in my conversion become an experience for many. Do not allow me to weaken; do not allow me to forget the burst of energy that accompanied your gift of faith. Allow me to share more and more in the life of your Son and confirm that it is truly your Spirit who speaks through me. Amen.

When he then begins to act and pour himself out, the innermost core of his faith loses a bit of its intensity. His prayers contain an incredible abundance of words, but they no longer possess altogether the same power of inner response as they did previously. He is like a famous speaker who has to give the same speech again and again and gradually begins to grow somewhat tired of it. Thus, Augustine grows a bit weary of his own eloquence, and he draws to some extent on his first impulse over and over again without receiving it in a fully fresh manner through sufficient contemplation. His first prayers were, to be sure, more awkward, but they were still more adequate than his last prayers; they may have been more abstract, but at the same time they had more intensity: he used the whole of his strength in order to adapt himself to what was new, however abstract it may have been for a time. He was like a thinker who seeks to master a new idea: although he is profoundly moved by the content that lies beyond his grasp, it is not yet within his power to develop the content in a logical way. Later, when his capacity increases, he is no longer inwardly moved by it to the same extent.

In relation to his mother, he is full of gratitude and tenderness. She brings about a new relationship to women in him. To be sure, he turns his attention primarily to men, but he now understands true love for a woman. In everyday life, his relationship to his fellowmen vacillates a good deal. Admittedly, he tries to love them, and he does indeed manage to love them from time to time, but it is often only with difficulty and with repeated failure.

At the beginning, speaking requires him to overcome himself, but later this is not necessary. At the beginning, he is so overwhelmed by grace that it is difficult to convey it, and work gives him trouble; later, it is much easier. He is able to write or to dictate an enormous amount, one thing after another, without slackening. He remains diligent in his studies, and they allow him to make contact with many important people. His zeal does not let up, even if his inner warmth lessens. He feels very much driven to write his confessions. That, too, costs him a lot at the outset, and it becomes possible only through much prayer and self-overcoming. But the more the work continues, the easier and the more unimportant it becomes to him. Finally, he scarcely has any interest in it anymore.

At the end of his life, he is much more educated and habilitated than he was at the beginning. He now knows how it is supposed to be done. Above all, he has a better understanding of the Church. But, personally, he is a bit exhausted. In the beginning, there was an enormous power, an impatience, to make an explosion. Afterward, it is like an outflow or an emptying.

Prayer from the later period: I come before you as one who is tired, Father, and I ask you to make yourself visible to me in all of my concerns in such a way that I understand what it is you desire from me and how I can carry it out. And also that I understand that the whole strength for this comes from you, that it is continuously transmitted to me by you; it remains yours even while it lies in me. You see what it is that I do, and you also see how tiresome everything becomes for me. I still desire to be able to measure my success by the contentment it brings you and by the fact that I truly do what you will. And success remains questionable. The preaching and assemblies draw more people than ever, and yet it often seems to me that my words are no longer able to penetrate; they are no longer alive; they seem to die the moment they are heard. And I see that I am filled with concepts and that the living element that constituted my initial faith has slowly died out over the years, being replaced by concepts, insights, and definitions. And I do not know how to return to the starting place. But you know, Father, not because your Son had to travel back, since he never in fact distanced himself, but because he always remained as if he were a person who had made the journey back, which means one who receives the entirety of faith and the entirety of strength from you alone and adds nothing of his own that could falsify it. Father, I beg you, allow my words to come back to life. Allow them to reach those who seek after you; allow them to awaken faith and to have such an effect that I myself am again humbled by it. For you know that, tired and discouraged as I am, I am not adequate to the task. At the same time, I desire to be adequate to it; I desire to be one of those people who remain faithful to you, and I know, indeed, that faithfulness does not mean being the same every day, but rather it means being new in you every day. Grant to me the newness of your faith; grant it to me in the name of your Son, who desires to see every day in us, his Church, a new proof of the mission he has accepted from you. I ask you this for the sake of his love; I ask you for the sake of the love of your Holy Spirit, and I ask you also for the sake of the love of those whom you have entrusted to me: Grant me this! Amen.

BENEDICT (ca. 480–545)

I see him in a cell. He is working and praying at the same time. He finds it difficult to pray and work at the same time. It costs him effort to persevere, much effort to keep his will in it. There is something that disquiets him, but he does not know what it is, and ultimately he does not want to know what it is. He has a book in front of him. It contains verses from the Bible, always accompanied by texts from the Fathers, and every time he comes to the end of a passage, his discomfort grows. Then he goes on ahead. At a certain point, he cannot go on any farther. It is impossible for him to pray anymore. Up to this point, he has read the texts as "work" and has interpolated "prayer" in the spaces between. He has done this with a sort of simplicity. Now he has come to understand where his unease is coming from. There is a point in him into which he does not want to enter. The insight is painful for him. But nothing is forcing him to risk the attempt at complete insight. It is only that he knows, with pain: There is something still amiss in me. Day by day the difficulty in prayer grows. In the morning, he is always fresh, and he thinks things will go smoothly. And yet every time they go less and less smoothly. Finally, it becomes clear to him: It cannot go on like this. There is no way to avoid pushing through to complete knowledge. That is what *God* proposes to him. And to the extent that he shows himself ready to perceive what God wills, he understands: God wills something new, a new religious Order ... And now, looking back, he grasps what it was that disquieted him as he read the stories of the Fathers and the monks: there was always an empty place there that needed to be filled, and he had the feeling that, in this, a task was being set aside for him in particular. Now he understands: He has to make a Rule, and he says Yes to God, although he cannot see anything. Other founders proceed on the basis of a plan. They see precisely what it is they would like to build. He does not see it at all. And thus he undertakes an extremely laborious work. He starts from scratch in everything he reads and looks for the places where a need could become visible. And, from here, he slowly begins to sketch out his Rule. Now he can pray again.

He is very obedient. But he is often tired, often hesitant. When he looks at other people, he is inclined to think: They could do it better than I. But because he said Yes and enters into the new obedience, he no longer has any internal obstacles. And externally there are not many. When some get in the way, the Church does not stand against his work. She grants her permission. The moment he seriously begins to undertake his work, he is already older, already transfigured, as it were. The fact that he did not say Yes earlier was not a fault in him but a failure to understand.

In relation to his fellowmen, he has the tendency to want to win them too quickly for the whole. When they run away from him, it is often for perfectly understandable reasons. He has externally promised more to them than he is able to keep. He lives too much on another level to be able to share their needs entirely. But he loves people as God loves them. In his love for God, he possesses a great equilibrium. In prayer, he experiences states of supernatural certainty and infallibility. *That* God has given him a particular task is almost more important for him than how. He has few visions. He practices a lot of penance; he probably started this already in his youth in order to mortify his body and its stimulations. He fights in particular against sleep, forces himself to get out of bed, which is for him a great penance.

First prayer, from the earlier period: In the name of the Father and of the Son and of the Holy Spirit. Lord, I have had such difficulty up to now in understanding that you require something new from me. And I feel myself completely incapable of carrying it out. Nevertheless, at the very moment I am saying this, I know you will it to be carried out. And that, if it is your will, I am not allowed to make excuses. I

345

know I must follow. And I know that all those things that struck me again and again in the books I read over the last few years were not in vain. From all the deficiencies I discovered, the things I knew had to change, I should also fashion something new in your name and with your help in the Order to come. Lord, I must ask you: Change me, transform me from the bottom up. Make me the sort of person who can truly serve you. You know my inconstancy, my unreliability: Again and again I start into things, and I think I cannot go any farther. And if I ought to make something new in your name, then it will have to bear the sign of your constancy. It must be yours. But if it is made by me, then it will risk giving evidence everywhere, from the beginning, of my own unreliability and not giving clear expression to your sign. Lord, change me! Lord, allow me to become new in you! Grant that I may become the instrument you need! And because I am certain that you desire to make use of me, and that error is impossible, I therefore swear to you: Make me, however difficult it may be and cost what it will, make me absolutely and completely into what it is you need; allow the new Rule to become your Rule, and have disposal over all my energies, over my entire spirit, over my entire body, over everything I have and what you ought to have in me. Bless everything that ought to happen in your name. For this I pray, in the name of the Father, in the name of the Spirit, and in your own name. Amen.

Second prayer, from the later period: Father, the work your Spirit gave me to undertake has begun. You see the difficulties I encounter, in spite of the efforts I make. And I know I am very much the cause of the difficulties: that I do not possess enough love and that my eternal hesitation and regrets that I cannot do better make it harder and harder for my followers to bear. Their trust wavers, because they see how little trust and faith I myself possess. And yet ever since I received your task, I have not doubted its authenticity for a moment. Because it is your will, it is also my will to carry forward that which has been begun. And because it is your will, it is also my will to become the proper instrument for what has been begun. It is difficult to establish the measure of prayer and the measure of penance that I have to offer you for the new work. It is also not clear to me how much I myself still have to learn from your books, from your whole teaching, in order to fashion the Rule and the life of those to come according to your will. There is uncertainty in me; and yet I can say with just as much justice: I possess the certainty of your faith. Father, have mercy on me; Father, help me, not only me, but also each one of those who come afterward. Form their life and mine too into a life according to the new

Rule, as you demand it from us and require it from us, in order to bring a new life into your Church. Lord, let your Mother help too; let her be with us. Let her be effective in us, so that we may create a unity out of the unity she has with you and out of the unity in which you live with the Father and the Holy Spirit, a unity for the work that we are beginning, a unity in which the only thing visible is the faith you give to us and the will that inspires us to do your will. Amen.

SCHOLASTICA (ca. 480–542)

A strikingly reasonable woman, who possesses general talents and is kind. She is very pure, with a perfectly childlike purity. She could end up in the most impossible situations without suffering any sort of damage. She simply trusts. Although she is very intelligent, she is perfectly *preserved* in her life. When she then has to give the new Rule to her cloister, she goes through a certain change with this Rule. But she allows a healthy reason to prevail everywhere, just as this reason seems applicable to her in prayer. She prays a lot. She did so already as a child, before entering the cloister. Her entry was for her the natural outcome of her prayer. She has no experience of anything like a struggle concerning her vocation. She lives in a sort of prayerful obedience, which always guides her and to which she entrusts herself like a child.

There are two things she sees in Benedict: first, he is the one who has provided the form for her Rule, the one who represents an authority for her and her cloister. But then, too, he is the one whom she has to help, and in this respect a strong, reciprocal relationship develops. Just as he does a lot for her, she too has to do a lot for him. She distinguishes the two things very well. She prays a lot for him; she is the epitome of the praying nun. She also knows that prayer in the cloister is something different from prayer outside, because here all the sisters pray with her. She has an exalted image of Benedict's calling, and in prayer she receives such certainty in this regard that she never doubts his mission. If it ever happens that all seems hopeless and he is at a loss about everything, then she is there to give him great consolation. She *knows* that things will work out. If she brings him the encouragement he needs, then it is not simply as one human being to another, but she brings it with the entire weight of the Church and the monastery. She brings him this consolation as the fruit of her prayer and in her complete femininity. He is sheltered and hidden like a child in her motherhood together with his Order. And she has to be such an expression of motherhood for him, because something of this has to exist in his Rule and in his relationship to his brothers. He is concerned about his brothers but is quite dry by nature. She has to broaden him in this regard, to fructify him and loosen him up by means of her femininity, so that he may understand the others better and also have the certainty that his own erotic temptations lie completely behind him. He has to learn that a femininity and a motherhood exist that are untouched by anything erotic. If Benedict had not known her, then woman would have seemed to him much more an embodiment of temptation. And in her prayer, she is able to give to God on his behalf what he would not have been able to give alone. In this respect, she is constantly ready to accept anything from him. She is very obedient; she never takes him to be wrong, even if she at first does not understand something he says. She learns from her interaction with him for her sisters, just as he learns from his interaction with her for his brothers. Each of them fructifies not only the other person, but moreover also the other's work and monastery.

First prayer, from the early period: Lord, I beg you to give me a share in the spirit of your young Mother, so that I can be young with my sisters. You see how different they all are and how much they need to be strengthened in their vocation. A strengthening that ought to lighten the life of each one of them as they realize everything: May their entry into the cloister, their acceptance of the new Rule, be something completely simple and unambiguous; may it be desired by you and required to serve you and, at the same time, serve your young Mother, who had the courage to accept you and indeed even to raise you. We ought all to be inspired by precisely this youthful spirit. And we believe, indeed, even more, we *know* that your Mother possessed this spirit in the very way we now need it. Need it in order not to be constantly horrified and put off by the weight of our task, in order to achieve obedience, the obedience to you and to that which will happen to us, the future you are preparing for us. Give us this spirit, out of love for your Mother, the spirit you gave to her and which, like all your gifts, is not used up in a single gift but which multiplies, so that, when your Mother received it from you, you thus showed that you are rich enough to lend it also to us. I ask you this in the name of the entire cloister, out of love for you and out of love for your Mother. Amen.

Second prayer from the late period: The hour has come, Lord, in which we come before you, in order to show to you, each in his own way, where we stand, what we need, what we have to offer. What I have to offer you is what I always have: my obedience, my readiness to do your will, and my entire life. What I also have to offer you, as always, is also the obedience of my brother Benedict, his readiness to do your will, and his entire life. What we both need is the strength to pour out your Spirit into our monasteries. Strength not to allow our eyes to depart from you in the obstacles we face daily. Strength to achieve the tiny everyday fidelity without forgetting the great fidelity of our promise. Strength to incorporate your Spirit and your life more and more into our Rules, so that the Rule becomes your Rule in truth and its implementation becomes a sign of genuine obedience to you. We need your assistance; we need your grace. Each one of us needs it for himself and for the other, for his monastery and for the other's monastery. By means of this grace, Lord, which has so tangibly accompanied us to this point, we feel that the life in our monasteries turns out to be stronger, that it has a share in your life; both of us, who are the leaders of our monasteries, see in all our followers the progress they are making—not externally, but indeed from the inside in a strengthening of the power of the vows, of readiness and simplicity, which allows all our sisters and brothers to accept from their superior what you will to give to him and thus to the entire monastery. I beg you, Lord, bless everything you do through us; bless our monasteries; bless them above all in the midst of your Church, together with the Church. They desire to serve the Church as a whole. Grant this to them, so that they may fulfill your will in this service and be permitted to live for the greater glory of the Father, the Spirit, and you. Amen.

GREGORY THE GREAT (540–604)

The period before his election to the papacy. He does not want altogether to believe he will be chosen, and yet he knows he will. A terrible confusion reigns in his soul. He has the feeling: if he is chosen, it would be wrong, if he is not chosen, it would be even more wrong, because he would truly be able to help the Church. He places the whole thing again and again into God's hands and is convinced that God will ultimately make the choice. He prays:

Prayer during the election: Father, I know that it is your Spirit who will determine the election. It is your Spirit who will determine the successor of St. Peter for your Son in his Church. You see, Father, how many people are for me, and you also see those who are against me. You know I am reluctant to assume the responsibility, that I want to implore you: Let this cup pass over me, and yet I have to say at the same time: Let your will, Father, be done, rather than mine. If it is your will that I be elected, then I ask you to deepen my understanding already now, to allow me already now to serve you much better, already now to make me so much a sharer in your Spirit that I might carry out your will also in the time before the election and in the days of the election, step by step, so that nothing of your will is obstructed, hidden, or otherwise changed by me. Father, the request is a great one, for you see what sort of sinner I am. You see me fall again and again into the same mistakes; you see me make no progress in perseverance and lose my courage again and again so quickly. And yet you expect courage, perseverance, and reliability from the one who stands as the head of the Church. How should I possess these things later if I do not have them now? And I am incapable of giving them to myself. I beg you, Father, enlighten me, give me as much a share in your Spirit as is necessary for the carrying out of this heavy office, if this office is truly intended for me; give me through your Son the mysterious grace of office, which no one needs more urgently than the one who must sit upon the papal throne before all Christianity. Father, be with all those who vote; be with the one who will be elected; and be in the prayers of your entire Church and all the believers. Amen.

Later, as pope, in a stormy time, he is entangled in a whole net of intrigues, great and small. For his part, he has an image of the Church that stands before him. He understands the unity of Christ and the Church; he understands the Cross and the fact that he must be taken up into this mystery and that he will be taken up. But then thousands of intrigues and obstacles place themselves between him and the Church and muddy the picture. And all of them together, both the smallest and the greatest, ultimately converge before his eyes into a general tragedy, or better still, into the woefulness of the situation, of *his* situation, which allows him to reduce all the difficulties to the same level, which allows them all to seem to be painted with the same color. The same mercy that he feels for the Church as a whole, he also feels in relation to himself. Then, he tries to grasp the Church in her origin in order to be able to heal her on this basis. He desires to take in hand, as pope, the threads that bind him with this origin, for example, with the individual parishes, with individual parish priests.

It is from this perspective, too, that one ought to understand his relationship to mysticism. It is conceivable that, from a person's confession of sins, a confessor might be able to tell where a starting point might lie in him for a deeper experience of God. For example, where a particular configuration of sins is absent or can be eliminated ... In a similar way, Gregory sees, on the basis of his own confession of sins, a possible starting point for himself in relation to mysticism, to a *possible* mystical gift, and he then projects this point into others. He is ultimately convinced that every person could be a mystic, if only he could set aside certain sins. There is a certain calculation in this: If I were to invest my money in such and such a way, I could become a millionaire ... The whole emerges for Gregory from the relationship between mysticism and sins. He thinks less about an ascent by stages in the spiritual life than about a certain density of sins in the soul that hinders the transparency of the divine light. But that can always be lessened through purification of the soul. And he imagines that a certain face of the soul, which is turned toward God, has to be completely pure in order to have a clean vision of God. And just as he is convinced that this holds for individuals, he is also convinced that it holds as well for particular religious Orders, indeed, for the religious state in general and, through this state, ultimately for the Church as a whole, the Church understood as the totality of all the individual missions for the vision of God or as their reciprocal supplementation. That is the ultimate goal of his pastorate. And he begins in complete earnest with himself first of all; he prepares himself for the vision of God. He seeks to emancipate himself from everything that can hinder the vision. He is outstanding in eliminating dross. He sees sin in himself not only where it in fact *is*, but also where it *could* be. Every failing, every lapse, every tiny little indifference seems to him all the more weighty for his filling the office of the papacy. What he says in this regard is not at all mere rhetoric, but pure experience. His zeal is boundless: he wants to purify everything, to create clear situations. His efforts and intentions exhibit a real magnanimity. He experiences every deficiency in the Church as a personal stain. He is permeated from top to bottom by the responsibility that has been laid upon him. He knows he must try to be worthy of it, even though he remains unworthy.

For him, mysticism is not just a theory; he has experienced some of it. But because he is so convinced of his theory, he will nevertheless never say of himself: I have seen, but rather: I would have seen if I had been purer. There can be unnoticeable transitions between the forms of vision: from a thinking about God to a thinking in God, to an imaginative conception of what God is like, in which it is God who gives the meaning and content of the conception, to a sort of dreamlike vision and, finally, to the clear evidence of seeing. Such transitions, such stages, exist, and if Gregory sees something, then there is one thing that is clear to him above all: that he *could* see more clearly with greater evidence. For this reason, he does not characterize what he encounters as vision in the proper sense. He is therefore also never completely secure in himself, whether he is at the moment actually seeing or not. It preoccupies him a lot, but he can never get entirely clear about it. Often, he feels sure he has seen certain things. But he suspects that he has seen them within a certain context and that this context is not clear to him. He takes all of this as a confirmation of his impurity. He worries himself quite a bit with questions. And he does not have anyone standing over him or even next to him. He has no one to whom he could really entrust himself. He also thinks that if someone were truly to see how things are in his soul, it could upset his trust in the papacy. He is like the doctor who avoids thinking out loud in the patient's presence.

Second prayer: Our Father, who art in heaven. Hallowed be thy name. May it be hallowed by the entire Church. May it be hallowed by each one of us. And may it be hallowed by your unworthy servant, who is now pope and who has so many difficulties. Father, I was halfhearted in my previous life, and so have I remained! The difficulties often come close to crushing me, and I am able to purify them not only in the stillness of prayer with you, so that they become bearable for the Church and so that I learn from you the path to follow. But I also again and again see how necessary it is for me to speak with others, perhaps even people who are unauthorized for such a thing, not only in order to ask their well-meant advice, but also to request from them a certain mercy. And I do this because I do not have the strength to stand before you alone; I do not have the courage to receive direction from you alone; I do not harbor the hope to be able to serve you in the way you expect. Nevertheless, Father, you have so often given me the evidence of your grace; you have accompanied me through all the hardships up to this point, so that this becomes a sign for me of how graciously you look down upon your Church. And you do not allow your servants to become isolated. Indeed, you are yourself; you help. And I should often allow your divine, fatherly assistance to suffice for things. But I always forget your readiness to open if a person knocks; I knock at others' doors and wait for them to open, and then I am disappointed when things turn out differently from the way people predicted or from the way they promised to do them. Father, teach me to place my trust more and more in you. Teach your entire Church through me to place her trust more and more in you. Teach us the Our Father, the prayer of your Son, in an entirely new way, so that in your Son's prayer, we might feel sheltered in you and try to do more emphatically and more genuinely whatever you expect from us. This I ask you, Father, in the name of your Son, in the name of your Spirit, in the name of your most holy Virgin, in the name of all the saints and of all those who have placed their complete trust in you. Amen.

ANSELM (1033–1109)

Anselm represents the perfect unity of prayer and work. It is completely the same to him, as it were, what it is he does; whether he works or preaches or holds a conversation: everything is prayer. And, indeed, such a pure prayer, so wholly surrendered to God, that it does not grow weak even during the times when he lingers for a long time in work. He never loses contact with God. He is filled with an incredible humility and never wants to add anything of his own to his work; rather, he never desires anything else but to articulate what he believes comes from God. He conceives a plan for the work he has in mind. Then he writes perhaps two or three sentences, and he is at a loss for the right word. He turns to God and asks him to give it to him, and then he seeks further for the right word in a union with God. There is a lot of pathos in the process. And when he then finds the right formulation after a certain time has passed, he sees this as nothing but God's work. He does not see it as his own, except when something does not turn out. He is completely convinced that everything good in his work comes from God, and everything bad from him. He would never claim to collaborate with God in doing the good. But the good that comes about takes complete hold of him. He totally forgets that he previously did penance, studied, prayed, and strove. God did everything, and it would certainly have been much better if he, Anselm, had not been there.

Although he lives so much in God, he is not the least bit familiar with God. Each time he turns to God, it always takes place with a new address, exertion, devotion, greeting, a new act of respect. As if he were not aware of the perfect unity in which he lived with God, he takes God once again into his activity. These "interruptions" do not disturb him in his work but only make it more fruitful. He only stands up, in fact, in order to kneel down. He always cuts his own recreation short, because, without this, he includes times of rest with God in his work. He uses God almost like a student who looks everything up in his dictionary that he does not know.

He is often somewhat unclear about his own mission. But he bears this unclarity as the price he has to pay for his work. And he does not want to appropriate anything or take anything out that was not given to him, but also he does not want to leave anything behind that was offered to him.

353

Thus he always prays at the start of his work more or less the same *prayer:*

Allow me, Father, to do everything the way you want it; make me your instrument, and forget, and allow me to forget, that I am and could be an obstacle. Each time things come to a stop in work, I understand that I am the source of the obstacles. Overcome them, if you will this work, and allow me to do nothing but obey you. Allow me to transmit your voice, so that the Church may hear it. Allow all those who ought to have a share in your doctrine, which it is my task to articulate in a clear way, to receive truly the share you have intended for them. They should not see the imperfection that comes from me but should glimpse more and more of your perfection. And you see, Father, how difficult it becomes for me to set to work and how I have to overcome myself in order to get started. Allow me to offer this act of self-overcoming to you; do not lessen it if it is useful to you, but permit me nonetheless to begin with your strength and to carry it out with your will.

After this a few traditional prayers follow. He prays from a book, the psalms, an Our Father, and so forth. And then he goes to work. Most of the time, he reflects at first on what he wrote and thought the previous day and utters a prayer of thanksgiving. Then he allows himself again and again to be overwhelmed by what he worked on. It is always more beautiful than he himself had thought:

Father, yesterday's work truly bears your stamp. I thank you for it; grant that all see it, recognize you, and forget your servant. And I beg you for the same grace for today's work.

Then he begins. He writes. After a period of time it becomes difficult. Then he prays:

Father, it is becoming difficult. Bestow on me something of what is yours in the Spirit of your Son. Your Son, too, overcame all his difficulties in your grace. And because he is God, he truly allowed you to be visible everywhere. But I know he invites us to attempt the same in his Spirit. Father, grant me a share in the grace of your Son; overcome these difficulties, in spite of my sinfulness.

Then he lays the problem before God, as a student might present a problem to his teacher, and he does it in such an eager way that he makes it clear to himself at the same time:

O Lord, where could the origin of my mistake lie? And it is like a conversation with God, as if God were to say to him: Think about it a bit ... , from what point on did the matter lose its foundation? And when he finds the mistake, he gives thanks and continues on in his work. This constant rising up with demonstrations, requests, and

354

invocations, followed by a concluding prayer of thanksgiving, seems a bit long-winded, but with Anselm it is altogether true and sincere and fruitful.

He also writes prayers, which emerge from his praying and which are intended to teach us how to pray. But one does not see as much good in these prayers as in the ones he himself prayed. They resemble his finished writings; they are too conclusive. While he is composing them, he frequently interrupts himself and fills the pauses with prayers that have not been written out, prayers of a very direct sort.

He does not seek mystical experience, because he feels himself too unworthy of it. He would have had more mystical vision if he had been guided. He does not open himself up in relation to the things to be seen; instead, he closes himself up a tiny bit; he experiences too much awe and distance. And because everything else in him is so correct, God does not insist any more on this with Anselm. Vision remains latent in him, as it were, like seeing through a veil, and there is no one there to take the veil away, to encourage him to go farther along this path.

In relation to people, he is the one who gives. They always expect things from him and give very little back to him. God does fructify what he possesses, but he lacks intellectual and spiritual exchange. People generally affect him a lot, but in this he remains completely humble and is always ready to abandon his work for the sake of his neighbor. He sees the obligation to one's neighbor just as clearly as the mission of his own work.

He practices a lot of penance at night. Getting out of bed plays a great role, particularly in his younger years when the temptations are great. He then does not give up his practice of penance until the temptation has been perfectly overcome.

BERNARD (1091–1153)

I see him in his monastery, together with those who entered with him. They have lived together for a period of time and are speaking with one another about their form of life and about the experiences they have had up to this point. The brothers are to that extent completely content. They only have to settle petty things, which in a certain sense correspond to their deficiencies of character. One would like to sleep more; another would like to eat more; the third one finds prayer too long. They are still very preoccupied with comfort. Bernard is the opposite: he finds that it would be possible to do a lot more penance, and so forth. And their love for him is so great that they are ashamed of their objections and come to agreement with him. And when he has brought them to this point, he begins to speak with them about his new plans, how a person could even better serve God, and they agree with him completely. Often, things do not come off without sharp arguments, above all with the older members, who have doubts about his mission. Many also succumb to his charm without noticing it, and thus there can be a waking up. On the whole, he ignites a great flame of burning love.

He has relatively little time for contemplation. He has a lot to study; he has to carry out his plans for reform, and so forth. He enters into contemplation, so to speak, on the ground floor, without special efforts, and it is from the first moment on so rich that he is as much elevated by it as he is rested. Up until the day when he begins to ask for suffering. He does so because he feels it was too easy for him; he was almost always able to achieve what he wanted through conversations with people, while his conversation with God did not seem to have been arranged altogether rightly, in spite of his contemplation. He thinks God would have to fashion and form him in a completely different way and that he would then, in that case and on the basis of his own suffering, be able to understand other people's suffering and difficulties much better. To be sure, he was not without external obstacles up to this point, but he was filled so full by the love of God that these were never able to bother him. They were nothing but fleabites.

God grants him the suffering he requests in the contemplation of the Cross. For example, he shows him Christ on the Cross and at the same time fills him with a boundless pain, which, in contrast to everything else in his mission, is completely undifferentiated. He suffers in a much more primordial way than he prays and than he thinks. In his thinking, he never loses vision; in suffering, it disappears from his sight. When he suffers, he no longer knows anymore that he had requested it from God. He suffers in a sort of identification with the Lord. In this moment, he ceases to be the sinner who stands over against the Lord.

After this experience, he knows much more powerfully than he did before that he has to lead people to him in unity with Christ and exhort them in Christ's place. He thus fulfills a task that he sees *within* the Son's task. For this reason, he seeks individuals, to whom he turns in order to situate them within the context of the overall setting of the New Testament: With whom could he compare this person? Where would the Lord connect with this one? and so forth. He also has a remarkable way of insisting on things until people have really grasped them. He never breaks things off prematurely. Perhaps that is what he

356

does the most carefully, namely, these exhortations. With his other achieve-ments, trips, and endeavors, he works up such a momentum that it sim-ply *goes*. With his exhortations, he really has to recollect himself in order to do it properly. And he often thinks while doing it: How must the Son have had to overcome himself in order to become a man and to enter into our society? Christ's existence among us is the mystery from which he draws the strength for his exhortations. With his other endeavors, he sets his eyes firmly on the goal and finds it entertaining to achieve. He takes enormous pains with this. But he is in fact also strong.

Thus, he can also carry out strict ascetical practices: the things he demands of others in the monastery are all things he himself has tried, and in fact he always has done more himself than he demands. Inter-rupting his meals, his sleeping, and very many corporeal penances. He has a certain fear of intellectual enjoyment. If the solution of a task fascinates him or if he experiences joy in intellectual work, in formu-lating things, he becomes distrustful. He pauses in his work and tests it. He is indeed happy to be with others, but more when he is tired and almost exhausted from his efforts. He is a bit goal-oriented. But he is constantly afraid of forgetting God for too long when he happens to be happy for a period of time. He certainly knows that God allows happiness. But he mistrusts himself because he is worried about dis-tancing himself from prayer. He is perhaps more inclined than most people to live heartily. But he does not give any space to this inclina-tion; he curtails it mercilessly.

In his interactions with his brothers, moreover, he always gives pref-erence to what runs contrary to his inclinations, so that it is almost impossible to figure out what his personal preference is.

He himself had no experience with any "stages" in his contempla-tion initially. But then he came to understand that he is able to lead others to perfect self-surrender only "by stages". Thus he makes con-cessions in the way he characterizes things. He himself lives in the core of his being in the way the apostles and disciples lived: he accepts everything the Lord gives, and indeed in the same way the disciples experienced it in the Gospel, without making any plans. They were not able to think up any "system" of revelation. Thus he too tries simply to be open and not to bind himself to any self-constructed system. Nevertheless, he realizes that misunderstandings come up for others in this way time and again; he sees their deficiency in the gift of discernment and in discretion. He himself has the absolute measure of intimacy, similar to John. But he sees how easily other Christians misuse this gift insofar as they seek enjoyment instead of intimacy. He even formulates this somewhere thus: that intimacy with the Lord has its justification in *service* and, thus, in the Father and not in us ourselves. That Christ opens his intimacy to us and gives it so that we might better come to know the Father, not in order to eliminate the distance between him, the Son, and us. If Bernard "constructs" stages, it is in order to assure proper intimacy, which is intended for others and tested out by himself. Assurances in work, in prayer and contemplation, and in the examination of conscience and self-control.

He lacks sovereignty in his spiritual direction; he is too distrustful to be completely superior. He has the tendency to allow people to stop perhaps a bit too early. It requires a certain patience in spiritual direction to lead people on "a longer leash"; this escapes him. For he also has an incredible amount to do, and the encouragements he gives are for him also time-savers. Finally, he is also plagued by a certain fear: a fear about his own prayer, when he is drawn too strongly into it. That, too, is a reason why he liked "stages" and approaches. When he constructs such "stages", then he never invents something new; he simply takes over things that were common practice at that time and that were much more commonly practiced by others before him than by himself. And, indeed, he adopts more and more from others the older he gets. When he entered the monastery as a young man, the only thing he saw was complete self-surrender, both for himself and for his brothers. As the years pass, he comes to see that "stages" can also have their value.

In this he has a certain exaggerated preference for precision and establishing things. He is also happy to speak frankly about problems; if things go poorly or not so well with someone, perhaps in prayer, then he becomes strict; he measures things off with precision, makes an effort to create order everywhere, and thus he lays a precise schema in his hand. Then these "stages" plague him again, because he thinks that he himself now also has to keep to them; and although he considers them to be nothing more than guidelines, he is worried about being arrogant if he leaves them out. He experiences genuine ecstasies, but because the people who are entrusted to him do not have these experiences, he is very afraid of taking something from these experiences that he is not entitled to take. At such moments, he almost alarms himself most of all, suddenly, regarding particular details. And he thinks that once he managed to settle certain things with precision, the whole thing would retain a certain form.

In relation to the Mother of God, he is to a certain extent comparable to Ignatius; he has a chivalrous respect for her. This does not keep him from harboring a tender love for her. This love is so alive, it is as if the Mother stood right next to him. He has a very beautiful way of surrounding her in prayers and offerings with little attentions. Quite often, when he feels afraid or petty again, he looks to her, and then everything is good again, because her own discipleship carries him back into the community of disciples around the Lord. If he no longer has the courage to move ahead directly, then Mary is there to set everything straight again, as a mother can lead her frightened or unhappy child back to joy with just two words. He prays special prayers to the Mother of God, not his own prayers, but those that have already been composed, for which he has a special love:

First Prayer: We, the whole community and I, now kneel before you, Lord, and beg you to deign to accept our request. You know we are convinced by the fact that it is your will that we undertake this new crusade. Nevertheless, the difficulties are great. The reports that come to us from the regions we must enter shake our resolve again and again. Is it right to put ourselves in such a great danger if we perhaps cannot achieve anything? If it is your will, see to it that we go there; we do not want to hesitate for a single moment; we desire to accept every trial, every setback, indeed, even death itself, without resistance, as something that comes from you. I have spoken with experienced men, and they have all pointed out to me that the danger is truly too great and that it may not be worthwhile. And yet we know, surely, that, at least in the immediate surroundings, we will have successes at the beginning of our journey. But we would also prefer not to have to give up suddenly and thus give others the impression that our undertaking was not worth the risk. We are worried about damaging your Church. Lord, we all ask you for illumination. Let it come to us! And let us recognize, when it arrives, that it is truly *your* illumination. Let us not be arrogant and overlook the signs you give us. All my brothers are of one mind in making this request of you. Bless their prayer; bless the prayer of the entire community; bless the prayer of all those who entreat you on behalf of this undertaking to proclaim your will. Amen.

It is only while A. is uttering this prayer that she realizes that it is about the actual Crusade. The political announcements had previously disappeared in Bernard's consciousness, as it were. Now, they appear in prayer and sharpen the hesitation by the hour. New announcements arrive. And he knows that even when he prays for certainty, things *can* remain uncertain to the very end.

Second prayer: Lord, allow me this night to be close to you. Allow me to experience the love you grant to those who believe in you. I thank you for all this love. Allow me to pass it on intact to those who are entrusted to me: in such a way that you yourself are it, that it is your love that comes alive in them. And grant me, Lord, I beg you, after all the joy you give me, after all the insight in which you allow me to share, the courage to spend the day, with its difficult decisions, wholly in your Spirit, to devote it entirely to you, and to allow every word I ought to speak to be a word that is ordered to you. Bless the monastery; bless the Church; bless all those who ought to come into contact with us, and allow many to come to faith in you. Amen.

DOMINIC (1170–1221)

A. first sees him under the immediate impression of a sermon that he heard, a sermon on hell and grace. Afterward, he is sitting in a sort of cell, but it is not a monastery cell, at least not a proper one. And he reflects: either grace or hell . . . The sermon he heard praised grace but presented hell in the background as a constant threat for those who do not want to accept grace and ended with a piercing appeal to everyone not to close themselves to grace. In this moment, Dominic makes a decision, one that can be understood quite simply: He decides, from now on, to let more grace be granted to those whom grace can reach, to whatever extent possible by means of all the channels of grace the Church has at her disposal; but he wants to damn immediately all those whom grace cannot reach, all those who deny and reject it . . . He wants to separate more clearly in the eyes of the Church those who have been graced from those who are lost, so that the Church may learn to discern better. In this, he does not want to anticipate God's judgment: God will always be able to save them if that is his will.

Night falls, and when Dominic now looks over the day and the evening, it becomes clear to him that they lay completely under the impression of the words of the sermon he heard. And he suddenly recognizes the power of words. How much wise words can be a source of grace. He decides to found his new community on the basis of this knowledge. Furthermore, it occurs to him how much his understanding has been fostered by this sermon, how he has received a new insight into God's mysteries. It is not clear to him how much of these mysteries the preacher himself understood, but it is clear that his preacher brothers absolutely will have to have extensive knowledge, both in philosophy and theology . . . They will also have to be able to draw from their inner treasury of learning and wisdom in order to fashion their words in an effective way.

Then A. sees him again, much later; the Order already exists at this point, and Dominic has in the meantime become much gentler, after

360

years of a bitter struggle with himself, with the world, and with his Order. This gentleness began for him inside his Order, with those who shared the same views and the same orientation with him—while he sharply rejected all those things that did not fit: everything that stood outside the Church or was not entirely orthodox inside the Church or was not very compliant within his Order.

He then sought to attenuate his abrupt manner and to extend the gentleness he felt toward those who shared his vision to other people to a certain extent. The intransigence, the complete aggressiveness, that characterize him, he now directs above all to himself. It is as if he had discovered gentleness as a new, effective weapon and now sought to wield it.

A. sees him pray the rosary. He sees Mary as the one who is so perfectly full of grace, as the gentle woman, that he presents to her, as it were, only the things of his that are gentle; he thinks about her when he himself is in a gentle mood; while in intellectual battles, thoughts about her would prevent him from having the requisite hardness. The Mother of the Lord is not made for battle. There are years in his life in which he prays the rosary very often, as if it were his primary prayer.

Prayer: Lord, you have said: "Whoever is not for me is against me." It is as though this, your truth, filled me more and more and brought me more and more to experience all the people I see and all the judgments I hear and everything I perceive inside of this division. I ask you: Grant that our entire work be dedicated to increasing the number of those who commit themselves to you. Grant that everything we do, the whole of our intellectual work, all our prayer and every word of our preaching, might contain so much life and possess so much power that it constantly leads new souls to you. But do not allow us, in this celebration of conversion, in this joy of work for you, to forget those who are against you. We must wage war against them; we must destroy them; we must make use of all the harshness we can muster; in our relentless pursuit, we must show them the teaching that we have to pass on to those who are for you. For perhaps there will also be a few who, by virtue of the horror of the knowledge of what it means to be against you, will confess to you. Lord, I ask you: Bless this work, increase it, and show us our faults. For we know that much of what we do proves to be deficient in your eyes. We fail to see what cannot stand up, what alienates us again and again from you, and so show us, we beg you, show us, your sons, show all those who are entrusted to us, more and more how we can live for you. Bless us; be with us and with your entire Church; and give your love and the love of your Mother to all those who ask for it. Amen.

ALBERT (1200–1280)

Already as a boy at school, he busies himself a good deal with conceptual thinking. From the beginning, he has a vivid need to communicate. When he hears the word "doctrine", he has a great desire to understand, to analyze, to speak with his peers about it, with intelligent people and with professors. He has a desire to back up his own perspectives and concepts with the understanding of other people. He is at once shy and temerarious. He assembles something, shows it to another person, who is delighted by it and who encourages him to continue on. Now he becomes audacious, defeats every objection with his idea. But then, suddenly, he sees a development, a new approach. He starts over in a very shy way, questioning, as it were, and when he sees that it works, he builds upon it again as if it were a dogma. This tension between hesitation and presumption, uncertainty and overconfidence, pervades the whole of his character. That includes his writing: in his first notes he is quite timid, but in the decisive communication he becomes bold. He has, so to speak, a powerful need for people, in order to carry out his mission and to give it its definitive form. Many things in his work have to be forced open by later ideas, because it was uttered too apodictically at the time.

He is quite progressive for his time. But he never went astray. If he ever has to break open his views, it is not in order to change them radically, but rather to broaden them, to give them more content. He himself often makes too emphatic a selection; he confines things too narrowly; he lifts a few particular details out of the fullness that is there; this is indeed the only limitation that one can ascribe to him. By contrast, there is his consistency in work, his fidelity; moreover, his respect for his fellowmen is admirable. Even when they are not particularly famous, they are considered by him. When he faces resistence, he takes a step back, reflects, perhaps comes to see where he was right, but then he constructs a very careful bridge from the foreign position that he rejects to his own, making an earnest effort to show his opponent how the path runs. If he is certain that his own opinion is defensible in relation to the Church, then he looks at the foreign point of view, which has not yet understood his opinion, as a task that has been entrusted to him. In addition to his great erudition, he possesses a great and touching humility and an attitude of prayer that never leaves him. The moment he is able to in the morning, he enters into

362

his contemplation. And it is in contemplation that he then goes to Mass. He thus allows himself in his contemplation to be led by just what the Mass of the day offers to him. Moreover, he carries into his contemplation whatever external events may offer to him, for example, a visit, and seeks to illuminate the situation that occurs there in contemplation. He has a great devotion to the Mother of the Lord and sees her very much as the contemplative who embraces everything within her contemplation of the Son. His love for the Son, his love for God in general, is also great, but he sees God more in broader contexts and abstract truths.

Prayer: Our Father, you see, indeed, that I desire to serve you, and this is how I understand my service: that your doctrine ought to be explained by me, yes, even by me, and so formulated that this articulated teaching may give the Church more and more support. But you also see that what I do remains deficient; the evidence of my incapacity shows up everywhere. In spite of this, I know for certain that you have given me this task, that it comes from you and not merely from me. It becomes difficult for me to carry it out when I am alone and easier when I see the enthusiasm of my students; but afterward, when I am alone again, everything seems impossible to me and full of thorns. I live in a vacillation between the affirmation and rejection of my own work. And I do not believe that this vacillation can be helpful to you. It is certainly a sign of my sin that this vacillation remains against my will and causes an increasing uncertainty. Take the sin away from me, Father; take this vacillation away from me if it should prevent me from following the path you have laid out for me and if it should find expression in my work, which ought to reflect the stability of your truth. Give me more fidelity; grant that I might forget myself more and never fail to recognize how much what I must proclaim in your name belongs indeed to you. Bless this work; bless everything that is done here in this house; bless the reception that is given to my—that is, your—work; bless all those who labor over the question of your eternal truth. Amen.

THOMAS AQUINAS (1225–1274)[1]

I see him in a period of growth and development: starting from simple truths, defining them more and more, bringing out their meaning,

---

[1] I requested this portrait of Aquinas from A., since the first one (see pp. 240–41 above) seemed all too negative in its brevity. The two portraits complement and reflect each other.

formulating them; before he even begins to write and offer something of his own, he is already extraordinarily occupied with the Christian truth and always with a laborious precision. He deals with the Christian truth according to a method with which I actually am familiar only from philosophy; he analyzes until he has nothing but pieces in his hand, each of which having become totally clear and evident, and in this clarity and evidence in the details he nevertheless does not lose hold of the whole. He does not dissect things to the point that everything crumbles away and gets destroyed, but he is quite careful every time to bring together the things that were separated. So that is how he is in his youth.

He attracts the attention of his teachers through his incredible clarity of mind. He has a sort of innate love for this intellectual activity in philosophy and theology. And in fact it is his primary interest in this that compels him to make out of himself and his life something that corresponds to his propositions. In prayer, he does not fly at a very high level, nor does he in faith. But in the clarity of his thinking, he flies quite high indeed. And because he cannot bear having this energy in thought and having to store it for further reflection, and next to this to have to cultivate prayer and contemplation, to which he does not feel particularly attracted, it is not hard for him to incorporate even his contemplation and prayer into his thinking, so that at the beginning he uses his contemplation like practice for the clearer vision of his reasonings. His prayer, too, is systematic practice for him. He arranges it into his work, and it serves as a preparation for the work. It is systematic in the sense that, if he happens to have been prevented from carrying the work out at the usual time, he will come back to it at the most impossible hours. The sobriety of his plan of work demands this, and he persists with a precision that was foreign even to Augustine, just as it will be once again to Ignatius. To be sure, he sees grace the right way, but because he thinks so precisely about grace, he somehow wants his prayer to share in this precision.

His vocal prayer consists above all in the Church's Liturgy of the Hours. But he does not allow himself to be led in this; instead, he forces prayer to say to him what he needs. If, for example, he happens to be at work on sanctifying grace, then he reads the daily psalms, and so forth, constantly in view of what they have to say to him in this connection. If a verse seems useful to him, then he makes a note of it, not in writing exactly, but certainly in his memory: that has to be used in that context; that can serve as an objection; this other thing is something I will come back to later once I have made the transition to this matter; this would require a chapter in itself; these verses can be left out; they are not profitable at the moment. This method allows him to feel he is not wasting any time. And, on the other hand, it corresponds to his system. Everything in him is ultimately subordinated to the intellect. And you would have to say that he is holy because he placed his enormous intellectual gifts entirely in the service of the Church's truth, because he allowed himself to be taken up into a greater context.

His contemplation is somewhat richer than his vocal prayer. But wherever possible he always contemplates things that fit in with the work he is doing at the time. Here, too, he is the one who leads God, as it were, rather than allowing himself to be led by God. He lacks a certain magnanimity. He contemplates, as it were, with pen in hand. But then God has mercy on him and gives him a share in genuine contemplation, gives him new insights again and again; lifts him up into regions beyond what his pen can transcribe. But when he returns from there, he settles accounts, as it were, with God: How is it that God did not allow him to retain everything he received, to take notes and translate it all into concepts? The one who tries to capture grace in his definitions, nevertheless, allows himself again and again to be surprised by grace, and it surprises him that grace can be so surprising.

His perseverance in work is hard to imagine. In his later years, he often gets sick and works in spite of it with the same perseverance. He has his heart set on bringing the whole, completed achievement to God. He overtaxes himself. He strains everything to this end, all of his energy, and renounces everything, simply to be able to complete his work. He pours himself entirely into his subject, which both he and God approved. He also has experience of prayer in work. He prays not only the obligatory prayers, but he also prays when he happens to run into difficulties in his work. However, he prays like a person who takes medicine in order to get his energies back. He prays in order to be able to get back to work.

With respect to other people, he is downright accommodating. He behaves toward them, in fact, in a more human and Christian way than he does toward God. In his behavior toward them, there is always a little bit of pity, that they do not know more than they do, that they are so intellectually impoverished, and there is therefore also a little bit of condescension. The person he is with somehow always feels some of his intellectual superiority. But he nevertheless has the smile of goodness when he speaks with this person. He willingly accepts God's cross in the form of his fellowman. What he is less sure of, however, is that he himself could become a cross: as a sinner. That the Christian has to bear his own burden and that this is a part of his cross. This insight is out of his reach.

By virtue of his constant mental activity, he has over time become very intellectual, even with respect to the Lord. Christ is God for him, the Son of God, who has become man; but he has little experience of how overwhelming, piercing, and devastating his personal love is. If he loves Christ, if he loves his neighbor, then it is, so to speak, because of his interpretation of the commandment to love. It is like a husband who loves his wife, not because of the personal qualities that make her loveable, but rather because of the "essence of marriage". He is for that reason not an egoist, but all of his thinking centers on "truths", and "essences", on God's truths that he has to defend. He is possessed by the idea that he has to fulfill his mission. His incredible diligence is, not a natural gift, but the expression of his will to direct all his capacities to service. God desired this service from him, charged him with the endless task of making things intelligible, but at the same time granted a meager subjective experience of grace. If someone like Francis of Assisi allows a stream of subjectively experienced grace to flow into the world, because this is the way he received it, then this is not a greater service than when Thomas makes manifest the little he received in his own way. There are different offices.

In order to allow what Thomas conveys to us to be truly fruitful and nourishing in a Christian way, one must always first allow it to dissolve, so to speak, back into Christian life: in grace, in prayer, and so forth. This is indeed what Thomas wants. He intends to offer nothing more than the structure and the framework. He takes great care to exclude the personal element from his work, in order to achieve an almost skeleton-like objectivity. He prepares the bones in such a way that not a trace of muscle is left on them. He is worried about not being able, otherwise, to allow the clear figure of the next bone to stand forth. This is all the more reason his work needs to be supplemented by Christian flesh and blood, in order to remain alive in the Church.

MECHTILD OF MAGDEBURG (1210–1285)

Initially, she lives a sort of tiny life of devotion, with an attachment to time, certain prayer obligations, and, on occasion, a lot of piety. It is "on occasion" because she does not yet experience her life as a genuine totality. She has fits and starts in this direction, and this is how she conducts things. Moreover, it occurs to her that she can pray with great interiority, and then, when she takes her place among other people again, she feels as if she had been yanked away from the atmosphere of prayer, almost as if she were sullied. At one point, she carries out a contemplation of spousal love, not on the basis of her husband, but starting immediately from the Lord as the Bridegroom and from his Bride, who is, first of all, the Church. During this contemplation, she sees in a sort of vision how much the Church burns in love and, then, how much the Lord burns and how a shared flame arises between them. But this occurs in such a way that the Lord's flame stands above the Church's flame, because the human element clings so much to the Church, an element that nevertheless can be obliterated by the Bridegroom's burning love. The vision ends in the Church's finally being set afire completely by the love of the Bridegroom. She sees this process as a sort of development, a growth of love, and indeed reciprocal love. She sees all the flames ascending up toward heaven and none falling back. Then she tries to understand where she herself stands in all this. And she discovers that she actually stands in a place where she is not permitted to stand: where there is still the possibility of falling backward. Now she engages in a contemplation of human nature. And she grasps that, in spite of her great solitude, she fails to satisfy a certain demand, because she lacks an ultimate attachment to Christ. Because her personal life still depends too much on nature and not enough on what lies above nature. And from this point on, every vision—and she has quite a few of them—turns into a demand from God for her to give herself more and more completely over to the law of the supernatural. And now she reflects. She sees that her present state is not enough; but she also knows she will never be fully adequate in the other state, in the strict life of the cloister. Nevertheless, the vows and Rules of the cloister would compel her to expose herself *in a more systematic way* to the Lord's fire. She would no longer be able to surrender herself, as she does now, to the love of God while thinking about a subsequent recuperation, a break in her self-surrender. She does not condemn the system she has followed up to this point. It is just that she does not find it suitable enough. She is not making a value judgment about those who continue on in this form of life. But she also knows that these people do not receive the same extraordinary graces that she does. Each time she departs from a vision, she poses a question to herself, as it were, that she does not answer. She has lost a bit of her initial naïveté in vision; she feels a slight unrest. She thinks: God wants more.

The visions themselves are like recreational walks. For example, she contemplates the Lord at a lake. He walks in this direction with his disciples, toward a village. Now her contemplation passes into vision. For a while, she sees the landscape, and she has time to move around a bit within it before the Lord appears. She has time to gaze at the grass and the trees and everything around. Now the Lord arrives, accompanied by his disciples. The events follow one another. Somehow, all of this is quite childlike. Like biblical stories that are recounted for children. At the end of the vision, it can be that the Lord might suddenly turn around and direct his eyes to her, with the question that is not articulated. And so it recurs, until she understands: she has to enter into the cloister proper.

From the moment of her entry, her visions become essentially more brief, not with respect to duration, but with respect to what is portrayed. They are still demands, but also fulfillments. The question at the end disappears. She gets so carried away that every question becomes superfluous. The visions that lie before her always remain the nourishment on which she lives in the interim periods. Everything reminds her of what she has seen and experienced before, and thus a sort of bridge is built to the next vision. She thus throws herself, as it were, into the new visions of her own accord.

These visions provide her with wonderful knowledge about surrender. She is in this respect very different from Mechtild of Hackeborn. This latter proceeds on the basis of the absolute supremacy of the love of the Lord, which always overtakes her human love. Mechtild of Magdeburg, on the other hand, sees how the Lord reduces himself at first to her measure and corresponds to her love, and it is only in the fulfillment that she experiences the boundlessness, which she cannot bear as a whole, but the pieces and fragments of which she holds within herself. The rupture comes first in that moment when the Lord finds us just as he in fact wants us.

Her surrender contains an entire rule, a process: she thinks, for example, about obedience. Then she sees the Lord's obedience, but as it is divided in us between the keeping of the monastery's Rule and her personal obedience to the Lord. She reflects until she reaches the point at which the two come together: the Lord's obedience and her own. And then comes the rupture and thereby also the fulfillment. She applies this rule to the tiniest things: the soup today is very bad; but when the Lord was on his journeys he also had to eat bad soup; God knows what the disciples' cooking was like ... Thus, her repugnance converges with the Lord's, and this ignites the love that can overcome.

First prayer, before her entry into the cloister (they are short prayers, because she always gets transported quickly into her visions as she prays):

Our Father, who art in heaven, you have given your Son to us all as your Bridegroom. I would like to express to you my gratitude for this. But I would also like to speak with you, Father, about your Son. A short time ago, there was nothing but love and surrender between the two of us, and every time we were together, every prayer, every offering I made to him, every vision, was inspiring and fulfilling. And now it seems to me as if a cloud were hanging over every one of our meetings. Something is no longer right. Your Son does not seem to be as happy as he used to be; the face he shows me is not the same. I pray to him as I always have; I offer myself to him as I always have; I try to love him as I always have. But each time it seems to me that he is disappointed when he leaves me. Father, I beg you, speak with your Son about this, and tell your Son he ought to show me what I should do so that he might be happy once again with his young bride. I truly want to do everything, and I beg you to allow me to do it. Amen.

Second prayer, much later, in the monastery: Father, I thank you for having led me into the cloister, where I can better serve your Son through the Rule. I see it in him now, and you will certainly also see it in him, that this is what he wanted and that he is not as disappointed as he used to be. But please, Father, do not let me grow lukewarm; never let me believe I have now completed everything your Son has asked of me, but rather show me, day by day, step by step anew, how I may please him more and more. This is what I want so dearly! And, behold! we are in a blessed house, where many people truly do everything in order to please him. And they are an example to me of surrender; they show me how they accomplish it; and I can learn a lot from them. I thank you for this community, but I ask you not to allow this human intercourse with my sisters, which to be sure is at the same time also a spiritual community, to become so pleasant that I therefore become less desirous of the company of your Son. I thank you for everything, and I ask you to make use of me more and more so that I might serve your Son more and more. Amen.

MECHTILD OF HACKEBORN (1241–1299)

She acquires the habit, quite young, of comparing all the events of her day-to-day life with what they would be if she were to surrender herself entirely to Christ. What meaning they would then have. For a long time, this is how she proceeds, and she has to allow what she imagines to take effect in her in order to measure the distance between her and the things she *would* experience if she were to surrender herself completely. And then she meets a person who attracts her very much and who is very much attracted to her, and she feels this love well up in her from one day to the next and fill her. But even in the

369

midst of this fulfillment, she has to compare herself again. How would it be if love were to acquire the measure of absoluteness? If she could belong to Christ? Now a new knowledge dawns on her: With precisely the same love with which I *could* love the Lord, the Lord in truth loves me, and not only me, but all those who have been given to him. He loves with a love that surpasses everything that could exist in the highest earthly love: with absolute love. And I can imagine my tiny human love allowing itself to be stretched to the utmost in love for God, but even at this limit, I have to realize that Christ's love remains infinitely greater. The distance between my greatest possible love and the Lord's love remains impossible for me to measure. The only thing I know is that my greatest love lies sheltered within his infinite love. For the Lord's love has inclined itself to me.

Already beforehand, the idea of the cloister was not foreign to her. In the first moment, she dismisses it, because she fears she would then have to let her spontaneous relationship to the Lord founder in a program of monastic norms; she fears she would have to give up her love—which she feels to be strong enough to be fashioned by her personally—for the sake of an impersonal form. She prays with great fervor and for a long time. The moment she enters into prayer, she loses herself entirely; she is enraptured the entire time. She herself feels she has entered another sphere. Coming back from this sphere is something she accomplishes in stages; she has to get used to the earth again gradually. As long as she is not yet in the cloister, it is always very difficult for her to find her way back; once the time for prayer has come to an end, she has to grope slowly through the transitional stages. Because of the extra time she needs, for which life in the world has no room, she decides she does indeed belong in the monastery. She has a subtle feeling for such things, which understands the delicate rules of the obedience of prayer very well. She thus knows that her rhythm of prayer does not fit in with a life in the world, because the precision of the obedience of prayer suffers here. She knows, moreover, that her chastity and her poverty would be endangered in the world. She understands that *at one point* the love of a man was allowed to serve her as a pointer to the love of God but that one is not permitted to repeat the experience a second time in the same sense. Although everything was completely pure, the danger would be too great if it were to be repeated. She also understood the lesson that it conveyed to her. For already then she directed everything to the perfect gift of her entire femininity. She sees the inclination in herself that points to totality. She did not take any step too far, but the inclination that became apparent sufficed to show her the totality of love. She observes the same thing with respect to poverty: in relation to this worldly love, she has envisioned all the property she would be capable of giving up and all the earthly goods she would be able to gather around herself in order to nourish this love. And she understands that the Lord desires one who is poor and stripped bare, without worldly goods, and that he spends everything in the cloister that he considers necessary for his bride. She is familiar with this concept of being a bride, but in a very different sense from, for example, the great Teresa. Indeed, she knows what woman in her totality means, but she immediately cuts away the whole sensual sphere in order to strip her spirit completely bare in God's presence. And at the same time in order to make herself completely tiny, in order not to create an expectation for more than she is able to give.

Her visions become more and more complex over time. Initially, the content is poor, but then it develops and acquires more spiritual substance. The other Mechtild travels the opposite path: her visions become increasingly simple, childlike, and lucid. Both encounter each other in a central point, and this encounter is for the other Mechtild not without influence. She is, so to speak, outflanked by the former, placed in her shadow, and she thus becomes inwardly smaller and more humble. This does not at all mean, however, that her visions are not as beautiful, and perhaps even more beautiful, than those of the little Mechtild. They know of one another before they first meet, and they feel a reciprocal attraction. But once they are together in the cloister, they are at first repelled by each other. The "little one" believes to a certain extent that she is not permitted to encounter the "great one" any differently than she encounters everyone else, that she may not extend more love to her. (Moreover, it is a strange cloister: the sisters tell each other everything; they talk about things that ought to be reserved for the confessor alone; they draw their sustenance from the exchange of confessions and experiences. This introduces disquiet and distrust among particular individuals who are not obsessed by God in the same way as others. On the other hand, there exists a certain enthusiasm for those who have the most beautiful visions, and so forth.) Thus, the "great" Mechtild is a bit put off; the "little" Mechtild finds that she permits herself too much for the beginning because of her visions, and the other Mechtild experiences this tension. Later, things go better; both carry out at the same time a return to the Rule in a strangely similar way. For both it is as if they were little lost atoms, a good distance from the Lord, because they collided with love in their relationship. And the Lord sends them a sort of life jacket, in the form of the Rule, adjusted to bind them closely together; and both are permitted to be bound only in the place where the Lord binds them. At the same time, both learn total surrender, although they have had mystical experiences for a long time. It is the moment when their mission is assured. As a mission, it was already beforehand quite in order for both of them. But their encounter was the great test for their mission. They had to allow themselves to be thrown into the very depths of nothingness and leave everything that came beforehand once again entirely in God's hands. In addition, they do not have any confessor who truly understands and educates. They have to learn things by trial and error, which would be self-evident in normal spiritual guidance. They are afterward all the more insightful for it, especially the "little" Mechtild. From that point on, she learned the true feeling of love, at every level and in every experience. In the relationship between the two of them, Gertrude is indeed present, but hers is only a quiet presence that hovers above them, and thus she is able to help untie the knot in which she herself is not caught up. Of the three of them, Mechtild von Hackeborn has the most reason and common sense.

Prayer: Let it be right, Lord, that I enter into the cloister. You see the hope I have to be able to serve you in earnest there, as you expect from me. But because I committed so many mistakes in the world, because I claimed to love you more than all things, and thus fell so short of your love, I have become fearful: I am afraid that I am promising more than I am capable of keeping, even though I know that the fulfillment lies in you and you grant it. Teach me to give myself in the way you will it, and accept my life from me, not as a gift of any significance, but merely as the tiny bit that I still have and am able to offer to your love. Grant that I may be faithful to you in the Order, that I may keep the Rule and also help those who belong to you in our cloister to lead the life you require of them. I ask you for your blessing for all those whom I leave behind in the world, people I had thought were so entrusted to me that I was not permitted to distance myself from them. Bless them, but bless no less the cloister that has now become mine. I ask this of you in the name of your Mother, who was indeed the first person to serve you for the whole of her life. Amen.

GERTRUDE (1256–1302)

Already before entering the cloister, she stands out because of her purity and surrender and because of a special virginity of soul. She is absolutely childlike and cheerful. She is not troubled by many questions while she is in the world; it seems perfectly natural to her to do the will of God. She prays like a child; she looks forward to the cloister and to everything that will happen ... She is incredibly sheltered. Sin makes no impression on her: it is something that belongs to the bad people with whom she does not feel much of a connection. Sin lies outside the world to which she belongs, a heavenly world. She possesses a sort of innate devotion; seen from the outside, this could almost make one think it was aestheticism—as if she were a person who saw only the beautiful and good in things, who had to take things selectively, as it were, and who turns her back to evil and harsh truths. But with her it is something different: this is how things were decided for her up to the time she enters the cloister, and during this time evil cannot reach her. She clings to the good and commits herself to it. Others see vice and seek, horrified, for ways to come to the aid of sinners. She sees the good and thinks about ways to make it accessible to everyone, and everything takes place in the context of great naïveté, goodness, and love.

In the cloister, she gets to know a lot of people. Very quickly, the common life in the cloister becomes a cross for her. She is deeply horrified: it is not what she thought it would be, being together with the pure, but it is instead a common life with a very mixed group of people. Many sufferings arise for her from this experience. She is extremely generous; she wants to give everything and in fact does give everything. Her life before her entry also becomes at the same time a cross, because she can no longer understand how she was able to live that way. She thinks she would have been able to accomplish more than if she had completely taken refuge in the good: if instead of adoring the simple beauty of the Lord she had contemplated him more in the Cross and in his absence in the hearts and minds of people.

This becomes for her a gateway into suffering. It is a spontaneous entry, but this choice itself corresponds to a task God has given her. Her discovery that community life is not the way she thought it was had a great *impact* on her. Whoever is so pure and at the same time so childishly naïve as Gertrude is will take the measure of purity not only from the Mother of God—which is perfectly natural—but also to a certain extent from herself. She fails to grasp that one can be different from the Mother of God, and if she sees the sisters so imperfectly, then she is not able to put herself inwardly in their place. But this is what she has to do, because it concerns the people who have been entrusted to her, and she herself is not permitted to form a party together with the Mother of God against the sisters. Thus, she is forced to stand there, where she is inwardly not able to stand, a place to which she has

373

no connection. This experience in the community suffices to reveal to her the essence of the entire world, to form her humility anew, and to place her will to give herself on a whole other level. Moreover, she practices a lot of penance. But in penance she becomes a child once more. In penance, too, everything is more a state than a reflection.

She is the bride of Christ, but in a completely spiritual sense, insofar as she understands that her nuptiality is made up of her feminine service. Everything in her gets transposed into service and prayer. The concept of nuptiality has no sensual aftertaste for her. Wherever sensual temptation might begin, she does not even need to formulate a No; it is already there formulated in her, so to speak, and she carries out spontaneously an act of spiritual assent. She also possesses a particular vision of things in the mystery of the Passion: while someone like the little Thérèse remains fixed on the way of the Cross, Gertrude is not fixed anywhere. She often proceeds from the departure scene in Nazareth: how the Mother has to let the Son go into the unforeseeable, and then again from the final moments on the Cross, where the suffering Lord looks down upon the few faithful who are there and behind them in spirit the mass of those without faith and without fidelity.

Her life as a visionary is again completely childlike. What she sees reminds one a bit of the pictures in a children's Bible, not in composition, but in the content that is offered to her and that she is able to grasp. She often sees a suffering, a joy, an encounter, a desire, and so forth, everything in the simplest shapes. Under the Cross and on the Cross, as she sees it, not much takes place, only a genuine and real suffering, which becomes very clear in the vision. It is as if in her pre-cloister life, when she was still in peace, she acquired the capacity to bear the later restlessness of suffering. Through a sort of being sheltered in the world, she gained at the same time "strong nerves".

First prayer: I thank you Lord, for the favor of having your Mother lead me to you. I am happy to be allowed to go into the cloister in order to serve you and in order to learn more and more from my sisters, from all your saints, and from your Mother what it means to serve you and what you desire from all of us. And I ask you: Show me your desires and make me able to fulfill them. You know, indeed, that I am not handy at many things. But I beg you, use everything I have; take everything useful, that which I do not yet possess and which you nevertheless need. Please fashion me in such a way that I am able to serve in this way, that I am able to correspond in a serious way to your wishes, and do not ever hesitate to show what you desire to have. Up to the moment I am able to come to you and your Mother in heaven, I truly want to do your will in everything and to renounce my own forever. Make my faith grow, so that you can broaden my service and put me in the place where you want me every day; allow me to pray in the way you want to listen and to do what you desire. I beg you: bless the world that I leave behind; bless the cloister into which I enter; bless your entire Church and every believer. I ask you this for the sake of your Mother's name; it is indeed she who leads me to you. Amen.

Second prayer: When I now contemplate your Cross, Lord—and indeed I contemplate it often, because you show it to me so often—I thus understand more and more that you make use of us precisely on the basis of your Cross. While I lived in the world, I thought I knew your desires, and when I begged you to express even more wishes and to use me even more, I thought I had some inkling about what the path looked like that you had determined for me. Today, I am once again horrified when I see where your demands lead and what you need. But the more I am horrified when I see how much we all hold back in our gift of self, how much we always seek to fulfill our own desires and fail to see yours. And if I now ask you: Express your desires, make of me what you will, then I know that the answer can be harsher than I would have thought bearable. Nevertheless, this is what I ask of you. I do not want to leave you lonely on your Cross. I want to stand there with your Mother and to suffer as much as you deem good. And I ask you: Do not see my weakness as a rejection, but take the whole of me; use me as you will; allow everything that was mine to become what your will requires. And bless, too, each of my sisters; bless them all so that they learn more and more, and I too, to do your will. Bless our house; bless your entire Church, and allow the sisters to gives themselves to you more and more through the goodness of your Mother. Amen.

ANGELA OF FOLIGNO (d. 1309)

She is a very simple young girl, but one who has very clear notions about things. She understands precisely what good and evil are. And she also understands why the good is good and evil is evil. Without a mystical insight, she has a very clear "vision" of the essence of things. She knows what things are, what value they have, what they want to say. She is very straightforward, but very upright. For her, no mixtures are allowed, no half and half. The good is simply good without qualification, and evil is evil without qualification.

She has a very rich prayer, which at times carries her whole soul away. She prays *totally*, in a unity of body and soul. She is merciless with herself, and she retains perhaps a certain harshness with respect to others as well, because compromise is completely foreign to her.

In the cloister, she becomes acquainted with a pettiness that was previously unknown to her. She experiences her acceptance into the cloister as a great grace; she expected to find saints in her sisters. But the blessed people to whom she comes are human beings with their failings. She suffers quite acutely from this, and in this suffering she actually makes the decision: God or human beings. Up to this point, the question did not arise in such a way. She did indeed want God, but she also took a lot from human beings. Now the demand comes to affirm God without remainder and to see human beings entirely from God's perspective. And not to want to communicate herself to human beings, but to bring God to them. That becomes the point for her.

Where the visions begin is difficult to say. There are various things that "help" her to come to vision. Sometimes the boundaries are not entirely visible between mere imaginative representations and super-natural vision. She is drawn up more and more into the supernatural, as it were, in natural stages. But once she arrives there, it becomes completely unhinged. It "changes into" the Lord's body on the altar; it "changes into" his voice; it "changes into" the bell that calls the sinners: when she hears the Mass bells ring, she hears supernaturally in them how this call passes from God to the sinner. It is actually heaven on the altar. The real presence of the Lord is not only limited to the bare Host; rather, the Host radiates this presence and draws all of the surroundings into heaven with it.

Over the course of a long period of time, she includes herself naïvely in her visions. She depicts herself and her states in order better to be able to depict what God is like. It is only very late that she learns to distinguish between her state and God in a clear manner. Her visions are strongly connected to her senses. She hears, she feels, she smells, she sees, and so forth. In a later period, she is also detached even from her senses. The transition corresponds in some sense to Christ's own transition from his state before the Cross to the state after the Cross. Christ, too, used his earthly senses before the Passion to see and to hear the Father and also to interpret him, while afterward he passes to the Father, so to speak, transparently. In the first period, Angela suffers many things during her mystical states; for example, she becomes sick when she looks upon evil, or she is enraptured and carried away while she looks upon God ... In the second period, she is separated from everything and, so to speak, inspired, although the earlier states were entirely correct and experienced in service and although she remains standing before good and evil in her simplicity even afterward and does not become overly sophisticated. The objects she uses in her service are included in her prayer; she cultivates toward them a peculiar relationship of love, and in this final period the things take on a certain transfigured character within the relationship.

She speaks very little about her temptations; but there are periods that are heavy for her. These are not only times when she sees the Lord suffer and suffers along with him, but also times when she herself becomes a question, which she experiences as a temptation. What sort of a creature is she, then?

Before her death, she sees everything once again, how it was. She is seized by a deep regret that everything was not better, and she takes unspeakable joy in God, but this joy is mixed with the bitterness of not being adequate to it. When she earlier saw the whole kingdom of God on the altar, it was connected with a feeling of perfect certainty: everything really is this way, it really is present. Now in death she experiences a great expansion, and that is very difficult for her. She had known that what she had seen and come to understand was only a small part; but she had become so accustomed to this that she came to take what she grasped of heaven for heaven itself. Now, everything opens up to her, and she sees that it continues on into eternity.

First prayer: Before her entry into the cloister. (There must have been certain concrete circumstances at the time of her calling that A. does not see: it is as if a decision had to be made again in the context of coercion.)

Father, I wish to approach you as your child. I desire to try as best I can no longer to choose my own way and to follow my own path. I know you lay claim to every thought and that, if I distance myself from you with a thought, the alienation would immediately become immeasurable. And the experiences of this most recent time have shown me more and more clearly the danger of alienation, of giving preference to my own existence. Father, give me your Son's hand, so that it may guide me. Grant that I might give mine to him in a childlike way and, because he himself has now pointed out the way, that I might truly enter in through the door that has been shown me, that I might be accepted and that through your love and the love of all my new sisters I might learn to do your will. Father, you know me; you know my obstacles; you know how I drag my feet in following you: transform, I beg you, all that belongs to me, so that it may become yours, and do not listen to my voice if I call out for some consideration.

377

Father, I thank you for the accompaniment you have given me up until now. I ask you once again to forgive me for everything I have done that was not right, and I give you the solemn promise to start over in earnest, if you give me the grace to do so. Amen.

Second prayer: before a holy Mass. (The sisters in this cloister apparently receive precise instructions regarding how they are to pray during Mass. For example, during the *Confiteor*, they are to call their sins to mind; during the offering they are to awaken certain impressions and images concerning the Lord's death. This produces to a slight extent the effect of something forced. Angela has to remember constantly what is now required of her. Her visions thus come about as agglomerations and disruptions of the schema she is asked to follow. She adheres to the required activity out of obedience. This prevents her from entering into a perfect unity with what the Lord shows her. The others do not understand, and she too does not understand, that she ought to have been left in peace in these moments. She stands restlessly in between the Church's prayer, the personally demanded additions, and the things that were shown to her immediately by God.) And now she sees and prays:

You do not grow tired, Lord, of allowing your sacrifice to be enacted day after day with your participation. You have given your share for all of us on the Cross, and you give it to us anew in each Host, to all of us who believe in you ... (In this moment, it is demanded of her that she reflect on her sins and on the sins of the world. Thus, a lapse occurs in her prayer. She is, as it were, drawn away from the Lord in order to enter into her sins. She pulls herself together, does what is demanded, and meanwhile the action on the altar continues, and she is flustered. At communion, it is once again demanded that she think first of all about her sins, but she already sees the radiant Lord coming upon her. It is only when the Mass has ended that she sees everything once again in unity, in the peace of thanksgiving. Her prayer does not lose its fruitfulness through this intrusion. But insofar as her naïveté in relation to God gets damaged, she is not able to keep her naïveté in relation to the cloister completely intact. Nevertheless, it ultimately does not get ruined; she remains a wonderful person, formed from a seamless cloth.) Her *prayer of thanksgiving:*

Lord, your first bride was Mary; she was permitted to carry you as Mother and as Bride at once. You dwelled within her. And now, Lord, because you come to us in your Eucharist, you dwell in us as if we were your mothers and your brides. In the Spirit, who allows us to understand that you are truly present in the Host, you allow yourself to be received as your Mother received in the Spirit and conceived you by the Spirit. Lord, although we know how unworthy we are, we are now filled with an infinite feeling of gratitude. You dwell in us; you are in is; you live in us and with us; you remain in us; do not leave us alone. You allow us in our imperfect way to do something for you that Mary did for you in her perfect way. Draw us deeper into your mystery. Lord, I beg you, take the whole of me; come to me with your entire mission; allow me to fulfill your will entirely. And I am certain: because you have arrived, you allow me to do at least *something*; you allow my sisters to do at least *something*; and you allow all of your believers to carry you. My gratitude, Lord, is like I am: weak and imperfect. And yet I wish that my gratitude were as great as my faith, for my faith is indeed not dependent on me; it is your gift to me. It comes from you with the entire fullness that God the Father lends to it; it comes intact, so to speak, through you to us all. And so allow gratitude and faith to be one, a unity that we desire to use for nothing else but to serve you. Bless all those, Lord, who have received you today, and grant that all who deny you or do not want to know anything about you may slowly begin to turn to you, all of them together with one another, and thus soon become open to your complete blessing. Amen.

Third prayer from the time of sickness, toward the end of her life: My Lord, through the days of sickness through which you lead me, show me that my time is coming near to its end. That it will enter into your time, that the time that belongs to me will cease to be mine in order to become wholly yours. Lord, you know I have little patience. I am not happy to be sick. Even though I have contemplated your suffering for the whole of my life, I have not learned to love it. And yet, precisely because I do not understand it and cannot bear it, I beg you to allow me to suffer as much as you think is good, to lay upon me as many days of sickness as you see fit. Do not let my groaning become bitter, but also do not pay attention to it; do not be put off by it. Show me the full measure of what it is you have laid aside for me. Lord, I do not know how near the hour of death is, how much lamenting I will yet make others listen to. But now, because there is still time, I thank you for all the graces you have directed to me, for everything you have given to me, and I beg you, perhaps for the last time, in earnest for forgiveness for everything I have done only with reluctance. I will try, Lord, in this final time, to contemplate the suffering of all those who have suffered for you; but I know that my suffering will seem small compared to the suffering of your saints and martyrs.

And how small indeed when I compare it simply with your own! Grant, Lord, that this contemplation of the suffering of your friends might become fruitful for all those who, like me, are tired of suffering. Bless my sisters; bless this whole cloister, the whole Order, the entire Church. And may you keep your blessing over me until the end. Amen.

BROTHER KLAUS (1417–1487)

A. sees him as he is making his decision to become a hermit. He finds it very difficult. But there is a sort of gradual adaptation. First, the thought runs through his head for just a moment: A person could ... a person should ... But he thinks it is crazy. The next day, it starts again and lingers for a while ... After a certain time, he gets used to the idea. He gets used to it in a completely childlike way, like a child who has learned something new and delights in it and thinks: This is really something neat! Quite naïve. At bottom, he got used to the idea; he even resolved himself before he realized what it actually means in truth. He simply goes; the meaning of things will become apparent soon enough. He hands himself over to God, who will certainly draw him into what is ever greater. The first "perhaps" that he utters does not contain any setting of limits in relation to God, and so it broadens him and prepares him for the total Yes, the surging Yes, and this is the way in which he sets out. His deed is greater than his knowledge, and his prayer is even greater than his deed. It is a twofold play of *exhortations*, but this is exactly how God wills it.

First prayer: The pathway up to this point that you, Lord, have led me upon with your kind Mother seemed to me to be a false path, when I did not know that it was you who were leading me, that your grace had chosen this path for me. Now, Lord, you will that I serve you in a wholly different way. It appears to me like a complete break with my past, and yet it is a continuation, because your grace chose it for me. Lord I always become frightened: frightened that I will not be able to sustain what you require from me, frightened that I am too old to adapt myself to it. And frightened that I understand too little about life in solitude, about the life of prayer, about the life of penance, to be able to fill the whole day with this new meaning. And yet, Lord, there was already a lot of penance here, a lot of renunciation, many things that I did again and again only in imperfect ways, even though I knew that you require more. Lord, grant me the certainty that I must tread this path, that I am no longer permitted to look back, that everything in my past was a preparation for this. Thus, I beg you, allow your Mother to accompany me. Allow her to be with me, so that I may learn anew to do everything according to your will. She is indeed the one who knows best what you require and how your expectations ought to be fulfilled. Thus, I beg you Lord, lead me and allow her, too, to lead me, and take everything from me that prevents me from coming to you, and let everything become such that you can use it, the way you want it. Do not abandon me. Accompany me. Give me the strength to remain. I promise you I will try to do your whole will, even there where I do not understand, even there where I am scarcely able to do any more. I beg you, grant a fullness to each of my prayers, and grant that everything truly be, not for me, but for the many people you have entrusted to me. Amen.

Then A. sees him in his hermitage. He has to return to the people in order to live with them. And it is hard for him. He prays:

Second prayer: O Lord, you see how difficult it is for me to speak to people. And yet they all come to me with their faith concerns, with things that you show to me so that I can and must give an answer to them. And now, Lord, I must go away from here in order to take on a task, one that I know you have given me, for it bears the signs of the other tasks that have been entrusted to me up to this point. Lord, I feel weak. Everything up to this point—the fasting, every penance, the vigilance, and all the prayer—was easy. But it will be difficult to fulfill people's expectations among the people. Nevertheless, I know you have taken my life; take it now once more, so that I do not become unfaithful but do what it is you require. I know I will not be alone; you accompany me, and our gentle Lady is always with me, and you give me the words I have to speak in order to carry out your task. I do not go forth with a hesitating faith, for I do believe. Rather, my hesitations are those of an old man who knows how regularly he fails; and yet I go, Lord, with confidence, because you will that I go. I beg you for the grace for those who will hear me and for the entire world that worships you. Amen.

He is driven by people into various forms that are awkward for him. God would in fact have wanted him to be more austere, more withdrawn. But he is forced into this, because people want to have a saint even while he is still alive. They want to test his holiness; they throw him into adventures, into public deeds, which are, to be sure, not able to ruin him, but are in a certain sense not appropriate to his being. He has a lot of visions, and he receives them in obedient childlikeness.

A. is reminded of the vision of the Mother of God she had when she was fourteen years old. There are things that are very beautiful to look at, things that simultaneously challenge and leave open. There are thoughtful visions, which a person can live on for a long time, as if it were nourishment. They offer immediate nourishment but also stores and reserves. One can remain with them, and often an answer takes shape from them ever so slowly. And they have the characteristic of never being used up. They are like a book that remains open, in which a person can always look something up, read on, and explore further. They are given like points of contemplation, which never dry up, but only give hints, so that the person praying has a supply for the following morning. This nourishment allows him to fast, just like living on Holy Communion. There can already be natural tasks that are so urgent a person simply forgets his hunger. The visions God gives him are the sort of work, the sort of task, that completely fills and absorbs him. Moreover, there is a fairly large amount of things in the visions that make his fasting and his penance easier. If ascesis is renunciation, then he possesses Mary's renunciation in his visions, which makes his own easier.

His greater consolation is the Trinity. He has a whole host of entry points, which direct him again and again, from all sides, to the Trinity. This is sufficient for his contemplation. He does not feel the need to see these points of entry gathered together in a connected theological system.

CATHERINE OF GENOA (1447–1510)

First observations concerning purity. She proceeds on the basis of her own temptations in order to attain an image of purity. She knows a lot about sin, for she lives in a crude environment. It arises in her like a discrepancy that dominates everything between her spirit and her body: between what she experiences on the outside and what she would like to experience from the inside. Everything that is not devotion, everyday life, she interprets as a temptation, and this is what gives rise to the demand to become pure. She has a lot of spiritedness in her blood, and temptation does not lie far from her; but she nevertheless also does not exaggerate her being constantly afflicted by temptation. She also experiences "states" of temptation. In confession, she goes into great detail about this. She does not see any peaceful path ahead of her. Wherever she sees the battle, she gets immediately involved in it, she ponders carefully over it, and takes her bearings from it. Not, of course, in order to dwell in it, but in order to overcome it for the sake of purity. This, however, results in something that is a bit cumbersome, something that gives her purity, which is in itself very beautiful

382

and hard-won, a certain rigidity over time. She has such a fear of getting even somewhat close to the danger zones that she immediately and vehemently braces herself against it. And thus she simply passes other things by without paying attention. She cannot simply let it be in peace. She suffers torment insofar as she wants to keep herself away from temptation. In relation to the tiniest failures, she thinks about what would have happened if ... and pushes her imagination to the point of her own damnation.

Her contemplation is heavily influenced by this attitude. She begins, for example, reading a verse: "Ask for it, and it will be given to you." Then she starts with herself. She first examines her conscience in contemplation. "I would like to achieve purity, and God will give it to me if I ask it of him. I ask it because I need it, because I do not posses this purity as a woman. I always have to struggle for it, and I have to achieve it as one who is incapable of achieving it in any other way than by asking. On my own, I do not possess it; I do not have the strength to arrive at it. But the Son, who himself was purity, shares with all of us what he possesses. Indeed, he himself says: 'Ask, and it will be given to you.' I imagine to myself how the Lord speaks these words, as he stands upon the mountainside, how his disciples watch him and slowly begin to grasp what it is he means to say. And each of these disciples sees what he himself would have to ask for. And because the Lord makes all those who believe into his disciples, I myself can stand among his disciples and do myself what the disciples do. To look into myself and see what I need in order to succeed, and to ask the Lord for purity, requesting it from him in just the way he wants it in order to please him. O Lord, you see that I constantly run into difficulties being the way you wish to have me, totally pure. I beg you, remove all the thoughts from me that are impure, and do not allow the impurity that I perceive again and again to touch me. Teach me to keep it away from me and not to take the least hint of it into myself, so that I may remain pure; with a purity I do not possess of my own accord, but which you give to me because you give to everyone what they ask from you." Then she continues on with her vocal prayer.

She sees sin not only in its being committed, but occasionally also in its effects. Each time she hears about a sin, it is to her as if she accompanied the sinner to the end of purgatory. She has explicit personal visions of purgatory. She sees a person she knows who recently died, the neighbor's son, who murdered his mother. And if she was not aware of his sin before then, she comes to know it in the vision of purgatory. She hears how the souls wail, how they cry out, how they come to understand, are actually led constantly from one sin to another, so that their understanding of the guilt they have incurred deepens. She sees the torture and at the same time the instruments of torture. Everything in her vision, which is quite genuine, is bound to her time period. She not only articulates it this way; this is also how she sees it. She does not translate it; this is just how it is given to her. She herself contributes only a little commentary. The explanation of the vision is rather clumsy, but quite loquacious, for she sees all the details in the simple facts. For her and for her sisters and for another person, who is perhaps her confessor, she carries out what amounts to interpretations of what she has seen, in which she digests and inwardly appropriates whatever belongs to some extent to her experience. For example, she saw the purgatory of a liar. In her interpretation, she will also speak about the purgatory she herself could have suffered because of a lie; she talks about what Scripture says in this regard; she adds exhortations to avoid lying, and so forth.

All these things remain bound to her person. But there is another part of her visions that is no longer bound to her. Ultimately, it is too little bound to her and, indeed, precisely because the first part was too much tied to her. That is the consequence of her modesty in relation to the body: the fact that her spiritual visions remain all too spiritual. There is a sort of rift that passes through her being. She is like a child at school who has only a little time available for his various tasks and who simply spent too much time on his first subject: now there is not enough time left over to do the rest in a basic way, and thus in the next lesson he cannot quite keep up any more. To be sure, he grasps what is going on, but not as sharply as he should have understood it. With Catherine, the heavenly vision remains without access, without a conductor, without an entirely adequate comprehension and interpretation. Of course, the vision of the Trinity is in itself already much greater than a vision of purgatory. With purgatory, there are always points of comparison. But in the Trinity, there are no other comparisons than God himself, so that it becomes extremely difficult to express something conceivable with regard to a vision like this. But in addition to this difficulty, Catherine does not comprehend everything. Afterward, she leaves a description of what she saw, as if she expected the teacher to whom she recounted it to understand completely what was meant, even if she herself did not entirely understand it. She provides a literal summary, which she expects will express in an approximate way what she saw. But there was a certain precision lacking in the vision itself, and thus this same thing is lacking in her expression. When she prays within her vision, she does not allow the vision itself to pray enough in her; she mixes too much of her own prayer in with it; she does not sufficiently understand that the vision itself is a God-given prayer. She thinks she has to carry out the particular intention she had carried with her into prayer; for this reason she does not remain silent enough within her trinitarian vision. There is a certain time for the *Domine non sum dignus*, but the time of vision is something else. She is unable to keep these sufficiently distinct. If she is given visions, she cannot get rid of the feeling that there must have been some misunderstanding, that she is not pure enough, and she busies herself with humbling herself and purifying herself, rather than being all eyes and ears. The whole thing is, as it were, very Italian and influenced by her education: a black and white painting of sin and holiness. She never manages to forget herself perfectly in what she sees. On occasion she attempts to bring a certain system into the whole thing: for example, she often has very similar visions, in which, however, something is different. Then she is able, under particular circumstances, to give particular attention to what has now become different, and thus she can be distracted from the main thing.

On the whole, there is quite a lot that is positive in her, also much achievement. It is just that it is connected too much with her own system of holiness. In her interaction with other people, she is extremely humble. But in God's presence she does not know how to surrender everything to the end. There remains something forced in her, which gives her the *appearance* that she is holding onto something, even though this is not what she wants to do.

Prayer in her vision: You have shown me a part of your heaven. You have shown me, Father, how you form the faith together with the Son and the Spirit, a faith that has to be triune, because it is also held in common by the Three, because you allow it to come to be among you and because you give it to us in the way you yourselves possess it. I saw the three thrones next to one another, and I saw a light that joined the thrones together, and the light was such that it appeared as if it came simultaneously from all three thrones at once. And the light was such that it illuminated everything and was so powerful that it cast its light into the hearts of all sinners. And the light was such that it burned; it sought out what it could consume with its flames, and within the Triunity there was nothing to burn because the Triunity is pure. And I offered myself to the light, so that it might burn in me what there was to burn. And when I offered myself, the light began to burn in me. My entire body turned into a fire; my head burned. There was nothing I could do but let myself burn. This burning endured for a long time, for all my sins stuck so closely to me that a brief fire would not have been enough to burn them. When the torment became so great that I thought I could not take it anymore, the fire began to burn in me as if from the beginning. For it had not only to consume the sins in me, but also to ignite a new, pure longing for purity in me. And insofar as this longing was ignited in me, something new, as it were, began in me: a life that allowed me more steadily to see into the light of the three thrones. And I saw the distribution of the triune prayer, but I did not grasp it, for it remained the ineffable. And my longing burned in such a way that I wanted to overpower this ineffable thing. But the ineffable remained ineffable. And the fire continued to burn in me, and the light continued to shine and burn. And I saw in the light something like a bright stripe: this stripe was hope. It ran from the Father through the Son to the Spirit and then back to the Father. And the stripe divided and ran again from the Father to the Son through the Spirit to the Father: and it was love. And this stripe divided again, from the Father to the Son through the Spirit back to the Father, and it was the triune faith, which was triune in its relationship to love and to hope, but also triune because it ran back out of the Father to the Son through the Spirit and to the Father. I should have perceived something I could grasp out of this triune faith, which I could then have passed on to all those who believe in you, O God. But I could not grasp it, because I did not understand the demand to grasp it; the burning continued on in me, and I remained absorbed in this burning. Father, you show me things that I am meant to pass on, but I know that I am not worthy to see them. And this accompanying feeling of unworthiness prevents me from seeing wholly the way you want me to see. Father, forgive me, I know that this unworthiness is an occasion, so to speak, for new sin. Father, forgive me in the name of this inconceivable Triunity that you are. Amen.

While she was saying this prayer, A. saw the vision, a radiant stripe that was like a belt, first one, then two, then three; and the second and third stripe emerged from the first and superimposed themselves on it.

A. says that what she saw was one of Catherine's visions, but Catherine had not so quickly understood and interpreted it; something in the way she interpreted it came more from her than from Catherine; it was above all an *illumination* of Catherine's mode of interpretation.

THOMAS MORE (1478–1535)

I see him as he studies Scripture. The Old and the New Testament. He does it almost always in connection with his office, in order to draw from the Bible the teachings and proverbs he needs. He looks in the Bible for the ideal image of what he ought to be. He studies with precision the righteousness of the Old Covenant and allows it to flow into the righteousness of the New Covenant. His office requires him to know what true righteousness consists in. He is aware that the religion of pure righteousness has been surpassed, but he also knows that the New Testament is built on the foundation of the Old. Thus, he starts to assimilate the Old Testament and then to transpose it into a Christian key. He always does this afresh in relation to everything that concerns his office. Also in relation to his behavior in his family, in relation to the tiny decisions he has to make day to day, and above all in relation to the big decisions of his office. For, without being aware of it, so to speak, he possesses the certainty that one day a great decision will be required of him, and he knows that he will not have the strength for the decision if he fails to recognize its necessity ahead of time. A long time before the great decision becomes actual, he is already at work on it. He speaks no Yes and no No without giving a precise account of what he is doing. His Christian conscience is what determines things. Once he makes his decisions, he does not budge from them, because he had weighed things for such a long time beforehand.

From a very early time, his prayer runs parallel with his spiritual development. There are people who almost always say the same prayers. Not Thomas. For example, he reads the psalms. He reads them systematically, one after another; he does not simply open the book up anywhere. His prayer, then, is a paraphrase of what he reads. He does not have any of his own contemplations. He fashions the words of Scripture into a personal prayer.

First prayer: "I want to lift up my soul to God." "You know, Lord, that I want to do this. Christ's new grace gives me the capacity to do it. Thus, through your grace, I wish to lift my soul to God. I wish to do it just as Christ taught us, when he said the Our Father ... And you know, Father, that this is what I intend to do today and that I would prefer if this small decision, which remains of no consequence to me but which has importance for those who stand under my judgment, would turn out entirely correctly." And then he says a second Our Father for the people, so that his judgment might be correct. "The third Our Father I pray for the great decision of my life, which I have been awaiting for so long already and concerning which you know that I would like to make it entirely your decision." And the fourth Our Father will be for those who belong to him, and the fifth and the sixth for the Church.

Now is the time before the great decision. He is in danger. In order to remain Catholic, he will have to offer his life. His prayer changes; it becomes more expansive. The prayer sketched out beforehand is actually preparation for the prayer that now takes place, which he begins to fashion in a much more personal way:

Second prayer: Father, you have given us your Son; you have handed him over to us, sinners, so that he might make your children out of the sinners we are. He founded the Church in order to glorify you. And he asks that we learn anew every day to glorify you with him. For us, there is only one way to glorify you: fidelity in the Church that was formed by your Son. Father, I would like to remain faithful to your Son, but I can do so only insofar as I fully acknowledge your Church and insofar as I, with all of the power you give me, on the contrary, keep anything from being done to your Church that does not correspond to your intention. You demand a sacrifice from me; you ask for my life; Father, my life has belonged to you from the moment I came to know you through your Son. There is no question for me but that I give it to you. Take it from me, just as I receive it from you: as a whole. Father, give me the strength to remain true to you up until the final moment; give me the strength to overcome, with your grace, the anxiety that befalls every dying person, at least to such an extent that the others who will be watching do not receive the impression that a coward is being killed, but rather see that they are putting to death a Christian, one who is your son. Father, difficult moments lie ahead. But they belong to you, because it was also you who gave me my good moments. You have been faithful to me for the whole of my life; you have made this fidelity visible to me; I have come to understand fidelity through you. Grant that I may hand over to you the proof of my fidelity in the little time that still remains to me. And to do this, not through my own strength, but through your grace. Father, I recommend to you those who are mine, my people, and my Church. Father, take care of all of them; be with all of them. And give to all of them your grace, which is the grace of your Spirit and the grace of your Son. Amen.

IGNATIUS LOYOLA (1491–1556)

Ignatius himself wants to show three prayers. The first one comes from the time at Manresa. He lives in a sort of superabundance of magnanimity and is inwardly not entirely flexible. A part of the Exercises is already finished. Now, he has gathered scriptural texts, two or three, expressing a particular thought and has added a few things of his own, then more biblical passages and his own thoughts for the next idea, and so forth. He sees somehow how the whole thing has to be brought into a unity, but he still feels incapable of bringing it about. He is still of the opinion that he cannot give it form. He receives without difficulty, but he does not have the capacity for passing on. He saw Mary and was powerfully affected by this appearance. Just as he knows what it means to serve a woman from his experience as a knight, so too he absolutely knows from this point on what it means to serve the Mother of our Lord. He draws certain comparisons in his mind between the show of favor from a lady whom one serves and what it means when Mary appears to a person. He understands this vision as the Mother's condescension to him. He understands that she has entrusted something to him with this and that this something is inside her; she gives what is hers to him; she gives it for the Church. And he intimates in a very unclear way that this something will be the Society. All of this is present at once: knowledge about a community, the incipient Exercises, which however still need to be melted down, and the vision of Mary. This vision represents the most absolute thing he has yet experienced in his life.

Ever since his conversion he has found himself in a state of readiness, which was something like a question. Manresa was meant to serve as a clarification of this question and a deepening of his faith. Then, at one point he discovers that Manresa changes into something completely different: the fact that he returns from this experience, not with a purified question, but rather with a new question that lays a much deeper obligation on him. To be sure, many things are illuminated, but the unilluminated region remains much greater. He will have to found something. But what this foundation will look like, he still has no idea at this point. He is heading toward an enormous risk. The idea of martyrdom lies in the near distance. And what if he were to fall into a total dead-end with all these new things? But he also knows that he is not collecting the Exercises for himself alone, that they are there, like Mary's appearance, for other people, for those who are to come. They are a seed, which will produce new seeds. How this will take place, he does not know. The fact that he himself, his own inner life, is something that is also given is very clear to him; nevertheless, this knowledge simply increases his lack of clarity. He does not yet see the obedience of the new community. He sees his own obedience to the Mother of the Lord, just as a knight obeys his lady, in freedom, and in doing so he advances his knighthood. He brings trophies home, in a certain sense, to his lady. In the same way he wants to bring to Mary the graces he receives. This is something quite settled for him. He begins by giving back to her the grace of her appearance—which he feels to be the greatest grace of his life—so that she may share it with the whole Church. For he has a precise perception of the connection between her and the Church as the Bride of Christ. For him, the appearance of Mary immediately turns into an ecclesial obligation. And Mary ought to allow the ecclesial grace, which she shares with him, to benefit the Church. The obedience in relation to the lady, that is, to Mary, to a large extent prepares for his later idea of obedience. This was never a theory for him, but rather the start of something altogether concrete. The Mother is now, for him, the new, concrete gateway to the Son, just as the Son is to the Trinity. The Son is like a stage between the Mother and the Trinity. And he sees this sort of heavenly hierarchy reflected in the worldly hierarchy. But this latter strikes him as rotten and decayed, the former as perfectly pure and intact. He also knows the hierarchy of the religious Orders—but only from a great distance—and he has vaguely in mind developing something like a religious Order or hierarchy in which both the heavenly and the ecclesial hierarchy would come together and would somehow be able to merge. The new picture would have to be a reflection of the divine image in the world and at the same time be built up in the Church by means of a form of perfect surrender; it would have to participate wholly in God's blessing in the Church. He would like to convey the spirit of the heavenly hierarchy to his followers, the spirit that will ultimately take for him the name of obedience and chastity (poverty is something he will see only later); he would like them to be so supernatural that they receive obedience and are able to practice it, just as it exists in God: absolute and perfect, independent of all human considerations, which he otherwise sees at work everywhere. Of course, he does not yet see anything of the "fourth vow" to the pope; he only sees the openness to the Church in a wholly indeterminate way. By contrast, chastity is something he sees very clearly, because he had to keep vigilance over himself to the point of the renunciation of his sensual powers.

He is extremely sensitive in Manresa, extremely vulnerable, and above all extremely lonely. That is the hardest. Everything would have been much easier if he could have simply entered already into a community that was created just as this new one would have to be. His vulnerability rests in part on the fact that he has his eyes on the absoluteness of service, but at the same time he feels himself to be a sinner and for that reason constantly doubts himself. He sees his mission, but he has no one to confirm it for him. This must always be kept in mind. Certainly, his mission is something explicitly masculine, and thus he has, as a man, a certain confirmation in Mary's appearance. But no earthly hand is there to help him. The fact that he is such a sinner, at least in his time at Manresa, is the particular cross that belongs to his mission. He has no possibility of setting the personal aspect aside somewhere in order to live out his mission in a free way. He has to carry himself along with it, without a break; he has to suffer from the contradiction between the burden of his sin and the heights of that to which he aspires.

The prayer in Manresa: Mary, Mother of God, I beg you to show me the way to your Son, my Lord, so that I can walk this path and so that I may be permitted to tell him that I wish to serve him in all things. That I wish to be a servant to him and will to carry out all the work that is entrusted to me in the joy of the servant who knows that his Lord is counting on him. Our Lord, it is not clear to me what you need us for, those of us who stand ready in the new community, about which I know only that it will come, though I do not yet know what it will look like. I beg you to give me the spirit to understand what you require of me; give your Spirit to those who come to this community, and do not allow yourself to be hindered in the carrying out of your plan through my unworthiness; instead, use me for whatever you wish, just as you wish, as long as you wish, and earnestly in every way. Though I may say Yes or No, hear only my Yes, which I draw out of the power that your Mother possessed in her assent; it is a promise I know I can keep only by means of your grace and your assistance. You see in my prayer, in my penances, and in the slow, laborious work that I wring from myself with so much trouble that I truly *want* to serve you. But, Lord, I am not alone; all those who are coming are present, those whom you see and whom I do not know. You know the work has to be accomplished as much by you as by me. And so I beg you to communicate your graces to all those who are coming, just as your Mother always gives each of her graces for the whole work, for the whole Church. Grant that I may love your Church more and more and that I may fill out the place I am meant to occupy in your Church, the place you have intended for me from eternity, according to your will. I beg you for your blessing, for the work, for the Church, for all believers, and I beg you at the same time to give me the favor to contribute whatever may come to your greater glory, for your Church, for me, and for the triune God. Amen.

In order to reproduce exactly the prayer that Ignatius said at that time, this prayer would have to be imagined as both more colorful and more awkward. It is a time when he prays only with many penances; he prays constantly, but he exaggerates the penance. From the experiences he has at this time, he will later draw the proper measure and the moderate attitude. It is not fanaticism that dominates him at this point, but he thinks he is not permitted to kneel down in prayer without having done some very powerful penance. His prayer has a very slow tempo; each of his prayers, even the vocal ones, contains an element of contemplation in it. When, for example, he prays before the table set before him, he waits until he has achieved a complete freedom from eating, a complete detachment. There was once in his little book of Exercises a passage that is no longer part of the book that ran: in prayer before confession, one ought to be indifferent to what it is God wishes to show a person. When one prepares for confession in prayer, one ought therefore at first to detach himself completely from his own intention and thus exist in such a way that God can show him what ought to be confessed, in a way that corresponds to man's confessional intention, but without this leading spontaneously to the examination of one's sins. Ignatius is convinced: If it is right that I confess now, then God will infallibly show me my sins as they appear to him himself, assuming I am prepared to hear him and thus that I am indifferent. He himself always enters into prayer with the specific intention to find what he is looking for. But within this will, he does not have any preference; he lets everything of his own go. The phrase "what I desire" means: "Everything that you desire". So much so that, if God wills it, my will can and ought to be prevented from being carried out. At the beginning of the prayer stands an act of pure surrender, in which one hands everything over to God's will. And it is only on the basis of God that one will receive back the "what I desire", *if* God so wills it and *just as* he wills it. This is what Ignatius intended for his followers. He imagines that his priests ought to forget their own intentions to such an extent when they begin the prayers at a funeral, for example, that they would be just as ready in that moment to bless a wedding. The intention is merely to do what God wills, and God fills this intention with his content.

Now in Manresa he has the time to pray in a contemplative way. He is able to do so ever since he saw the Mother of the Lord. He also receives a particular insight into the essence of the Trinity, into the unity of the three Persons. He hears this unity in the image of three notes: it is a single chord in which one can distinguish the three notes but cannot separate them. Each note has its meaning and its justification by its relationship to the two others, in order to form a threefold harmony with them. Just as he grasps the unity of the Persons of God here, another time he grasps the unity of God's totally comprehensive providence: the fact that all things and events work together, from the tiniest to the most essential. At that time it seemed to him that the one Word of God comprehended everything, but in such a way that individual notes rang out, in the words of the prophets, in the Church, in nature, everything flowing into a unity in the direction of the Father. Through this vision of the unity of the Word of God in all things, he receives a particular sensibility for variety, for what is safe, deliberate, indispensable, and unexpected, for what is humorous and picturesque in God's individual pathways. It is as if he were so fundamentally anchored in unity that he no longer had to have any fear about multiplicity.

What he lacked above all in Manresa was a spiritual director. He considered certain things to be right at that time that he later let fall. On the basis of negative experiences, the essence and breadth of guidance opened itself up to him.

In Paris. He studies with his companions. There are a few who already feel they form a community together; for some it is hard; others have an easier time of it. There are many things that cause Ignatius some difficulty: the fullness of his contemplation in Manresa has disappeared. He no longer feels the grace. The supernatural certainty that he still does have for the Society, he no longer has for *himself.* And however wise he is able to be for others in understanding that there have to be periods of testing and dryness, it is nevertheless difficult for him to grasp this in his own regard. For he has the absolute awareness that his followers ought to be educated, and at the same time he sees what trouble he himself has in his studies and worries that God's whole plan could founder on his incapacity. Finally, he is not certain whether his brothers are truly and thoroughly convinced by the necessity of willing to serve God in the way he intends. And he is bodily exhausted and unwell.

Second prayer. Triune God, Father, Son, and Spirit, I wish to direct this prayer to your greater glory, just as I wish that everything I do and my companions do may redound to your greater glory. I am often afraid, because so many things have changed, and I even no longer experience the facility in prayer and contemplation that I had earlier, but I have to struggle with difficulties and inhibitions. It is possible that my service does not completely suffice. It could be the case that the service the Son requires of me could have been meant to be different from what I am able to do or even willing to do. I therefore beg you, Lord: conform my will to your will by giving me your will in order that the Father's will may also be done in me and that I may learn better to do what he requires from me. Even without seeing him. In Manresa, the contemplation was easy for me; the days of dryness came seldom. Each time I stood up from prayer, I was filled with a grace that had an effect on my work and allowed me to walk my path step by step. The path was easy to see; it was a path given to me through contemplation. One event linked up to the next, with hardly a gap. And now it costs me a lot to contemplate. The difficulties of my studies seem so great that they make themselves felt even in the midst of my contemplation, and they distract me. If it were your will, God, that this is the way it ought to be, then I would accept it so. But I am unable to see whether this lack of peace in contemplation comes from me or from the evil enemy, or whether you will it so for your mysterious ends. And so I beg you for clarity, if it is indeed your will to grant me such clarity. If it is your will that everything remain just as it is, in unclarity, then change nothing. In my studies, the difficulties grow, in such a way that I again do not know whether the peace that is lacking in contemplation is due to this or whether you take away from me the opportunity of peaceful work and understanding because you somehow see infidelity in me. If this is the case, then I beg you to show me this infidelity. But if this difficulty in study could be useful in some way to you, then leave me with it. I am also often afraid that I might offer my brothers an occasion for doubt because of my lack of peace and the difficulties that are so hard to master. I worry that I will not provide them with the example you wish to give them and that they receive misgivings about the rightness of our founding. If you need these misgivings, then let them be. But if you do not need them, then I beg you to take them away, so that my companions may see more clearly and serve you better in their clearer vision of the new Society. Do everything according to your will. Grant that I may serve your will constantly with everything I am, for your greater glory, just as the Son has shown us, and grant that our tiny Society may grow to your greater glory and serve you. I beg you, triune God, do this; do it also out of love for our dear Lady, who also desires this new Society for her Son. Amen.

In his later years: He sees the many resistances to the Society, especially in the Church, among her representatives. To be sure, he has experienced certain alleviations and continues to experience them; he has been granted a certain limited authority. But it is not enough. He wants to give more of himself. He would like at the same time to become the ground for the new Society, with everything that he is and possesses; he would like to be a field out of which the seed shoots up; he would like to immerse himself, to be extinguished, spent, and absorbed.

And he first prays three Our Fathers, with a particular intention: the first for the Father, the second for the Son, and the third for the Holy Spirit. Then he prays three Hail Marys: the first as homage to the Mother, the second for the Society, and the third for the Church. His own prayer comes only after this. This prayer occurs within a contemplation after Mass. He has contemplated a small part of the way of the Cross—specifically, how the Lord, carrying his Cross, took a few steps and is so weary under the burden that he scarcely knows whether he really took these steps, whether he has somehow come nearer to the place of the crucifixion. It is his custom, at the end of his contemplation, to pray these three Our Fathers and Hail Marys in the following prayer in order to produce some clarity, in light of the contemplation, about the path of his Society and his position in it:

Triune God, you allow our Lord, in his carrying of the Cross, which is meant to lead to the redemption of the world, nearly to collapse from sheer exhaustion. And, in doing so, you allow him no longer to know whether he comes closer to his goal and makes progress in the redemptive suffering. We struggle with so much opposition in our tiny Society that we practically do not know whether we serve the Church and help the Son to carry his Cross through our service and bring the Church closer to the world. Encouragements also occur, but so too do many setbacks and obstacles, so that our vision is taken from us, and I do not know whether the last months have brought any progress. And, as always, I am also unable to say now whether your will is being fulfilled or whether I and perhaps also my followers are an obstacle to your will. In the grace that you have given me, I see the confirmation: You will our Society. But I beg you: Use your graces as nourishment for the Society so that these graces may, through the Society, become nourishment for the Church. Take from me everything: that which you give me and which I could perhaps pass on by means of your grace. Take it from me, if it be your will, in order to give it to the Society and to allow it to be taken up into it as your seed; for I know that everything you have given me was intended to be a seed for others. I beg you: Bless in me everything that is yours and that comes from you, and destroy in me everything that is not in unity in you, and leave everything that remains and is blessed to benefit the Society and through it your Church. If you willed to give me confirmation in a way that I might have experience of it, it would be a great consolation for me. But if you do not will to give me this consolation, then do not give it to me. Nevertheless, teach me and my followers and also your Church, which often prepares such difficulties for us, to understand your will more and more, to carry out your service, and to be obedient in service to you. Grant your blessing, triune God, and allow us to live in your blessing. Amen.

PETER OF ALCANTARA (1499–1562)

A. initially sees him a long time before he meets Teresa. He is studying and praying at the same time. He possesses a lot of theological knowledge, none of which is particularly genial, but it is knowledge that he constantly nurtures and increases to a certain extent in view of his spiritual guidance. Right at the beginning of his activity as a spiritual director, he had to confront something: he had for a long time become accustomed to getting by on the knowledge he had as if it were a standing resource. He had not yet grasped at that point that spiritual guidance is precisely something that demands a lot from the spiritual director in terms of cooperation. To be sure, he prayed and made a lot of effort, but it was still without a total personal engagement. He did not understand the necessity of constantly broadening one's prayer as much as one's knowledge, in order to encourage the seekers and the restless with the help of one's living experience. And what results is a certain slackening of his effectiveness. He now understands that nothing Christian is ever "finished". And he begins a new life of prayer and study in the service of his spiritual guidance.

A. sees him later, once he has already known the great Teresa for a while. He is completely in her confidence and receives a lot from her, since she has a gift for describing to him the things she has experienced in such a way that he receives a share in them, and he too is made fruitful by them for his prayer. He himself has visions, and they now acquire another aspect. Before, they were much more rigid than hers; they involved virtually no enjoyment at all. They were like exclamation points, like sudden bolts of lightning, which make one cringe because they unveil an awful truth. And he, the spiritual director, himself lacks a proper director and yet would need one. For he has a certain dread or fear about the things he experiences. Now, since Teresa recounts things about herself to him, he loses this dread, and his visions become less abrupt. The light of his vision expands, and he becomes more willing than he was earlier to communicate it. Teresa also teaches him what he had previously known only in a textbook sort of way: namely, that all of his inner experiences belong to the entire Church. He will later also maintain an extreme discretion regarding his own experiences; nevertheless, they no longer contain inwardly anything more for himself; but they stand instead at the Church's disposal. He helps Teresa in any way he can, but she is perhaps stricter with him than he is with her; she does not transfer the sort of pleasure she takes in her own states in any sense to him. She does not put up with anything like this in him, precisely because she knows the things from her own experience. To be sure, she can also be very strict with herself, but she tends, in her work of reform, to be stricter with her sisters than with herself. To some degree, she never loses the feeling that she has already done so much; it has already cost her so much; she is moreover the person who knows about mystical things ... She also tells herself that a man can bear strictness more easily than a woman. Toward the end of her life she is no longer very childlike, but she is extremely deliberate and reflective.

They both fructify and help one another. He recognizes the correctness of her states and ecstasies and thus frees her from many human anxieties. From then on, her visions become significantly freer and also more correct, because she no longer has to struggle against them. For her, this is the foundation of guidance: that he acknowledges her. Moreover, he also speaks very openly about a lot of things, especially in confession, where he can be harsher than usual. And if it does her infinite good that he recognizes the genuineness of her visions, then she for her part allows him to say everything in confession; even the harshest word is never felt as anything other than proper. She allows herself to be led, but through her visions and their content she also leads him. She also communicates many things to him that he can use in his hearing of confessions and his spiritual direction. For in prayer she exhibits a great magnanimity: she gives things away freely. When he has difficult cases, when he is in need, then no sacrifice is too great for her. He learns from her that a person has to pay if he wishes to be a guide. He is now very far from his beginnings, when he drew simply from his existing resources. He has experienced a significant broadening. His magnanimity has grown through hers. Previously, he had also thought that, in spiritual direction, one would find a particular number of regularly recurring types. Now he knows that God has personally entrusted him with each individual and that he must guide each one in a personal way.

First prayer: Lord, your servant stands before you and begs you for the grace of your enlightenment. It is so difficult to lead when one has to be led oneself. So difficult to hear confessions when one is a sinner oneself; so difficult to distribute communion when one feels oneself unworthy to hold you, Lord, in unworthy hands. And yet, you demand all of this from us. And I can console myself only with the thought that you, who are pure, you, our God, you who established the sacraments, in every operation and indeed in every single word you uttered, you saw yourself placed before sinners who had no desire to understand, so that even you had to struggle with great difficulties in every moment of your earthly life, even if they were quite different from the difficulties we face. But, Lord, my difficulties are such that I scarcely know anymore whether I am truly adequate to them, whether I ought to remain, whether I ought to continue to serve you where I am. For I see that up to this point I have made things too easy for myself. I have allowed many living things from your doctrine to die in me. I feel as though I myself willingly put death where you had intended there to be life, and I also thought you had created in your twelve disciples twelve types, as it were, which embodied the personalities that are entrusted to us. This false opinion led me to divide my penitents into twelve arbitrary categories and to treat them correspondingly. I saw in them, as it were, a Judas and a John, a Peter and a James, and I thought I could justify these divisions on the basis of what I drew from your words and from what I understood of your teaching. I did not understand that you did not create any categories, but in the commandment to love one's neighbor, which applies to us all, you have given something to us to stand as a model for our spiritual direction. We ought to imitate this model so that each and every person might come to understand love and to long for love, so that each person, wherever he is, might be seized by your word if we communicate it to him in truth and, in addition, offer our prayer for him. Lord, I beg you: Give me new courage, which means, renew my faith; may it come alive so much that it becomes useful for you, and give me love so that I may learn from you to love all those who belong to you. Amen.

Second prayer: My Lord and my God, I wish to thank you today, just as I do every day. To thank you from the whole of my hope, from the whole of my faith, from the whole of my love. You surround me with so many visible graces that I can scarcely find the words to say to you how much I love you and thank you. And you do not want me to turn away at all from what you give me. I must accept all of it, in gratitude, in order to pass it on further, as you show me that it needs to be passed on. And if Sr. Teresa has now entered into my life through your grace, then I see indeed what this means for me and for those who have been entrusted to me. Through her, you have taught me to stand before you with a much firmer hope and also to carry a much firmer hope and much greater love into the tasks I must accomplish. I thank you for having given me so much through Sr. Teresa. Grant that I, too, may teach her to use all the graces she so rightly receives altogether exclusively in the sense of the mission you have given to her. I know that I cannot receive so much from her without on my part also giving her as much as you allow. Lord, the task is difficult, but it is also so beautiful that I am always forgetting its difficulty. I also know that this difficulty means nothing more than participating in your difficulty. Grant that all the graces we receive in common might be used by us as well as by all those around us, who are visibly touched by them, in such a way that the entire Church receives her share of them, which is indeed the whole. And receive our common gratitude and our common love; use it as you will, but grant it the vitality that always characterizes everything that belongs to you. Amen.

FRANCIS XAVIER (1506–1552)

A. sees him at the time of his decision to work with Ignatius. He is aware of the difficulty of what he is taking upon himself. It will not be easy for him to stand by and become the co-founder of the new project. He throws himself into something wholly without seeing where it will take him. To be sure, he knows he is called "to something particular". But will the difficulties not overwhelm him? In all humility, he also knows he is gifted and that he could undertake completely different things; he could use his talents for some completely different service, perhaps for something much more visible, which would lead to quick success. At this point in time, he utters the following prayer:

First prayer: Father, I desire to serve you. You and your Son and your Spirit and our most blessed Virgin. And I desire to give my life to you in such a way that you might never think I desire to give you only a part or that I intermingle what belongs to me to a certain point. I want my life to be a service; I want this service to be made use of by you just as you require it, so that your concern, whatever it may be, may be better brought to fruition. Indeed, you know the plans I have for my life; you also know the joy I take in my own talents and in the development of my abilities and knowledge. Now I wish to hand this joy over to you without remainder, a joy that was in fact not pride, and to surrender to you all I have, so that I may do nothing other than what you have planned for me. You see this new thing that is coming into existence and how these men seek and pursue only what belongs to you. And I believe I understand unequivocally that you want me to be one of them and that our powers are to be used by you in such a way that none of us knows anymore how far his own power extends, whether it be mine or someone else's. This might be a sacrifice for me, because I am used to observing myself. But this, too, lies in your hand, Father. I wish to entrust to you also all my habits, just like everything else upon which I apparently or truly depend, and to do everything together with the others in the perfect obedience you desire, if you only show me that this path is the right one. But I believe you are already showing it to me in the path the others are following, which seems to me clearly to be the right one. Bless what is coming into being here, Father; bless each one of us and allow your work, through us, to benefit the entire Church. Amen.

Later in the missions. He has just had a great success; he is deeply moved, overwhelmed, grateful, and at the same time he feels a sort of suffering in not being able to stay with the people he has converted. Their Christian life will be only slightly different from their previous life; the conversion seems to him to be the effect of an all too powerful momentary influence, and there is not any possibility for him to fortify and build up the work with a subsequent mission. And then he has a personal problem: the fact that he participates in a much greater truth than those whom he converts. To some extent, he envies them the simple, round wholeness of their faith, which they have now received, a quality he never experienced in his own faith, for his is much more differentiated and subtle. Thus, the two forms complement one another in a sense, without being absorbed by one another. Nevertheless, he wishes that the old believers could have a share in the advantage of the newly converted, but also, contrarily, that the new Christians could participate in the culture and the established breadth of the faith in the lands of origin. Herein he also sees one of St. Ignatius' desires: to communicate, not a stagnant, but rather an educated faith and to work toward its greater formation.

There is a point at which Ignatius and Francis stand very close to each other: respect for sober work, and indeed not so much in theory, in theology, as in serious personal commitment to one's station in life, whatever it might be. Francis is at times nearly blinded when he contemplates the ways the faith could be developed. All the things a person could make out of these simple propositions, these stones that lie adjacent to one another in the building structures! A person could build fantastic towers—and yet ultimately, if one were to cultivate the stones, everything again, like before, would fit into the coffers of the one Church and her doctrine. The most objective and sober thing can be developed into the most personal without threat to its substance.

Second prayer: Father, grant that the work of our mission may prosper just as you and our superior desire it to. You see how it expands, how the task becomes more and more comprehensive every day. Often, it seems very hard for me to move on from one place to the next, for I know each time that I leave things behind that are unfinished, and the newly converted experience too little help. It will be hard for them to persist in this fullness of faith in which they now stand, and they run the danger of becoming disappointed. On the other hand, I know that elsewhere people are waiting for us to arrive; many people hope in us whom we are not permitted to disappoint because we have to bring *your* message and that of the Son, the Spirit, and our gentle Lady. Father, I beg you: bring to completion what is imperfect; do not allow the zeal that the believers now evince to slacken. Fill them every day anew with your truth and your love. And allow many people to pray to you for those in our company, so that they may help us, and you can use their petitions in order for the work that ought to belong to you to be clearly recognizable as yours. Father, I beg you also for all those whom I must leave behind, those who wait for my return, for your entire Church, with the many facets of her face, and for all those who do not yet believe, those who are meant to come to faith through your mission. I beg you also for me, Father, give me the strength to remain true, and give me so much love that all those with whom I interact might feel your love through me and thus be won for you. Amen.

TERESA OF AVILA (1515–1582)

A. sees a young girl with awakening desires. She knows she is not permitted to live for herself. And in purity she simply gives everything over to God. She does not touch a thing. She refrains from opening the wrapped present that she hands over. Perhaps the little girl does not even know to whom it belongs, the present she is handing over. She does not think it either important or unimportant. She simply knows that it is something over which she does not have disposal, even in thought, something a person neither increases nor decreases, something on which a person also cannot draw interest. A person knows only that it could be misused, even already by one's thoughts. One leaves it over to God: "Guard it, or allow it to unfold at the proper time, or allow it to atrophy and disappear, for in any event it is yours."

As she gets older Teresa does not distance herself much from this young girl's attitude. But then she begins nevertheless in prayer to underscore certain things. She prays with every fiber of her being and also of her body. Her entire physiological womanhood prays in her. For A. this is almost unintelligible. She thinks the physiological dimension is simply something one hands over to God. Teresa, by contrast, contemplates it as something that belongs to her, something to which a human being has a right by virtue of his constitution. Including the delight that can lie in it. And to be sure with Teresa, this does not come to a head in the sexual sphere, but it is spread out, as it were, throughout her entire being, her entire body. She understands quite a bit about the erotic. She does not want to transfer the sexual element altogether over into her mystical life. Nevertheless, she does want even these possibilities of her being to resonate in her surrender to God. In her renunciation of the erotic element on earth, she sees something like an anticipation of a corresponding fulfillment. In this there is nothing at all that is dirty in her, as it is in so many wholly or partially false mystics. It is her will that the spirit take possession also of her chastity. She would have been somehow sad if her sensuality had been taken away from her. She would have thought that she could no longer serve the Lord anymore with the whole of her being but would be like someone who was castrated. And the whole configuration of questions is for her quite significant. She gathers her body into her prayer, into her ecstasies. She does not forget for a moment in ecstasy to hold out and offer even her body to the divine light, to the divine truth. Taking "nuptiality" seriously in this relationship remains from this point on a danger for Carmel.

Prayer (spoken by A. only with serious reservations):

Lord, love for you is burning me. It burns me more than practically any woman has burned in love for a man. I feel this burning in my entire body, nothing in it is untouched by this flame. Lord, come to me; quell this burning with your presence; come to me, for I can no longer bear being apart from you! Come to me, for I am your bride, who has but one longing: the longing for her bridegroom. Come to me, and look at what you can make out of me, for you see that the longing for you is so great that it occupies all of my thoughts and fills me so that, henceforward, I can carry out what the cloister and my sisters demand from me, and what is also your demand, only with the greatest effort.

And yet, Lord, this burning, because it springs out of the inability to wait anymore until you are there, is so full of delight that I do not want to renounce it. And I hardly know anymore what I ought to long for from you: that you quell this burning or that you, on the contrary, allow it to become even more fierce. Do what you will, but do not allow me to neglect any part of your service on account of this burning. Give me daily the insight that I need in order to lead my sisters, to show them the way to you, to accustom them to the new religious Order, to lead them into the new love, to educate them in your service, and to make out of each of them your bride. Be effective in me in such a way that I can have an effect on others, but be at work just as much in all of them so that they can have an effect on me, too. Lord, remain with us; fill us more and more; be with us, and be in the path that you have prepared for us and that we sometimes walk laboriously enough, so that we might truly fulfill your will and so that our cloister, together with all the other cloisters of our Order, might become homes in which you are happy to dwell. Lord, bless this house, bless the entire Order, the coming foundations, but bless also your entire Church, who is perfectly your Bride. Amen.

STANISLAUS (1550–1568)

A. always sees him only in prayer, in a prayer that constitutes the whole disposition of his life. He is much more childlike than his age, and his prayer is even more childlike than he is himself. He is, as it were, completely untouched by life. And yet he knows many things about it, many things, too, that are not beautiful. But this knowledge does not penetrate into him. What he knows about sin and what is hateful remains stuck to the shell, as it were. His inner life fends off everything evil, and indeed it repels it from the spirit of contemplation. Just as contemplation takes an objective truth of God into itself and allows it to turn into an experience in the soul and something one lives through, just as the objective truth of God thus at the same time penetrates the soul from the outside and becomes subjective truth in it, in the same way out of the same contemplation Stanislaus drives the experience of evil from his soul. Not in such a way that the objective knowledge of the thing is forgotten or gets lost, but in such a way that its subjective existence is pushed outside, becomes objectified. Not every Christian has such a relationship to evil. There are others who are afflicted by it in their innermost being, others who are made "sick" when they experience certain things. There is no possibility for Stanislaus of getting involved in an experience of evil in himself; he pushes it outside.

He is so pure in his relationship to the Lord that he has nothing but readiness in him, but readiness exclusively for God, so that he does not measure any of the things that reach him, but he accepts everything in

403

the perfect readiness of purity. He would be immediately ready to do impossible things if he knew God had demanded them. All his other gifts—his intelligence, his cultivation, and so on—are, so to speak, taken up into this purity: something has a value for him only if it allows itself to be transposed into readiness. Whatever he learns, sees, or experiences is immediately transposed into readiness. This readiness is not at all theoretical but is absolutely straightforward in pure faith; it is spontaneous.

First prayer, spoken with the strength one presumably has, for example, at the beginning of one's novitiate: Lord, I thank you that I am permitted to live in the community of those who have given to you their entire life and whom you use and form according to your pure will. I know I still have no oversight and stand as a young disciple among the experienced. I beg you, allow the experience of others to benefit me, so that their service might teach me how a person serves you, how he sees out of your love, in what sense a person loves you, experiences your faith, how one believes in you. Lord, I would like to give you everything I have; I would like to give you my play and my study and everything that occupies me, all my thoughts, so that you may see, in everything, that I love you. And Lord, you know I am indeed not strong; I am not gifted; I have not been favored by some gift, but have always been in some sense average. And yet you allow me to live among the gifted and the capable. Allow me to remain ungifted, if it serves you so; allow me to become more gifted, if this were to attain greater glory for you, but grant me one thing in any case, Lord: Allow me to be ready always to thank you for having called me to be one of your followers and together with them to venture the effort to do your work. Amen.

Second prayer: Today I come, Lord, as a sick and a weakened man to you. And I believe I do not have the strength anymore to lead the life you have shown to me. Nevertheless, peace and confidence dwell in me, which you give to me every moment anew, because your love is so great that it also allows us to belong to you even as we lie on our sick bed. And if you have nothing else in mind for me anymore than to allow me to suffer, then let me suffer, Lord, in memory of and in gratitude for your suffering; allow my prayer always to accompany you; do not permit any other thought, intention, or word to arise from me that does not serve you. Grant that everything of mine may be yours. Grant that my increasing weakness may become a witness for me and for others that your love continues forever and is so great that it can fashion something out of this unspeakable weakness in love for the Father. Amen.

JOHN EUDES (1601–1680)

His entry into the community: he wants to serve God completely and is perfectly distrustful of himself. He believes community life would be the sole possibility for him to come nearer and nearer to doing what God wills. He abandons all his previous plans for the future in order to become completely pliant in God's hand. His prayer, at this stage, is one that has not yet passed through the crucible; it is childlike, trusting, kind, and believing. But his trust in God does not yet overcome entirely his distrust of himself, which compels him again and again to look back on himself. If his trust in God were greater, if it led to the overcoming of his distrust of himself, things would be even more correct. On the whole, he is pure and good.

First prayer: Lord, I know you are calling me and that you want me. I also know that your love can completely embrace me. I may perhaps often experience your love as harsh, because it aspires to burn away all my resistances, to absorb all my weaknesses into your strength, and my vision is thus taken from me. But Lord, I offer myself to you, and I implore you: Take me. Take this offer of myself seriously. You know me; you know I am hesitant; you know I become weak and experience doubt and infidelity. But I know you are fidelity itself. And if I feel like I am taking a risk in giving myself to you as I am, I nevertheless do it once and for all, irrevocably, in the name of the love that unites you with the Father and with all of us.

He abides inside this prayer; he allows himself to be carried away, but always in such a way that the chasm remains visible for him: the chasm between his unworthiness and the greatness of grace. Then years pass of increasing self-surrender, but also filled with increasing disquiet, because he feels more and more that his mission is a different one. He feels it in a more personal and more differentiated way; he knows he would have to stand at some sort of beginning and not in the center. This awareness of having to stand at some beginning occasions the greatest difficulties because of his distrust of himself. He understands that he has to break with this center in order to go to the required beginning.

To this is added the entire situation with Marie des Vallées, who simultaneously confuses him and reinforces him in the direction in which he is going. Her confessions confuse him on account of their excessive detail; he feels there is absolutely something true here, the center, and that this center concerns him; but he feels just as strongly that not everything is in order. Still more, he knows he has to take his new beginning out of the center of this woman's mission. At first he believes he has to accept the whole thing that is offered to him, to eat the whole plate that is set before him. After a little while he begins to understand that he is only being asked to eat *from* this cake. And because he knows how to pray and his prayer is true and somehow "pleasing to God" in the Old Testament sense, God thus sends him vision and the gift of discernment as an answer in prayer. He receives a sense, given by God, for what God wants and what God does not want. He discerns Marie's mission in prayer. He would not trust this clear vision at all outside of prayer. Everything is initially done to confuse him. He is like a director who is offered a play: the third act is magnificent; the second and the fourth a bit weaker; and the first and fifth are simply out of the question. And yet the play is offered to him as a whole. Of course, he also has moments in which the third act awakens doubts in him, and no one can object that he took it over without criticism. But he comes along with a few criteria, which are in his possession. One of these criteria is whether what is offered holds up in his prayer and, indeed, in his prayer that is led by God. He traces out a path, as it were, within his contemplation: he posits a starting point and an endpoint, some truth that he develops at the end, a truth that ought to come out reinforced. Between these points he inserts what he wants to test. And when he comes through, if this middle section allowed him to traverse the path from the beginning to the end, then that is the assurance that this middle section comes from God and holds up in God's truth. If it presents an obstacle, by contrast, then he throws it away as false. This leads him to discussions with Marie. She is unhappy when he makes a selection out of what she offers him. She is not unconditionally obedient. She wants to be able to help make the decisions, as it were. She does not simply lie out in the open. He feels this, and it makes him again unhappy, for he recognizes that if she were to let this go, she could be completely true and transparent. She does not manage completely to stand before him in the Spirit fully naked. And yet he is again and again fructified from the central point and compelled from this point to find his true beginning; the truth in her mission is so true that it allows him to find his own truth in spite of all the muddiness.

Second prayer: It is your love, Lord, that leads me to you, your grace that allows me today to place my entire weakness before you. It is a weakness that was always so great that I had difficulty remaining in the easier mission of the Society, because I found it too heavy. Today, Lord, I recognize your love in the fact that you lead me to stand with the whole of my weakness there where I do not wish to stand and to break with everything. I had entered in obedience to you, in the same obedience in which I ought now to risk the new thing you demand from me, which I cannot oversee, which I fear, in the presence of which my weaknesses seem abysmally deep and more opaque than ever. But, Lord, you have always shown me in prayer that I cannot serve you in any other way than by following the path you have indicated to me and by accepting the mission anew just as you give it to me and attempting in defiance of my weaknesses to allow what you will to come to pass. You bind me in a new obedience so tightly to yourself that everything before seems easy and enviable. Lord, without your grace my weakness would be unable to take this new path. But your grace will teach me to bear it. I beg you, Lord, accept all of me each day, and grant that I may do your will and that this new task will help all the people who are included in it to draw nearer to you. Lord, take from me the human things that still cling to me, so that I may become for those whom you give me what a superior ought to be in relation to those who follow him: a hand that leads to you, a will that seeks to do yours, a love that comes from your own. I beg you, Lord, bless everything we undertake; bless it as you will, and bless it in such a way that we recognize your blessing—or do not recognize it, if that would better serve you. But I implore you for one thing: Allow us to bring to fruition in your love everything we do. Amen.

Later, more difficulties arise and great inner struggles. But he knows without any hesitation that he did the right thing in leaving his community. He knows he is on the right path, although on occasion he wishes he would not have had to leave. And precisely in the hours of great inner need, doubts grow about the value of Marie des Vallées' visions. He is aware of her non-transparent sides. But he also has the consoling thought: If such a woman maintains so much purity that she retains the ability to communicate so much of the truth in spite of everything, how much purer, then, must be the central mystery of Mary, the Mother of God!

He also has many lukewarm members in his new Order. When he contemplates them, he is seized by the fear that he is guilty for their mediocrity. He does not radiate the light properly. But he is a great man of prayer; he bathes entirely in God, in his grace, and does this in great humility and purity.

Before his encounter with Margaret Mary: He is the experienced spiritual director; he knows many things, especially about missions and
what advances and hinders them. He leads many people, and people
are generally amazed at the certainty of his judgment. He is in this
respect similar to the Curé of Ars: he sees what state souls are in. Not
in a visionary way, but with a straightforward knowledge about what
he has to do. People often have the experience that they immediately
fall apart in his presence, like meticulously constructed systems and
buildings, that they dissolve into nothing in the presence of his glance
and his words. He is imperturbable. He prays a lot and very well. He
is completely disinterested and gives everything back to God that belongs
to God. He also has the gift, in leading souls, of breaking things off at
the proper moment, if it has become senseless to continue any farther.

The encounter with Margaret Mary. He comes to this encounter
filled with an inner certainty that there truly is a mission here, but it
is also accompanied by a certain fearfulness. He cannot quite explain
this latter. At their first meeting, he knows he is the one for whom she
has waited; he knows this with perfect certainty. And he understands
that it is correct like this, and nevertheless something seems to grate
on him inside. He cannot bring these two feelings together. In everything they discuss, he has the feeling they are speaking past one another.
In confession, this gets resolved, and he feels that it is correct. Outside
of confession, he cannot get rid of a feeling of distrust. Somehow he
has come to doubt the whole thing. Then, when he is with her again,
the doubts disappear, but he enters into extreme disquiet in this regard.
It is as if there were a sort of *suffering* bound up with this acquain-
tanceship. He understands that he cannot allow this suffering simply to
rest upon him, that it is nothing that could be compared with a natural irritability. If he had known Margaret from the beginning and had
been able to guide her, he would certainly have noticed the unbal-
ances and would have been able to remedy them. But he takes over in
the middle of things, and thus it is extremely difficult for him to distinguish between what is genuine and what is false. He sees the mission with perfect clarity. But he also knows that the true saint ought
to possess the same distance and the same closeness to his mission;
Margaret, on the other hand, has a whole variety of distances at every
point: at one time far away, the next moment very close, the next
moment in the middle ... And thus he is unable to determine which
is in fact her true distance. She withdraws the transparency from him
that she ought to offer him. With the same evidence, it is clear that

something is correct and something is not correct. And one ought to salvage what is correct at any price. He cannot do anything but pray as resolutely as possible and to *pour* his own mission into hers. He knows about his own mission. But he also knows that she possesses a more arduous mission than his. Thus, he begs God to add his mission to hers, to place his equilibrium in a helpful way at the service of her disequilibrium.

Later, he feels a restlessness all over again. He sees that things have become better in the effects of her mission. But now he is overtaken by the thought that he should have shown her, not how she was, but rather how she ought to have been . . .

He suffered from all these things. His many vows are like an augmentation of his readiness to give himself; he takes them as necessary in order to give what he can, as an attempt to give more. And he also stores up experiences in himself in order to be permitted to expect them of others. He makes a gift of things he acquires in prayer in order to preserve what is best in Margaret. Sometimes these vows bring him into a certain conflict: between a vow and obedience, between a vow and love . . .

First prayer: Before he undertakes the guidance. (A. says: "I hear it in French. In which language should I say it?" She speaks it in French; but in order to follow it, I write it down in German.)

Mon Dieu, vous m'envoyez dans un champ nouveau. Et je sais que la moisson vous appartient. [My God, you are sending me into a new field, and I know that the harvest belongs to you.] And yet I do not know whether it will truly be brought to harvest. One thing is clear to me: that it ought to be a harvest in your name, even if it is not a harvest in the eyes of others. I go forth, not knowing whether this mission is genuine, a mission you have given and that you protect and arrange. I know that my decision, my Yes or No to this mission, has wide-ranging consequences. And yet it ought to be a harvest even if my decision is No. Then there will be disappointments, and you also desire that these disappointments become fruitful according to your will. But the Yes also has many implications, for then the Church will have received something that, to be sure, she already possesses but that will become her property in a heightened sense. The decision does not lie only with me, and yet it has been handed over to me, as it were, personally; it has been handed to me as to one of your servants, who attempts to live from your obedience, to me as one who ought to receive wisdom from you within this obedience, the wisdom to make decisions in your name and with the help of your grace. I beg you,

Father, allow the decision to pass through me in such a way that it is not influenced by me, but finds and takes what belongs to you in me, what you place in me, so that the word of the decision might be your word. Allow this word to be uttered in my office; grant me the grace of office, so that I may be able to utter a word of your grace. You know how precisely people receive a word spoken in one's office, as if it were already a part of an irrevocable judgment. Thus, Lord, take my prayer and everything that belongs to me; give me only what belongs to you, as much or as little as you wish, but give it to me so that it may be recognizable already in the first conversation and in everything I will have to do in this affair until the end. Grant that everything may happen for your greater glory, and give your blessing to everyone involved. Amen.

Second prayer: In a moment of unclarity: Father, everything I thought I knew up to this point has come unhinged. It is as if every discussion with Sister contained a contradiction to the previous one. In every Yes I utter, there lies at the same time a No, and in every No the Yes does not allow itself to be smothered. And thus I am completely lacking in insight; I cannot distinguish things; I do not understand how, every time something becomes clear, something unclear arises right in the center of what was clear and does not allow itself to be distinguished altogether from the clear. I believe in the mission, and at the same time I do not completely believe in her. I believe in the words Sister says, and at the same time I recognize that they do not ring perfectly pure. And yet it is impossible for me not to believe them, because these words are a part of your truth and allow themselves to be assembled together, but only once they have been passed fresh through a crucible, as it were, which is someone other than Sister, though I have no idea where I could find him. Father, I beg you to allow me, if you will, perhaps to become a crucible, to allow me to suffer, and grant too that each of my uncertainties, which now plague me so severely, may be used by you in such a way that they serve as a crucible and genuine suffering. If it pleases you, Father, then give more clarity to me, and if the lack of clarity lies in me because of my sin and my inadequacy, then let whatever you wish to remain in unclarity, but free me nevertheless from sin and inadequacy, insofar as these hinder me from saying the word that my brothers expect from me and which ultimately has to become the word of the Church. I desire to place myself again at your service, to offer everything to you that you can use; I beg you, bless what is good in the Sister; separate her from what seems to me unclear, and bless our conversations; bless me and our entire Order, and allow everything we do to redound to your greater glory. Amen.

ELIZABETH OF THE TRINITY (1880–1906)

It is difficult, with her, to say where her prayer begins and where it ends. She has really long stretches of prayer. And then she has moments when she falls out of contemplation, and these moments are in fact the most painful she knows. This happens to her suddenly, while she is in the middle of her day's work; she sits, for example, in her cell sewing something, and in doing so she could be very well in complete contemplation. But then suddenly everything is harshly interrupted. But it also happens in the middle of her actual contemplation times or during her prayer in choir: at once, the whole thing comes apart. That is the most acute torture for her, but it is at the same a great grace, because this is how she becomes more and more acquainted with the *misère de la nature humaine*. She knows that she is the one guilty for this breakdown because of something still unclean in her. This causes her to feel a certain repugnance in relation to herself, in relation to everything that is unclean or sinful in human beings. It is this repugnance that drives her again and again to God. Not in such a way that she turns to God from the repugnance she feels regarding what is human, for she goes to God out of love for him. But the repugnance powerfully increases her need for purity, for love. It is for her an occasion, so to speak, to *want* to ascend to such heights. She knows that God needs adoration, and she thinks: if she were to allow this adoration to take place somehow above in the light of the Trinity, then she would be torn away from the impurity of the human; otherwise, she would be reminded too much of the sinfulness of nature, and her adoration would lose some of its purity. There is a choice in her contemplation, in her thoughts: the choice of the pure sphere of God.

She sees a lot in her prayer. Because she truly wants it, because she loves and pushes herself, she receives much insight from God, especially into the mysteries of the Trinity. What she writes, what she says, are not empty words, not abstractions, even if they seem occasionally empty and schematic. It sometimes seems that she is at bottom afraid of the concrete. She does not want to let things fall into the complete impurity of the lower spheres. In relation to knowledge and experience, the abstract in her corresponds totally to something concrete. When she moves within the heights of the Trinity, then it is because she cannot remain below and does not want to.

There is in this not only a being carried, but also a *striving*, even if this striving is quite pure. A striving that is nevertheless not perfectly detached and therefore remains painful. There is perhaps a parallel here to what aridity was for the little Thérèse. She suffers immensely in this striving, and God allows her to pay the price for it, insofar as he allows her to fall out of contemplation. For example, she is never able to write more than a few lines at a single time. Then she breaks it off and is at a loss. A. utters the following prayer in explicit suffering. The beginning of the prayer is very difficult. She starts off, there and then, and nothing is right. It is supposed to be done like this; . . . no, first like this! . . . It is a suffering to live the way she does. She has no sense of humor at all. She is very earnest, but not at all hysterical. She establishes a beginning again and again, but she does not need to establish it because it has already been established. She seeks a way of overcoming the distance when there is in fact no distance to overcome. Again and again she discovers: This is not the right thing. She selects the places where she could perhaps make her contemplation; she chooses what seem to be the appropriate texts. She avoids others, because she has the feeling that they would not offer the proper starting point. And in the middle of her contemplation, completely abstruse things occur to her, not like a little distraction over which a person is led, but like a dramatic, definitive break. Then she has to look again for new points of entry. In her writings, she records only the heights and leaves invisible holes, as it were, standing between them, the places at which she falls away. She is compelled to do it this way, because she is writing for others and has to fashion what she presents in an acceptable way.

Prayer: Triune God, Father, Son, and Spirit! If we, Father, are permitted to call you Father, then we thank your Son, who has humbled himself and has come to us as a man in order to bring us the Spirit. And you, Father and Son, have created a relationship before us for yourselves, which corresponds in a certain way to human relationships. But you have shown it to us in such a way that no earthly relationship between father and son would ever be adequate to what you have revealed to us. For we are sinners. Father, let us forget that we are sinners, and let us draw our sustenance from the fact of being permitted to be with you, of being permitted to adore in our contemplation all the mysteries of your threeness, your eternal threeness, your constant becoming three. In your threeness you show us that there is no beginning and no end in your life; through the three among you, you show us that everything in you is all or nothing. There is no beginning and no end, because in fact everything is a beginning and in fact everything is an end, an end so that the beginning may ever be new, a beginning, so that the end may be visible. And there is no rest in this not-being-the center, which you disclose to us, no rest, because everywhere there is the same challenging love, the same self-giving love, the same receiving love. Father, we say "love", and we have learned this word from the Son, but we are using an expression we do not understand, which we are unable to fulfill, which only arrives at its proper meaning in the Triunity of heaven. For only what lasts eternally has meaning. Father, if we contemplate your eternal being next to your love, then we are carried away by something that overflows us at every point, something that would completely submerge and drown us if your saving, triune love did not come to our aid in order to draw us into the participation in the triune worship in heaven. And every worship on earth is a foretaste of the heavenly worship. Father, I beg you, allow me, allow our entire cloister, allow everyone who is bound to us, to participate in your heavenly adoration, now or when we arrive in heaven, but do not push anyone away, for all our followers belong to you, and whenever we say "ours", may you allow us instead to say "yours". Amen.

THE COMMUNITY OF SAINTS

Of the many saints that we have "done", each had his personal way of praying. For all of them, it became possible to see what was peculiar to them; and for many it was also possible to see whatever was inadequate in them. We were able to see precisely where their deficiencies lay, but we also saw the will to self-gift in all of them who were holy, even if some of them perhaps did not know exactly how to carry out this gift. Often it was less their own fault than it was the failure of those who did not guide them properly. The power of office then did not have a powerful enough effect on their lives.

In the Church, the predominant tendency in many ways is to see the saints as manifestations that have fallen straight from heaven, to take their words as untouchable oracles, and therefore, especially with more modest missions, with the "lesser prophets", not to contribute very much to their success. If everyone, especially the people holding some office, had been more aware of how much they were permitted and in fact supposed to participate in the administration of the saints' missions, then they would have engaged themselves and their offices more emphatically in those missions. Priests need to be trained very differently in this regard. They have to understand how many missions founder on account of being insufficiently cultivated by those in office, both in their lives and in their prayer. The priests thus neglect not only their own prayer, which is required by their priestly mission, but also the prayer of the person entrusted to their care, which they are meant to keep alive. If a priest does not know how to pray himself, how is he supposed to teach it to others who have to learn it from him!

There is something I have witnessed again and again: people become preoccupied with the authenticity or inauthenticity of visions, with the accuracy or the inaccuracy of prophecies, but they do not keep watch over what is most important, namely, a person's interaction with God in prayer. Of course, this does not mean we ought to spy on them, as it were. But an earnest look into whether there is a conversation with God, and what it is like, is indispensable for those who are sent. And to a great extent the quality of prayer can also be determined. For the most part, priests are not missing much in their knowledge of sin. But the penitent ought to appear to them as a fellow human being whom the Lord loves and with whom he would like to have an exchange in prayer. In the advice and spiritual direction priests give, there is so much talk about people that there is scarcely any time left over to talk about God—about what God expects from the person and what the person ought in turn to proclaim to his neighbor about God.

If no one teaches Christians how to pray, then they will attempt to do it on their own in one way or another. But in doing so they run into difficulties that they do not have sufficient insight to eliminate. Many will think that the difficulties lie above all in human nature, and all one needs is a certain technique in order to be done with it and make one's way to God. They overlook the fact that God decisively fashions the answer in man with his cooperation, just as he expects it and requires it. In heaven, there are also angels of prayer, who live so much in adoration that this is what gives them their office, namely, to form the prayer of the saints in a way worthy of heaven. Man's personal prayer becomes perfect to the extent that the angel prays it along with him, to the extent that he newly establishes it and draws it upward. And with those who no longer need the purgatorial fires, because God desires to take from them whatever remains imperfect and unsuitable in heaven without trouble, there is the same mysterious translation by the angels, the saints in heaven, and by God himself, from an earthly prayer to a heavenly one. And it often becomes clear in such a translation and guidance of the earthly into the heavenly that the same thing would have been possible for the person at prayer already on earth if it had only been pointed out properly to him.

Whoever arrives in heaven has to introduce himself. This introduction, however, is not one-sided; those who introduce themselves are at the same time the ones who are introduced. God had been waiting for us, just as we waited for him. And now that we are those who have been received, there is no longer any talk about sin and unworthiness. Confession lies behind us. Now there is only the augmentation of grace, so that we no longer need to confess anymore; the Lord's grace has settled sin for us along the way. But now the prayer of eternity must be planted in our hearts and on our lips, the prayer within the vision of the Trinity, a prayer we ourselves say in such a way that the Mother of God and all the saints and angels can say it with us. All those who have long been in heaven experience the joy of arrival anew with every newcomer. For the joy of arrival is itself eternal joy, and therefore it is common to all. And thus the prayer in which we are led upon our arrival is also always the common prayer of heaven, never the private prayer of Mary or of an individual saint. We were expected in this communal prayer among the saints, in which we are now being led. It does not overwhelm our personal prayer; indeed, one could say that our personal life only now truly begins for the first time. We observe how much that is foreign falls away from us and how what belongs to us is set free. What we are being led into is again, not something foreign, but in the highest sense natural, although one cannot say we had expected it to be this way rather than some other way. When it arrives, it is simply the right thing, that which is far and away the best.

In the prayer that unites all into one, which is not difficult to understand, each person at the same time comes to understand his own prayer. Whoever had previously had trouble in prayer now understands how easy it is. And whoever had prayed with ease, like a child in relation to his father, continues to do so, but with a new depth that surprises even the person himself who is praying. He is permitted to be a child in a completely different way, because the Father is so infinitely greater. For each person who is initiated into the prayer of heaven, it means a new fulfillment, and each eternal day is eternally new, because we ourselves are always newcomers in eternity.

In this prayer, it is perhaps remarkable that the Son's earthly journey is not mentioned. Each one knows he has dwelt among us and taught us the prayer to the Father. And yet the prayer of the Cross and the prayer of death are not repeated, nor is the prayer on Mary's knees. A new prayer takes shape, wherein the relationship between the community of heaven and God is established. If this prayer of the community of saints were not there, which pervades all the personal prayers as their measure, then there would be the danger that too much of the particular would have carried over from the world. And if we now pray in heaven for the sinners on earth, then we do so indeed as people who once knew sin; but the connection between sin and the Cross lies behind us. The Cross remains alive for us, but not insofar as we have put the Son on the Cross; it is rather that we are permitted to participate in his loving desire to sacrifice himself. And the Son takes us with him into the world as his heavenly saints; he takes us with him into the effects of his love. We are permitted in a Christian way to work together with him among men. From this perspective, it is not true that the Cross loses its significance for us. For each saint remains open to the world's suffering. It is only that the openness has become different. How could the Lord allow people on earth to participate in his Cross when he himself has nothing more to do with it? But how could the Lord, who still has something to do with the Cross, exclude his saints in heaven from it? How could the little Thérèse let her roses rain if she no longer possessed a sense for the world's suffering? To be sure, it is not possible to express how a person can retain this relation to the world's suffering in the midst of the happiness of heaven. But it is there. Indeed, the joy of heaven is so great that it takes everything, including the Lord's suffering, up into its superabundance, which belongs to the Lord. The gratitude, the eucharist of heaven, is so great that Good Friday is included within it along with everything men have suffered through in the Lord's Spirit and in connection to him: not something that has become ineffectual, but as a reality that has been entirely embraced in glory.

The Prayer of Adoration in Heaven

Father, we all come into your presence in order to give you thanks. To thank you for the earthly life you have given us to live in hopeful expectation of the vision of you. And you have given us your Son, communicated your Spirit to us, in order to accompany us and to show us the path to you, the triune God. We thank you for everything earthly and for drawing our temporal life to yourself in such a way that we are henceforward allowed to share in your eternal life for eternity. For all this we thank you, and now we begin to adore you with the new words of eternal life. We see how your Son and your Spirit adore you in the reciprocal triune adoration, which fills heaven from the beginning of the ages; we see how the Mother of your Son adores you and is honored by the triune God and how the whole heavenly court, all the saints, all the angels, all the redeemed, adore you with her. They all show us that this adoration knows no end, that we are permitted to love you endlessly, and everything up to this point now becomes a new present in perfect fulfillment, in a grandeur of love we scarcely dare to imagine. We ourselves, who learned slowly and hesitantly to pray and serve on earth, find ourselves so welcomed as if there lay for you, the triune God, in our arrival the fulfilling conclusion to a long expectation, as though the joy for you were as great as it is for us who arrive. It is the joy of Christian love, joy over the fact that the children have returned home, that they are all there and no longer have to be regarded as alienated souls, but they are there, in the place that was intended for them from before the foundation of the world, a place they adopt with such joy for themselves that no one can say where the joy is greatest.

We beg you, Father, keep us in this joy of arrival, and allow us all throughout eternity to repay our gratitude, which is indeed the content of our faith, in this adoration, to which we are now invited and belong and out of which we are no longer able to fall. Allow us to join in the celebration; allow us to join in the vision; allow us above all to join in the love by virtue of the love that comes from you, the love that is perfect in you, the triune God, and returns perfectly back to you from this day forward, because we are now with you as your own. Allow us to call you Father together with your Son for all eternity in the sense that the Holy Spirit gives to this name. Amen.

ALPHABETICAL INDEX

John the Apostle, St. (*continued*)
215–19 passim, 267–71, 274,
283, 289, 357, 398
Don Bosco and, 175
Gregory the Wonderworker
and, 35
Ignatius Loyola and, 3–4
John XXIII, Pope, 21, 201–2
John Vianney, 225, 256, 408
Joseph, St., 27–28, 147
Joseph of Cupertino, St., 254
Judas Iscariot, 278, 284–86, 288,
398
Jude Thaddeus, St., 278–79
Julian of Norwich, Bl., 245–46
Justin Martyr, St., 219–20

Kempis, Thomas à, 89–90
Kierkegaard, Søren, 173–74
Klaus, Brother (St. Nicholas of
Flüe), 380–82
Konnersreuth, Therese von, 21,
209–11

Las Casas, Bartolomé de, 102–4
Lataste, Marie, 264
Lateau, Louise, 189–90
Lazzari, (Maria) Dominica,
176–77
Leo I (the Great), Pope St.,
228–29
Leo XIII, Pope, 263
León, Luis de, 116–17
Leseur, Elisabeth, 199–200
Lippert, Peter, S.J., 313–14
Louis IX of France, 72–73
Louis Marie Grignon de
Montfort, St., 256–57
Lucie Christine, 186–87
Lucy of Narni, Bl., 105–6
Luis of Grenada, Fr., 120n
Lukardis of Oberweimar, 74–75

Luke, St., 16, 275, 292–93
Luther, Martin, 106–7

Macarius (Pseudo-Macarius),
36–37
Manning, Henry Edward
Cardinal, 172–73
Margaret Colonna, Bl., 73–74
Margaret Mary Alacoque, St.,
155–56, 408–9
Marguerite de Beaune, St.,
148–49
Maria Celeste Crostarosa, Ven.,
165, 309–11
María de la Visitación, 21,
120–22
Marie de Jésus, O.C.D., 192–93
Marie de la Trinité. *See* Jacques,
Louisa
Marie de l'Incarnation, Bl.,
143–45
Marillac, Louise de, 142–43
Mark, St., 16, 290–92
Marmion, Columba, Bl.,
197–98
Martin, Pauline, 198–99
Martin of Tours, St., 226–27
Mary, St., 5–6
See also John the Apostle;
Joseph; *individual names*
Mary Baouardy (Mary of Jesus
Crucified), Bl., 187–88
Mary Frances of Naples, St.,
165–66
Mary Magdalen, St., 286–88
Mary Magdalen dei Pazzi, St.,
114n, 129–30
Matarrelli, Palma M., 178–79
Matthew, St., 275–78
Matthias, St., 288–89
Maximus the Confessor, St.,
230–31

Simeon Stylites, St., 227–28
Simeon the New Theologian,
    St., 233–34
Simon the Zealot, St., 283–84
Speyr, Adrienne von, 1–24
Stanislaus Kostka, St., 403–5
Stein, Edith (St. Teresa
    Benedicta of the Cross),
    207–9
Stephana Quinzani, Bl., 100–101
Stephen, St., 137, 217–18
Suarez, Francisco, 303–4

Tauler, Johannes, 77–78
Teresa Benedicta of the Cross,
    St. (Edith Stein), 207–9
Teresa of Avila, St. (Teresa of
    Jesus), 4–8 passim, 59, 84,
    110–11, 129, 184, 371,
    396–403 passim
    Marie de Jésus and, 193
Tertullian, 221–22
Thaddeus, St. See Jude
    Thaddeus, St.
Theophane Vénard, St., 179–80
Thérèse of Lisieux, St., 69, 184,
    186, 292, 374, 412, 416
    Margaretha Ebner and, 81–82

Marie de Jésus and, 193
    Pauline Martin and, 198–99
    Pius XI and, 197
Thomas, St., 281–83
Thomas à Kempis, 89–90
Thomas Aquinas, St., 9, 21,
    240–41, 301, 363–66
Thomas Becket, St., 237–38
Thomas More, St., 386–88
Thurston, P. Herbert, 21
Timothy, St., 29–30
Tintoretto, 112–13
Titus, St., 29–30

Vallée, Irénée, O.P., 193–95
Vallées, Marie des, 140–41,
    405–7
Veronica Giuliani, St., 127–28
Vincent de Paul, St., 142n, 252
Vincent Ferrer, St., 85–86
Vincent Pallotti, St., 260–61
von Spee, Friedrich, 141–42
von Speyr, Adrienne, 1–24

William of Saint-Thierry, 57–58

Zebedee, 268–69

424

INDEX BY HISTORICAL PERIOD